GOLD AND FREEDOM

A NATION DIVIDED

Studies in the Civil War Era

———

Orville Vernon Burton
and Elizabeth R. Varon,
Editors

GOLD AND FREEDOM

THE POLITICAL ECONOMY
OF RECONSTRUCTION

Nicolas Barreyre

TRANSLATED BY
ARTHUR GOLDHAMMER

UNIVERSITY OF VIRGINIA PRESS • CHARLOTTESVILLE & LONDON

University of Virginia Press
© 2015 by the Rector and Visitors of the University of Virginia
All rights reserved
Printed in the United States of America on acid-free paper

First published 2015

3 5 7 9 8 6 4 2

Library of Congress Cataloging-in-Publication Data
Names: Barreyre, Nicolas, 1975–
Title: Gold and freedom : the political economy of Reconstruction /
Nicolas Barreyre ; translated by Arthur Goldhammer.
Other titles: Or et la liberté. English
Description: Charlottesville : University of Virginia Press, 2015.
Includes bibliographical references and index.
Identifiers: LCCN 2015019358 | ISBN 9780813937496 (cloth : acid-free paper)
ISBN 9780813937755 (e-book)
Subjects: LCSH: Reconstruction (U.S. history, 1865–1877) | Southern
States—History—1865–1877. | United States—Geography—Political
aspects—History—19th century. | Spatial analysis (Statistics) | United States
—Politics and government—1865–1877. | United States—Economic
policy. | United States—History—Civil War, 1861–1865—Influence.
Classification: LCC E668 .B25513 2015 | DDC 973.8—dc23
LC record available at http://lccn.loc.gov/2015019358

Cover art: "This is a white man's government,"
Thomas Nast, *Harper's Weekly,* September 5, 1868.
(Library of Congress, Prints and Photographs Division,
LC-USZ62-121735)

CONTENTS

ACKNOWLEDGMENTS

A FIRST BOOK is a long intellectual journey, and along the way one contracts many debts that no gold can repay. They are debts of mentorship, friendship, and moral support. Unlike other debts, they are a pleasure to acknowledge.

I owe a great deal to four outstanding historians for their mentorship: Gilles Pécout, my undergraduate advisor at the École Normale Supérieure (ENS); Jean Heffer, my master's advisor, and François Weil, my Ph.D. advisor, at the École des hautes études en sciences sociales (EHESS); and Olivier Zunz, at the University of Virginia. Their generosity and intellectual rigor are inspiring, and their friendship honors me.

EHESS in Paris has provided a matchless environment for intellectual growth, and its Center for North-American Studies is a unique place to discuss ideas. I especially thank my colleagues Cécile Vidal, Gilles Havard, and Pierre Gervais for the many conversations that informed my thinking. My years training at the University of Virginia and the University of Chicago have also been seminal. I extend my heartfelt gratitude especially to Michael Holt, Kathleen Conzen, Richard John, and Michael Perman, who have generously guided me during my stays. I have also enormously benefited from critical discussions of my research in progress at the University of Illinois at Chicago, Oxford University's Rothermere Institute, the University of Paris I Panthéon-Sorbonne, the Centre Maurice Halbwachs (ENS-EHESS), and the University of Heidelberg, as well as conferences of the Social Science History Association and the Journal of Policy History.

Historians would be helpless without the assistance of librarians and archivists, and I am no exception. My gratitude goes to the geospatial staff at the University of Virginia's Scholar's Lab; to Christopher Winters, Franck Conoway, and Sandy Applegate at the University of Chicago's Regenstein Library; to the staff at the Library of Congress Manuscript Division; to Susan Swaide at the New York Public Library; to Nan Card at the Hayes Presidential Center; and to Paul Erickson, Vincent Golden, and Lauren Hewes at the American Antiquarian Society.

Being an Americanist in Europe requires many long-distance trips to far-away archival repositories and other institutions. I am thankful to EHESS and ENS in Paris for providing travel funding, and to the George Lurcy Educational and Charitable Trust, the Fulbright Program, and the American Antiquarian Society for generous scholarships.

Many colleagues have kindly read parts of the manuscript in some form or another, and given me invaluable feedback. I especially wish to thank, besides those already mentioned, Richard Bensel, Michael Caires, Romain Huret, Claire Lemercier, Annick Lempérière, Alan Lessoff, Nicolas Lyon-Caen, Vincent Michelot, Natalia Muchnik, Scott Nelson, Elizabeth Varon, and Richard White, as well as the anonymous readers at the Éditions de l'EHESS and the University of Virginia Press.

This book was first published in French by the Éditions de l'EHESS. I am particularly grateful to Christophe Prochasson, its director, and to Caroline Béraud, my editor there, for their welcome. I extend my thanks to the whole team who made such a beautiful book out of my manuscript.

Translation is also an adventure in itself. My thanks go to the University of Virginia Press, and especially Richard Holway, my editor there for a warm welcome. The Florence Gould Foundation provided generous financial support. And I owe an enormous debt to Arthur Goldhammer, who provided a flawless and elegant translation; working with him is an absolute pleasure.

Finally, I am grateful to friends and family for their presence and support throughout the years. I dedicate this book to my parents, in humble homage to their unfailing trust and support.

NOTE ON STATISTICAL AND
GEOGRAPHIC ANALYSIS

PART OF THE interpretation proposed in this book is based on a statistical and map analysis of congressional roll-call votes between 1865 and 1877. It uses the database put together by Howard L. Rosenthal, Keith T. Poole, and their team.[1] For parties, I have simplified affiliations by grouping Conservatives and Independent Democrats with Democrats, and Unionists, Unconditional Unionists, Independent Republicans, and Liberal Republicans with Republicans. For sections, I have grouped states along the conventional understanding of sections at the time shown on map 1. The Northeast includes New England (Connecticut, Maine, Massachusetts, New Hampshire, Rhode Island, Vermont) and the Mid-Atlantic states (New Jersey, New York, Pennsylvania); the West is mainly made up of Midwestern states (Illinois, Indiana, Iowa, Kansas, Michigan, Minnesota, Missouri, Nebraska, Ohio, Wisconsin, with Nebraska added in 1867), as well as the three Pacific states (California, Nevada, Oregon). The bulk of the South comprises the secessionist states (Alabama, Arkansas, the two Carolinas, Florida, Georgia, Louisiana, Mississippi, Tennessee, Texas, Virginia), as well as the former slave states that remained in the Union and, therefore, did not undergo Reconstruction (Delaware, Kentucky, Maryland, West Virginia).

The roll-call analysis in this book is based on these groupings. A *partisan vote* describes a vote where the majority of Democrats opposes a majority of Republicans. A *sectional vote* describes a vote where a majority of Northeasterners opposes a majority of Westerners, irrespective of parties. The cohesiveness of each group is measured with a simple Rice Index, going from 0 (perfectly divided group) to 1 (perfectly united group).[2] The polarization between two groups is calculated as the mean of the Rice Index of each. I have termed it a *polarization index*.

The mapping of the roll-call votes in Congress is based on the atlas edited by Kenneth C. Martis.[3] Each congressman's vote is represented as his district. Maps mapping one particular vote thus show the districts. Maps showing series of votes spanning several Congresses do not show the districts, as they saw their boundaries change over the Reconstruction period. For those maps, I devised a *sectional index:* each sectional vote is assigned 1 if the vote aligned with the majority of Western votes, -1 if it aligned with the majority of Northeastern votes, 0 if no vote was cast. The total was put on a scale from -100 (systematic alignment with the Northeast) to 100 (systematic alignment with the West).[4] Only states with entire series from 1865 to 1877 are included, which explains why most of the South does not appear in those maps.

GOLD AND FREEDOM

Introduction

There were only four witches in all the Land of Oz, and two of them, those who live in the North and the South, are good witches. I know this is true, for I am one of them myself, and cannot be mistaken. Those who dwelt in the East and the West were, indeed, wicked witches; but now that you have killed one of them, there is but one wicked Witch in all the Land of Oz—the one who lives in the West.
—L. Frank Baum, *The Wonderful Wizard of Oz*, 1900

L. FRANK BAUM'S *Wizard of Oz*, published in Chicago in 1900, met with immediate success. Written for children as a classic coming-of-age story, the book resonated in specific ways with the society of its time. One of its attractions was to echo the great political debates that had mobilized Americans in the years leading up to its publication, thus lending itself to an allegorical interpretation of the contemporary United States. The book recounts the adventures in the Land of Oz of Dorothy, a typical American girl from Kansas, in the country's heartland. Along the way she encounters a scarecrow (symbolizing farmers), a Tin Woodman (allegorically representing workers), and a Cowardly Lion (William Jennings Bryan, the Populist candidate in the 1896 and 1900 presidential elections). All four must go to Oz, the capital of the kingdom, to find a solution to their problems. They must travel the Yellow Brick Road (gold) to reach the Emerald City (the color of the dollar), where the man in charge is a Wizard who wields power through illusion (the president). After many adventures, the characters discover that they already have what they are looking for: common sense for the farmer, humanity for the worker dulled by mechanization, and courage for the silver-tongued candidate. Dorothy learns that the Silver Shoes she has been wearing since the beginning of the story have the power to take her back to the America she loves, with her family. Together, farmers and workers, aided by the populist candidate Bryan, are thus led to the discovery that silver—that is, the remonetization of the silver dollar—is the answer to the heartland's distress. The tale thus echoes a narrative popularized by the Populists in the 1890s, which blamed the economic woes that many Americans were experiencing on the orthodoxy of the gold standard.[1]

Although the capital of the Land of Oz has the color of money, the most powerful personages in the kingdom are in fact four witches. Set at the four cardinal points of the compass, they embody a symbolic geography that reflects the American spatial imagination. In the late nineteenth century, Americans thought of their country as comprising four large regional blocs, known as sections. Covering vast stretches of the map, these sections were also charged with a potent but malleable political meaning—a meaning that Baum transferred to the witches in his book. Thus, the Good Witch of the North stands for the Midwest: a friend to honest workers, whom she tries to help, she is not powerful enough to defy the Wicked Witch of the East, who embodies the Northeast, the home of industrial and financial capitalism. When the story opens, she is in possession of the Silver Shoes (whose power she has usurped). She is also responsible for transforming the worker into the Tin Woodman by forcing him to work like a machine. The South, like the Midwest a hotbed of Populism, is also represented by a Good Witch, who reveals to Dorothy the power of the Silver Shoes (the remonetization of silver that was at the heart of the Populist programs in the 1890s). The Wicked Witch of the West, for her part, represents the mining barons of the Far West: allied with the Wicked Witch of the East, she governs with her Golden Cap (financial power) and seeks to possess the Silver Shoes.

Echoing the myths forged by Populism, *The Wizard of Oz* attests to the broad public's extraordinary investment in the monetary debates of the late nineteenth century, which culminated in the famous "battle of the standards" (gold versus silver) in the election of 1896. It is also the key to understanding that investment: for Americans, the money question was not only political but also geographical. It involved not only the parties but also the sections. Hence there is an inherently *spatial* dimension of politics in the United States. That is the subject of this book.

BEFORE SILVER there was paper. The money question originated well before the 1890s. It was a product of the Civil War, when the Union, to finance the enormous cost of its military operations, turned in part to the printing press. Thus was born the "greenback." Although legal tender, it was not convertible into coins (reserves of gold were too low for that). This exceptional situation, justified by the emergency of war, became problematic after peace returned in 1865, because the United States now had two official currencies of different values. This gave rise to a heated political controversy: the greenback became a touchstone in much broader debates in which rival conceptions of the economy, justice, and the role of the state were forged and competed. In this sense, the money question—a story of greenbacks before it was a story of the silver dollar—would last thirty years.

The emergence of this debate, as well as its intensity, may seem surprising in a political context dominated by a single issue: Reconstruction. After winning the war, the Union was left with the task of setting the terms on which the secessionist states would be readmitted to the Union. The goal was a just and durable peace—a tricky thing to achieve after a civil war. The issues that had triggered the war—secession and slavery—had been settled by force of arms. But numerous other thorny issues had arisen. What place should the newly freed blacks have in the new American society? What role should white Southerners who had taken up arms against their country be allowed to play? Should the Southern states be reformed, by force if necessary, or simply readmitted to the institutions of the federal government as they had existed before the war? All of these questions made for impassioned political debate, all the more so because they in fact called for a veritable redefinition of the American nation, citizenship, and the relationship of the people to the body politic.

Reconstruction was therefore a formidable business, as the vehement confrontations and even physical violence of the era attest. In such a context, it is remarkable that the money question gained any traction at all, let alone became such an important political issue. In the aftermath of the Civil War, the United States was consumed by two debates that touched the very definition of society: the first had to do with the republican system and the limits of democratic participation, while the second involved the economic model and the type of social relations on which it depended. Both were legacies of the war. Both brought the same cast of politicians to engage in debate with the same set of citizens. It was impossible for such closely related debates to proceed independently.[2]

Thus the two major American political debates of the last third of the nineteenth century flowed from the same crucible. Their long trajectories were linked. On the one hand, the money question emerged in the context of Reconstruction, which influenced the nature of the debate surrounding it. In return, the course of the economic debate influenced the reform process in the South, shaping the political possibilities of the time. In short, it is impossible to understand Reconstruction apart from the economic debates that engulfed the nation. Conversely, the nature of those debates and the role of the money question cannot be grasped apart from Reconstruction.

This book explores the intersection between Reconstruction, the central issue of the postwar period, and the economic debates epitomized by the money question. It does so on two levels. The first is a detailed analysis of the inter-actions and cross-influences of Reconstruction and political economy. This re-quires broadening the history of Reconstruction beyond the reform of the South (prominently including racial relations), to include the dynamics of the economy throughout the country. The second involves a more systemic approach to poli-tics. It proposes an analysis in terms of political configuration, asking how debates were shaped by the political field. More precisely, it looks at the ways in which parties (organizations) and sections (spatial categories) interacted to successfully (or not) embody contending political positions. Thus the emphasis is on the spa-tial dimension of American politics and, in particular, on the key phenomenon of *sectionalism*, that is, the geographical expression of antagonistic regional interests in a national framework.

THIS FOCUS ON the spatial dimension brings with it two benefits. First, it shifts the center of attention in the study of Reconstruction to a truly national context. Second, it makes it possible to relate Southern reform to changes occurring at the same time in the North, which Northerners were attempting to understand. Because the two approaches are complementary, the book brings together two historiographical realms that are often separate.

Traditionally, Reconstruction has been studied as a continuation of the Civil War: "It was essentially a postwar political and constitutional settlement—the peace treaty ending the Civil War—the terms of which would define and con-solidate the gains of the victor over the vanquished."[3] It therefore prolonged the clash between the North and South: by reforming the South, the North sought to ensure that the results obtained on the battlefield would endure. In this his-tory, the end of slavery, together with the social and political transformations it implied, plays an absolutely central role. The political history of the institutional reforms that the Republicans attempted in the South and the social history of racial relations in these newly post-slave societies define the backbone of the vast historiography of Reconstruction in all its avatars, and were masterfully weaved together in Eric Foner's 1988 synthesis.[4] Since then, historical interest in this period has not flagged, and there have been many studies of economic changes in the South, of gender relations among whites as well as blacks, of social change in various places, of the recourse to violence, and so on. What all these studies have in common is that they place race relations at the heart of Reconstruction.[5] With good reason: this is a fundamental question, and the interpretation of Re-construction that follows draws heavily on this body of work. But this approach depends on a specific geographic focus on the South (whether on a local or regional level) or on the political interplay between North and South (generally focusing on federal policies). Attention is therefore concentrated on one of two places, either the secessionist states or Washington, DC.

In this confrontation, the North is often forgotten, as Michael Holt points out:

> Since the term *Reconstruction* refers primarily to a readjustment between the North and South and of economic, social, and political relationships within the South, most historians would agree with Eric Foner's contention "that events in the South remain the heart of the Reconstruction drama." Nonetheless, over three-fifths of Americans lived in the North, where much of importance occurred between 1865 and 1877 that ostensibly had nothing to do with race relations or the South. The experiences of that northern majority require assessment. Since the power base of the Republican politicians who undertook the reconstruction of the South lay in the North, they had to pay close attention to the demands and grievances of their northern constituents, lest they lose power to the Democrats. Thus northerners' reactions to their own postwar experiences often helped shape and complicate Republicans' attempts to formulate and implement Reconstructions policies.[6]

Indeed, the recent revival of American historians' interest in political economy has fostered new work on the ways in which people's lives, ideas, and above all economic thinking changed in the United States after the Civil War, especially in the North. The main lines of inquiry include the intellectual history of economic thought, a reexamination of the role of elites in redefining the general interest toward a laissez-faire model and intransigent property rights, and works dealing with an activist state and the efforts of various groups to obtain (or block) federal government intervention. Often focused on the North, these works are rarely concerned with Reconstruction, and each adopts its own chronology.[7] Nevertheless, those that do consider the battles over the postwar Southern social model propose stimulating new interpretations. Concentrating on the labor question, Heather Cox Richardson suggests that the convergence of race and class tensions can be seen as fundamental to the elaboration and success of a free-market ideology that became dominant at the end of the century. Focusing on the state, Gaines M. Foster sees the experience of Reconstruction and the reaction against it as key elements in the emergence of a Christian lobby that sought to enlist the federal government in the regulation of individual behavior.[8] Such works thus incorporate Reconstruction into the broader scheme of American history, from which it has often been isolated. Because they look at extended periods of time, however, they avoid saying anything about Reconstruction itself, and even broaden the definition of the word way beyond its original meaning, to refer more generally to the modernization of all or part of the American social, economic, and political systems after the Civil War.

The approach proposed here is different. It retains the definition of Reconstruction as contemporaries understood it, namely, the attempt to establish a republican system of government in the secessionist states—republican as Northerners in power in Washington saw it (which in the post-abolition South had to do primarily with race relations). It links these processes to the whole range of political issues that roiled the United States in the same period in order to uncover the ways in which they influenced one another. The goal is to situate Reconstruction in a truly national framework so as to arrive at a better understanding of Reconstruction itself. It is in this perspective that it becomes relevant to analyze the situation in terms of political configuration, by which I mean the structure of power relations in a period when the consequences of the war were being worked out.

ONE CANNOT make sense of nineteenth-century American politics by looking solely at political parties. Secession itself is the most visible indication that other forces were at work. The event was the climactic moment of a geographical division: sectionalism. The word can be understood as "an intermediate stage between regionalism and nationalism. Sectionalism was more than the defense of regional interests: in the case of the South, it was a matter of defending a social system, a way of life, and forms of thought. But it was situated in the framework of a nation and did not question the region's participation in that nation." Secession came at the peak of this tension.[9]

Because of these extreme consequences, sectionalism was no small matter. Nor was it a one-time occurrence. On the contrary, it was deeply rooted in the workings of the American political system. The political scientist Richard F. Bensel, who has devoted several books to the phenomenon, sees it as a "'massive fact' of both extreme complexity and basic spatial or geographical simplicity." Its simplicity arises from the fact that Americans took sectionalism for granted. In the nineteenth century, it was a self-evident fact that there existed a South, a Northeast, and a West, and that these sections had their own identities and interests. Its complexity comes from the fact that it is difficult to characterize these sections precisely in either geographical terms or in the meaning they held for Americans. Sectionalism has an economic dimension: Bensel argues that "the historical alignment of sectional competition in America is primarily a product of the relationship of the separate regional economies to the national political economy and the world system." But it also has a cultural dimension, because each of the sections carried an identity, an often vague, sometimes contradictory set of images and symbols that defined it for both its denizens and others.[10] To understand the political impact of sectionalism, we must therefore first isolate these various aspects of the historical construction of the sections.

Reconstruction is an interesting moment to attempt such a study, because it provides an opportunity to escape the confines of the North-South confrontation that preoccupies most works on sectionalism before the Civil War yet without overlooking the fact that Southern reform was central to the politics of this period. The situation was peculiar: on the one hand, it was essential to draw the consequences of a war fought because one section had attempted to declare its independence from the others; on the other hand, that section no longer participated in the normal operations of the federal government. Simply put, the relations between North and South were being renegotiated, even though the South was no longer participating in national affairs. This made more room for another, less strident sectionalism, that which divided the Northeast from the Midwest.

The word "Midwest" calls for a comment. It did not exist in 1865. At that time, one spoke of "the West." In today's parlance, the word "West" conjures images of wide open spaces, high mountains, canyons and deserts, cowboys and roaming herds. At the time, it referred to the whole region that begins in the Ohio Valley, runs from the Great Lakes to the Mississippi, and then continues beyond. But even if it included peripheral territories still farther to the west, the word "West" primarily meant what we call the Midwest today. For reasons of geographic clarity, I therefore use the word "Midwest" in this book (apart from quotations in which the original wording is retained).

This Midwest took on special political importance during Reconstruction. For example, a historian as attentive to space as Frederick Jackson Turner saw East-West sectionalism as the major force behind the North-South clash, and therefore its settlement. Over the course of his career, Turner's thinking followed an interesting path, beginning with the concept of "frontier" and ending with a conceptualization of sections. He concluded that a section was a "faint image of a European nation," and that Congress should therefore be seen as a "League of Sections," a sort of diplomatic arena in which the nation's representatives negotiated something that bore "a striking resemblance to treaties between sections."[11] Another major American historian of the early twentieth century, Charles A. Beard, thirteen years younger than Turner, also made use of the idea of sectionalism in his work. Like his elder, he grew up in a period when the sectional phenomenon was so visible in the political arena that it was hard to ignore. It therefore played an important role in his and his wife, Mary's analysis of the Civil War and its consequences as a "second revolution," drawing on his economic interpretation of Reconstruction. For Beard, the Republican Party was the vehicle of a capitalist revolution led by the Northeast and imposed on the other sections of the country. His student Howard K. Beale interpreted Reconstruction in this light. It supposedly enabled the Radical Republicans to hold on to power by delaying the South's return to the Union and separating it ideologically from the Midwest. With the agrarian majority of the country thus divided, it was conquered, and the capitalists of the Northeast were able to impose economic measures that would never have been accepted in "normal" circumstances. Beale concluded that the disastrous policies of the Radicals had reinforced the power of wealthy capitalists, delivered the South into the hands of a single party, and created the conditions for Populist agitation and its ultimate failure.[12]

This strong interpretation met with a whole series of refutations in postwar historiography. Republicans were divided on economic policy, and there was no correlation between politicians' positions on Reconstruction and their economic policies. Similarly, businessmen did not constitute a homogeneous group, and there was no consensus on monetary or tariff issues. This was true even within each region. The financial debates were revisited to bring out the views of different interest groups in order to escape from an overly simplistic dualism (East vs. West, capitalists vs. farmers, etc.). In short, postwar historians emphasized the variety of positions rather than massive oppositions, drawing a nuanced portrait rather than a canvas in black and white.[13] The subsequent generation lost interest in these issues.

Nevertheless, Beard's interpretation of Reconstruction contains an important insight: the major issues of the time were indeed couched in sectional terms, and although the rhetoric of the day was varied, it was seldom nuanced. In short, the Northeast/Midwest dichotomy should be taken seriously for the simple reason that it was forcefully raised by contemporaries. The question thus remains: How did such diverse interests come to be subsumed in two simple—not to say simplistic—antagonistic positions? In other words, how did the sections come to be so prominent in the economic imagination of Americans? This is the new basis on which I propose to reevaluate the role of economic sectionalism in Reconstruction.

THIS BOOK REFLECTS two ambitions. The first is to make sense of the sectional logic, that is, the transmutation of certain themes of political economy into geographical oppositions. The second is to reinterpret Reconstruction in this light and to evaluate what Southern reform, the redefinition of citizenship, and the transformation of race relations in the United States owe to these sectional economic issues. In fact, these two ambitions are inseparable, because they share a common terrain. They require a new mapping of America's shifting political landscape. On the one hand, sectionalism shaped the major economic debates of the time. On the other, party politics shaped Reconstruction. In both there was a geographical dimension—the North versus the South and the Northeast versus the Midwest—and an ideological aspect more or less coincident with the division between Democrats and Republicans. Each of these two phenomena had its own dynamic, but the two dynamics were not independent of each other.

The goal, then, is to make sense of the advent and operation of a specific constellation of political forces in post–Civil War America, a constellation that involved the parties and sections in a constant back-and-forth among the national, regional, and local levels. Party organization and sectionalism, the forces that simultaneously shaped the political field, are considered here together, in relation to each other, in order to measure their full effect. To put it another way, Reconstruction and political economy are not treated separately but rather in interaction with each other. This is possible only on the terrain of national politics, where I analyze how the geographical dynamic complicated the more familiar interactions of the parties.

The book is divided into two parts. The first looks at sectionalism and considers the ways in which major debates in political economy revolved around an opposition between the Northeast and Midwest, with the South largely absent from the discussion. The goal is to uncover the political logic behind this geographical pattern. Chapter 1 adopts the perspective of the Midwest to examine the emergence of a sectional identity that eventually took on a national role. I evaluate this development and examine how it worked. Chapter 2 then takes up the money question, which became one of the most important political issues of the remainder of the nineteenth century. The consolidation of a myriad of financial problems under a single rubric owed a great deal to sectionalism—an opposition between the Midwest and the Northeast that divided and destabilized both of the major parties. Turning to taxes and the tariff, chapter 3 shows how the sections could take definite positions despite the complexity of shifting coalitions of interests. It also examines the political logic of the various economic positions, which cannot be understood in purely ideological or intellectual terms. Political interaction was capable of dissolving the contradictions of political thought.

Part 2 then proposes a reinterpretation of Reconstruction that places it in a truly national framework by incorporating issues of political economy. It examines in detail the political interactions of the two blocs in order to reconstruct the chronology of the reshaping of politics in a period of great fluidity. Three moments stand out, and each is the subject of a separate chapter. Chapter 4 explores the way in which the emergence of economic sectionalism in the North between 1865 and 1869 disturbed the balance of forces in relation to Reconstruction, allowing certain groups to seize the levers of power to try to block a Southern reform policy they opposed. Chapter 5 focuses on a second moment, when sectional conflict between the Northeast and Midwest divided the parties and thus paradoxically favored a reinforcement, indeed a radicalization, of Reconstruction policy, which served as the ideological core holding the parties together. This strategy worked up to the point where it provoked an ideological backlash, turning some Republicans against Reconstruction. This opened a third phase, which is the subject of chapter 6. Starting in 1873, sectional pressure became so intense that it soon led the Republican Party to turn its back on Reconstruction. Buffeted by crisis, the parties then underwent a partial geographical realignment that coalesced in the major electoral crisis of 1876. The resulting political configuration ended Reconstruction, and established a new precarious balance of forces between parties and sections that would endure until the end of the nineteenth century.

By integrating Northern sectionalism into the history of Reconstruction, I hope to clarify the geographical underpinnings of the new political configuration that emerged in this period and to show how it shaped the range of political possibility, the limits and constraints on what could be done in the United States in the latter part of the nineteenth century. In short, the history recounted in this book is one that emerged from the intersection of two major post–Civil War debates: one about the economic consequences of the war and the other about the political, racial, and social consequences of the abolition of slavery—gold and freedom.

PART I

Sectionalism

1

Sectionalism

THE VIEW FROM THE MIDWEST

———————— • ————————

> The first day's review, Wednesday, May 23, was given to the Army of the Potomac. . . . On the ensuing day the Army of the Tennessee and the Army of Georgia, constituting the right and left wing of General Sherman's forces, were reviewed. There was naturally some rivalry of a friendly type between the Eastern and Western soldiers, and special observation was made of their respective qualities and characteristics. The geographical distinction was not altogether accurate, for Western troops had always formed a valuable part of the Army of the Potomac; while troops from the East were incorporated in Sherman's army. . . . It was true, however, that the great mass of the Army of the Potomac came from the eastern side of the Alleghenies, while the great mass of Sherman's command came from the western side. —James G. Blaine, *Twenty Years of Congress from Lincoln to Garfield*, 1884

ON MAY 23 AND 24, 1865, Washington witnessed the greatest military parade of its young history. For two days, around 150,000 soldiers of the victorious Union marched before an immense crowd and a full complement of government officials. Regiment after regiment, the Army of the Potomac, led by General George Meade (the victor at Gettysburg), and then the Army of the Tennessee and the Army of Georgia, led by General William T. Sherman, marched in step down Pennsylvania Avenue from the Capitol to the White House. The spectators, of whom there were many—75,000 on the first day according to the *New York Herald*—tirelessly cheered the troops: they shouted, applauded, sang to the music of marching bands, threw flowers and wreaths, waved handkerchiefs and flags. The soldiers were impressed by the enthusiasm of the crowd: "We was proud that we belonged to Sherman army," one of them recounted, "and it paid us for all the hard marches that we have endured and the dangers we have passed through."[1]

The Grand Review was an unprecedented ceremony. For the first time, the United States honored its troops—and not just the officers—with a military parade of this kind. The capital had never seen so many soldiers, and it left a strong impression on the public. Newspaper accounts waxed lyrical:

> It is the army of the desolation of the South, that has made its mark of blood and ashes for two thousand miles, littering the whole line of its tremendous march with graves and the ruins of the habitations of its enemies. These are the men who brought the war home to the South, and brought the first wail of despair from the enemies of American nationality; and you can read something of this grand and terrible history in the dark faces of the heroes.

The ritual gave the people "a 'triumph' as demonstrative, if not as formal, as that given to a conqueror in Ancient Rome," marking the birth of a united and indivisible nation.[2]

In retrospect, it was obvious to the spectators at the Grand Review that what was treasonous in the behavior of the South was to have renounced membership in this nation. In this respect, the presence of black men, marching in the parade in meticulously aligned ranks, was symbolic. Their presence made visible the meaning of a conflict set in motion by slavery and transformed into a war of emancipation. It offered an eloquent illustration of the new nationalism that united everyone living within the borders of the United States.[3] The Grand Review put the new nation on display: "The whole country claimed these heroes as a part of themselves, an infinite gratification forever to the national self-love."[4]

In this great patriotic communion, the sectional rivalry between the soldiers of the Northeast and those of the Midwest that the Republican James G. Blaine described in his memoirs was all the more remarkable. It can be seen, for example, in the common desire of the officers and enlisted men of the Army of the Tennessee and the Army of Georgia, primarily made up of Midwesterners, to demonstrate as much discipline as the Army of the Potomac had shown the day before in order to refute their reputation as crude and savage warriors. Orders were given to clean their rifles, polish their shoes, and hand out as many new uniforms as possible. General John Geary bought white gloves for all the men in his division. Sherman issued the following instructions: "Be careful about your intervals and your tactics. Don't let your men be looking back over their shoulders. I will give plenty of time to go to the capitol and see everything afterward, but let them keep their eyes fifteen paces to the front and march by in the old, customary way." By the time this order reached the ranks, it was often simplified: "Boys remember its 'Sherman' against the 'Potomac'—the west against the east today."[5]

To be sure, this tension should be seen primarily as a military competition between rival armies. The Army of the Potomac, commanded by the various generals-in-chief of the Union forces, had the honor of defending the capital and of confronting Robert E. Lee, the prestigious commander of the Confederate forces. Yet many of the soldiers and officers on the Western front felt, not without reason, that their victories in 1863 were decisive in breaking the military impasse in which the Union Army had been caught, and that by marching across the entire South from Tennessee to Georgia, they had struck into the heart of the Confederacy in a way that gave the North the upper hand. It was his success in the West that won Ulysses S. Grant the post of commanding general of the Union armies, which he led to victory. The desire to outshine the other armies in the parade reflected a competition among the different troops to claim the glory of the victory.[6] In this respect, therefore, it was "'Sherman' against the 'Potomac.'"

This competition was reinforced, however, by a more general rivalry between sections, the Northeast and the Midwest. This resulted in part from the organization of the army. For both legal and practical reasons, the Union left it to the governors of the states to provide troops—volunteers initially, conscripts later on. Regiments were formed by each state and bore the name of that state: the 31st Ohio, the 69th New York, the 104th Illinois, the 54th Massachusetts, and so on. The system seemed natural to everyone. Salmon P. Chase, then secretary of the treasury, said in 1861 that he would "rather have no regiments raised in Ohio than that they should not be known as Ohio regiments." The mobilization of the first mass army in American history, along with patriotic competition among states, reinforced the attachment of the troops to their communities of origin. In battle, the soldiers were defending the honor of those communities as much as that of the Union.[7]

Sent to the nearest theater of operations, these regiments found themselves grouped by region. Thus in 1865, despite many troop movements during four years of conflict, only 30 of the 186 infantry regiments under William T. Sherman did not come from the Midwest. The organization of the military forced units from the same geographical area to share a common experience of war and therefore reinforced the sectional pride of the soldiers. Inter-army rivalry (over which units had achieved the most glorious victories) blurred easily into inter-sectional competition (over which section had demonstrated the greatest patriotism). The day of the Grand Review was indeed a day of "east versus west" for the soldiers of the Army of the Tennessee and the Army of Georgia.

The same Midwestern pride could be seen among the spectators. People came from all over to honor the boys who had fought for the Union. While some banners proclaimed the gratitude of the nation ("The Pride of the Nation," "The Nation Welcomes Her Brave Defenders"), others proudly affirmed local or regional sentiments: "Ohio Welcomes Her Brave Boys Home," "The West Is Proud of Her Gallant Sons," "We Welcome Our Western Boys: Shiloh, Vicksburg, Atlanta, Stone River, Savannah, and Raleigh." It is striking that in this celebration of unified nationalism, unwilling to tolerate a section (the South) that felt so distinct it had tried to secede from the nation, such expressions of sectional loyalty poured forth spontaneously without raising any eyebrows. National pride could be expressed locally, and the public interpreted what it saw through a sectional lens. The Western soldiers seemed taller and darker according to the *New York Herald*, which remarked that the West could be proud of its "tall, sinewy, iron-framed warriors." Sherman had feared that the city dwellers of the Northeast would take his men for uncivilized savage brutes, but in fact they impressed the crowd with their virile strength and military discipline.[8]

The section was thus a shared category, used by soldiers and spectators alike to make sense of the Grand Review in which they were participating. When the Army of the Tennessee and the Army of Georgia marched down Pennsylvania Avenue, people saw soldiers from the West. All were Americans—they had demonstrated their patriotism on the battlefield. They came from various states, whose names their regiments bore. But what identified them in their own eyes and the eyes of the public was that they came from the West. The few exceptions only proved the rule. At first sight, this phenomenon is difficult to explain: the Union had just fought against the assertion of sectionalism by one section, and that secession was based on the existence of a fundamental difference between the seceding states and the rest, slavery. No institution underpinned or reinforced Midwestern sectionalism. There was little objective basis for the distinction between the Midwestern states and their neighbors to the east. Yet even amid the most fervent expressions of patriotism such as the Grand Review, the men and women of the Midwest proudly proclaimed their allegiance to a section distinct from the rest of the country.

What "Midwest" Means

In his annual message to Congress of December 1862, Abraham Lincoln saw a definite link between section and nation in trying to explain the imperious necessity of preserving the Union, for which the country had been at war since April 1861:

> The great interior region bounded east by the Alleghenies, north by the British dominions, west by the Rocky Mountains, and south by the line along which the culture of corn and cotton meets, . . . already has above 10,000,000 people, and will have 50,000,000 within fifty years if not prevented by any political folly or mistake. It contains more than one-third of the country owned by the United States—certainly more than 1,000,000 square miles. . . . A glance at the map shows that, territorially speaking, it is the great body of the Republic. The other parts are but marginal borders to it. . . . In the production of provisions, grains, grasses, and all which proceed from them this great interior region is naturally one of the most important in the world. Ascertain from the statistics the small proportion of the region which has as yet been brought into cultivation, and also the large and rapidly increasing amount of its products, and we shall be overwhelmed with the magnitude of the prospect presented. And yet this region has no seacoast—touches no ocean anywhere. As part of one nation, its people now find, and may forever find, their way to Europe by New York, to South America and Africa by New Orleans, and to Asia by San Francisco; but separate our common country into two nations, as designed by the present rebellion, and every man of this great interior region is thereby cut off from some one or more of these outlets, not perhaps by a physical barrier, but by embarrassing and onerous trade regulations.[9]

Born in Kentucky before moving to Illinois, Lincoln embodied the "typical" Westerner: tall, sober-looking, of strict moral character, he was a self-made man celebrated for his birth in a log cabin. This image was widely publicized in his 1860 presidential campaign.[10] In this passage, however, he is by no means an apologist for his section. On the contrary, he links the future of the Midwest to the fate of the Union, relying on a familiar representation of his region. His words reveal the Midwest as a political category, and convey a construction of the national space inextricably intertwined with the economy. In this passage, the president avoided the term "section"—the war, after all, was a consequence of sectionalism pushed to the limit. Instead, he based his argument on a shared spatial imagination from which he drew arguments in support of the political and military struggle he was waging.[11] The context suggests that his description of the Midwest was by no means polemical but widely known and accepted. With great economy of language, the president summed up the characteristic features of his section: its geography, its place in the nation, its destiny, its agricultural economy and agrarian culture.

A Geographic Truism

Lincoln did not invent the "great interior region" he described in his message to Congress. The existence of this geographical entity—"the West"—was taken for granted by his contemporaries. Examples of its omnipresence abound. A meeting held in Chicago in 1869 to advocate for the right of women to vote was called the Western Women's Suffrage Convention. Two years earlier, a group of former slaves (of whom there were few in the region) formed a Western Freedmen's Association. In June 1868, John A. Logan, who headed a new and soon-to-be powerful veterans' organization known as the Grand Army of the Republic, presided over a meeting of the Armies of the West in Chicago. Two years later, he came under attack by a newspaper whose name leaves no room for doubt about its readership: the *Western Soldier's Friend and Fireside Companion*. In 1866, a group of newspapers formed the Western Associated Press, which complained about the quality and price of the news supplied by its monopolistic competitor, the New York Associated Press. Numerous professions organized sectional associations: the North-Western Fruit Growers Distributing Association, the National Bankers of the Northwest, the Woolens Manufacturers Association of the Northwest, and so on. Some of these groups, such as the Northwestern Agricultural, Mechanical, and Manufacturing Association, were distinguished solely by their geographical identification.[12]

Newspapers organized articles by section, under headings such as "Washington News," "The West," "The East," and "The South." This kind of classification seemed "natural," sometimes in a literal sense. As in Europe, where people often claimed to find "natural" borders for countries, Americans found warrant for their sectional divisions in contemporary technical works, such as the first statistical atlas of the United States, published in 1874, which included a survey of American forests by a Yale professor who relied on a human rather than botanical geography: "For convenience in discussing the kinds of wood, we may divide our domain into ten geographical divisions, viz:— 1st. New England; 2d. The Middle States; 3d. The South Eastern region; 4th. The Northwestern region; 5th. The Southwestern; 6th. The Plains; 7th. The Rocky Mountain region; 8th. Arizona, New Mexico and the Great Basin; 9th. The Pacific region; and 10th. Alaska." None of these regions was distinguished by a single forest type, as the text demonstrated in quite some detail. Whether this geographic classification was reproduced unthinkingly or chosen for pedagogical purposes, the fact remains that the writer simply could not escape the standard division of the country into regions.[13]

The fact that sections were so ubiquitous indicates that they were deeply rooted in the culture, though the precise limits and even the names of the various sections remained quite vague. Lincoln's "great interior region" was not yet called the "Middle West," a term that did not become popular until the end of the century.[14] At the end of the Civil War, the idea of a Far West distinct from the West nearer the East Coast and settled in the years after the Revolutionary War had not yet taken hold. The region called the Midwest today was then referred to as the West or the Northwest or sometimes the Old Northwest.

This semantic instability tells us something about the historical construction and transformation of the territory. "West" hints at a geographically open definition in relation to the old colonies of the Atlantic Coast. It was clear where the West began but not where it ended; the term was open enough to encompass the whole territory from Ohio to the Pacific.[15] "Northwest" was more circumscribed: it referred to the Northwest Ordinance of 1787, which defined the new territories acquired under the Treaty of Paris and specified how the region would be transformed into states. In this sense, the Northwest comprised the territory from Ohio to Illinois and Minnesota.[16] Time has altered this definition, however. After all, this "Northwest" ceased to constitute the Northwestern portion of American territory after the conquests of the 1840s. Some people therefore began to refer to it as "the Old Northwest" to distinguish it from the Oregon Territory obtained from Britain under the treaty of 1846, which included all the territory from California to the 49th parallel.

The terminology points to both the geographical openness and historical rootedness of the definition of the postbellum Midwest. The openness is obvious in light of the vague boundaries that contemporaries attributed to the section. Lincoln's message portrayed a region that stretched from the Alleghenies to the Rockies and from Canada to the boundary line between cotton and corn regions—a definition that combined mountain ranges with political boundaries and agricultural practices. In 1870, James A. Garfield, an Ohio Republican and future president of the United States, lumped together the "states that extend west from Ohio, north from Arkansas, and east from the Rockies." In 1874, the *North American*, a magazine based in Philadelphia, published a portrait of American industrial production in which the West extended southward into Kentucky

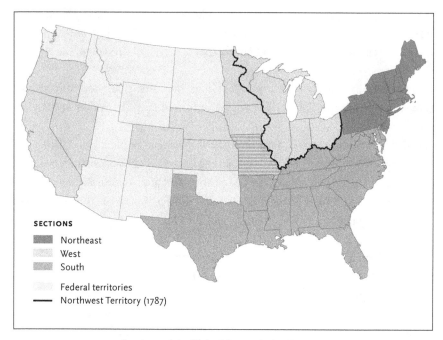

MAP 1. Sections of the United States during Reconstruction

and Arkansas. Sectional boundaries did not always coincide with state boundaries: the western portion of the vast state of New York was sometimes included in
the West, as indicated by the names of various firms located in the area.[17]

Map 1 indicates the most common sectional boundaries of the post–Civil War
period. It shows that the Midwest traced its historical roots to the Northwest Ordinance but began to stretch farther to the west. It also highlights the ambiguous
position of Missouri, which resembled the Midwest in many respects (economic,
demographic, and political) but shared a slave past with the South—this pivotal
role would prove crucial in the rise of the Liberal movement in 1870 (see chapter
5). Finally, the map illustrates a crucial point: although the South expanded westward, the Midwest was construed as a section distinct from the Northeast. Even
though its existence was obvious to Americans at the time, there was nothing
self-evident about it a priori.

The Midwest therefore had no intrinsic geographic meaning. Indeed, its uncertain boundaries and fluid verbal definitions show clearly that it was a shared
cultural construct. Other sections were equally vague: the territorial extent of the
South was not even defined by secession, as boundaries of the region continued to
shift after the war. Sections were blurred about the edges.[18] Indeed, these unclear

boundaries resulted from the fact that the sections had no institutional existence yet constituted a strong cultural presence.

The absence of any institutional structure for sections is one of the key distinctions between nation and section in the United States. As a nation-state, the United States has a government to govern its territory and an army to defend it. Under the federal system, each state has a precise jurisdiction, beyond which its legal authority ends. This structure is embodied in concrete institutions (departments of government, police, courts). By contrast, the sections have no institutional form: there is no intermediate level of government between the federal government and the states. In practice, therefore, the sections exist only in contingent, voluntary associations. They are therefore "imagined communities" without official institutional correlates. Their strength does not derive from law or institutional practices but rests, rather, on "a sense of common interest and identity across an extended, if indeterminate, space."[19]

In this respect, the sections were the geographical expression of a positive content. They caught on because they made sense. Since they were not sustained by everyday institutional practices or inscribed in law, they endured because they remained relevant to the way Americans understood the space they lived in—their territory. In this perspective, the vagueness of sectional boundaries was a plus, because it meant that the geographical definition of each section could adapt to its semantic content.[20] For example, it allowed for a distinction to emerge between a Far West and a Midwest when the Civil War and its consequences changed the definition of the section.

The semantic content of the Midwest as a section, its raison d'être as a category, was at that time essentially economic. The dominant representation was that of an agricultural region, the breadbasket of the nation and the world. This was a historical construct based on an economic reality. It was this construct that infused cultural—and political—life into the section as the Civil War drew to an end.

Access to Land and Market

In his annual message of 1862, Lincoln singled out two important characteristics of the Midwest: its stupefying demographic growth and its abundant agricultural output. These two features, which are easily quantified, accurately described the states west of the Appalachians. At the time of the Civil War, however, they had become *defining* traits of the Midwest itself, constituting its meaning and identity. In the national political crisis, a dominant interpretation of the region crystallized around a vision of its destiny that rested on two pillars—access to land and access to the market.

Access to the land was at the heart of the Land Ordinance of 1785, which established procedures for the survey and sale of public land. Although lots were initially large and expensive, prices tended to fall as time went on, until the Homestead Act of 1862 granted property titles to anyone who cultivated public land for a period of five years. The Land Ordinance, like the Northwest Ordinance of 1787, came to stand for the availability of land to anyone willing to farm it, as many people did, even without a clear title.[21]

The Ordinance of 1787 also outlawed slavery of any kind in the Northwest Territory. This ban, uncontroversial at the time it was passed, was inherent in the logic of the text, which envisioned the settlement of the territories by immigrants from Europe. This did not mean that slaves were totally absent from the region. Those who inherited their status from the French regime were still there, while thousands of others were brought into Indiana and Illinois as indentured servants. Once the territories became states, moreover, they were free to reestablish slavery, a possibility that was raised numerous times until 1824, when the voters of Illinois defeated it once and for all by a large majority.[22] Across the Mississippi, however, Missouri became a slave state when the first North-South tensions arose in 1820, and the case of Kansas in the 1850s became one of the main bones of contention in the crisis.

Indeed, it was amid the political turbulence of this period that the anti-slavery clause of the Northwest Ordinance took on symbolic value. Faced with the expansion of the "Peculiar Institution," the absence of slavery came to be intertwined with access to land. "Free land and no slavery" was the slogan associated with the free-labor ideology that spread in the North: "free soil" and "free labor" were two sides of the same coin. This equation of economic opportunity with absence of slavery was at the heart of the crisis that gripped the United States in the 1850s. For many, the West was open and expanding, developing thanks to a substantial influx of immigrants, who cultivated an ever-growing acreage of farmland. To introduce slavery into the new territories won from Mexico was tantamount to blocking this growth (territorial as well as economic) and challenging the section's very identity.[23] This view was far from unanimous, however, as shown by the series of debates held in 1858 between Abraham Lincoln and Stephen Douglas, both of Illinois.[24]

The anti-slavery sentiment that emerged in the Midwest takes on its full meaning only when linked to access to land. The latter was the force behind a massive immigration, which was one of the most important factors in the brief history of the United States. The Midwest, where only a few hundred white settlers lived in 1790, was home to nearly 9 million in 1860.[25] The availability of fertile soil (once the Indians had been driven out) was a key factor in attracting new settlers, be it the Germans who settled in Wisconsin, the Norwegians of Minnesota, or the Anglo-Americans who put down stakes in Illinois. Not only was there room in the Midwest to build communities similar to those they had left behind, but the abundance of good land also encouraged them to engage in more productive and commercial forms of agriculture.[26]

Despite certain ambivalent feelings, the new citizens of the Midwest were ardent promoters of integration into regional, national, and international markets. Many of them mobilized for internal improvements. The opening in 1825 of the Erie Canal, which linked the Great Lakes to the Port of New York, marked a turning point. Frenetic canal-building ensued, followed by railroads in the 1840s. Popular support can be seen in the generous aid that cities and states granted to railway companies. The role that the canals and railroads played in integrating the region into international trade networks is reflected in the influx of European (mainly British) capital to finance these construction projects. The results were impressive: by 1860, the Midwest alone accounted for a third of the nation's railroad network. New lines stretched throughout the region, ending the isolation of many areas. Map 2 reveals the extent of the changes, which left virtually no farmer more than 20 miles from a canal or railway line.[27]

The economic and social consequences of this transportation revolution were colossal, as was its impact on the structure of space. The entire region was linked to a few central cities, which served as markets and grew at an impressive rate. Chicago was the most spectacular example of such growth. Barely a village in 1830, the city counted more than 100,000 residents in 1860. But St. Louis, Cincinnati, and Cleveland also prospered. The Great Lakes region and later the land west of the Mississippi became a vast, fertile hinterland serving these new cities, which thrived on trade in the region's agricultural products (including wheat, corn, and beef). New York became a major international port. Cotton was no longer the only king.[28] These rapid economic and geographic transformations, fueled by immigration and burgeoning new means of transportation, reshaped Americans' understanding of their own geography. They thus contributed to the birth of the Midwest as an "imagined community": a region conceived as such by its inhabitants, for whom it quickly came to seem "natural."

A Political Construction

Demographics and economics are important factors for understanding the construction of the Midwest as a section and especially for comprehending its image and the positive content it conveyed. By themselves, however, these two factors cannot explain how this part of the country became differentiated from other

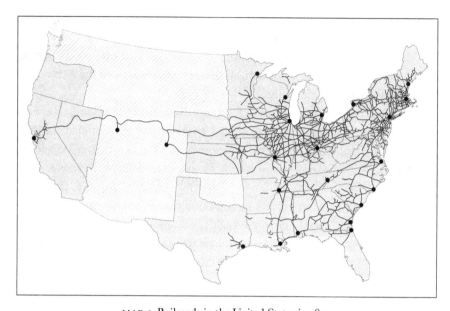

MAP 2. Railroads in the United States in 1870

Source: Charles O. Paullin, *Atlas of the Historical Geography of the United States* (Washington, DC: Carnegie Institution of Washington, 1932).

regions. For example, map 2 shows clearly that the railway network tied the Atlantic states to the Great Lakes region in an unbroken chain. Nor was agriculture a distinctive feature of the Midwest, even though the share of the workforce engaged in agricultural work was greater there than in the Northeast. There were more farms in New York and Pennsylvania in 1860 than in states farther to the west. The ratio of population to number of farms suggests that all of the states remained largely rural. Nor was attractiveness to migrants a distinguishing feature of the region that came to be the Midwest: among the ten states whose population doubled (or more) in the 1850s were not only California, Iowa, Wisconsin, and Illinois but also Texas and Arkansas (and this is true even if we count only the free population). In that same decade, Ohio's population grew less than that of Massachusetts, and Indiana's less than that of New Jersey.[29]

Even the cultural attributes ascribed to the "Westerner" had much in common with the cultural attributes of other Americans. The Western ideal type was slow to emerge. The earliest migrations into the Northwest Territory, just after independence, came mainly from the South. Migrants from the Northeast did not arrive in large numbers until the 1820s. In the early years, there is little evidence of identification with a "Northwest." Indeed, migrants defined themselves, and

even more their neighbors, in terms of their region of origin, reviving old prejudices. Southerners were said to be too independent to be sociable and too lazy to
be industrious; "Yankees" were said to be crafty and dishonest. Little by little,
however, people began to think that by rubbing shoulders with one another, the
migrants acquired a new character, combining the qualities of Southerners and
Northerners: thus was born "the Westerner." He was supposed to represent the
true American, stripped of parochial (European) characteristics. Clearly, however, this attempt to define a region not by its difference from other regions but
by its representativeness was not devoid of ambiguity. The distinguishing feature
of the Midwest was precisely that it had no distinguishing feature.[30]

Demographic, social, and economic phenomena all played an important part in
the development of the Midwest. It is nevertheless important to point out that the
crystallization of the Midwest as a distinct geographic region despite its similarity
to other regions owed a great deal to politics. It was politics that differentiated the
Midwest from the Northeast, whereas the Southwest remained part of the larger
South. A thorough study of this phenomenon is beyond the scope of this book,
but it is important to recognize two processes that are crucial for understanding
the sectional rivalries between the Midwest and Northeast and their post–Civil
War consequences. First, the advent of mass political parties made it possible to
include diverse cultural groups in the same political conversation. Second, the
promotion of local and regional economic interests aroused opposition to other
sections of the country. Here, negative contrasts were as influential as positive
identifications with a common destiny.

The advent of politics played a fundamental role in creating a sectional identity.
Migrants arrived with a strong sense of attachment to their homelands, whether
in Europe or the United States. Southerners, for example, consciously cultivated
their customs, partly to preserve their identity and partly to distinguish themselves from other groups (especially New Englanders). The same type of behavior
was perhaps yet more pronounced among European immigrants, whose native
languages and customs were even more different. Many migrants, whether Norwegians in Minnesota or New Englanders associated with the Ohio Company,
settled in small, homogeneous communities that reproduced the housing styles
and customs of their home region. Yet autarky was impossible. Since many decisions were taken at the state or federal level, people could control their local exis-
tences only by participating in politics. The influence of mass parties after 1820
meant that cultural identity receded in importance compared with a more broadly
defined political participation. The process was not without ambiguities, because
homogeneous communities sometimes traded support for a political party for

autonomy and other compensatory benefits. Still, politics brought many different groups, each with its own identity, into a common dialogue at the state and national levels.[31]

This integration took place in part on terms inherited from the revolutionary period and from conflicts that erupted in the wake of the Northwest Ordinance. All the states of the Northwest had experienced territorial government direct from Washington. On the one hand, this aroused opposition (particularly in Ohio) to the "colonial" system as long as the territories were not yet states. On the other hand, republican discourse encouraged an antagonistic vision in which the original states were pitted against the Northwest Territories in a battle that echoed that for independence. In the early years of the American republic, the settlers of the territories conceived of their situation as similar to that of the thirteen colonies vis-à-vis the British Crown in 1776.[32]

The Land Ordinance of 1785 reinforced this distinction by encouraging the emergence of yet another conflictual discourse. A struggle broke out between squatters who occupied and cultivated land to which they held no title and the federal government, which sought to survey, regulate, and extract revenue from the sale of public land. The settlers defended what they felt they had won by dint of courage (against the Indians) and hard work against the arbitrary decisions of a government that favored wealthy absentee speculators by selling lots that were too large and expensive. The ensuing discourse insisted on the economic and political benefits of establishing "a hardy, independent, industrious yeomanry" rather than "principalities for the rich." The point was to defend smallholders against rich, greedy speculators from the East. The common identity that emerged from this political conflict stemmed in part from the image of the small, independent farmer, owner, and entrepreneur versus the common enemy, namely, the East, which controlled the federal government and was personified by the figure of the rapacious speculator.[33]

The shared identity that developed around the issue of public land crystallized in a campaign for public subsidies needed for internal improvements. There were of course some mixed feelings, and disputes inevitably arose about the precise routing of a canal or railroad, but Midwesterners were by and large ardent defenders of these projects. In the national arena, however, in Congress or in dealings with the president, they quickly realized that federal resources were limited and choices were inevitable, with the Midwest in competition with other sections for money. Under Andrew Jackson's presidency (1829–1837), for example, many Midwestern Democrats grew impatient with Jackson's ambiguous attitude. The president sought to keep the Southern states, generally opposed to subsidies, happy without alienating the Midwest, which wanted them. He claimed to be in favor of projects that were in the national interest but rejected those he considered to be of purely local concern. Many Midwesterners saw his veto of the Maysville Road in Kentucky as a betrayal. They indignantly portrayed the Midwest as a region deprived of federal aid, despite the fact that federal money derived from the sale of public land in the West had financed the economic development of the South and Northeast. Millions of dollars had been spent to help Atlantic commerce, they argued, yet the federal government refused to pay for the improvement of Midwestern rivers and the building of canals on the grounds that these were local projects. Such controversies helped to solidify the idea of "the West," as settlers from New England, the South, and elsewhere joined together in defense of what they saw as the common interests of their new section. This newfound unity was reflected in bloc voting by congressmen on bills dealing with internal improvements.[34]

Out of these political battles emerged a section, then known as the West, in opposition to other sections (which themselves were not fully unified).[35] I do not mean to imply that "the Midwest" was a perfectly unambiguous category. Indeed, visions of its future varied widely. The boosters who promoted the region's economic development and sought to attract investors stressed the importance of cities—the vision of a great metropolis.[36] Others preferred the agrarian ideal of a citizenry of yeoman farmers. The sectional identity was not uncontested: it coexisted to one degree or another with other identities. In this region of immigrants, loyalties of origin were powerful. In the 1850s, Nativists attacked European immigrants, especially the Irish, as un-American. They viewed them as rootless and unassimilated, refusing to become "Westerners."[37] But the greatest challenge to the new Midwestern identity was the growing sectional crisis between the North and South, between slave and non-slave states. During this period, political tensions revived older loyalties of Midwestern migrants. Yet even those attachments had changed. For instance, the Southerners of Illinois, Indiana, and Ohio believed until 1861 that the Union could be saved from two extremisms—the intransigence of Southern planters and New England abolitionism—by unifying the West and strengthening its ties with the border states. Remembering their blood ties to Southern cousins and their regional ties to other Westerners with cousins in the Northeast, they hoped to ward off secession. In the end, the war forced most former Southerners to think of themselves first and foremost as Midwesterners, while the Confederate South became the enemy. Even when identification with the West was at its most fragile, however, it continued to sustain the image of a veritable American melting pot.[38]

At the end of the Civil War, the Midwest was therefore a section that existed, in the sense that its inhabitants—and others—were aware of it as a distinct, shared reality. This mental construct or shared image was made possible by massive immigration and the development of an impressive transportation network. These processes set the terms of political debate and defined the stakes of an economic system that had to be defended politically, financially, and culturally against other sections with their own distinct interests. Two factors shaped this evolution: the first, which can be characterized as positive identification, allowed people to imagine a common destiny for the entire region beyond that of simple locality or state; the second, which we might call negative identification, defined and reinforced the community in opposition to other groups. Both were indispensable to the emergence of a shared identity. The distinction is similar to one that Patricia N. Limerick used to distinguish the terms "region" and "section": "Regions, by this arrangement, unite, while sections divide. Regions can both complement and compliment one another; sections can only compete. Regions have their roots in a warm and hearty connection between distinctive people and distinctive places; sections have their roots in political and economic struggles for dominance." The contrast drawn here is valid insofar as it reflects a lexical reality rooted in American history.[39] But in truth, "section" and "region" are two sides of the same coin, because differentiating between self and other is part and parcel of recognizing the existence of common interests and a shared destiny. In the nineteenth century, it was primarily the word "section" that was used to denote the parts of the country known as the Northeast, the Northwest, and the South.

A Spatial Category in Politics

Born of politics, the section as a spatial category was a key feature of the United States after the Civil War. Even as the North-South confrontation remained central to the political debate, the opposition within the North between the Northeast and the Midwest helped to shape the political landscape. The next two chapters explore how the major economic debates of the day became sectional and shook up the "usual" game of parties. First, however, I discuss how sectionalism emerged and played out in national politics.

Let us start with Congress. A statistical snapshot of voting there offers a good first image of the importance of sectionalism. Table 1 covers all roll-call votes throughout Reconstruction (December 1865 to March 1877).[40] Unsurprisingly, voting divided along party lines in most cases, meaning a majority of Republicans voted one way and a majority of Democrats the other. This is what we would expect, and was true of roughly two-thirds of roll-call votes in the House during this

TABLE 1. Roll-call votes in Congress during Reconstruction, 1865–1877

Congress	39th (1865–67)	40th (1867–69)	41st (1869–71)	42nd (1871–73)	43rd (1873–75)	44th (1875–77)	Total
HOUSE OF REPRESENTATIVES							
Total roll-call votes	613	716	634	517	475	328	3,283
% sectional votes*	19	15	26	18	17	17	19
% very sectional votes[†] out of sectional votes*	41	29	36	15	46	7	31
% sectional votes through abstention[‡]	18	22	9	12	12	20	15
% partisan votes[§]	62	59	67	65	66	56	63
% very partisan votes[‖] out of partisan votes[§]	82	82	83	75	81	88	82
SENATE							
Total roll-call votes	501	716	742	803	420	434	3,616
% sectional votes*	23	27	20	11	22	12	19
% very sectional votes[†] out of sectional votes*	47	37	43	42	61	38	44
% sectional votes through abstention[‡]	19	17	32	33	25	26	26
% partisan votes[§]	41	43	45	42	51	47	44
% very partisan votes[‖] out of partisan votes[§]	75	69	68	84	73	87	76

* Sectional votes are defined as votes where the majority of Midwestern congressmen voted yea, and the majority of Northeastern congressmen voted nay, or vice versa.

† Very sectional votes are defined as sectional votes where the majority in each of the two groups was above 60 percent.

‡ Sectional votes by abstention are defined as votes where the majority of one sectional group voted either yea or nay, and the majority of the other abstained.

§ Partisan votes are defined as votes where the majority of Republicans voted yea, and the majority of Democrats voted nay, or vice versa.

‖ Very partisan votes are defined as partisan votes where the majority in each of the two groups was above 60 percent.

period. Voting in the Senate followed a similar, though less clear-cut, pattern: there were fewer senators than representatives, and the culture and rules of the Senate afforded them greater individual autonomy.[41] The power of the partisan imperative is also evident in the strong cohesiveness of the parties in most of the partisan votes (four-fifths of them in the House).[42] In sum, in most partisan votes, a very unified group of Democrats opposed a similarly unified group of Republicans.

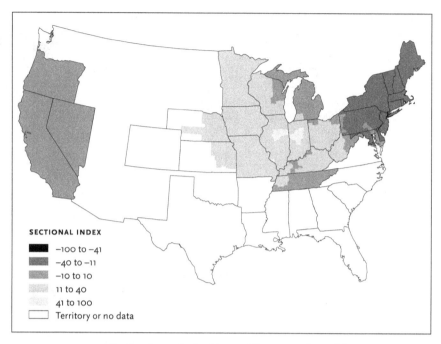

MAP 3. Sectional votes in the House of Representatives, 1865–77

But the table shows a second influence also at work: geography. In both houses, one-fifth of the roll-call votes (roughly 1,300 votes over 12 years) pitted North-easterners against Midwesterners, regardless of party affiliation. This is quite a striking number. This sectionalism was less important than partisanship. It was also less polarizing: in the sectional votes, the opposing groups (representatives of the West and those of the Northeast) were often less solidly united than the opposing groups in partisan votes.[43] This suggests that sectionalism, though common, was more fragile politically, or at any rate that the cost of breaking ranks was lower. Unlike Southerners on the eve of the Civil War, postbellum congressmen felt less pressure to line up with their section than with their party.[44] Still, a large number of votes followed a sectional pattern.

A glance at map 3 confirms the importance of the section as a spatial category. Projecting sectional votes onto congressional districts, it shows that the Midwest and Northeast were veritable voting blocs. There is no transitional zone between the two. We see rather a juxtaposition of two clearly distinct regions. On sectional votes, Ohio's representatives were closer to those of Iowa or Minnesota than to their colleagues in nearby Pennsylvania. This finding is all the more remarkable in that the map represents an aggregate of all sectional votes, no matter what the issue, including even the least polarizing ones. Furthermore, although the average cohesiveness of each sectional group is not very high, the correlation between the behavior of House members and the culturally defined sections (as contemporaries saw them and as represented in map 1) is remarkable. The map underscores the cultural and therefore political force of sectional affiliation.

In Congress, sectionalism was a recurrent, relatively stable phenomenon that was well-defined geographically and culturally. It was nevertheless less important than partisanship in terms of both frequency and average intensity. Sectionalism emerged most frequently in connection with economic policy debates, as table 2 makes clear. The issues included the financial consequences of the war (currency, banking, and public debt), the tariff, taxation, and subsidies for internal improvements. This last set of issues had been around for a long time and played a central role, as we have seen, in the crystallization of the Midwest as a distinct section. By contrast, the other issues emerged in or were transformed by the war. But all of them involved the role of the federal government in the economy. To understand how they became sectional, we need to zoom in on the precise political mechanisms that, in Congress, would suddenly turn debates on a particular topic into a conflict between the Northeast and the Midwest.

How Sectionalization Worked

The Bankruptcy Act is a good place to begin an examination of how economic debates became sectional conflicts. Discussed in 1866 and 1867, this bill was designed as "a code of positive law—embracing the relations between debtor and creditor in every State—superseding the local laws, and intended to be uniform and national in its operation."[45] Previously, the regulation of bankruptcy and debt recovery, although an expressed federal power in the Constitution, had mostly been left to the states. The new law established the first comprehensive nationwide system.

The bill was introduced partly in response to economic problems raised by Secession and the Civil War. Many Southerners had incurred debts to Northerners that became impossible to collect. The wartime economy disrupted normal credit channels, and bankruptcies multiplied. When peace was restored in 1865, the problems did not end. Among the factors making for a more volatile economy were large-scale destruction of property in the South coupled with general insolvency, the fluctuating value of paper money, and wartime inflation followed by a postwar policy of deflation. For Republicans, "the circumstances in which the country is now placed, owing to the terrible convulsion through which we have passed" called for "the passage of a general bankruptcy law."[46]

TABLE 2. Main themes of sectional votes in Congress, 1865–1877

Themes	Roll-call votes	Polarization Index
Money and banking	80	0.43
Internal improvements	75	0.26
South and Reconstruction	53	0.14
Tariff	48	0.37
Appropriations	40	0.26
Taxes	37	0.30
Public debt	22	0.40
Session calendar	18	0.23
Bankruptcy Act	14	0.33
Public land	14	0.19
Military pensions	11	0.52
Census and apportionment	11	0.55

Note: This table lists the themes of the bills that have given rise to sectional roll-call votes. It only lists the main themes and represents about 67% of all sectional roll-call votes.

The Polarization Index measures the polarization in a vote or a group of votes between two groups (here Midwest and Northeast), on a scale from 0 to 1. It is the means of the Rice Index for both groups.

The idea of a federal measure "superseding the local laws, and intended to be uniform and national in its operation" represented a continuation of the economic reforms that the Republicans had pursued since 1861. They shared the vision of a nation in which all interests would harmoniously coexist. The government should intervene in the economy in order to liberate and stimulate economic growth based on free-labor principles.[47] Thomas Jenckes, a Rhode Island Republican who had promoted these goals for several years, described the bankruptcy law as "an attempt to establish the law of debtor and creditor upon an equal and just system, based upon the Constitution, and which shall have a salutary and satisfactory operation in all parts of our country," and saw it as part of a broader vision of a unified national economy. It would be followed by "recognizing and enforcing a code of commercial law, and above and beyond all declar[ing] by the plain language of statute-law what we believe to be, and what we are prepared to maintain, as the law of nations."[48]

At first sight, such a reform was not sectional but national, if not nationalistic. Boards of Trade throughout the North, from Boston to Detroit to New York to Cleveland and Chicago, supported the bill.[49] But sectional rhetoric soon cropped up in congressional debates. Homesteads were the crucial issue. In all the Midwestern states, laws existed to protect homesteads (family-owned and -occupied farms) from seizure by creditors. In Iowa, for example, 40 acres of homestead were protected in this way, regardless of the debt incurred by the owner. But the bankruptcy bill proposed to eliminate this exemption, "touching a question as precious to the judgment, conscience, and heart of western men as this idea of a homestead exempt from violent seizure under the law," according to John A. Kasson of Iowa. William Stewart, a senator from Nevada, argued that "these homestead exemptions have so far entered into the system of the country, particularly in the West and on the Pacific, and have operated so beneficially, that it will be a great calamity to disturb them." Alexander Ramsey, Stewart's colleague from Minnesota, warned that even though he favored a national bankruptcy law, he would vote against the bill if the homestead exemption was not preserved.[50]

The homestead exemption was not specific to the Midwest, however. It existed, in one form or another, in nearly all the states. "In the State of Vermont the homestead is limited to $500 in value; in New York it is limited to $1,000," Eugene Hale, a Maine Republican, observed. Nevertheless, a sectional association emerged. Ramsey explained, "We have in our State a very moderate exemption, consisting, I think, of eighty acres of land in the country or a town lot in a city or town, and upon these little sanctuaries families have enshrined themselves. Driven out by the exactions and persecutions of heartless creditors in the East, they have sought an asylum in the West, and by these liberal laws of our States have been protected." The homestead exemption thus became a sectional problem because it was interpreted in terms of already well-established representations. "The free and easy but honest and true men of the West . . . are an agricultural people, interspersed with mechanics. They have not the highly developed commerce of Boston, New York, or Philadelphia. Nor have they the manufacturing peculiarities of Massachusetts, Connecticut, or Rhode Island. The farmers and mechanics of the West are, as a people, inferior in intelligence, enterprise, honesty, and patriotism to no portion of our fellow-citizens."[51] A historical legacy, this image of an agricultural people explains the reflexive instinct to see the homestead exemption as a sectional issue. The idea of protecting the core of what a family needed to survive from seizure by creditors was not inherently sectional, and in any case, it was included in the laws of nearly every state. But the very word "homestead" encouraged a sectional interpretation, because it generally referred to a farm, and Western representatives had fought hard for the Homestead Act of 1862 in order to facilitate access to public lands.[52]

The debate about bankruptcy stirred sectional feelings as it touched on a key feature of American representations of the Midwest. This, in turn, completely changed how congressmen viewed the bill. Although the text had been conceived as a way of standardizing bankruptcy laws across the country for the benefit of all, it suddenly took on the aspect of a threat to local liberties that would use the long arm of the federal government to enhance the power of Northeastern financial interests. Some Midwestern Republicans resorted to anti-federal rhetoric. Halbert E. Paine of Wisconsin denounced the "engine of oppression" that "a Federal court may be in the hands of a man holding office for life, free from the salutary checks of responsibility to, and swift punishment by, the people." In his view, "the Federal courts . . . are, in some parts of the country, hardly less terrible to the people than the Star Chamber or the Inquisition itself."[53] This astonishing diatribe might sooner have come from a states-rights Democrat than a Republican. Paine's inflamed rhetoric reveals the effects of the political lens at work here: the threat the proposed bankruptcy law posed to homesteads created a sectional identification. Because the homestead exemption required that state laws be taken into account, Midwestern congressmen insisted that the federal standardization of the bankruptcy code be circumscribed to allow for needed local adjustments.

Midwestern sectionalism thus disrupted the Republican effort to redefine the federal system. That project was shaped in large part by a series of negotiations in a time of political emergency. Because sharp divisions existed among Republicans, we cannot speak of a uniform ideology. Nevertheless, the Republican Party presided over an institutional rebalancing in favor of the federal government during the war and Reconstruction.[54] In this political context, the sectional anti-federalism that erupted among Midwestern Republicans amused both Democrats and the most conservative Republicans. Senator Lafayette S. Foster of Connecticut remarked that it was

> very popular on this floor to talk about, I will not say the omnipotence of Congress, but the absolute power of Congress and perfect weakness of the States. States rights, under certain circumstances, are sneered at exceedingly in certain quarters, and the man who talks about States rights is in danger, I have thought at times, of being regarded as being in sympathy with traitors. But now if the Congress of the United States undertake to say that a man who is in debt shall pay his debts or rather that his property, except a certain amount, shall be applied to pay them, . . . they are exceeding their legitimate powers and trampling on State sovereignties.[55]

Was it possible both to defend state-by-state exceptions to the Bankruptcy Act while at the same time asserting federal power over the Southern states? For at the same moment, Congress was devising its Reconstruction policy, imposing reforms on the secessionist states. Many controversies erupted over the respective limits of federal and state power. These contemporaneous debates inevitably influenced the bankruptcy debate. On the one hand, the same nationalizing impulse that militated in favor of limiting the autonomy of the defeated South also called for a uniform bankruptcy law. On the other hand, maintaining the homestead exemption for Midwestern states created an obstacle to enforcing such a code in the South. Massachusetts Republican Senator Henry Wilson thought that the law could be "construed [in such a way] that the stay laws which have recently been passed in some States" with the support of Southern planters would allow debtors in those states to avoid paying their debts. To allow the states to establish exemptions was to permit Southern debtors, many of whose creditors were in the North, to use their local political influence to evade their obligations. Would this not be tantamount to surrender on the issue of Reconstruction?[56]

It was in the tension between the local and the national scale that the bankruptcy debate became sectional. The federal bill was amended in response to local (Midwestern) demands for the protection of homesteads. This exemption, however, opened the door to local Southern evasion of debts owed to nonlocal Northerners. The only remedy was a national law depriving Southern debtors of the legal means to escape their financial obligations. This contradiction in federalism could not be overcome in the bill alone, and it proved impossible to pass the Bankruptcy Act without including the exemptions demanded by Midwestern representatives, as the sectionalism in the voting attests. This conundrum was solved when Congress adopted the Military Reconstruction Acts of 1867. The new Southern policy promised to give Republicans control of Southern legislation locally, thus removing the objection to the homestead exemptions in the Bankruptcy Act, which was then passed by a party vote.[57]

It is important to note the role of federalism in transforming a law with national ambitions into a sectional issue. Because states had their own bankruptcy laws, comparison with the federal bill was possible. Federalism thus led to a dialogue between the federal and state levels wherever shared jurisdiction existed. Yet the interaction of institutions at these different levels is never predictable. Rather, it is historically contingent, as people make it work, day to day, in practice. In this case, representatives from different states debated the terms of a uniform law for the entire country. Each representative brought his own analytic categories to the debate. Among them, it is striking to see how readily sectionalism influenced the political judgment of the participants. The homestead exemption was not specific to the Midwest, yet the issue was formulated in sectional terms *from the beginning* of the debate. This fact attests to the political potency of sectional thinking, which shaped the geographical interpretation of federalism.

Sectionalism and Patriotism

Sectionalism created tension between the local and the national. It should never-theless not be interpreted by analogy with the Southern secession as being in con-tradiction with pro-Union patriotism, which the Civil War significantly strength-ened throughout the North. Sectionalism pitted the Midwest against the Northeast rather than one of these two sections against the nation. Unlike the antebellum confrontation between slavery and free labor, this new sectionalism did not involve a confrontation between two systems. Continuity prevailed within the North. In-deed, the defense of regionally defined economic interests involved claims of higher patriotism.

Sectionalism here can be understood as a geographic overdetermination of Americans' economic relationship to their nation. In this respect, it was not in contradiction with nationalism. A bill debated in 1866 to equalize veterans' boun-ties is a good place to observe the way sectionalism served as a prism refracting federal policy. Initially, the bill was purely national in character. It proposed dis-tributing aid in the form of cash bonuses and land to all soldiers and sailors who had served the Union, with deduction of bonuses previously paid. The bill thus offered both social assistance (responding to the many veterans who found them-selves in difficult economic circumstances) and a reward for patriotism.[58]

This legislation anticipated the veterans' pensions of $100 per year of service that would involve the federal government in large-scale social assistance a decade later.[59] But because the bill proposed deducting bonuses already received, it was not a simple distribution of equal bounties to all veterans; rather, it attempted after the fact to express equal gratitude to each man who did his patriotic duty. Wartime bounties had never been uniform. Paid by states, counties, towns, and even private organizations to encourage men to volunteer for service, these boun-ties varied widely, depending on the date and place of recruitment. The bill's sponsor, Robert C. Schenck of Ohio, explained that "Some soldiers [had] received $1,000, $1,200, $1,500 bounty from various sources." But if "the United States [is] the *alma mater* of all the soldiers," such favoritism would have to be corrected by paying bounties to those who had not received any.[60]

At first sight, such a purpose should have drawn unanimous support from a Republican Party accustomed to seeing its actions as motivated by patriotic virtue. Yet objections were immediately raised. Edward H. Rollins, a Republican from New Hampshire, professed not to understand the rationale behind the pro-posed law: "If some States or local organizations have been liberal and patriotic enough to pay additional bounties to their soldiers, why should those bounties be deducted from the amount now to be paid by the United States?" This objection can be seen in ideological terms, as a clash between two rival conceptions of federalism: on one view, an effort should be made to treat all soldiers equally throughout the country; on another view, the federal government, by dealing directly with individuals, would be interfering with what had already been done at the state level. In fact, however, the objection expressed a sectional interpretation of the situation. Listen once more to Rollins: "Why should States like New Hampshire and other eastern States, who have paid their soldiers liberal bounties, be now required to assist in making up deficiencies in this respect on the part of other sections of the country?" Were not Midwesterners trying to use federal taxes to make the Northeast pay bounties to Midwestern soldiers that they had been unwilling to pay themselves? Hamilton Ward of New York agreed: "In New York the towns and counties and local associations generally were very liberal to the soldiers. . . . I believe that under this bill not one in twenty of the soldiers from the State of New York will receive a dollar of bounty."[61]

Sectionalization transformed the debate, and people soon stopped talking about equalizing bounties among soldiers of the united North and focused solely on balancing federal subsidies between the two sections. The objection arose because representatives of the Northeast were unwilling to vote for a law that, in their view, would primarily benefit the Western states, which had paid smaller bounties. The Western response minced no words: "In many of the poorer States of the Union soldiers have enlisted without State or local bounty, and in some instances without any national bounty." But this simply proved that "our soldiers . . . entered the Army through motives of patriotism, and did not wait for any high bounties, and are entitled to the benefit of this bill."[62]

Once again, the political argument rested on crystallized representations of the sections. The West was essentially agricultural and still a region of pioneers, while the East was industrial and rich.

We of the West in furnishing soldiers labored under much greater disadvantages than other sections. Our people were engaged chiefly in rural pursuits. They were occupied in the cultivation of new farms and in the development of new industries. They were not wealthy. They were acting under the disadvantages of pioneers, and our counties and our States could not afford to pay volunteers the immense bounties which were paid by the eastern States . . . richer in accumulated capital as three to one to the western States. If the older States with their large means have acted liberally, we commend them for their liberality. They had the capacity to pay largely where we had not.

The Democrat Francis C. Le Blond spoke less gingerly in accusing his colleagues from the Northeast of seeking to rob the West twice, since, in his view, "the very wealth they possess they have wrung from the West by high tariffs." In referring to the sections, the congressman set the debate on bounties in a much broader economic context: "I understand, from the vote already cast upon this proposition, that it is a contest in this House between the West and the East, between labor and wealth. The vote already taken has indicated that such is the issue; and we shall see when the final vote comes whether the East is to control the West in regard to all legislation."[63]

While conflict was sectional, political legitimacy was national. The arguments clearly set up a patriotic competition: which section was the most American? "It is known as a fact few of our soldiers deserted," Iowa Republican Josiah B. Grinnell maintained. "It will be found by references to the records that desertions among the troops from the eastern States and middle States were as three to one compared with the desertions from the soldiers raised in our rural communities, which is no reproach to the States, but to those who accepted the bounties and escaped." Two patriotic discourses clashed: one side claimed that the Northeast was the more patriotic section because it generously rewarded its volunteers, while the other responded that Western patriotism was truer because it was more disinterested.[64]

The example of the bill to equalize bounty payments shows that, within the North, sectionalism, aroused by economic interests, was conceived in relation to the nation and not against it. The invocation of patriotism was no mere rhetorical flourish, although that aspect is not to be neglected. In the aftermath of the Civil War, it was a powerful political weapon that Republicans knew how to wield to perfection.[65] In fact, Americanness was an integral part of sectional identity and invoked in speeches throughout the Reconstruction period. In 1869, the *Chicago Republican* marveled at how rapidly Kansas had ratified the Fifteenth Amendment. It was "a model of legislative promptness and expedition. A Saturday afternoon telegram from Congressman [Sidney] Clarke in Washington announced the language of the proposition at Topeka, and the same gentleman received a return dispatch, at 8 o'clock in the evening, communicating the fact that both branches, the Senate unanimously, the House by 67 to 7, had ratified. This is an example of American—especially of Western—decision and performance." A few days later, the *Joliet Republican* noted the stark contrast with Pennsylvania, which failed to ratify the amendment for want of a quorum. The conclusion was inescapable: "The time is fast coming, nay, more, it is already upon us—when the West will control the politics of the entire country, and it will lead as it leads in business and everything else, with prompt and decisive vigor. The old day of dallying and delay will have gone by when the West comes into power. It will govern as it has fought."[66]

The Spatial Dimension of Politics

On January 22, 1870, two Illinois congressmen, Jesse H. Moore and John A. Logan, spoke at length on the floor of the House. It was time, they contended, to consider the "constitutionality, practicability, and expediency of changing the seat of our General Government." Both men rose in support of an idea that had been discussed for the past several months in a number of Midwestern newspapers, Democratic as well as Republican: moving the nation's capital to the geographic center of the country.[67]

According to the *Joliet Republican*, "That the great Mississippi valley—the destined seat of empire, the heart, the strength, the power of a mighty nation—will also take within its broad and massive bosom the capital of the government is but a mere question of time, and without doubt the sooner it is done the better." Furthermore, "the Western press is generally endorsing the proposition started anew a few days since by the *Chicago Tribune* in favor of removing the national capital from Washington to St. Louis." The Midwest was "the destined seat of the Empire, the heart, the strength, the power of a great nation." "Westward the Star of Empire and the Capitol of the Republic must make their way," insisted the *Chicago Republican*. The *Cincinnati Enquirer* made a similar argument on demographic grounds: "Washington has had its day. Since it was made the capital, in 1800, a West has grown up, which, by the late census, will have a larger population than the East. The tide of population has swept across the Alleghenies to the Mississippi and to the Rocky Mountains, and every year in the future but adds to its strength. The capital of the future in this country must be a thousand miles west from Washington at least."[68]

Many reasons were offered to persuade readers that a western move was inevitable. Recent wartime experience showed that in order to defend Washington, so close to the South, it had been necessary to divert large numbers of troops that could have been put to better use elsewhere. Furthermore, the city was too close to the ocean, which exposed it to a naval attack, as the English had proved in 1814. Geography was of course the root of the problem. A glance at the map was enough to show that

> in those early days of the formation of our government, Washington was comparatively the center of our inhabited country. Then the national heart, throwing out its healthy, vigorous arteries of patriotism and wise statesman-

ship, was where it ought to be—in the center and vital part of the national body. Now, the comparison would be more complete were we to imagine a wreck of a man with his heart in his great toe. How could such a violation of nature thrive?

On this view, the centrality of the capital was crucial. For the *Quincy Whig* (Illinois), it was only "an act of justice to the more remote sections of the Union, especially that on the Pacific Coast." Above all, "a Capital centrally located" would provide "the bond of Union" for "the whole country."[69]

If everything—history, geography, and demography—called for the federal capital to be transferred to the Midwest, the ultimate argument was political. "Can anyone doubt that, had the Capital been surrounded by the free States of the West in 1861, instead of located between two slave states in sympathy with treason, that the rebellion would not have been permitted to assume such proportions before the attempt would have been made to crush it out and restore peace and tranquillity to the country?" asked the *Quincy Whig*.

> It would be peculiarly appropriate that the National Capitol should be located among a people who faithfully sustained the Government during the war and contributed to the preservation of the Union, besides giving to the nation the President [Lincoln] and the Commander-in-Chief of the armies [Grant] under whose administration these results were secured. And when the removal of the Capitol from its present site near the tomb of the Father of His Country shall take place, what would be more appropriate than that it should be planted near the spot where repose the ashes of him who saved and regenerated the Government which Washington founded?[70]

This campaign to move the capital may seem silly in retrospect. Nevertheless, it is revealing of the spatial dimension of American politics. It confirms that conflicts of interest on specific issues crystallized into a permanent distinction rooted in stereotypical representations. The section then became a quasi-institutionalized political category: even though it had no legal existence, it organized the way political actors perceived policy and understood how it worked, and therefore it influenced the way they acted. Like the parties, but in a secondary fashion, the sections structured the political field and introduced a spatial dimension. In this perspective, moving the capital would have been a sign of changing geographical power relations in the United States.

All of this influenced the bargaining that is the daily stuff of political life. Take, for example, the distribution of leadership posts, a matter for negotiations in which sectional balance was a major consideration. At the end of 1868, the Republicans had to find a person to fill the vacant position of Speaker of the House. "It looks as though it will be conceded to the East," James A. Garfield remarked. He was a contender for the post himself, but he was from Ohio. Only "if it comes west, I think it could easily be brought to me."[71] The same sectional considerations played a part in the choice of presidential candidates. In 1875, a Democrat observed that "the election of a western Speaker would almost ensure the nomination of an Eastern personage to the Presidency," thus improving the chances of New York governor Samuel J. Tilden. These calculations showed how important sectional balance was in each party.[72] Failure to maintain this balance could not only lead to internal recriminations but also expose a party to political attack. The leading Midwestern Democratic paper, the *Cincinnati Enquirer*, was quick to reproach Republicans for awarding all congressional committee chairmanships to New Englanders after the war. "The present condition of the United States is that of a country ruled by one of its sections," the paper alleged. "New England is a virtual oligarchy in the political state, and the rights and interests of the West are subject to New England measurement, to be ordered and arranged by a power incapable to look beyond its own."[73] From the beginning, Democrats had accused the Republican Party of serving as a vehicle for Puritan abolitionist fanaticism. The rhetorical strategy is clear: to confine a party to one section was to suggest that it would not represent the entire country. In other words, national legitimacy required a party to represent every section to some degree. In the aftermath of the Civil War, politics was also a matter of geography.

IN A LONG ARTICLE entitled "Eastern Jealousy of and Aggression on the West," the *Cincinnati Enquirer* devoted one and a half columns of its December 7, 1874, edition to Midwestern complaints about the Northeast. The paper looked all the way back to the Treaty of Ghent (1814) that ended the War of 1812 with England, in which the American negotiators, drawn from the Northeast, allegedly sacrificed the interests of the nation as a whole to those of their section. The article concluded,

> We are the Great West in our population and wealth, *but the little West* in our participation in directing the councils of the country. We tell you the truth when we say that the tariffs are made by the mill owners of Massachusetts and the furnace owners of Pennsylvania. They make them for their own interests, and with the distinct knowledge that it is robbery of you. Your currency laws are dictated by Wall-street bankers, brokers and bondholders.

They declare what the amount of the currency shall be, and of what it shall consist. The East owns the bonds, and the West has to pay the principal and interest. The East has the most of the National Banks. Our Eastern friends so contrived it that the main income duties should fall upon whisky and tobacco, which are mainly Western productions. . . . Nor is this amount collected back from the consumers. The Eastern people don't drink the Western whisky. They, on the contrary, use an article called rum. . . . We thank God that, by the census of 1870, the political power of this Union passed from the East to the West, across the Allegheny Mountains, and that it will never return through all the cycles to come.[74]

Here, in the space of a few lines, we find concentrated all aspects of the sectional conflict between the Northeast and the Midwest. These regional categories, constructed in the first half of the nineteenth century, were accepted as fact by the time of Reconstruction. The political situation of the country and the political economy of the period were viewed through this lens. In this period, sectionalism arose mainly in connection with economic issues, with currency and tariff policies foremost among them. The persistence of these debates only established the sectional category more securely as a lens of political interpretation for which one reached whenever there was a need to adjust political balances. In short, power was a matter of parties but also of sections. Like parties, each section stood for certain values and defended certain interests. Like parties, sections also fought for more power: the question of relocating the federal capital was highly symbolic in this regard.

During Reconstruction, sectional conflict between the Northeast and Midwest was an inherited phenomenon. Although the Civil War did create a wave of nationalist sentiment, it did not submerge these sectional differences. On the contrary, it crystallized them and brought them into sharper focus, most notably by heightening the distinction between the Midwest and the western portion of the South. As we have seen, sectional reflexes were easily triggered by political debate. In this context, major economic issues such as the war debt, paper money, and the tariff eluded the grasp of the parties, products of the upheavals of the 1850s, and were transformed into sectional controversies, sometimes virulent ones. The war had restored the Union, but sectionalism remained a major political phenomenon.

2

Gold and Paper

HOW MONEY BECAME SECTIONAL

———————.———————

The two great questions into which politics are now divided are, restoration of the Union and the management of the finances and taxation.
—George H. Pendleton, speech in Cincinnati, July 24, 1868

SECTIONAL DIFFERENCES between the Midwest and Northeast became important after the Civil War owing to the introduction of a new issue into political
debate: the money question. As the months passed, the money question claimed
a growing share of attention, jostling with Reconstruction, then the central political issue of the day. The consequences of the war had to be dealt with. Military
victory had settled the great questions at the heart of the conflict. The South's
secession had failed, and slavery had been abolished. But some issues remained
unresolved, and new problems arose. Now that all blacks were free, what was
their status to be? Should American citizenship be redefined? Should the Southern states be reformed, or was it enough to admit them back into the Union as if
nothing had happened? Had the war changed the role of the federal government
and its relation to the several states and their citizens? The challenge, it seemed,
was to rethink the American nation—nothing less. Reconstruction was at the
center of heated debates involving the parties, the newspapers, and the public.

Little by little, however, the money question came to the fore. The war had
been very costly, and the United States faced a colossal debt of $2.3 billion. "Noth-
ing can be found in history to compare with this," declared one Republican congressman. "Never before, within the same space of time, has so large an amount
of money been raised by loans."[1] In addition to this unprecedented debt, half a
billion dollars in paper money (greenbacks) had been issued. This paper was legal

tender but not convertible into specie. With peace restored, the American government, and above all Secretary of the Treasury Hugh McCulloch, were confronted
with two titanic tasks: to pay back the public debt and restore the convertibility of
paper money to gold.

Unlike Reconstruction, there was consensus around these goals in 1865. For
Roscoe Conkling, the influential New York Republican, to satisfy both was "what
nearly all discreet and patriotic men desire." In December, the House of Representatives declared almost unanimously "that this house cordially concurs in the
views of the Secretary of the Treasury in relation to the necessity of a contraction
of the currency, with a view to as early a resumption of specie payments as the
business interests of the country will permit; and we hereby pledge co-operative
action to this end as speedily as practicable."[2] This consensus soon fell apart,
however. By 1868, newspapers were reporting that "next to reconstruction the
currency is what most interests the mind of the American people." Leaders of
the workers' movement spoke of the currency issue as "a question that must destroy the power of a monster moneyed aristocracy, or bind the whole labor of the
nation, white and black, in fetters to gold." From the pulpit many Protestant ministers fulminated against a financial "heresy" worse than "atheism in religion."[3]

Such was the inception of one of the most virulent and contentious political
issues of the late nineteenth century. The money question aroused passions and
divided the nation. It served as a symbolic catalyst for competing conceptions
of political economy in a rapidly industrializing society.[4] Its sudden emergence
destabilized political parties that had coalesced in the 1850s around the issues of
slavery and federalism. In the midst of clashes over Reconstruction, they suddenly found themselves divided about the economy.

This chapter explores how the money question became one of the central issues
of American politics, crystallizing opposing, not to say Manichean, moral visions
of society and mobilizing large numbers of citizens. It asks why this ideological
debate was organized not around the major parties but on a geographical basis.
While Republicans mauled fellow Republicans and Democrats assailed fellow
Democrats over the issue, the sections—both the Northeast and the Midwest—
came together around distinct and antagonistic positions. The goal here, therefore, is to understand the *sectionalization* of the money question: how did the
spatial structuring of the political field disrupt the Reconstruction of the South
and transform the parties?

The Financial Legacy of the Civil War

When the Civil War ended, there was no "money question." The state of public finances and the economic effects thereof were not a major issue of political controversy. Nevertheless, when Hugh McCulloch became secretary of the treasury in March 1865, he inherited a very complicated situation. To finance the war, the government had resorted to three expedients: it had borrowed money, it had printed money, and it had harnessed the banks for support. It had taken these steps to deal with the enormous cost of military actions at a time when money was hard to find, but most people believed that they were temporary. The survival of the Union had been the priority. When hostilities ended, the United States found itself with a colossal debt, paper money that could not be converted into coins, and a functional but unbalanced national banking system.

It was therefore a time of difficult choices, because the economic consequences of the war could not all be dealt with at once. The debt was too large to repay rapidly. The value of paper money was too different from that of gold to return immediately to convertibility. Priorities had to be established. And on this point, McCulloch's action roused increasing resistance as soon as 1866. The collapse of the broad consensus around public finances gave rise to the money question, which would become a major issue for the next three decades.

How to Finance a War

At the outbreak of the Civil War in 1861, the federal government quickly recognized that, with an empty Treasury, its usual sources of revenue would not suffice to finance the necessary military operations. An emergency session of Congress met to give Secretary of the Treasury Salmon P. Chase the means he needed, and enacted measures already tried in previous conflicts. The idea was to raise taxes to meet with the ordinary expenses of the government, and to borrow the money necessary to wage the war. Yet this first salvo of financial measures fell well short of what was needed. The new tariff, already raised twice, did not yield the anticipated revenue as imports declined. The direct tax on land created resistance. Chase himself was slow to implement a new income tax he disliked. And the new loan proved difficult to market.[5]

With no end to the war in sight, Republicans soon realized that it needed resources at an unprecedented level. Tens of thousands of soldiers and officers would have to be equipped, armed, clothed, fed, and paid.[6] Those needs strained the country's financial resources. The banks that remained solvent saw their gold reserves dwindle and suspended convertibility of their notes (in New York on December 30, 1861). Coins also vanished from circulation, as Americans hoarded them in the face of an uncertain future. The government's problem was twofold: it had to find buyers for its bonds, and it needed cash to pay for the war effort. Under pressure from the dwindling gold in circulation, Congress, under the leadership of Elbridge G. Spaulding and Samuel Hooper in the House and William Pitt Fessenden and John Sherman in the Senate, developed a three-pronged plan: a comprehensive system of taxation to pay for general expenses and interest on the debt (see chapter 3); paper money to make up for the shortage of specie; and a system of national banks to support the sale of U.S. bonds.[7]

"Greenbacks"—as they quickly became known, due to the green ink, harder to counterfeit, with which they were printed—were born on February 25, 1862, when Congress officially authorized the issuance of "Treasury notes" (or "United States notes") as "legal tender for all debts, public and private" and, therefore (it was hoped), "as good as gold." There were serious doubts about this move, however, not least by Secretary Chase himself. The historical precedents, such as the continentals during the American Revolution, or the *assignats* during the French Revolution, did not augur well. Meanwhile, the South had already issued its own paper that immediately depreciated. Cautious, and to ensure an influx of gold to the Treasury, Congress required customs duties to be paid in specie. But gold remained scarce, and the government was forced to authorize a series of greenback issues that by the end of the war totaled $431.5 million.[8]

The third part of the Republican plan was to set up a national banking system. After Andrew Jackson vetoed the renewal of the charter of the Second Bank of the United States in 1832, the federal government had removed itself from the banking sector, leaving regulation of the banks to the states.[9] But the war destabilized the banks, partly because all the money invested in the South suddenly evaporated and partly because the mobilization and transition to a wartime economy had placed enormous demands on the system. In the Midwest in particular, many banks failed. In Illinois, two-thirds of the banknotes in circulation were backed by reserves of Southern bonds. By May 1862, 93 of 110 banks had been liquidated.[10] Banks everywhere suspended convertibility of their paper, thereby undermining the value of their notes. To float the necessary war loan and stabilize the value of banknotes, Congress created a national banking system in February 1863. Despite the opposition of leading New York bankers, the new system managed, after some delay, to establish itself on a firm footing by 1865. To be certified as a national bank, a bank had to invest a minimum of $30,000 and one-third of its capital in Treasury bonds, to be deposited in the U.S. Treasury, which in exchange issued

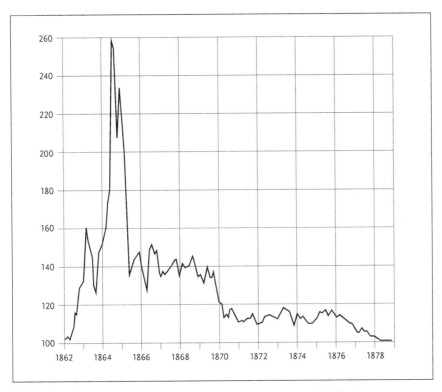

FIGURE 1. Market value of greenbacks (for 100 gold dollars)

Source: Wesley C. Mitchell, *Gold, Prices & Wages under the Greenback Standard*
(Berkeley: University of California Press, 1908).

banknotes worth 90 percent of the face value of the bonds on deposit. The law limited the total quantity of notes in circulation to $300 million.[11] This system ensured that banknotes would be backed by the full faith and credit of the U.S. government and that the banks would have an interest in the financial health of the state.

These steps profoundly altered the monetary system of the United States. In 1865, the country's money supply included both gold dollars, which were used almost exclusively to pay customs duties and settle international transactions (except on the West Coast, where gold remained in circulation), and paper dollars (greenbacks), whose convertibility was suspended at inception and whose value varied widely in relation to gold (see figure 1). Strictly speaking, the official currency of the United States included both greenbacks and gold. Also in circulation, however, were national banknotes, which were not legal tender but were guaranteed by the government, and state-bank notes, although in diminishing amounts after Congress taxed them to their death.[12]

When peace was restored, leading to a sudden drop in public expenditures, the newly appointed Secretary McCulloch deemed two issues to be of the highest priority: the existence of two inconvertible official currencies of different value and the existence of an enormous debt, part of which was nearing its term. The steps he took to remedy these problems stirred up a debate and launched "the money question."

The Implosion of the Monetary Consensus

Hugh McCulloch was a banker. Born in Maine, he moved to Indiana at the age of twenty-five and there began to work for the state's central bank, working his way up until he became its president in 1857. Although initially opposed to the issuance of greenbacks, he decided in 1862 that they were necessary to the financing of the war. He helped to manage the new legal tender, first as comptroller of the currency and then as secretary of the treasury.[13] He nevertheless believed that "an irredeemable currency [is] an evil which circumstances may for a time render a necessity, but which is never to be sustained as a policy." Like most of his fellow bankers, he thought that "gold and silver are the only true measures of value . . . prepared by the Almighty for this very purpose."[14] Greenbacks were only a promise to pay in gold, and as long as the government could not keep that promise (that is, as long as these notes were not convertible into gold), their value would be subject to damaging fluctuations. In the summer of 1864, when the Union's military fortunes were at a low ebb, it took no less than $258 in greenbacks to obtain $100 in gold. In 1865, the spread narrowed (to $145 in greenbacks for $100 in gold), but McCulloch remained convinced that any delay in a return to convertibility posed an immense economic threat to the nation's well-being.[15]

The secretary of the treasury therefore initiated a deliberate deflationary policy. The theory was simple, based on the law of supply and demand: there were too many greenbacks in circulation, so in order to increase their value, they had to be made more scarce. Once greenbacks came close to parity with gold, specie payments could be resumed (in other words, the Treasury could announce that greenbacks would be exchanged freely for gold and vice versa). McCulloch made this policy his top priority and withdrew from circulation any greenbacks that came into the possession of the Treasury. Between October 31, 1865, and June 1, 1868, $72 million in greenbacks were destroyed.[16]

At this point the general public was not much interested in these technical matters. The few newspapers that discussed the issue at all, both Democratic and Republican, unanimously approved: "The country will receive this information with unqualified pleasure. All classes of society will be benefitted by a cautious and gradual reduction of the currency."[17] The secretary's action was also well received in Congress, where, as Vermont Republican Justin S. Morrill noted with satisfaction, it was "approved not only by a vote in itself unexampled, but a vote of unexampled unanimity."[18] At McCulloch's request, the Republicans introduced a bill in February 1866 to formalize and extend his authority to withdraw greenbacks from circulation. The enthusiasm for this measure shows that views converged across the political spectrum: the goal was to stabilize the federal government's financial situation by restoring convertibility as soon as possible.

Nevertheless, dissent soon emerged. Some began to wonder whether such rapid contraction was really a wise policy. "Is it worth while in the present condition of affairs," Maine Republican Frederick A. Pike asked, "when the tendency of things is all right, to interpose, and for the purpose of avoiding a supposed catastrophe run the risk of hurrying the country into commercial difficulties that may be serious?" Although everyone shared the goal of specie payments, some were alarmed that a sudden contraction of the money supply would bring growth to a halt at a time when the economy was already having difficulty adjusting to new peacetime conditions. It would be better, they argued, to allow the excess money supply to be absorbed as business expanded.[19]

The devil was, of course, in the details. In early 1866, Congress generally agreed that "the important question to be considered is, how to restore the currency to a sound and stable condition at the earliest practicable time with the least possible disturbance of the value of property and of the substantial interests of the industry of the country." But many clearly were unwilling to allow McCulloch to do as he pleased, objecting "to the details of the bill, and the extent of the powers conferred by it."[20]

Some congressmen, for example, did not understand why the withdrawal of greenbacks, which cost the government nothing, had to be financed by the issuance of U.S. bonds at 6 percent. "Why, sir, the bare mention of such a transaction provokes a smile of incredulity," remarked Hiram Price, an Iowa Republican, who objected to the annual burden on the budget that the interest would entail. Certainly sound management of the Treasury should strive to reduce expenditures related to the debt and not increase them, in order to reduce taxes. "A species of currency everywhere popular and satisfactory surely might be left out until the interest-bearing unfunded liabilities have been retired or provided for," his New York colleague Calvin Hulburd added.[21]

The more important objection voiced at the time, however, had to do with the authority granted to the secretary of the treasury. Thaddeus Stevens of Pennsylvania, a Republican leader in the House, warned, "This is a tremendous bill. It proposes to confer, in my judgment, more power upon a single man than was ever before conferred upon any one man in a Government claiming to have a Constitution." Hulburd went even further: "Under this bill his absolute control of the currency, and of course of the business and the fortunes of men and of the country, is perfectly tremendous."[22] These men had no qualms about extending the powers of government. Many of them had voted during the war for measures that accelerated the centralization of the state.[23] But they saw danger in manipulating the currency: "This question of the currency is one that affects so intimately all the business relations of life, the property of every man in this country, his ability to pay taxes, his ability to earn food and acquire a living, that no man ought to have the power to vary the volume of currency."[24] Money was involved in every transaction and thus set the value of both property and labor. Hence, a majority of Congress refused to grant McCulloch all the latitude he wanted, despite assurances from his supporters regarding his honesty and competence.[25] To have done otherwise would have been to grant too much power over the economy to a single individual.

Ultimately, the Contraction Act of 1866 authorized the secretary to withdraw greenbacks from circulation but limited his power to do so to $10 million in the first six months and then $4 million per month thereafter until convertibility was restored.[26] This outcome reveals the dynamics of the debate. There was agreement about ends but disagreement about means, details, and above all about how much trust to place in the secretary of the treasury—the office and the man. We witness the emergence of themes that presage a change in focus from restoring convertibility to a more sweeping "money question," that is, from a technical problem of finance to a major political issue. In view of the size of the debt, the first questions that arose concerned the relative priority of contraction versus debt repayment. Political decisions regarding public finances quickly took on a moralistic tone that favored polarization of the debate. For James A. Garfield, a Republican from Ohio, the choice was simple: "On the one side it is proposed to return to solid and honest values; on the other, to float in the boundless and shoreless sea of paper money, with all its dishonesty and broken pledges."[27] Thus was sown the seed that would within a few months place the money question at the center of American politics.

The hardening of positions can be seen in the growing polarization that pitted representatives of the Northeast against those of the Midwest. Initially, this polarization was weak. An analysis of the votes taken early in 1866 shows a few preliminary signs of sectionalism affecting Republicans, little noticed at the time. Sectional arguments were absent from the debate, and the list of speakers on the contraction bill shows no particular pattern. At this stage, the situation was not yet seen in geographic terms, although Midwestern representatives on the whole seem to have been more sensitive to the possible negative consequences of rapid contraction.[28]

The situation evolved very rapidly over the course of 1866. By the December session, sectional divisions on the money question were increasingly evident. In the face of economic difficulties, some congressmen called for a halt to McCulloch's strenuous efforts to withdraw greenbacks from circulation. It was not easy to pass such a bill, however, and several attempts were required before a modest version made it through. At each step, the voting became more polarized, even though sectional rhetoric was still muted. There was now a clear convergence of views on the issue among representatives of the Midwest, along with a hardening of opposition to the Northeast.[29]

The Emergence of the Money Question

It may be difficult to believe that debates on subjects as arid as floating a government loan or regulating the supply of paper money could rouse the passions of voters across the United States, from the big cities of the East Coast to the vast corn and wheat fields of Iowa and Minnesota. During Reconstruction, however, the money question became the touchstone of American economic policy. The broad spectrum of financial problems bequeathed by the war required complex technical solutions, but the whole discussion was boiled down to a debate about monetary norms, which served as a metaphor for social norms. The money question inflamed the American political imagination because it embodied antagonistic moral visions projected onto a society undergoing rapid change following the end of slavery and the transformation of the economy.[30]

At times, congressional debate illustrated to the point of caricature the gap between the technical complexity of the issues and the moral certainties of the day. In February 1867, for example, congressmen discussing a "bill to provide ways and means for the payment of compound-interest notes" could not even agree whether the bill was deflationary or inflationary. "It ought to be distinctly understood that the proposition of my colleague is for the direct expansion of the currency," assured John M. Broomall, a Republican from Pennsylvania. "On the contrary," his colleague William B. Allison of Iowa replied, "I regard it to a certain extent as a measure of contraction." Clearly, congressmen were not at all clear about the consequences of the measures upon which they were called to vote.[31]

Despite this—or perhaps because of this—the political and moral stakes seemed clear to everyone. For the supporters of specie, inconvertible paper money was the root of all evil, and contraction the only salvation. To repay the government's debt with greenbacks, as some wanted, would be tantamount to theft, John Sherman thundered in the Senate: "It proposes to pay to the creditor of the Government who now holds the interest-bearing obligations of the United States a note not bearing interest, and compel him to take that note against his will. It thus proposes to confiscate the property of the citizen." In the House, James A. Garfield was harsher still: "Business men and legislators have taken paper money in such overwhelming doses that they are crazed, and like the lotus-eaters wish to return no more to solid values. Forgetting the past, forgetting their own teachings, their votes and their records of a year ago, they join in the crazy cry, 'Paper money,' 'Oh, give us more paper money!'" On the other side, the moral certainties were expressed just as forcefully but in political rather than symbolic terms. "The only question to be settled in this matter," Iowa Republican Hiram Price observed, "is the question whether the country is prepared . . . to place upon the statute-book of the nation a declaration that we will pay out of the pocket of the people to the bankers of the country four or five million dollars in the shape of interest when it can be just as well and wisely avoided by passing a bill for the issue of non-interest-bearing notes."[32]

Parties are often underpinned by great moral oppositions. In this case, however, the two contending parties did not succeed in translating the political debate on the money question into institutional language. Both Republicans and Democrats had coalesced in the 1850s around the slavery issue. On economic matters, however, neither party was homogeneous, to the point that some observers predicted their disappearance.[33] In this context, sectionalism soon became the touchstone for political regrouping on the money question. Yet there was no a priori reason why greenbacks or government debt should lead to geographic alignments. In both the Midwest and Northeast, one could find proponents as well as adversaries of a speedy return to convertibility or the use of paper money to pay down the debt.[34] In order to understand how financial debates became sectional, we must look at how they crystallized initially in a series of binary oppositions and analyze which groups came to identify with the positions thus staked out.

The Terms of the Debate

The money question emerged when a complex series of distinct but related problems of political economy were boiled down into two broad positions soon characterized as "soft money" versus "hard money." When political actors took positions on the issue, they did so in relation to a whole range of subsidiary questions, even though they may have considered certain aspects more crucial than others. Four major themes stood out: the definition of money, the reimbursement of the debt, the priorities of financial policy, and the relative merits of greenbacks versus banknotes. The construction of a single political cleavage common to all these issues was at the root of the money question.

The first disagreement had to do with the very nature of the notes the federal government had been issuing since 1862. What was a greenback? Was it real money? According to the dominant school of classical economics, the answer was no. "Money, which is a universal measure of value and a medium of exchange, must not be confounded with credit currency in any of its forms," James A. Garfield insisted. "Value can only be measured by that which in itself possesses a definite and known value." If gold and silver served as money, it is only because they had *intrinsic* value. "The coining and stamping are but a certification by the Government of the quantity and fineness of the metal stamped."[35] According to this view, "a greenback is a promise to pay a certain number of dollars." Taking a bill from his pocket, Senator Charles Sumner read to his colleagues the words the Treasury had printed on it: "The United States promise to pay to the bearer *five dollars*." The fact that greenbacks were legal tender but not convertible into "real" money was merely an expedient, justified only by exceptional circumstances. "The suspension of specie payments was originally a war measure, like the suspension of the *habeas corpus*. . . . As a war measure, it should cease with the war, or so soon hereafter as practicable." To do otherwise would be to break the promise printed on the bill.[36]

On the other hand, the negative effects of contraction and the positive experiences of using greenbacks in daily life had led a growing number of Americans to reevaluate their thinking. For them, money was simply an instrument of exchange made operational by the authority of the government. For the *Cincinnati Enquirer,* "The authority conceded, the Congress can issue stamped paper . . . and make that stamped paper a legal tender, the same as it can make gold pieces, stamped and marked by the Government, legal tender in the payment of debts. . . . There is no distinction between gold legal-tenders and paper legal-tenders."[37] Greenbacks were money in the full sense of the word simply because the law made them legal tender. For the defenders of greenbacks, the real scandal was that the law itself created a hierarchy by insisting that customs duties be paid solely in gold. "It is idle to talk of paying specie," one of Sherman's correspondents sputtered, "until Congress shall have set aside its gold humbug; until it shall have ceased to *discredit* its own paper. Let Congress repeal the law requiring duties to be paid in coin, and then it may talk about resuming."[38]

This concept of money as a socially determined instrument of exchange is closer to today's way of thinking than the bullionist theory of the intrinsic value of gold and silver.[39] In the post–Civil War period, however, it had to overcome several hurdles. First, it was new, whereas classical economics had been around since the late eighteenth century. And second, all the historical precedents presaged the failure of any paper currency. It was therefore easy to "array the authorities against inflation by quoting a number of extracts in chronological order giving the opinions of leading statesmen of the last hundred years." Furthermore, gold, along with silver, was "the recognized standard of value in the whole civilized world."[40] International trade was based on the weight of metal corresponding to units of exchange in different currencies. The international monetary conference held in Paris at the time of the World Fair of 1867 was intended to standardize these exchange rates.[41] There was little room in such thinking for a paper currency that could not be converted into specie.

TO DECIDE WHETHER greenbacks were money was all the more important as the government owed a huge amount of money to its creditors. This is why the U.S. debt became central to the money question, turning it into a fundamental matter of economic justice and morality. At the war's end, everyone agreed that the debt ought to be repaid as quickly as possible. "A permanent national debt is not an American institution, as our history has already twice proven," Vermont Republican Justin S. Morrill observed in 1866. "And though it may take a number of years to wholly extinguish the present debt, the policy of gradual extinction can and should be steadily pursued." No one contradicted him at the time. But the war debt was colossal—$2.3 billion as of March 31, 1865—and it soon became apparent that it would take a great deal of time to pay it all off: probably no fewer than thirty-five years, according to John Sherman, chairman of the Senate Finance Committee. Clearly, the Republicans would have to resign themselves to the existence of long-term debt.[42]

In this context, two specific problems became major political issues in 1867:

the payment of the "five-twenties" and the taxation of U.S. bonds. The "five-twenty bonds" had a maturity of twenty years but were callable after five, hence their name. They made up the largest part of the war debt. The law provided that the principal should be paid in "lawful money of the United States," an ambiguous designation that might include greenbacks as well as specie. Clarifying the situation became a major issue, because the value of the greenback dollar was markedly different from the value of the gold dollar. The choice of whether to pay the five-twenties in one or the other currency could have a significant impact on the federal budget as well as on the portfolios of bondholders.

The problem was immediately put in terms of economic justice and honor. Some vehemently protested the thought that the loan might not be repaid entirely in specie. "I am ashamed to have a proposition made at the close of the Thirty-Ninth Congress to pay off the debt of the United States or any portion of it otherwise than by bonds payable, principal and interest, in gold, or else by gold itself," Theodore M. Pomeroy of New York exclaimed. Henry W. Corbett of Oregon resorted to the classics: "Public credit should be 'like Caesar's wife, above suspicion.'" They pointed out that all other bonds were payable in gold, and that the public had bought war bonds with the idea that they would be as well. Was that not how they were sold? Jay Cooke, the financier chosen by the government to float the loan, had emphasized this point in his publicity campaigns. Most of the people who held this view believed that greenbacks were not "real" money but merely acknowledgments of debt. To pay bonds in greenbacks was thus "to compel a loan without interest" and "simply robbery." For Timothy O. Howe of Wisconsin, greenbacks were "an active and bitter reproach upon the integrity and good faith of the nation, because they constantly flout the business world with promises which are as constantly broken."[43]

Hard-money financiers protested a proposal that struck them as a swindle on government creditors. Their opponents objected to the idea that the nation's elected representatives, charged with watching over the people's money, would even contemplate granting such a windfall to bondholders. "Every man in the country purchasing a bond is presumed to know the character of the law creating the bond or the existence of any other law affecting the bond either as to time, manner, or mode of its payment," Oliver P. Morton of Indiana observed. The advertisements published by Jay Cooke, a private agent, were not to be taken as commitments by the government: "It would be a monstrous doctrine that the right of the nation . . . could be varied or changed by the illegal or unwarranted declaration of a public officer who has no power to say or do anything, except that which is conferred upon him by law."[44] Indeed, it would be an immense gift to bondholders to repay in gold bonds purchased with greenbacks at a time when those greenbacks were trading at a considerable discount.[45]

In 1867, positions hardened as Ohio Democrats made it a campaign issue (see chapter 4). A nuanced approach became almost untenable. For instance, John Sherman believed that the letter of the law authorized reimbursement of the principal of the five-twenties in greenbacks but that it would be impolitic to do so because it would make it difficult to float any future loans at a reasonable rate of interest. He was immediately accused of flip-flopping, as fellow Ohioan James A. Garfield pointed out: "Sherman has twice boxed the compass on the greenback & bond question, and each time we supposed he was catching the wind of popular favor." Invective filled the columns of newspapers, which branded some politicians as "bondocrats" and others as "repudiators."[46]

Whether the five-twenties would be paid in specie or greenbacks was not the only question, however. In fact, the issue of reimbursement symbolized antagonistic political and moral positions. For one side, the public debt was as sacred as the blood shed by soldiers in the war, since it had saved the country in its hour of peril. Timothy O. Howe, noting that "the cause in which that debt was contracted is one to which three hundred thousand volunteers gave their lives," asked, "Who is he who dares stand by the graves of the patriot dead and say that the cause would warrant the sacrifice of their lives but is not worth the tribute of our money?"[47] For others, however, repayment in gold would make the government guilty of unequal treatment. "The soldiers who risked their lives in their country's quarrel could be paid with greenbacks, but the bond holders must have gold," a Democratic newspaper protested. Repayment in gold would rob the soldiers of the fruits of victory for the benefit of a small group of bondholders, whom some branded an "aristocracy." Bondholders "are exempt from all State and local taxation," another Democratic paper complained.

> They are thus a favored and protected class, with peculiar special privileges and immunities. . . . The wealthy nabobs who have invested largely in these securities labor not, neither are they engaged in any business; yet Solomon, in all his glory, hardly lived more sumptuously. . . . All they have to do is, once in six months, to receive the money wrung from the hard earnings of the laboring poor upon their coupons. If this does not constitute the essential features of an aristocracy, maintained and kept up by the public, what is?[48]

Those who defended the payment in gold of both principal and interest on the five-twenties challenged this view. According to them, "a very large majority of our national securities, representing more than half the public debt, are $500 and less in denomination, mostly $100 and $50," owned by "the thrifty mechanic, farmer, retail dealer, washerwoman . . . and so on."[49] Indeed, the war bonds had been marketed to the general public: Jay Cooke relied on advertising and a network of brokers to sell the bonds, which were issued in notes with face values as low as $50 or $100 (at a time when a New York mason earned $2 a day).[50] We do not know who bought these bonds during the war or who held them afterward, in view of the considerable trading that went on.[51] The criteria invoked here are clearly political and moral in nature, however. One side pointed out that workers were paid in greenbacks while capital was remunerated in specie that traded at a premium, leading to charges of injustice. The other side insisted that war bonds were held by ordinary patriotic citizens, whose financial sacrifice ought not to be punished by repayment in devalued paper. In the end, both dogmatic positions rested on moral claims about the nature of the greenback.

The payment of the five-twenties was the central theme of the money question in 1867–69, until passage of the Public Credit Act in March 1869 and subsequent measures to fund the debt resolved that particular issue. This was only one aspect of the debt problem, however. The other, which soon came to the fore, had to do with a proposal to tax the interest on U.S. bonds, which enjoyed a tax exemption. Wartime federal taxation, still in effect, had spread to so many corners of economic life that this exemption could easily be denounced as "an invidious distinction in favor of capitalists. . . . While the farm of the farmer, the merchandise of the merchant, and the workshop of the mechanic are all taxed for county, State, and Federal purposes, the holders of these securities can look on with perfect indifference." Was this not proof that "the present Congress . . . are mortgaged, body and soul, to the bondholders?"[52]

Those who saw the public debt as a sacred trust viewed the attempt to tax Treasury bonds as a roundabout way of repudiating part of the Union's financial obligations. For them, taxing the bonds was tantamount to theft, because it would alter the initial contract specifying what interest the government promised to pay. Since the government was simultaneously seeking ways to finance its debt, many observers felt that imposing a new tax would make it more difficult to float a new bond issue with longer maturities and lower interest rates. Nevertheless, some representatives saw political danger in this position. Benjamin F. Butler, a Massachusetts Republican, stressed the political imperative to present the matter in a favorable light: "We have discounted our taxation on that bond in advance, and . . . we have taken payment in advance, as we shall do if we pass this at a low rate of interest and fund under it." Others dwelled on the antipatriotic nature of a tax on the bonds. Since it would be impossible to tax foreign bondholders, would the tax not favor them at the expense of Americans?[53]

On both aspects of public debt management—the mode of reimbursement and the taxation of interest—the debate was transformed into a unique political and moral confrontation. For one camp, it was the dignity of the government and the honor of the nation that were at stake, while for the other, the issue was the creation of a new aristocracy, something Andrew Jackson had fought in his day by vetoing the Second Bank of the United States, an act that had acquired mythical status. Technical matters of finance came to symbolize rival visions of political economy: scrupulous defense of the government's obligations to bondholders came to be identified with hard money, while the attempt to oblige bondholders to help pay the expenses of the federal government came to be identified with soft money. These opposing views became increasingly polarized, all the more so in that the technical issues were complex and had to be simplified and coarsened for electoral purposes.

THE SAME LOGIC quickly led people to contrast two types of paper issued by the Treasury, greenbacks and bonds, and to oppose one as *morally* superior to the other. Such beliefs explain why some gave priority to the reimbursement of the debt while others thought the resumption of specie payments more urgent. It is on this very question that McCulloch's actions exploded the monetary consensus of the immediate postwar.

For those who believed that an inconvertible paper currency was the greatest danger, the priority was to withdraw as many greenbacks as possible from circulation in order to restore parity with gold. Several arguments were advanced to justify this position, the inevitable consequence of which was to prolong the existence of the public debt, since the Treasury's resources were to be directed toward another goal. One of these arguments was the claim that because Treasury bonds paid interest, they were morally superior to greenbacks. For Wisconsin Senator Timothy O. Howe, for example, greenbacks were "all debt and all due": not to repay them would dishonor the nation. To try to make people believe that greenbacks were in fact money was nothing but a dishonest way of shirking one's debt. For Howe, the choice was simple: "And in every human nature it is said the angelic and the devilish constantly struggle for the mastery, so the Treasurer found there was a war in the members of the greenback between the principles of debt and of cash." On the contrary, the bonds were imbued with the honor of the war itself. Radical Massachusetts Senator Charles Sumner argued, "The added glory of removing this great burden . . . justly belonged to another generation, in aggrandized population and resources, in presence of which the existing debt, large to us, would be small."[54]

In any event, all these arguments relied on the idea that the burden of the debt constituted a much less present danger than a paper currency, whose "deep-seated and far-reaching evils cannot be overstated." According to Senator Reuben E. Fenton of New York, paper money

> takes from men their property, by putting it upon a capricious and changing basis and measuring it by a false standard of value. It withholds from labor its just reward, by paying it in fictitious money, or compels it to resort to higher demands as the only protection from the reduced purchasing power of its compensation. It introduces uncertainty and anxiety into all business operations, wantonly changing contracts suddenly affecting prices, injuriously taxing all interests, producing violent fluctuations, and building up airy and delusive structures of hope, only to topple them over in disastrous ruin.

This apocalyptic image—ironically put forward by the very men who less than a decade earlier had voted to create the paper currency—led to only one conclusion: these evils were to be avoided at all cost. Some took this literally. Horace Greeley, long a champion of Whig ideas, did not hesitate to call for merciless contraction in 1866, "even if it should 'shut down the gates of half our mills, close some of our stores,' and drive 'a half million or so workers' to the West to grow corn."[55]

By contrast, those who viewed greenbacks as indispensable inevitably saw the extinction of the debt as the most urgent task facing the nation. "With such heavy interest-bearing liabilities constantly and rapidly maturing, why should the power be asked to call in and pay or fund the non-interest-bearing notes," asked Calvin T. Hulburd of New York.[56] The debt cost the federal government astronomical sums every year, and these sums could be paid only by levying taxes, which inevitably weighed on the country's producers. The resulting vision was just as binary as that of the anti-greenback camp: Treasury bonds were identified with idle rentiers, while greenbacks were linked to producers—those whose labor and investment contributed to the creation of wealth. Greenbacks oiled the wheels of production and perfused the economy as blood perfuses the body, whereas Treasury bonds constituted an intolerable burden, enriching bondholders at the expense of everyone else. Why, then, should the government favor bonds, which were costly and for the most part had to be reimbursed in gold, over paper money, which cost nothing? Why withdraw greenbacks, leading to deflation and thus discouraging production, when there was a colossal debt needing to be paid off?

A SIMILAR BINARY opposition emerged later during Reconstruction, between greenbacks and national banknotes. The national banking system had been explicitly created to help float loans and establish a more homogeneous currency through the national regulation of banks. So the government issued two types of paper money: greenbacks, which were legal tender and rested directly on the faith of the government, and national banknotes, which were not legal tender but whose value was supported by a reserve of U.S. bonds and thus indirectly guaranteed by the government. Soon, however, the debates on the money question came to oppose those two types of notes.

Apologists for the national banknotes argued that they were better than greenbacks because they reacted to the needs of the market: national banks were subject "to a higher law — the law of supply and demand — pervading and covering all." Since the amount of outstanding banknotes varied with the deposits of the bank's clients, it infallibly adjusted to market demand. By contrast, it was "far above the wisdom of one man, or a thousand men, to determine" the proper amount of currency. Hence the Treasury was not capable of regulating the money supply, and Congress even less so. That was, according to the banknote apologists, the main problem with greenbacks. The national banks could regulate the money supply, however, because they responded to market demands. The only flaw in the system, in the apologists' view, was the ceiling on the total circulation of national banknotes imposed by law. But proponents of "free banking," that is, of removing that ceiling, were hard-money men. For them, the system would only be safe with a return to specie payments, because then the banknotes would be ultimately based on "true" money: "First make our money stable in quality, then let its quantity fluctuate with the tide and currents of trade. But if its value is not fixed, fluctuations in its amount operate as a perpetual inducement to speculation."[57]

The champions of national banknotes were in the hard-money camp, in that they viewed gold as the only legitimate monetary base, but they were more moderate than some others who remained wary of banks and rejected the idea of abolishing the limit on the circulation of national banknotes backed by Treasury bonds. For those who argued that money was too abundant, free banking looked like inflation in disguise. By contrast, those who believed that the money supply was insufficiently elastic, so that at certain times in certain places there was not enough cash to meet the needs of commerce, saw free banking as a way of solving that problem without encouraging inflation.[58]

Nevertheless, all agreed that greenbacks were the worst type of currency and opposed those whose understanding of finance rested on that form of money. By contrast, soft-money men saw greenbacks as the people's money and balked at allowing a coterie of bankers to control the money supply, thereby putting producers at their mercy. "If we increase the power of these national banks," Indiana Republican John Coburn warned, "they will constitute such an enormous and dangerous monopoly that the liberties of the country may hereafter suffer from their influence." To some, the national banking system smelled suspiciously like the notorious Second Bank of the United States. "Nick Biddle's 'monster' — for the destruction of which the whole country was aroused to desperate effort in Jackson's day — was no more beside its sixteen-hundred-headed successor of our times than a guinea-pig beside an elephant," the *Cincinnati Enquirer* opined in 1869. Others extended wartime patriotism to the monetary domain: the federal government, being the instrument of the people, should take control of the economic sphere, they argued, and with the issuance of greenbacks it had done so. Furthermore, the national banking system cost taxpayers dearly because it was based on bonds that paid annual interest to the banks. "Under the present system about twenty million dollars improperly go to these favored few from our taxes collected," complained Pennsylvania Democrat Samuel J. Randall. The bankers thus reaped an undeserved windfall.[59] Greenbacks, on the other hand, cost the people nothing. Why tax citizens for the benefit of bankers when a better and cheaper system already existed?

THUS, WITHIN THE space of a few months, the complex debates around the currency, the public debt, and banking lined up on either side of a single cleavage. It became possible to treat the money question as a single moral and political issue involving broad visions of the economy, about which Americans had passionate feelings. Books, brochures, and pamphlets proliferated. Politicians received countless letters from citizens, known and unknown, offering more or less far-fetched solutions to the difficult money question. Paradoxically, it was precisely because the subject was so technical and confusing that positions divided into two broad camps, "hard money" or "soft money."

Economic Interests and Political Stakes

In the aftermath of the Civil War, the money question came to symbolize a much broader debate about what sort of economic relations Americans really wanted. The victory of the North had consecrated the "free-labor" ideal, which had emerged in the 1840s and 1850s in opposition to the slave system that dominated in the South. Already, however, this triumph was called into question by the transformation of American society through the acceleration of industrialization, the growth of capital markets, and the first creations of big corporations, with the railroads leading the way. All these new facts of life were not compatible with the free-labor ideology, and Americans were forced to reconsider their beliefs concerning what economic system was most desirable for the United States. In this context, the money question stood for the vanishing of old economic certitudes and the need to establish new ones.[60]

In these debates, economic interests jostled with rival conceptions of a just economy. Ideas of what the economy was or ought to be were measured against concrete economic situations (with all participants taking their own situations to be the norm). Positions were elaborated and expressed in terms of the broad categories that defined the economy at that time—farmers, workers, industrialists, merchants, and financiers. The way these groups approached the debate, developed more or less common views, and took stands (or refrained from doing so) largely explains why positions on the money question divided into hard-money and soft-money camps. Even more important, we can begin to see why positions divided along sectional lines: in other words, why the Northeast and Midwest came to symbolize hard money and soft money, respectively.[61]

NO ECONOMIC GROUP was unanimous on the money question because the members of each group did not share identical economic interests. Broad commonalities emerged, however, because (reputedly) representative institutions encouraged the expression of common views, and because polarization increased the pressure to choose sides. Broadly speaking, the financiers, merchants, and a minority of industrialists joined the hard-money coalition, while other industrialists, workers, and farmers opted for the more heterogeneous soft-money side.

It is best, however, to begin with the rather loosely organized group of intellectuals, academics, and Protestant ministers whose involvement did much to harden positions on the money question, linking it to "natural" laws and thereby turning it into a moral issue. Numerous professors of political economy went all out to defend the dogmatic view that gold and silver have intrinsic value and therefore constitute the only true monetary base. The theoretical basis for this view was drawn from classical economics, while England served as a practical model for the iron laws enunciated by these academics. At Princeton, Yale, and Harvard, the leading lights of the discipline—Lyman Atwater, William Graham Sumner, and Francis Bowen—insisted on the "sound principles" of "honest money." Textbooks such as Arthur Perry's *Principles of Political Economy* (1866) taught the nation's elite, educated in the great universities, the immutable laws of supply and demand, value, and money.[62]

Popularized by talented pamphleteers, these economists were the first to introduce a moralizing tone into postwar financial debates. In the 1870 revised edition of his textbook, Bowen assured his readers that "the prolonged use of Paper Money . . . [had] done even more harm to the morals of the country than to its commerce, its reputation, and its financial well-being." His colleague Perry proclaimed that "a paper money is only tolerable when it is actually and instantly convertible on demand into gold and silver." With consummate scientific rigor he added, "Taking all things into consideration, every way the best money is the gold and silver which God has evidently designed for that purpose." Political economy was at that time a branch of moral philosophy. For Lyman Atwater, a Protestant minister, "economics and ethics largely interlock." His colleague Leonard Bacon maintained that "financial questions are also, and equally, moral questions." Even the least religious of the professors, those who embraced the new social science inspired by Auguste Comte and John Stuart Mill, did not regard the detachment and objectivity required by their commitment to science as reasons to refrain from normative moralizing. On the contrary, their scientific goal was to discover the laws by which God imposed order on the world. Bowen, a professor of "natural religion, moral philosophy, and civil society" at Harvard, conceived of his work as "a general science of Human Nature, of which the special sciences of Ethics, Psychology, Politics and Political Economy are so many distinct and co-ordinate departments."[63]

The link between economics and ethics was reinforced by the involvement of numerous Protestant ministers and religiously oriented periodicals in the debate. The *Boston Christian Examiner* (Unitarian), *Chicago Standard* (Baptist), *Chicago Advance* (Presbyterian), and *New York Christian Advocate* (Methodist) vied with one another in denouncing the danger that paper money posed to public morality. "It is hardly an exaggeration to say that to the disordered condition of the currency we owe the chief part of the extravagance and dishonesty in mercantile circles, and so much of the corruption in public offices as is not due to our imbecile method of filling these offices," asserted the *Boston Christian Examiner.* And many pastors, including the celebrated Henry Ward Beecher, did not hesitate to preach sermons on finance from the pulpit.[64]

The involvement of clergy in the money question varied from denomination to denomination. The activists were mostly of the Calvinist persuasion. Episcopalians, on the other hand, remained true to their tradition of avoiding political controversy. Rural churches, whose parishioners might have been hostile to orthodox financial views, generally remained silent. When a minister did take a stand, however, it was always in dogmatic defense of the gold standard. The only moral path was a resumption of specie redemption and payment of principal and interest in gold. Such doctrinaire absolutism led in some cases to a fetishization of gold that might not seem very Christian. Although it is hard to say what influence these pastoral interventions had on the debate, they undeniably lent a moral tinge to the hard-money position that helped to unify its adepts while complicating the path to legislative compromise.[65]

The discourse of these intellectuals served the economic interests of other groups. Among the most contractionist were merchants, especially those engaged in import-export trade. The daily fluctuation of the gold value of greenbacks added to their risks: the purchase and sale of goods abroad required payment in gold, as did the payment of customs duties, while transactions on the domestic market were settled in greenbacks. The instability was felt not only by importers in the major ports (New York, Boston, and Philadelphia) but also by merchants all along the distribution chain. For an importer, if the price of gold (in terms of greenbacks) fell, the value of his stock decreased, but he could buy new merchandise abroad more cheaply (in terms of greenbacks). Conversely, if the price of gold increased, imports also became more costly in terms of greenbacks, but the value of the merchant's stock increased. Yet it also became more difficult to sell that stock, especially if substitutes were produced domestically at a price that did not vary with the price of gold. Finally, all foreign transactions required an exchange where greenbacks could be traded for gold, and the Wall Street Gold Room was subject to speculative activity that further increased the merchant's risks. In short, the existence of two inconvertible currencies was a source of instability for merchants.[66]

For these reasons, merchants demanded a rapid return to convertibility. Across the country, boards of trade regularly petitioned the secretary of the treasury and Congress to urge the contraction that alone, in their view, could lead to a swift resumption of specie payments. In February 1868, as they gathered in Boston to form a new National Board of Trade, they wasted no time before calling for a contraction of the money supply and a return to the gold standard.

Merchants did not form a monolithic group, however, owing to the wide range of their activities and interests and the diversity of their backgrounds. In New York, for example, a small minority led by George Opdyke—merchant, banker, and former Republican mayor of the city—succeeded in persuading the local Board of Trade to moderate its annual resolutions. In the Midwest, merchants were less directly involved in international trade and therefore less directly

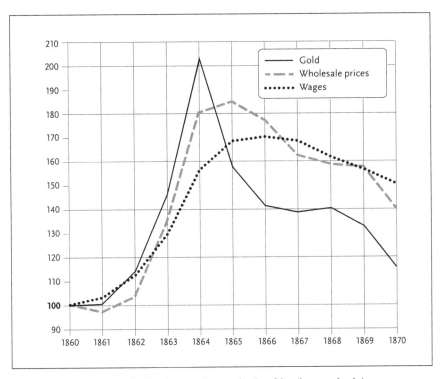

FIGURE 2. Gold, prices, and wages in the 1860s (in greenbacks)

Source: Robert P. Sharkey, *Money, Class, and Party: An Economic Study of Civil War and Reconstruction* (Baltimore: Johns Hopkins University Press, 1959), 146.

concerned by fluctuations in the price of gold. Some worried about the consequences of too rapid contraction and found the "gentlemen on the seaboard" all too blinded by their "calculations on gold." Another suggested, "Domestic commerce may be worth of some consideration." Despite these differences, however, most merchants agreed that convertibility was desirable, and few defended the principle of an inconvertible paper currency.[67]

All in all, merchants formed the most strongly contractionist interest group, more so, ironically, than bankers. They too had an obvious interest in anything that increased the value of capital. When the price index decreased, and greenbacks appreciated (see figure 2), the purchasing power of the income from capital increased, benefiting bankers. Broadly speaking, contraction favored creditors, since it increased the value of money and therefore of the capital reimbursed by debtors. The very substantial dividends that the New York banks distributed to their stockholders after the war show why bankers had an interest in contraction.[68]

Nevertheless, not all bankers favored a rapid contraction of paper currency. Some were in a greater hurry than others. The large bankers of New York took the lead. James Gallatin, for example, had opposed the creation of greenbacks in 1862 and urgently called for "the funding or payment of the interest-bearing notes and a continual contraction of the paper currency." He was an unusually uncompromising hard-money man, however, just as he was a staunch opponent of any state intervention in the nation's monetary affairs and banking. Many bankers did not wish to see unduly rapid contraction, which would impair the economic health of their clients. A panic leading to widespread bankruptcy would cause them no end of trouble. In an 1867 petition to Congress, a group of rural Midwestern bankers warned that a "further reduction of the volume of currency at present would prove highly injurious to the banking, manufacturing, and mercantile interests of the country, and would entail suffering upon nearly every member of the community." Hence any number of bankers, especially in the Midwest, where bank credit and national banknotes were in short supply, called for a moratorium on contraction. "Let the currency alone!" wrote one in the March 1866 issue of *Bankers' Magazine*. "Its diminution to any considerable extent would . . . plunge [the country] into a deeper abyss of financial calamity" than the war itself.[69]

These disagreements had to do only with the opportunity and pace of contraction, not with the ultimate goal. The majority of bankers agreed with George S. Coe, one of the most influential figures in the world of finance: greenbacks "represent no real value." Gold was a changeless object whose intrinsic value made it suitable for use as money. Paper was viable only if convertible. For bankers, only banknotes were truly useful, because they reflected the country's output. By contrast, greenbacks were arbitrary and therefore ineffective. The entire banking profession could thus rally around the bullionist principle. Some favored rapid contraction while others preferred to allow economic growth to do its work, but all agreed on the virtues of the gold standard and rejected any inflationary policy, and all agreed on the superiority of banknotes and the desirability of retiring all greenbacks at some point in the future.[70]

In short, most bankers joined the hard-money group alongside merchants, academics, and clergy. Nevertheless, a small but active minority campaigned for abundant money. Jay Cooke was emblematic of this new type of financier. He had made his fortune selling war bonds. After the war, he invested heavily in industry and railroads. Forced contraction went against his basic interests. "As to getting back to specie payments, the least said about that the better," he wrote to his brother Henry, "as it is the premium on gold that enables us to sell the 5–20's."

Cooke directly profited from the difference between greenbacks and gold, since investors could buy bonds with greenbacks while collecting interest in gold. In a broader sense, for reasons of both self-interest and ideology, and although he was not an inflationist, he shared with many other investors the conviction that it was best not to shrink the money supply too rapidly. "Why should this Grand and Glorious Country be stunted and dwarfed—its activities chilled and its very life blood curdled by these miserable 'hard coin' theories—the musty theories of a bygone age—These men who are urging on premature resumption know nothing of the great & growing west which would grow twice as fast if it was not cramped for the means necessary to build RailRoads and improve farms and convey the produce to market." These financiers were rarely fervent proponents of the greenback, however. They insisted that Treasury bonds be paid in gold. They generally favored banknotes, partly because they profited from the national banking system but also so as not to be at the mercy of Treasury operations intended to influence the price of gold. They nevertheless opposed contraction, which increased the cost of capital and hindered investment in industry.[71]

OWING TO THESE concerns, this small minority of financiers stood closer to the soft-money side than other bankers. For a variety of reasons they stressed the need for easy money in order to foster economic growth. Rhetorically, they did not defend financial orthodoxy on moral grounds, emphasizing instead the patriotic virtues of developing the domestic economy in the face of foreign competition as well as the role of the federal government in defending American producers, just as it had saved the Union during the war. The soft-money camp was far from homogeneous, however. In terms of rhetoric and interests, it was less cohesive than the hard-money group. Its members all thought of themselves as *producers*, however. Industrialists, craftsmen, workers, and farmers could see themselves as having convergent interests and sharing a common future because all were creators of wealth, in contrast to other groups, which they readily conceived of as parasitic.

Broadly speaking, industry suffered greatly from the end of the war, and industrialists reacted against McCulloch's contractionist policy, which they believed would compound their difficulties. The years of conflict had been good for them, but the transition to a peacetime economy cut into their income. The general decrease of prices due to the sudden curtailment of government consumption affected them directly, while the fall in the price of gold made imports more competitive on the domestic market. At the same time, wages continued to rise owing largely to worker pressure. Figure 2 shows how this combination of factors affected industrial incomes. In some sectors products had to be sold at a loss.[72] Many industrialists attributed these problems to the secretary of the treasury's monetary policy. In December 1865, the conservative *Commercial and Financial Chronicle* of New York deplored the fall in the price of gold, which "totally defeated the anticipations of those who looked for activity and buoyancy with the commencement of the new year." Iron makers, especially in Pennsylvania, vehemently attacked a policy that they deemed "the most vicious that has ever been proposed by any finance minister the world as yet has seen."[73]

The views of heterodox economist Henry C. Carey appealed to this group. Well-known for his steadfast defense of protectionism (see chapter 3), Carey took a close interest in the money question as a second axis in his championing of an active national development policy. In his view, a large money supply was necessary to stimulate entrepreneurship, whereas tight money implied higher rates of interest and a shortage of credit. Furthermore, the premium on gold served as a protective wall against imports, since it automatically increased the prices of goods purchased abroad, making domestic substitutes more competitive. Finally, in Carey's eyes, paper money served the cause of achieving monetary independence, which in his nationalist, neo-mercantilist view was a desirable goal. He pointed to the panic that followed the 1866 collapse of the London bankers Overend, Gurney & Co. in extolling the benefits of an inconvertible currency. When the price of gold rose suddenly on the London exchange, a large quantity of the precious metal quickly found its way there from the United States. "The crash was terrific, yet it never affected our domestic operations for even a single hour. Our monetary independence had been established. Our machinery of exchange being a non-exportable one, we had no use for gold, and if it were needed abroad, we could say, 'Why let it go!'"[74]

Industrialists shared with Carey the idea that they were producers (along with farmers and craftsmen) and therefore belonged to the class of borrowers in need of cash to finance their activities.[75] They preferred a system that would encourage domestic production and investment for development. They were nevertheless likely to prefer banknotes to greenbacks, largely in reaction to the campaign to repay the five-twenties (which many industrialists had acquired during the war) with paper money. The industrialists' preference also reflected their confidence in the banks as instruments for investment. In any case, they preferred easy money to tight money, regardless of the composition of the money supply: gold by itself would not suffice. There were of course substantial disagreements within this group. Iron manufacturers (centered in Pennsylvania) inclined more to the soft-money side, while textile manufacturers (primarily in New England) leaned in the other direction. Their industry was more mature and better established, and therefore less in need of investment, and making investments more difficult tended to tamp down domestic competition. Still, as a group, industrialists were clearly on the soft-money side until at least the Panic of 1873.[76]

This same "producerist" ideology served as a rallying point for the postbellum workers' movement, which came to share the views of the soft-money industrialists but with significant differences. Traditionally, workers had always preferred coin. Before the war, organizations of craftsmen and workers had staunchly opposed any kind of paper money, which they associated with banks. The war changed their outlook, however. In the absence of coin, the choice was between banknotes and greenbacks. Longstanding anti-monopolist and anti-bank sentiment led the National Labor Union, formed in Chicago in 1867, to opt for greenbacks. In a "Declaration of Principles" modeled on the Declaration of Independence, the union denounced the national banking system as an unjust "delegation by Congress of the sovereign power to make money and regulate its value to a class of irresponsible banking associations, thereby giving to them the power to control the value of all the property of the nation, and to fix the rewards of labor in every department of industry. . . . This money monopoly is the parent of all monopolies—the very root and essence of slavery."[77]

The money question led the workers' movement onto rather unexpected terrain involving interest rates. Influenced by the writings of two reformist businessmen, Edward Kellogg and Alexander Campbell, some trade unionists became concerned about the interest that banks drew from their loans. In their view, "money is the public measure of value," but value itself was created by production. From this they deduced that the only legitimate interest rate was one linked to growth, that is, to the creation of additional value through development of domestic production. Both Kellogg and Campbell put this rate at about 3 percent and alleged that any interest above that level was a tithe taken by bankers from the labor of producers. "Interest acts like a tax-gatherer," explained William H. Sylvis, one of the principal union leaders. "It enters into all things and eats up the price of labor. . . . It produces nothing; all it does is transfer the products of labor to the pockets of the money lenders, bankers, and bondholders." In this respect, the interests of bankers were opposed to those of both workers and industrialists. The fact that they could charge so much for the use of their money could only be a consequence of monopoly. The national banking system exacerbated this feeling of injustice.[78]

This anti-monopolistic vision converted the organized workers' movement to greenbackism. Banks were the enemy. In contrast, greenbacks were the money of the people, by the people, through the intermediary of the federal government. The most influential union leaders called for retiring national banknotes from circulation and replacing them with greenbacks. The *Workingman's Advocate*, a Chicago labor newspaper, wrote,

> The question is whether the government shall furnish the paper issues, which shall have all the qualities of money, and which, in fact, shall be made money by the same unquestionable authority which makes gold and silver money or whether the government shall abdicate this power . . . into the hands of a small class of men chartered by act of law to furnish a wildcat currency, to engross and speculate upon the products of labor, to swindle and cheat without restraint.

Workers also campaigned for fair reimbursement of Treasury bonds, which from their point of view meant payment in greenbacks wherever possible. The income from capital was not "real income," since it did not arise from the process of production, so that exorbitant reimbursement of money invested in government bonds could only come at the expense of producers, the only true creators of wealth.[79]

The labor movement was not uniform. It included men barely distinguishable from the industrialists who followed Carey as well as radical socialists. Some found it difficult to shed their antebellum bullionism. As late as September 1868, union leader Lewis Hine still believed that specie was "the workingman's currency, and the only honest currency." Local conditions likewise played a role. The militancy of Sylvis and Campbell made Illinois the spearhead of working-class greenbackism, whereas trade unionists in Massachusetts campaigned for the eight-hour day and viewed monetary issues as secondary. Despite these variations, the workers' movement's postbellum commitment to anti-monopoly politics writ large resulted in strong support for the greenback and for "fair reimbursement" of Treasury bonds.[80]

Insofar as farmers constituted an organized movement, they, too, moved from bullionism to greenbackism. As was the case with antebellum craftsmen and workers, the farmers' attachment to specie originally reflected their wariness of banks, which was as much a product of Jeffersonian and Jacksonian agrarian republicanism as of practical concerns. The banking system, which varied from state to state, was often unreliable, with notes that were not universally accepted and too many bankruptcies to inspire confidence. After the Civil War, however, farmers, unlike the trade unions, took no interest in the money question.

Although they, too, were affected by the changing economic conditions, they did not feel the effects immediately. The end of large-scale orders from the military together with increased competition from Argentina and Australia reduced demand on national and international markets, while mechanization stimulated by the war along with the cultivation of new land in the wake of the Homestead Act eventually increased output. But prices did not begin to fall until 1868.[81]

Farmers then organized. The National Grange of the Patrons of Husbandry, founded discreetly in Washington in December 1867, witnessed a rapid increase in the number of its local committees. Sharing some characteristics of cooperatives and some of unions, these Granges numbered nearly 800,000 active members in 1875. In the face of economic difficulty, their first response was to contest the freight rates charged by railroads. In some states, the Granges were relatively powerful. In Illinois, for example, they succeeded in imposing substantial reforms, including a provision in the new 1871 constitution authorizing the state government to regulate railroads. The ensuing court battle led to *Munn v. Illinois*, a Supreme Court decision that would be the basis for future federal regulation of transportation.[82]

It was not until after the Panic of September 1873 that the Granges took up the money question, rejecting their bullionist past in favor of greenbacks. In December of that year, the Illinois State Farmers' Association called for elimination of the national banking system and a new issue of greenbacks. Once again, anti-monopolism played a pivotal role in this change: it was because the banking monopoly became a pressing issue for farmers that greenbacks came to be seen as the "right" money. There were several reasons for the hostility to the banks, including the permanent threat of foreclosures on mortgages. In addition, the interest the banks demanded from their rural clients, coupled with the recurrent shortage of money during harvest seasons, affected farmers directly by limiting their access to credit and their ability to pay back loans when due.[83] Still, the rural bullionism of old did not simply vanish. The most militant farmers, those involved with the Granges, were the quickest to make the leap, however, and many rural newspapers followed suit. Thus despite the diversity of opinion, the overwhelming tendency in the 1870s was for farmers to go over to supporting greenbacks and opposing national banks. Farmers joined the soft-money camp.

As is evident by now, interest groups played a large role in shaping the money question. Americans conceived their economy around those groups—bankers, merchants, industrialists, workers, and farmers. Yet none of them were homogeneous in either their understanding of their interests or their conclusions concerning the money question. Variations and even divergences of opinion were common. The existence of institutions that either were or could plausibly claim to be representative, however, made the construction of reasonably coherent positions possible. In all those debates, it is striking to find that all of these groups found it important to take positions on the money question at all. It says something of the potency of this political issue that combined economic interests with ideological underpinnings, shaping it into a battle between two firmly opposed camps, hard money versus soft money. The money question was thus more than a simple matter of public finance: it became a window into the very structure of society.

The Sectionalization of the Money Question

The hard-money/soft-money dichotomy, based on well-defined economic interests and consolidated into competing moral visions, might at first glance seem to have nothing to do with geography. Soon, however, the Northeast and Midwest became identified as sections with one or the other of these two positions. The transition from ideological polarization to sectional confrontation was a twofold process involving, first, a change of scale in which local differences were smoothed out at the national level, and, second, the discovery that sections, as a category, were useful for framing the money question in political terms at a time when the parties were unable to develop consistent positions on the issue. Because the sections had already acquired economic identities, they served as the most "natural" way to frame the debate.

The sectionalization of the money question was facilitated by a built-in geographical bias of the national banking system, in both its design and the hazards of its implementation. To begin with, the $300 million in national banknotes authorized by the law of 1863 were distributed in a highly unequal manner. The urgent need to organize the system, the poor health of Midwestern banks, the decision wherever possible to convert existing banks into national banks rather than create new ones, and the choices made by the comptroller of the currency all help to explain why some states found themselves with no national banks after the war while others claimed more than their legal quota of banking capital. States from Maryland to New York received on average $14 to $20 of national banknotes per capita, and Connecticut, Rhode Island, and Massachusetts received $42 to $77. By contrast, the farther west one looked, the scarcer national banknotes became: around $8 per capita in Ohio, Indiana, and Minnesota, but only $5 in Iowa and $3 in Missouri. The South had virtually no national banks.[84]

This imbalance was reinforced by the very design of the system, which was built around a three-tiered "pyramid of reserves": at the bottom were the country banks; above them stood the reserve city banks, distributed among seventeen cities; and at the top, the New York banks. All of these institutions were subject to minimum reserve requirements, but the law allowed them to deposit substantial portions of these mandatory reserves in banks at the next higher level of the system.[85] This encouraged the transfer of a large fraction of bank deposits to the Northeast, and especially New York, not least because it became customary for the New York banks to pay interest on the reserves entrusted to them. This "pernicious practice" came in for growing criticism after the war, because "it produces a scarcity of capital for legitimate trade at one point [and] . . . a temporary plethora of money in the cities," thus encouraging speculation.[86]

These structural imbalances in access to money were reflected in the interest charged on bank loans. Throughout the period, rates varied from 10 to 12 percent in most of the Midwest, while in New York, they hovered around 6 to 7 percent.[87] Cash was thus in short supply in precisely those regions where alternative means of payment, such as checks, were still rare. In 1874, only 5 percent of transactions were settled in cash (specie, greenbacks, or national banknotes) in New York, whereas in rural counties, the rate was above 50 percent. The development of checking made it possible to increase the number of transactions completed without recourse to cash, but checks were used only in the Northeast, where banks were numerous and well-capitalized.[88]

The financial system that emerged from the Civil War thus exhibited a definite geographical bias. In the great banking centers of the East Coast, money in all its forms was abundant, while in rural areas (especially in the Midwest, far from New York), money was scarce and credit difficult to obtain. This situation became particularly critical in the fall, when moving and selling crops required a substantial amount of money on hand, triggering a vast flow of the nation's monetary resources. Local banks recalled their reserves in anticipation of a large volume of withdrawals, while big-city banks lent abundantly throughout the Midwest, where, the demand for cash being high, they could charge high rates of interest. These enormous capital flows destabilized the American financial system every year, while the concentration of capital in a few banking centers of the Northeast during the remainder of the year encouraged speculation.[89]

The American financial system was thus geographically biased. These regional differences partly explain the divergence of views on the money question—on the origins of the country's financial woes and the means to remedy them. It was easier to believe that money was too readily accessible if one lived in New York than if one lived in Kansas. Nevertheless, the sectional bias was only one among many others. Economic groups had different interests wherever they were located, and we find advocates of contraction in the Midwest as well as champions of the greenback in the Northeast. Some newspapers delighted in pointing this out: for example, in 1874, the *Cincinnati Trade List and Commerce Bulletin* denounced "western and southern bankers [who] united with eastern capitalists to prevent an increase in circulation," while the *Quincy Whig* in Illinois maintained that "the most radical of inflationists in Congress from the West have uttered nothing more extreme or irrational in favor of expanding the volume of irredeemable paper currency than has been advanced by Mr. Kelley and some other Representatives from the East."[90] Even though these newspapers were trying to convince their readers that the money question was not a sectional issue, the terms "West" and "East" had become unavoidable. The transformation of the issue into a sectional dispute proved irreversible. It became virtually impossible to discuss the subject without invoking the division between the Northeast and the Midwest.

Several factors were involved in transforming the money question into a sectional issue. The first was simply the existence of the sections as pre-established categories ready for use. Their availability made them easy to mobilize for the purpose of analyzing a new political issue such as the money question. Thus it was only "natural" that in September 1866, a conference of Midwestern bankers was held in Chicago, which the *Chicago Republican* described as "an event in our history worthy of more than a passing notice." The paper hailed the "assemblage of Western bankers [who] met in convention in the metropolis of the West for the express purpose of protecting Western interests." If the banking system was national, it was nevertheless also experienced as regional.[91]

It was particularly easy to view the money question through a sectional lens because a geographic bias did in fact exist. But that cannot be the whole story: like their colleagues in the Northeast, Midwestern bankers did not have confidence in greenbacks—paper currency that had no coin basis and no reserve backing. But with fewer national banks in the Midwest, these same bankers also wanted to see the legal quota abolished and free banking authorized. Bankers as an interest group shared some common interests at the national level, such as the resumption of specie payments, but there were also regional differences, such as a desire for a redistribution of banking capital.

As preexisting political categories, sections could easily be mobilized to make sense of reality. In the minds of Americans, the Midwest and the Northeast already existed as geographic entities, ready-made to frame a question for comparison. This proved particularly potent in the transition from the local to the national level. Locally, we find the same interest groups more or less everywhere, and yet their relative weight differed from place to place. This is why, for instance, the editor of the *Chicago Republican,* a tireless promoter of Midwestern industrial interests, felt compelled to explain over and over again that the future of the section could not rest on agriculture alone: "The West is capable of something more than being a mere farm. . . . We have room in our cities for the highest degree of excellence in the finest productions of mechanical skill, and room for the population engaged in those pursuits." It would be senseless "to make agriculture its exclusive pursuit, and leave its iron, its coal, and all its countless natural opportunities unemployed." Midwestern farmers were apparently such a powerful group that unstinting effort was required to prevent the region from identifying exclusively with agriculture.[92]

The relative power of the various interest groups in each region partly account for the sectionalization of the money question. In Massachusetts, traditional elites exerted considerable influence. In New York, the influence of financiers was amplified by "Boss" William M. Tweed's corrupt political machine. There the balance of power fell on the hard-money side. By contrast, in the Midwest, the radical agrarian tradition found a more favorable terrain among farmers mobilized by a difficult economy and high freight rates, and by workers more concerned with the money question than their counterparts in the East.[93] Joining the soft-money camp was easy.

The balance of power worked out as it did all the more easily because it was reinforced by each section's established image. Throughout the country, people were prepared to believe that the Midwest would defend agrarian interests precisely because it was *already* identified with those interests. This was apparent during the first congressional debates on the money question. At that point, farmers were already mobilized in favor of regulating the railroads.[94] On currency questions they were more reticent but rather conservative. Among Midwestern congressmen, however, an agrarian reflex was quite apparent as early as 1866–67. One Northeasterner expressed his irritation: "I have heard the agrarian sentiments . . . too often upon this floor to be alarmed by their expression at this time."[95] This was a clear sign of the political force of the term "section"—it referred not only to a region but to a whole range of ambiguous yet widely understood issues that influenced the positions of everyone involved.

The pertinence of the section as an analytic category was most evident at the national level. Interest groups, when they met and deliberated as such, were not sectional, even though sectional variations existed. Locally, moreover, there was no unanimity on any of these issues. But the transition to the federal level simplified this heterogeneity and transformed the controversy into a clash between the

Midwest and Northeast. This transformation did not occur all at once. Section-alism in congressional voting was slow to appear and solidify. Once it became a recurrent phenomenon, however, it seemed irreversible—and at times vehement. "Why," John B. Henderson of Missouri angrily asked, "should the people of my State be compelled to stand by and listen to such a speech as the Senator from Massachusetts [Henry Wilson] has made, with his pocket full of bonds . . . ? He has got an iron rule fixed upon us, and . . . the West must submit to it." As early as 1868, debate had already crystallized around sections, and the financial ortho-doxy of a senator from Massachusetts could only be interpreted as favoring the Northeast over the Midwest.[96]

With each new political confrontation we see a series of correspondences being established. The section was not so much a geographical region as a Russian doll, encapsulating a whole set of political issues. Although these metaphorical dimen-sions varied with the partisan objectives of the moment, sectionalism remained pregnant with significance precisely because each section's image conveyed an ideological freight that transcended by far the literal geographical definition. For example, in mid-1866, the *Cincinnati Enquirer*, one of the leading Democratic newspapers in the Midwest, began contrasting New England and the Midwest, Republicans and Democrats, bondholders and workers, banknotes and greenbacks. Through a series of semantic linkages, the paper sought to set forth a coherent po-litical system articulating the sectional economic interests of the Midwest. Article after article established correspondences and equivalences whose intent was to accuse Midwestern Republicans of favoring the rich at the expense of the majority while at the same time betraying the interests of their own section for the benefit of the Northeast. "The party to which they belong has its head in New England and its tail in the West," the newspaper wrote in a revealing passage. "There can be no hope for the West until she emancipates herself from this radical thralldom. It must until then, like Issachar, continue to bear the burden of the ass; and must be ridden by New England masters, whose spurs at every step of the journey will draw blood from the jaded and exhausted people."[97] In these few sentences, the focus shifts first from New England to the Republican Party, then back to exploit-ative New Englanders versus the people of the West. We see how sectionalism could be mobilized for partisan ends: because the sectional category was dense with meaning, it could be used to rally support and shape political debate.

IN THE EARLY YEARS of Reconstruction, the money question was shaped more by section than by party. The compression of the wide range of opinions on this complex subject into vast regional blocs came about largely through the use of political metaphor. To be sure, there was a genuine geographical bias in the financial system established during the war. But the crystallization of complex technical issues into sectional alignments was the effect of a *political* process. Each section was a historical construct whose significance transcended mere spatial extent. Each section projected an economic image, and these images governed the course of debate.

For that reason, the clash of interest groups and ideologies did not hinder the sectionalization of the money question. The parties were built around a very different set of issues and, given the coalitions of which they were constructed, could not put together coherent positions on the money question. Sections could. Although there were farmers throughout the country, they were far more numerous in the Midwest, and above all, the Midwest was *identified* as an agricultural section. Similarly, bankers and merchants existed everywhere, but the Northeast was incontestably the center of financial and commercial power, so that its sectional interests were seen as identical to the interests of those two economic groups. In any case, debate continued to rage at the local level, and developments there had an impact on national politics. In Congress, sectionalism did not supplant the parties, which remained the primary force shaping political debate. It was precisely in the transition from the local to the national scale, however, that the sections exerted their influence on politics. When the money question became the central political issue of the day, section threatened party.

3

Economic Policy and Spatial Justice

TAXATION AND THE TARIFF

———— • ————

Now, suppose a poor man goes to work on that land, just see how the country protects him. He first undertakes to fence in his land, and the spade with which he digs the hole for a post is taxed; the ax with which he cuts the post to put in the hole is taxed; the boards he puts on the posts to make his fence are taxed; the nails with which he fastens on the boards are taxed; and the hammer with which he drives the nails is taxed. When the fence is done and the man goes inside to work, his plow is taxed, his hoe is taxed, his cultivator is taxed, his reaper or mower is taxed, and everything he uses is taxed. And for the benefit of whom? For the protection of American manufacturers. . . . He fights the battles of the country and pays its taxes, too, and this is the protection you give him.
—John Wentworth (R, IL), speech in Congress, July 5, 1866

TO FINANCE THE WAR, the federal government established a tax system without precedent in the nation's history. Although it relied primarily on loans, it had to back them with an efficient and credible tax system. High customs duties, taxes on all products and services, and a tax on high incomes—American citizens suddenly felt the tangible presence of federal power. During the war, few contested taxes that were seen as a patriotic duty. Once peace returned, however, the rise of a fiscal "leviathan" did not fail to provoke debate.[1]

It was in this new context that the old question of the tariff once again reared its head. Since the beginning of the Republic, customs duties had been a regular source of income for the federal government. Abetted by the war, however, those same duties became what they had never previously been for long: a protectionist instrument. Whole swathes of American industry were sheltered from international competition. These protectionist measures were also redistributive.

Protected sectors were subsidized by unprotected ones, and by consumers in general. Everyone understood this, and when the military emergency ended, the issue of the tariff once again became acute, and with it the issue of economic justice and the government's responsibility in this area.

As with the money question, so with the tariff question: neither of the two political parties was well-equipped to deliver a coherent response. Their leaders, one observer bitterly complained, "are afraid that by introducing new issues into their political program, they may cause dissension in their own ranks."[2] Debate therefore developed along lines of sectional opposition in the North (at first the defeated South had no say in the matter). The tariff lent itself to the defense of local interests, to lobbying, and to congressional horse-trading, but in the broadest sense, the Midwest came to be identified with free trade and the Northeast with protectionism. This sectionalism would force the parties to make internal compromises and eventually established a political configuration that would persist until the end of the nineteenth century.[3]

Taxation and Protection

Americans had been debating the tariff from the earliest days of the republic, customs having been made the primary source of federal revenue in 1789. Import duties served a dual purpose, at once fiscal and economic. They both provided the federal government with revenue and increased the cost of goods imported from abroad, thus encouraging domestic producers of the same products. Throughout the first half of the nineteenth century, tariffs were the focal point of clashes over the economic role of the federal government. The Civil War transformed the tariff issue, however, because duties were sharply increased and the tariff became part of a more elaborate tax system. Once peace was restored, the old debate was revived in new terms.

As early as 1866, a movement arose to quickly retrench the wartime tax system, which was losing legitimacy now that the hostilities were over. *Harper's Weekly* spoke for the movement: "It is grand to think that our Government is the richest in the world. . . . It is not quite so grand to realize that we pay man, woman and child, white and colored, twice as much money to support our free republican government as is paid by the 'downtrodden masses of Europe' (we are anticipating the orators next week) to maintain their 'worn-out, bloated despotisms.'" Was there still any good reason to bear the burden of taxes tolerated only as needed to wage a war for the survival of the Union?[4] In this first election year after the war, pressure mounted for the government to trim its sails. The need to cut taxes

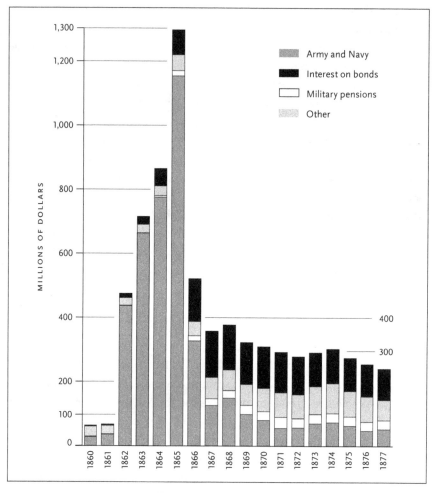

FIGURE 3. Expenses of the federal government

Source: U.S. Bureau of the Census, *Historical Statistics of the United States from Colonial Times to 1970* (Washington, DC: Government Printing Office, 1970), 2:1114.

was all the more apparent in view of the fact that federal expenditures had been cut by two-thirds (from $1,218 to $386 million) in a single year (see figure 3). The army had demobilized, cut spending drastically across the board, and canceled the large orders for uniforms, food, and munitions that had sustained the war effort. It was nevertheless impossible to pare the budget to prewar levels: a military presence was still required in the South, even though many among the reduced number of troops were being redeployed against Indians in the West, and bonuses and disability pensions had to be paid. Above all, the enormous public debt had to be financed and paid down. Interest payments alone became one of the largest items in the federal budget, $133 million for fiscal year 1866.[5]

The government therefore needed to maintain its sources of revenue in order to meet these expenses. Various financial imperatives had to be prioritized. Should taxes be cut or the war debt paid off? Hugh McCulloch, the secretary of the treasury, made the withdrawal of greenbacks from circulation his top priority (see chapter 2), and this in turn made it necessary to raise substantial revenues. How quickly to pay down the debt was also an issue. It was therefore impossible to dismantle the wartime tax system. So which taxes were to be lowered? The 1866 polemic over the tariff grew out of this debate.

In the first half of the nineteenth century, a pragmatic distinction had been made in regard to taxation: local authorities taxed property, while the federal government met its needs through customs duties and the sale of public land. The federal government's fiscal power was a central feature of the Constitution of 1787. As early as the 1790s, with Alexander Hamilton's economic plan, and even more with the so-called Tariff of Abominations of 1828, which was at the root of the constitutional crisis of 1832, protectionism versus free trade had been a major political issue. But the principle of using customs as the main source of federal revenue had never been challenged. This system, however, proved woefully inadequate to pay for the Civil War. Under pressure, the Republicans therefore revamped the federal tax system.[6]

When conflict broke out at Fort Sumter on April 12, 1861, the U.S. Treasury was empty, although preliminary steps had been taken to remedy this situation. Despite initially optimistic predictions, it soon became apparent that the war would be long and costly. Senator John Sherman worried that "the problem of this contest was not as to whether we could muster men, but whether we could raise money." Even though war is always costly, lenders have to be convinced each time that they will be reimbursed when the conflict ends. A happy ending was not obvious in the early months of the war, and it proved difficult to sell Treasury bonds even at a steep discount.[7]

At the outset of the war, Republicans resorted to traditional methods copied from previous conflicts: in addition to customs duties, they imposed a direct tax on land and housing property. But the measure aroused considerable opposition. Because it did not take financial and industrial assets into account, it "must fall with very heavy, if not ruinous effect, upon the great agricultural States of the West and Southwest," one politician warned, and yet would spare the wealthy industrial states of the Northeast. To compensate for this and in order to avoid a dangerous division in the North, Congress decided to tax all incomes above $800 a year at the rate of 3 percent.[8]

These early measures proved inadequate, and how to finance the war remained a major concern throughout the lengthy conflict. Bill after bill, the Republicans expanded the fiscal system, striking a political compromise between efficiency and acceptability. On the one hand, the tariff was extended to nearly all imported goods and regularly increased up to an average effective rate of 48 percent. Excise taxes were also levied on most goods and services, especially alcohol and tobacco, along with a 3 percent tax on industry, fees for certain professional licenses, and a tax on high incomes (5 percent for incomes above $600 a year and 10 percent above $5,000 a year). The collection of the direct tax on land was suspended in 1862 except as a confiscatory weapon against the South. By the end of the war, the system generated enough revenue to pay for about 20 percent of government expenses, but its most important contribution was to enable the federal government to borrow money by reassuring lenders that it would have the ability to repay their loans. For political reasons, Republicans favored indirect taxes, which were not subject to the constitutional requirement to apportion among the states according to their populations. Indirect taxes could be collected in less obvious ways, moreover, because they could be hidden in the prices of everyday goods and services and were therefore "less painful" to pay. Nevertheless, the creation of a Bureau of Internal Revenue staffed by tax collectors assigned to measure the output of every farm, shop, workshop, and factory in the country dramatically revealed the enhanced powers of the federal government.[9]

The Republicans, who in April 1866 began the transition to a peacetime economy, logically turned their attention first to the most visible taxes. The political reasons for this were clear. If "we want revenue," John Wentworth of Illinois explained, "those means of revenue are the most popular which are the least felt in collection." Experience, he continued, has shown that the "inquisitorial" aspect of tax collection was "as odious as it is cruel." Justin S. Morrill, a Republican leader on economic issues, insisted that only "imperative necessity" could justify "an excise tax on manufactures. . . . But the exigency has passed, and measures designed to be but temporary must be replaced."[10] Between 1866 and 1872, most of the tax system established during the war was therefore dismantled. The income tax was gradually reduced, dropping from 5 percent on incomes above $1,000 a year in 1867 to 2.5 percent above $2,000 in 1870 and finally to zero in 1872. Excise tax rates were also lowered, and the range of products covered was narrowed. After 1872, federal taxes were limited mainly to tobacco and alcohol for both practical and ideological reasons (see figure 4). This concentration on a small number of products, along with drastic cuts in the personnel and budget of the Bureau of

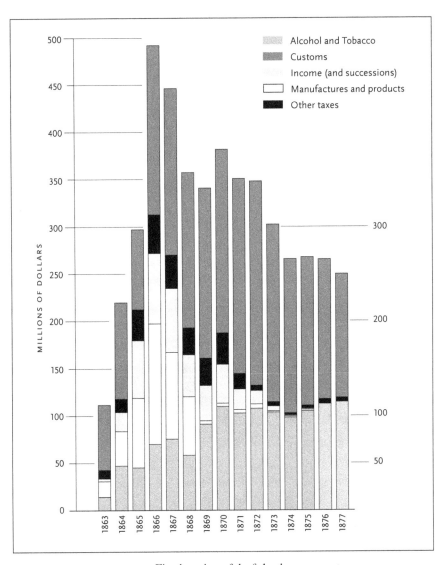

FIGURE 4. Fiscal receipts of the federal government

Source: U.S. Commissioner of Internal Revenue, *Annual Report of the Commissioner of Internal Revenue for the Fiscal Year Ended June 30, 1877* (Washington, DC: Government Printing Office, 1877), 153–76.

Internal Revenue in 1872, made it clear that the federal government was cutting back and curtailing its intrusion into the private affairs of its citizens.[11]

The dismantling of the tax system stirred little protest apart from the stiff tax imposed on alcohol, which was challenged in certain areas for economic and cultural reasons.[12] One tax escaped the cutbacks, however: customs duties, the

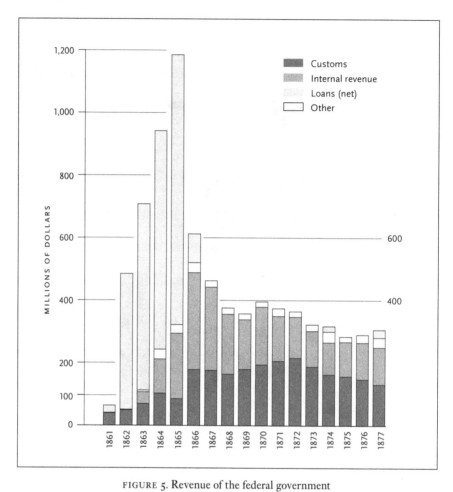

FIGURE 5. Revenue of the federal government

Source: U.S. Secretary of the Treasury, *Annual Report of the Secretary
of the Treasury on the State of the Finances for the Year 1877* (Washington, DC:
Government Printing Office, 1877), 10–13.

revenue from which increased significantly between 1865 and 1872, as did the
share of total federal revenue generated by the tariff (see figure 5). In short, a
decision was made not to decrease tariffs. In part this reflected a return to traditional forms of federal taxation. "We must pay as far as practicable the ordinary
expenses of our Government from duties upon imports," John Wentworth explained to the House. "Our debt and interest are so excessive that we are now in
no situation to" consider a cut in tariffs. Nevertheless, given that the secretary of
the treasury had just announced a budget surplus of more than $130 million, and

the cuts in other taxes were estimated at $75 million, other options were available.[13] Why exempt the tariff from the broad tax cuts?

The answer came in June 1866, when Justin S. Morrill introduced a bill to *increase* customs duties. The bill failed to pass, and no significant adjustment of tariffs occurred before 1872, when nearly all other federal taxes were eliminated. The importance of the Morrill bill lay, however, in its abandonment of the political argument used to justify tariff increases during the war. Morrill proposed instead to transform the wartime tax system into a permanent system of industrial protectionism, independent of the financial needs of the federal government. He then reopened a debate that immediately provoked divisions within both major parties and pitted section against section.

The war had transformed the tariff question. The battle between protectionists and free-traders, which went back to the early days of the United States, had long defined a fundamental political cleavage separating Whigs from Democrats. But the crisis of the 1850s changed the political dynamic. The nascent Republican Party was a broad coalition organized around the issue of slavery. It included fervent protectionists (among them many Pennsylvanians deeply affected by the crisis of 1857) as well as proponents of free trade. The first tariff passed under the aegis of the Republicans, the "Morrill Tariff" of 1861, was a moderate fiscal measure approved before the war and justified by the fact that the U.S. Treasury was empty. The Morrill Tariff's average effective rate of 20 percent was comparable to the average effective rate of the tariff of 1846. In other words, it was not a protectionist measure but a "revenue tariff," whose main purpose was to generate revenue for the federal government.[14]

The need to finance an immensely costly war changed everything, however. It justified a series of tariff hikes: first in August 1861, then again in December of that year, followed by additional increases in June 1862 and June 1864. In fact, the tariff brought in relatively little money (see figure 4), partly because the high duties discouraged imports and partly because of inflation. But it played a pivotal role in funding the war through its association with indirect taxes. On the one hand, the "increase of excise duties" was meant "to provide the needed revenue for the Government," while on the other hand, higher customs duties served to "protect the manufacturer or producer against the consequences of such increase and save him from ruinous competition."[15]

By the war's end, the tariff stood at an unprecedented level, with an average effective rate of 48 percent and only a short "free list" of exempt articles.[16] Protectionism was no longer a distant political goal, as it had been before the war, but an economic reality. More important, perhaps, was the fact that four years of fiscal reform had linked the protection of domestic industry to the financing of the federal government. It therefore became possible to pass bills that would have been impossible to pass in different circumstances. Morrill and his colleague Thaddeus Stevens, both key Republican leaders, were protectionists, and the laws they pushed through bore the protectionist stamp. The change in tariff policy during the war was not due to any Republican consensus on the issue, however. High wartime tariffs were justified as necessary compensation for other taxes or obtained as quid pro quo for favors to other socioeconomic groups (such as the Homestead Act, which benefited farmers).[17]

Because the Morrill bill of 1866 no longer linked high tariffs to other taxes, it exposed the protectionist motive more clearly. Cutting taxes on industry while maintaining high tariffs put money in the pockets of protected manufacturing sectors. Politicians who had voted for higher wartime tariffs without embracing protectionist goals now faced an altered political landscape. As one Midwestern senator complained, "I did not suppose that the arguments enforced against me for four years would now in a moment be reversed."[18] The restoration of peace changed the political context. Protectionists could no longer claim that high tariffs were required to meet the needs of the federal government, so they claimed instead that domestic industry needed protection, thus reviving the prewar debate. But the new postwar political configuration changed the nature of that debate.

As in the days of Henry Clay, protectionists like Morrill claimed that vulnerable domestic industry needed protection from international rivals in order to "place the American laborer, producer, or manufacturer upon a level of fair competition with foreign capital and foreign labor." Protection was necessary for economic development: rather than "bring in the manufactured article," it was better "to bring in the laborer himself," who by his labor would enrich the country. Congressional protectionists insisted that their primary motive was to protect not "the manufacturer and the capitalist [who] can get along with or without the duty," but "the man who digs the iron, the man who chops the wood, and the man who burns the coal." Did these workingmen not deserve "a fair day's wages for a fair day's work"? "Does any gentleman here wish to bring the American mechanic and laborer in his daily wages down to the miserable starvation pauper prices of Europe?" thundered Benjamin F. Wade on the Senate floor. "Who here is the advocate of trampling down the American mechanic and the American laborer?"[19]

The adversaries of protectionism pointed out that the protection of certain industries imposed a direct burden on all other Americans. "Does the gentleman from Pennsylvania [Thaddeus Stevens]," Iowan James F. Wilson harangued in the House, "expect the consumers of the country, who are to pay these exorbitantly increased rates under the duty now proposed to be laid for the purpose of sustaining the theory which he has advanced here to-day of building up at some future time manufactories of these particular articles?" Many openly doubted that "the manufacturers [would] become liberal toward those they employ," warning instead that "the more margin you give them the more money it puts into their pockets." Meanwhile, protectionism imposed "an onerous and excessive burden upon the consumers . . . the toiling millions of the country," and especially farmers. Was this not, Hiram Price of Iowa asked, "discrimination against the agricultural interests and in favor of the manufacturing interests?"[20]

Although these arguments recapitulated the terms of the prewar debate, the conflict had injected new ingredients. One of these was patriotic rhetoric. Invoked in defense of the Union, it partially undermined the legitimacy of free-trade discourse, especially since Southerners had used it in defense of states' rights since the 1820s.[21] William D. Kelley, a Republican with overt ties to Pennsylvania iron interests, was quick to argue that to reject the tariff increase would be tantamount to high treason. For example, a failure to increase the duty on Canadian coal would, in his view, reward those who "went out of this country and invested their funds in an enemy's territory," even though American manufacturers would benefit. Protectionists vied with one another in denouncing "British gold [which] is operating to secure American legislation for British interests." In other words, nationalism bolstered the economic defense of the nation against "foreign artificers of brass and iron and even of clay." But the patriotic argument could also be stood on its head: for example, Illinois Republican John Wentworth asked why manufacturing interests should be favored at the expense of farmers, when farmers made up the majority of those who fought in the Union's armies.[22]

Another legacy of the war, the fiscal and financial situation of the country also changed the terms of the tariff debate. Morrill, for example, linked the need for protectionism to the "unusual taxes" and "disturbing flood of an exclusively paper currency." Once again he was making use of the dual role of tariffs, as both a source of revenue and a protectionist barrier. On the one hand, reducing imports, for which "we pay . . . by sending abroad gold and silver," made it possible to conserve the coins needed to restore parity between greenbacks and gold. On the other hand, tariff protection ensured that "our own fields, factories and workshops [would be] fully manned and the men constantly employed," and on these conditions, "our great revenue from internal taxes [was] wholly dependent." In order to reduce the debt and work toward a resumption of specie payment, the federal government needed to secure its fiscal base.[23] Morrill's adversaries rebutted this analysis. Francis C. Le Blond, a Democrat from Ohio, argued that "not one gentleman has offered an argument why [the tariff] should be raised for the purpose of increasing the revenue" at a time when Congress was lowering other taxes. John B. Henderson, a Missouri Republican, remarked that, "as you increase the tariff, so you increase the paper currency of the country and increase prices, and one merely urges on the other" in a vicious inflationary circle that would make it almost impossible to return to the convertibility of greenbacks.[24] The tariff thus became one of many taxes, and this changed the terms of the debate. Its fiscal and financial incidence was as controversial as the advisability of sheltering certain American industries from international competition.

Ultimately, the 1866 bill, introduced at a time when reducing the tax burden was the order of the day, bared the protectionist intentions of one segment of Republicans. The bill figured as part of a broader strategy of economic development based on federal intervention. What was possible in wartime, however, became problematic in peacetime. The conflict changed the debate. It also simplified the work of the protectionists, since high tariffs were already in place. By seeking to go still further, however, they provoked a reaction that put them on the defensive and divided both parties, especially Republicans.

The 1866 bill thus renewed a sectional view of the economy that the war had attenuated without eliminating. The first half of the century had seen a heightening of the contrast between the South and the North, slavery and free labor. This split had ramifications in every aspect of political economy: the role of government, taxation, internal improvements, and the tariff.[25] By seceding, however, Southerners removed themselves from the political equation of the Union. Protectionists, many of whom were from the Northeast, were therefore able to revive an understanding that dated back to the 1820s with Midwesterners, who called for infrastructure investment and access to public land. Votes in favor of building a transcontinental railroad, the Homestead Act of 1862, and the financing of agricultural colleges in every state were so many signs of sectional log-rolling for which the quid pro quo was higher import duties.[26]

The 1866 bill marked a move away from this dynamic, and rekindled sectional tensions. "Sir, look at the free list" (that is, the list of products exempt from customs duties), Le Blond exclaimed. "Does it inure to the benefit of the West? Does it benefit any western man, except with regard to two or three articles? Why, sir, that long list inures almost exclusively to the benefit of the State of New York and the New England States." Many others also viewed the bill through the lens of geographic interests. The high protectionist Thaddeus Stevens had the opposite complaint—that the bill was too timid. He characterized it "as a free-trade bill from beginning to end. . . . This is a tariff particularly fitted for the eastern market." (This last comment implicitly associated Pennsylvania, which Stevens represented, with the Midwest.) Farther west, many people found that, on the contrary, the bill proposed import duties that would have been far too high. What all these reactions had in common was that they singled out a primary beneficiary of the measure based on section as well as economic sector. The Democratic *Cincinnati Enquirer* summed up the debate: "Here is anything but protection, either to the Western agricultural or the Western mechanical producer." The conclusion followed: "The country is governed for the benefit of New England."[27]

By breaking with the fiscal logic, the 1866 bill isolated protectionist economic policy, stripping it of legitimacy except in the eyes of those interest groups that it favored. Despite its partial failure, it transformed the tariff question into an explosive political issue by reviving an economic sectionalism that divided the two major parties.

The Geographical Underpinnings of the Tariff Issue

Tariff policy was all in the details. The law did not set a uniform rate but rather imposed specific duties (in dollars or percentage of value) on each type of imported article. Hence the tariff schedule determined a precise degree of protection for each sector of the economy. As such, the tariff laws encouraged bargaining over specific details and the formation of ad-hoc coalitions (what congressmen call "log-rolling"). This situation explains why economic justice was a central theme of the tariff debate. It contrasted with the debates on the money question, filled with good-versus-evil moralizing rhetoric. Here the issues, though technical, were simpler in that there was a limited number of levers Congress could adjust, thus they lent themselves more easily to black-and-white rhetoric, while the tariff divided in a myriad of products, each individually considered. At first sight, tariff policy might not seem to be a sectional issue. Yet the conjunction of interest-group competition with the question of the justice of federal economic intervention allowed sectional differences between the Midwest and Northeast to reshape the debate.

The Effects of Industrial Geography

Since the early days of the Republic and Alexander Hamilton's *Report on Manufactures*, protectionist policies aimed at developing domestic industries had found many advocates in the United States. Its strongest support came from politicians in the Northeast, the first region of the country to industrialize. In the postbellum period, however, sectional differences transcended economic geography. Heavy industry is an interesting case in point. Its advocates called for strong protection against foreign imports. The location of mineral deposits and sources of energy largely determined where firms in this sector chose to operate. For instance, the iron industry was concentrated in Pennsylvania and Ohio, where coal was abundant—that is, in the transitional zone between the Northeast and Midwest.[28] Although the politicians representing these particular districts were on the whole protectionist, that fact alone cannot explain why one section was broadly identified with protectionism while the other was not. Economic geography and section did not match.

The past had something to do with it: the older states industrialized earlier. But the second industrialization may have confused the picture to some extent. Many Midwestern boosters thought so. In 1868, when experiments with "reducing Missouri iron ore to pig metal with Illinois coal" at Carondelet, Missouri, near St. Louis, proved successful, the *Chicago Republican* was quick to predict "the inauguration of one of the most useful and the most developing industries of the age." The technical advance showed that it was possible to use locally mined coal to produce high-quality iron. The proximity of the coal mines to the source of iron ore made this experiment interesting. The newspaper nevertheless warned that without "the principle of protection," this potential "would be neglected."[29]

The need to industrialize was one of the major arguments advanced by Midwestern protectionists. "It may cause some surprise to people at the East," wrote the *Quincy Whig*, a central-eastern Illinois newspaper, "to learn that the West is likely to become a vast emporium of industrial production rather than a mere grower of breadstuffs for others." The paper attributed the region's rapid development to the customs barrier: "Without further protection, not only would the progress of manufactures cease, but those interests that are but yet in their infancy would inevitably sicken and die." Borrowing an idea from theorists of protectionism such as Henry C. Carey, the paper emphasized what it saw as the fragility of a nascent branch of industry: "It is for western manufactures that protection is needed more than it is for those of the East."[30] Along this line of thought, it is easy to find many protectionists in the Midwest. One of the most visible was the *Chicago Republican*, which in April 1867 counted in the section "some thirty or more of our Republican papers [that] have recently come out for protection." Protectionism was in part an ideology of development inherited from the Whigs and reinforced by the new nationalism. But high import duties also found champions in interest groups that profited directly from them. Ohio iron manufacturers were perhaps the most extreme case: even moderate protectionists were too tepid for them.[31]

Conversely, even though the Northeast was identified with protectionist interests, some groups there, starting with merchants, staunchly opposed protectionism. New York import-export firms correctly saw the closing of American markets as a direct threat to their businesses. These businessmen were a mainstay of the American Free Trade League, founded in New York in 1865. A highly active group, it published numerous pamphlets and sponsored speaking tours by experts such as Edward Atkinson, Francis Lieber, and Roeliff Brinckerhoff for the purpose of promoting lower tariffs.[32]

Even some interests more closely tied to manufacturing rejected protectionism. Railroads faced higher construction costs at a time when new lines, including the transcontinental railroad, greatly increased the demand for steel rails. "Without a stiff duty upon iron they could get a far superior article for railroads at half the price they now have to pay," the *Cincinnati Enquirer* asserted in 1871, echoing railroad managers. Their stand against the high tariff on steel imports was shared by those who hoped to accelerate the development of the transport infrastructure. Among them, according to James F. Wilson, "the farming interest in the West is interested" in making sure that "the construction of railroads . . . shall not be retarded by the legislation of this Congress."[33] This startling convergence of interests among railroad magnates and financiers on the one hand and farming interests on the other was not limited to any particular section.

Finally, even within the manufacturing sector, not everyone supported protectionism. Although New England was identified with the protectionist cause, many industrialists were in fact ambivalent about it. It partly had to do with coal from Nova Scotia, where many New England manufacturers, protected by a reciprocal agreement between the United States and Canada, had invested in low-cost sources of fuel. When the United States ended the agreement with Canada in 1866, Pennsylvania mine owners had every intention of claiming the market for themselves by eliminating "the only Coal that competes with the American Anthracite" and other domestic coals. Some New England congressmen sought to restore access to the Nova Scotia mines, but many were protectionists who found their anomalous position on coal difficult to justify. Justin S. Morrill of Vermont, whose name was attached to every tariff bill since 1861, nevertheless tried to minimize the affront to the domestic preference principle: "We have drawn moderate supplies of bituminous coal from Nova Scotia. . . . Most of the pig iron used . . . comes from Pennsylvania. Is it now to be insisted upon that no coal shall be used in those regions but that which is dragged over a thousand miles of railroad?" For free-traders, the irony was delicious. This episode shows that geography alone cannot explain sectionalism on the tariff question. Within each section, important economic interest groups opposed protectionist measures. Even within the manufacturing sector that high tariffs were meant to encourage, interests diverged from branch to branch and locality to locality.[34]

The Grand Bargains

The structure of the American tariff encouraged congressmen and senators to champion special interests. In 1871, the tariff list covered some 180 articles, from plaster ornaments to epaulettes and galloons (luxury articles), from butter to carpets, glass to magnesium, vinegar to earthenware, and salt to lead type (necessities). Each item on the list was subject to a specific duty set by Congress. With such a system, it comes as no surprise to learn "that men act on the tariff mainly as local interest requires and without a general, consistent principle," as James A. Garfield complained in 1872. Whatever a politician's ideological stance, it was essential to defend producers in one's home district. This was particularly true of House members, whose electoral base was more localized than that of Senators, who had to strike compromises among potentially competing interests at the state level.[35]

As noted above, iron producers were the most militant proponents of tariff protection. In the wake of the crisis of 1857, Pennsylvania had fully embraced the iron industry, and all the state's representatives, Democrats and Republicans alike, spoke with one voice on the tariff question. Congressman William D. "Pig Iron" Kelley owed his epithet to his devotion to the cause. Iron and steel producers were less powerful in Ohio, but their ire toward Garfield despite his generally protectionist stance says a great deal about what manufacturers expected from their congressmen. Indeed, Garfield did not deny that he "faithfully represented the manufacturing interest" in his district, though he believed that his more flexible position was more likely to succeed than the intransigent attitude of "the Iron men."[36] Mining firms, which were both cost-sensitive and geographically localized, also expected their local representatives to defend their interests vigorously. In 1866, Fernando C. Beaman of Wisconsin and Zachariah Chandler of Michigan intervened on behalf of "the copper mines of this country, and especially those in the Lake Superior region," and fulminated against the idea of buying copper abroad "when [our] mountains are full of it." Amasa Cobb, who represented "the northwestern lead-mining district," championed the zinc and lead interests: "There is no metal in commerce . . . that costs so much to produce it in proportion to the price at which it sells as lead." Hence, in his view, lead deserved strong tariff protection.[37]

Competition among different branches of industry, and consequently among different localities, gave rise to bidding wars for congressional support and created tensions. Many congressmen felt that if some of their constituents reaped economic benefits from tariff protection, there was no reason why others should not also profit. If iron and coal could be protected, why leave copper without government support? Protectionist rhetoric could not justify limiting the benefits of protection to just one sector of the economy. This inherent expansiveness of the protectionist position served them well, because it made it possible to build the necessary legislative coalitions. It also created tensions, however, because any artificially created rent comes at the expense of other social groups. In 1866, John H. Hubbard of Connecticut argued on behalf of manufacturers who used copper as a raw material and complained of not being able to get enough of it. "I am strongly in favor of a protective tariff, but a proper discrimination must be made," he insisted. "All agree that the tax should not fall on the 'raw material.'" John F. Driggs of Michigan immediately objected to this idea, warning that "to strike off the duty on ore is to rob the poor miners of the necessaries of life and the Government of so much revenue." Was it possible to protect both the miners of copper and the manufacturers of products that made use of copper? Their interests were contradictory, and protecting one came at the expense of the other.[38]

Settling such disputes was difficult, and victory generally went to the stronger party rather than being decided by a comprehensive vision of the national interest. In 1866, the *Louisville Democrat* complained that "the most profitable part of the foreign commerce of this port [New York] is now in the hands of 'our foreign relations' . . . thanks to our New England high-tariff masters." To remedy this situation, "a bill to revive the navigation and commercial interests of the United States" was introduced in Congress. On the grounds that the tariff had made shipbuilding in the United States too expensive, and thus damaged the interests of U.S. flag shipping, the bill proposed to subsidize the industry to compensate for the burden imposed by customs duties. Competition among various types of products soon hijacked the debate. William B. Allison of Iowa noted that "they have confined the bounty to 'iron, steel, or composite' vessels." But why not include "the [Michigan] copper interest"? Why should there "not be paid to the copper interest a bounty corresponding to that which is paid to the iron-masters of Pennsylvania"? Meanwhile, John F. Farnsworth of Illinois expressed surprise at being asked "to enact heavy tariffs to obstruct or prohibit commerce, and then vote large subsidies to foster commerce!" The bill failed in large part because of these clashing economic interests.[39]

Clearly, the existence of a high tariff inherited from the war drastically altered the terms of the debate. It set different branches of industry in competition for the favors of the federal government. Because certain products were subject to import duties, congressmen sought compensatory subsidies for other products manufactured in their home districts, leading to a bidding war. Even those who favored free trade were caught up. James W. Grimes fought hard during debate on the 1866 tariff bill for duties to be lowered along with other taxes. But at the last minute, when he realized that his efforts had failed, he tried to insert a provision that would benefit the farmers in his state: "I propose to raise up the duty on wheat or barley or some other agricultural product that may be stricken down by the bill to something like an equality with, or to the level of, the protection given to the manufacturing interest."[40]

These tensions among competing economic interests could be quite powerful, especially within the same sector. For this reason, protectionists enthusiastically welcomed an 1865 accord between the National Association of Wool Manufac- turers and the National Wool Growers' Association to join together in asking for tariff protection. The accord solved two problems. First, it simplified the issue of striking a compromise between possibly competing economic interests. Morrill, who chaired the House Committee of Ways and Means, was forthright: "The duty proposed in this bill . . . is a duty with which the wool-grower himself is entirely satisfied. It is proposed by him and nobody else." This remark was in- tended to silence critics of the bill. Second, the accord on woolens became the model for a successful conversion of an agricultural sector to the protectionist cause. According to the *Chicago Republican*, "it has generally been assumed that the agricultural class in this country should oppose protection as a principle, while the manufacturing class support it." Now, however, "in the single article of wool the principle of protection is already quite as important to the farmer as the manufacturer."[41]

Accordingly, Congress was quick to approve a high tariff bill on woolens, even though a more comprehensive tariff bill failed to pass. It soon became apparent, however, that the Woolens Act was more the result of a successful lobbying effort than of a truly unanimous demand coming from a specific sector of the economy. In 1872, a group of manufacturers of woolens sent a memorial to Congress de- nouncing the maneuver:

> This tariff was devised by carpet and blanket-makers, who pretended to be
> "The National Woolen Manufacturers Association," in combination with
> certain persons who raised fine bucks and wished to sell them at high prices,

and who acted in the name of "The National Wool Growers' Association." The former demanded extravagant duties on foreign blankets and carpets, and low rates on carpet wools. The latter demanded the exclusion of foreign clothing wools, in the mistaken idea that the growth of fine wool here would thus be promoted. Between the two, the real grower and the cloth manufacturer found little consideration of justice, but were ground between the upper and nether mill-stones.[42]

The economic stakes and potential profits of tariff protection were high enough to generate intense lobbying activity, which elicited growing numbers of complaints from Congress. In 1867, James W. Grimes denounced "the methods that have been adopted to secure the passage of this bill. . . . The manufacturers of iron and a few wool agriculturists and speculators . . . have organized associations, contributed large sums of money to mold public sentiment through the press, and have formed combinations with other interests to control the legislation of the country." Senator William Pitt Fessenden, former secretary of the treasury, urged his colleagues not "to leave the formation of a tariff to the manufacturers themselves. They have too much interest in it. . . . We must exercise our own judgment upon the question." This appeal to political responsibility went largely unheeded, partly because certain congressmen had conflicts of interest. The *New York Evening Post*, a Republican newspaper, published this attack in 1866:

> There is Mr. Stevens — he demands a higher duty on iron, which, of course, will raise the price of that article: he is an iron master. There is Mr. Griswold, who demanded a heavier duty on railroad iron, which would of course increase the price of the commodity. Mr. Griswold is a manufacturer, at Troy, in this State, of railroad iron. There is Mr. Morrill, who imposes higher duties on foreign marble. Mr. Morrill, we are told, is interested in marble quarries in Vermont.[43]

In subsequent years, "the power of great corporations" in Congress became "more strikingly exhibited" and "disheartening." It was responsible for any number of political-financial scandals between 1869 and 1877, which undermined the presidency of Ulysses S. Grant. It fed growing wariness on the part of some of the elite with respect to federal intervention in the economy, and explains a great deal about the evolution of tariff policy in the post–Civil War period.[44] Interestingly, however, what allowed industrial lobbying on the tariff question ultimately served to limit its influence. The complexity of the law, which set duties item by item and combined both fixed and proportional levies, required a technical competence that only industrial experts could provide, and Congress depended on them to learn about the state of affairs in each branch of industry. But the same complexity fragmented the decision-making process and encouraged politicians to defend their local interests. In the end, only coalitions of interest groups and representatives could win a majority in both houses. Meanwhile, neither of the major parties had a unified and consistent position on the general question of protectionism. Once again, the sections played a pivotal role in structuring the debate. It was because of this, far more than because of the South's return, that the Republican-dominated Congress voted to reduce tariffs in 1870 and 1872.

The Sectionalization of the Tariff

A sectional vision of what was at stake became inevitable in the immediate postwar debates. It was much in evidence in congressional speeches regarding the 1866 tariff bill. For instance, Samuel Hooper of Massachusetts complained that "it would be more justly designated as the 'Pennsylvania and western tariff.'" By contrast, John B. Henderson of Missouri believed that "New England has a very great interest in it," even if "our friends in the central States find themselves strong enough to make New England begin to pay" duties on Nova Scotia coal. William Pitt Fessenden, who reported the bill in the Senate, felt compelled to act as arbiter, stating explicitly that "each section of the country is thoroughly and perfectly protected against the other as the law stands."[45]

This sectional interpretation was partly the result of an aggregation of local interests. It reflected the complexity of the debate and thus transcended a straightforward clash between free trade and protectionism. Edward Atkinson, a New England manufacturer who favored an end to tariff protection, took note of this in a pamphlet he wrote for the American Free Trade League:

> The difficulties of the Protectionists have been much complicated, of late, by the claim made by the Western and Middle-States for protection to agricultural products and upon materials in their primary or secondary condition, such as copper ore and regulus, raw and lined flax, hemp, jute, linseed, hides, goat-skins, etc. It would seem as if the West had suddenly come to the conclusion that New England, by means of protection to manufactures, had been making money out of them, and that it was time for them to get a return in kind from New England.[46]

This was a consequence of the bidding war noted earlier. The point to note here, however, is that the insistence on protecting not just finished products but raw materials as well was imputed to *sections*.

TABLE 3. Roll-call votes in the House on the tariff

Total number of roll-call votes	83
Number of sectional votes	48
AVERAGE COHESION BY REGION	
Northeast	0.38
Midwest	0.35
AVERAGE COHESION BY PARTY AND REGION	
Republicans	
Northeast	0.64
Northeast (minus Pennsylvania)	0.60
Midwest	0.32
Democrats	
Northeast	0.46
Northeast (minus Pennsylvania)	0.76
Midwest	0.82

Note: Cohesion is measured with a Rice index, going from 0 (very divided) to 1 (united).

We find the same sectionalism at work in congressional voting. Most decisions were made in committee or on the floor without a roll-call vote (and therefore cannot be analyzed quantitatively), but between 1865 and 1877, there were eighty-three roll-call votes on tariff questions in the House (see table 3). In three out of five of these, congressmen from the Northeast were on opposite sides from their Midwestern colleagues. The map clearly demonstrates the political potency of sectionalism—the dividing line between Ohio and Pennsylvania is almost perfect (see map 4). Broadly speaking, the Midwest appears to have been less unified than the Northeast, where the protectionist center of gravity lay in the primary coal-mining and iron-producing areas, confirming the influence of that industrial sector.[47]

When we look more closely at the situation, several political dynamics emerge. First, the Midwest's opposition to strong protectionism, though not without historical precedent, was not something that could be taken for granted in the immediate postwar period. In 1866, representatives of the section were divided, as a glance at the voting map reveals. Representatives from the more agricultural districts of the Midwest opposed higher duties, but many others, most notably from Michigan and Ohio, favored them (see map 5). Nevertheless, a consistent sectional response was beginning to emerge partly in reaction to a more unified Northeastern bloc and partly in connection with other conflicts that were taking on a sectional coloration (like the money question). What was specific to the geographical pattern associated with the tariff was the pivotal role of Pennsylvania:

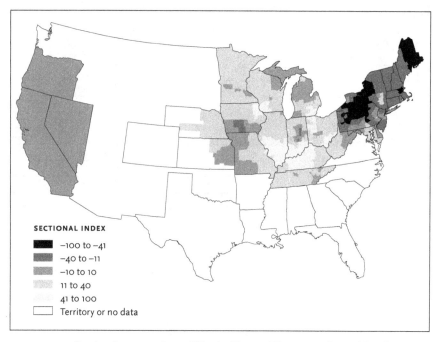

SECTIONAL INDEX

■ −100 to −41
■ −40 to −11
▨ −10 to 10
░ 11 to 40
   41 to 100
☐ Territory or no data

MAP 4. Sectional votes on the tariff in the House of Representatives, 1865–1877

as a bastion of protectionism, the state played a role in rallying Northeastern Republicans to the protectionist cause (after the failure of the 1866 tariff bill, which revealed latent tensions) while dividing Northeastern Democrats (see table 3). The 1872 compromise was forged without the help of Pennsylvania, however. The map of the voting on the bill to reduce tariffs by 10 percent across the board shows that Pennsylvania remained intransigent in the face of an accommodation for which other Northeasterners recognized the need (see map 6).

Note, finally, that Democrats were sectionally divided on the tariff question less often than Republicans. There are two possible reasons for this. One has to do with the history of the Democratic Party, which had long championed free trade. The other has to do with its minority position in Congress, which tended to unify it. The evidence shows that the influence of sectionalism was stronger on the Republicans when it came to voting, but we find sectional rhetoric contrasting Midwestern and Northeastern interests in speeches by members of both parties.

Both the voting pattern and the rhetorical content of speeches suggest that the sectional divide was closely associated with the identification of the Midwest with agricultural interests. There was of course a factual basis for this. Illinois,

MAP 5. First vote on the tariff bill, July 10, 1866

Note: Illinois's at-large representative voted nay.

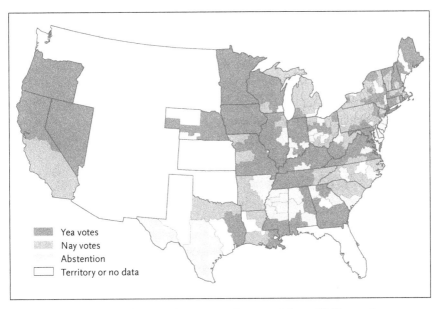

MAP 6. Vote on the general 10-percent decrease of the tariff, May 7, 1872

Note: Illinois's at-large representative voted yea.

Iowa, and Missouri alone produced two-thirds of American grain. In the mid-1870s, the Midwest produced 2.5 times as much wheat as it consumed, while the Northeast produced only half of its consumption. Thus there was a stark contrast between the two sections: the Northeast's agricultural sector was much less productive than the Midwest's. In addition, Midwestern grain producers depended increasingly on exports. The domestic market no longer sufficed as the acreage of improved land increased, and as the army's sudden cessation of orders closed out an important market. The region's sudden emergence as a major international supplier had already earned it the title of "granary of the world."[48] Protectionism did nothing to favor export goods. For one thing, import duties could not raise domestic prices, because domestic supply largely outpaced demand. For another, the risk of closing "our ports to foreign importations by a prohibitory tariff" was that it might force "foreign countries" to retaliate by "exclud[ing] our productions." The South's experience during the war had proven that it was illusory to think that foreign countries had no choice. Those who believed that the "cotton famine" would be an effective diplomatic weapon had only offered European nations an incentive to diversify their sources of supply. Might not the same thing happen to Midwestern wheat?[49]

Furthermore, protecting other sectors of the economy increased costs paid by farmers, whose tools and supplies became more expensive. The increase in the price of iron, largely due to the tariff, had a direct impact on the cost of tools and agricultural machinery. Many Midwestern papers expressed discontent with "the beauties of the protective tariff which has been fastened upon the country by the revolutionists" and which served only "to pamper a Pennsylvania iron lord." More broadly, duties on items of daily consumption such as clothing inevitably reduced the farmer's purchasing power while leaving him unprotected from international competition. The *Chicago Tribune* viewed the protection of manufacturing as a tax on farmers:

> The duties and the middlemen's profits on the duties add eighty to one hundred per cent to the cost of the imported goods which the consumer must pay. It takes two barrels of flour to purchase a given quantity of cloth—one barrel is exchanged for the goods, and the other is consumed in paying the tariff and the profits on the tariff charged by the importers who advance the duty to the Custom House officer. The tariff, therefore, acts exactly as a duty on exports.[50]

The political weight of farmers explains why arguments in favor of protectionism continued to focus on agriculture even after the war ended. "A purely agricultural people is a dependent one," the *Chicago Republican* asserted. "The farmer is the most prosperous when his market is at his own door, and this latter cannot be the case where all his neighbors are producers of the great staples of food." The war had shown that "when the bulk of our produce was consumed at home, when our manufacturers were most vigorously and remuneratively employed and protected," there was no difficulty finding markets for the products of agriculture. Higher tariffs would allegedly reproduce these conditions. One Pennsylvania iron manufacturer claimed that he alone redistributed $1.7 million to agriculture, of which $1 million went to Western farmers. Furthermore, he argued, "agriculture and manufacturing industry united in the same nation, under the same political power, live in perpetual peace!"[51]

Many farmers remained unconvinced. In part this was because they worried about their economic situation. Several years of falling prices in the wake of good harvests in various parts of the world, along with the emergence of new exporting countries such as Argentina, had decreased their purchasing power, or so they believed.[52] At the same time, high tariffs had apparently yielded juicy dividends for certain industrial sectors: these "protégés of the present tariff laws" included "the owners of coal and ore beds, and manufacturing capitalists, who exact contributions from consumers to swell the profits of their investments. . . . They ask life pensions." It was more difficult to reduce tariffs than to increase them, it turned out, because to cut the tariff was to deprive someone of an acquired bonus (legitimate or not). Senator John B. Henderson compared the situation to an addiction: "It might be asked why the inebriate, whose frame has been shattered by draughts from the intoxicating bowl, yet thirsts for that which has well-nigh destroyed him."[53]

The opposition to protectionism thus took on a moral aspect, directed against those who profited from a system that gave them undeserved income at the expense of others. Midwestern Democrats in particular denounced those "who cannot do business without begging of [their] neighbors—living on their hospitality —it would look more manly to work by the month for a livelihood. But this would not be necessary. In this great and powerful West, so prolific of natural advantages, are plenty of profitable channels for capital and labor, and we need no protection, and all we now ask is for all classes to do business without special protection."[54] This statement shows a clear understanding of the redistributive effects of protectionism. The differentiation of duties on an item-by-item basis produced unequal rents, so certain branches of industry could increase their prices more than others. Over the last third of the nineteenth century, the tariff was responsible for a net redistribution of income corresponding to 8 percent of

GDP.[55] Many people saw it not as a legitimate policy of national development but as a law authorizing some "to take from the pockets of the consumer and put it into those of the manufacturer, the importing merchant, and the jobber." It was a way to "compel the many to cater to the few."[56]

And among the many were large numbers of farmers. The Granges, cooperative associations of farmers that had formed after the Civil War, took a public stand on the tariff issue. In the early years of their existence, their main goal was to regulate the freight rates charged by railroads, whose pricing policies, they charged, were unfair. But a sector with such a high stake in exports could not avoid the tariff question. The Grange convention held in Springfield, Illinois, in April 1873 met "to discuss questions of taxation, of tariff and of banks in so far as those questions affect their agricultural interests," the *Cincinnati Enquirer* reported. From that moment on, the Granges continued to elaborate an anti-protectionist position, although they were never free-traders on principle, nor did all farmers agree.[57]

As with the money question, Midwestern sectionalism on the tariff emerged through the region's identification with farming interests. This was partly due to a division within the agricultural sector itself, because it seems that many farmers in the Northeast, endowed with less fertile land and mostly specialized in growing perishable goods destined for nearby urban markets, had converted to protectionism before the war.[58] Midwestern agriculture was more productive and therefore more dependent on foreign markets. Farmers were also more influential in the Midwest, where they constituted a larger share of the population and economy (although the agricultural sector dominated the nation's economy as a whole).[59] Politics alone made sense of this identification, however, at a time when farmers were just beginning to organize. During the war, despite the fiscal pressure, Midwestern congressmen demanded compensation for voting to increase tariffs, including the Homestead Act of 1862, which was clearly favorable to agrarian interests.[60] After the war, they opposed the attempt to expand protectionism in a similar spirit.

The identification of the Midwest with agriculture was so powerful that even proponents of the tariff felt called upon to show that it would help develop the American economy across the board. But the arguments they chose only reinforced the sectional dynamic. Two approaches dominated: one was to insist on the industrialization of the Midwest, while the other was to maintain that agriculture itself would soon be in need of protection.

One tactic was to begin with the Midwest's supposed industrial backwardness to justify protectionism on nationalistic grounds. Given that the section's industry was still "in infancy," the argument was that "the older States of the Union need this protection against the competition of foreign cheap labor and cheap capital far less than do the newer States of the West and South." The *Chicago Republican* explained that "the iron masters of Pennsylvania can far easier do without [a protective policy] now that their own enterprises are established," while New England textile manufacturers "ask for just enough discrimination to protect themselves, but would resolutely hold it back from full benefit to those whose needs are greater." It then followed that the way to defend the interests of the Midwest was to demand higher tariffs: "Tariff laws have made the manufacturers of the East, as they did those of England, opulent and strong. . . . Not a few of these must inevitably come to regard the West and the South with that jealous apprehension with which it once looked upon transatlantic competitors," and are ready to "organiz[e] opposition to the influences that would build up, in other parts of the country, competing furnaces, mines, machine-shops, cotton-mills, woolen-mills, factories, and other industrial undertakings." Never mind that the majority of protectionists were in the Northeast. The Chicago newspaper did not hesitate to play the economic sectionalism card in an attempt (albeit unsuccessful) to mobilize support for protectionism against "the ungrateful designs of that newly arrogant and self-aggrandizing section."[61]

A second argumentative tactic was to insist that economic development would lead to a situation in which farmers rather than manufacturers would require tariff protection. Here, the English example was useful:

> In England, protection was first invoked in behalf of manufactures, but when manufactures had grown to the point where they began to consume foreign food and fabrics to any great extent, free trade became the doctrine of the manufacturers, and the agricultural classes fought for protection. In this country we are verging toward this second stage of the question, where protection will be ardently contended for by the farmers, while the manufacturers, selfishly mistaking their true interests, will favor free trade as a means of getting the food and the raw materials for their manufacturing more cheaply from abroad.[62]

Since agriculture was so dominant in the Midwest, the argument ran, it was only logical for Midwesterners to demand a high tariff before the manufacturers changed their mind, on the grounds that in the future, the economic situation of the two sectors would be reversed.

In other words, the debate about protectionism was built around a vision of the sections in which the Midwest was identified with agriculture and the Northeast with manufacturing. This explains how people in the wool sector were able to reach an agreement on a protective tariff in 1866. It proved possible to move beyond the opposition of "the agricultural class" and "the manufacturing class" because "in the single article of wool the principle of protection is already quite as important to the farmer as the manufacturer. . . . We ought to raise every pound of wool manufactured in this country." Protectionists hoped that the wool accord would serve as a model for agreements in other sectors, especially "stock-raisers, corn-raisers, and wheat-growers."[63]

Ultimately, in order to move beyond the opposition of manufacturing and agriculture, the protectionists sought to put the sectional cleavage, which they deemed unfavorable to their cause, behind them. "Protection is not sectional," declared the *Chicago Republican*, the primary Midwestern proponent of higher tariffs. "The great West with its mineral and agricultural wealth, with its cotton, wool, hemp, and flax fibers, is as vitally interested in and benefited by protection as the ingenious, enterprising, and industrious New Englanders."[64] But even this argument showed how difficult it was to escape the sectional framing of the tariff debate.

The American tariff debate thus hinged on sectionalism. As with the money question, this came about because the sectional idea embodied a political significance that transcended its geographical definition. The interplay between section and political economy imposed structure on a discussion complicated by the range of interests involved and the technical nature of those issues. The agrarian image of the Midwest and the identification of the Northeast with manufacturing served in a powerful way to polarize the debate. Despite all the log-rolling bargains struck in the corridors of Congress, the sectional idea took hold in voting behavior as well as political rhetoric.

Sectional Pressure and Partisan Unity

The sectionalization of the tariff debates represented a danger for the parties, which were divided on the question. From the 1820s to the 1840s, Democrats and Whigs had managed to create national coalitions on the issue in spite of sectional differences, so that the tariff could become a platform plank. The party realignment of the 1850s changed the situation. The Republican Party emerged as a coalition based on the issues of slavery and federalism but proved to be quite divided on tariff policy.[65] Some former Democrats, such as Lyman Trumbull of Illinois, were now important members of the new party. The sectionalization of the tariff debate threatened to blow the party apart. "It is clear that there are great and serious differences among the leading members of the Republican Party in regard to it, and the most careful and prudent management is now needed," James A. Garfield remarked in 1870. A correspondent of Senator John Sherman went so far as to suggest that "the party is so far from a unit on that, that the result could be an explosion." Even those who saw "protection or free trade" as "the largest question of public economy now before the people of the United States" were convinced of the need for a new party realignment: "It is startling proof of the desperate and unnatural condition to which party politics have arrived—of the utter misuse and debauchery of partisanship in politics—that this question can exist in the bowels of the Republican party, and yet that party not dissolve. It actually nominates and supports protectionists and free-traders indifferently: the paramount question being who can be elected. Still, bad as the Republican Party may be, the Democratic is much worse."[66]

The Democrats were also divided, even though their postwar ideology was more in line with their prewar ideology. Pennsylvania stood apart, where Democrats, responding to local conditions, were as much in favor of protectionism as Republicans. This put them at odds, however, with "the Democratic organs of the West," as rival newspapers were quick to note: "The Democracy, which proposes to make goods cheap, to open the doors to competition, and to break down New England, has no abiding place in Pennsylvania."[67]

The danger that sectionalism might fracture the parties was the main reason for the (relative) decrease in tariffs that occurred in 1870 and 1872. Although there were many protectionists in the Republican Party, they were unable to win party approval of their program. With broad tax cuts underway and sectional divisions intensifying, compromise became necessary. Garfield expressed concern that "a very high tariff would raise the hostility of the consumers throughout the country and lead them to become Free Traders." Certain obvious excesses weakened the Republicans. For instance, in 1870, the United States experienced "a coal famine, and the sufferers, without regard to party, charge their misfortune, in a great measure, on the duty of $1.25 per ton on coal. . . . A great body of the people complain that Congress taxes the fuel they burn." To Garfield, it seemed "very unwise to let the whole revenue system suffer, in consequence of this duty."[68]

Most scandalous of all, perhaps, was the tariff on salt. A basic necessity, it was nevertheless subject to a high tariff, which the 1866 bill had even proposed to increase "to the very respectable figure of 299 percent." As any number of newspapers pointed out, "there is but one place in the United States where solar or coarse salt is made to any extent, namely, the Onondaga Salt Springs" in central New York. When it was revealed in 1869 that the firm earned enormous profits of "700 percent on their capital," it "raised great indignation in the minds of the people." Other manufacturers, particularly in the meat-processing industry, which used a great deal of salt, could be heard "crying out fiercely against the injustice thus done them and the undue protection given to the salt interest." Such scandals threatened to undermine the legitimacy of protectionism, which could be seen as a way to reward the friends of people in power and thus as a form of corruption. Under political pressure, Congress enacted a sharp decrease in the salt duty.[69]

Mobilization against the tariff originated in the Midwest. In 1871, the majority-Republican Wisconsin legislature passed a resolution declaring that "any duties levied upon imports, which tax one section of the country for the benefit of the other, or protect one class of citizens at the expense of the other, impose an unjust system of taxation; that tariffs levied for any other purpose than the revenue necessary to meet the wants of the Government, are unauthorized by the Federal Constitution." The following year, the Republican Party in Ohio, a key electoral state, rejected "the principle of fostering any industries" with the tariff and "declared the primary object to be to raise revenue, guarded by the duty to so adjust the rates of imposts, as not to *injure* the interests of any particular class."[70]

A sectional compromise was then forged in response to anti-protectionist pressure within the Republican Party in order to preserve the tariff barrier around the domestic market. One slogan summed it up: "Tariff for Revenue." Ironically, this was the phrase that Democrats had used before the Civil War to justify low import duties. Availing themselves of these connotations, the Republicans announced a reduction of the tariff to adjust it to the government's fiscal needs. Henceforth, any protection of industry would be merely "incidental." Once again, the Republicans used the fiscal aspect of the tariff as the basis of their political stance. Protectionists were thus able to limit the impact of the tariff reduction that Congress passed in 1872.

The complexity of the tariff, which imposed different duties (sometimes levied in dollar amounts and other times in percentages) on each product, lent itself to a variety of maneuvers, such as the abolition of the duties on tea and coffee in 1872. This measure, which was debated and passed just before the general revision of the tariff was taken up, dealt with products not grown in the United States, so that the bill did not injure any American producers. It nevertheless allowed Congress to make a great show of its desire to alleviate the burden of the tariff on taxpayers. The bill, supported by cries of "No taxation of the breakfast table!" dealt with a highly symbolic commodity. The tax on tea imposed by the British Parliament in 1767 had been among the issues that triggered the American Revolution. "The breakfast table" continued to be taxed, however, as some representatives were quick to point out: "In the first place you must have a table. . . . On the wood of which the table is made the duty is thirty per cent *ad valorem*."[71]

Be that as it may, the bill's symbolic import was great, and it did reduce revenues by $20 million, or one-fifth of that year's budget surplus. This left that much less room to reduce duties on other products. This stratagem, the brainchild of lobbyist John Hayes, left "the great industries almost intact." Still, protectionists were unable to prevent a broader revision of the tariff. After lengthy debate, Congress in 1872 passed a bill reducing it across the board by 10 percent and moving a good many articles to the free list while correcting the most glaring and therefore politically dangerous excesses. The salt duty was halved, while the duty on coal was reduced from $1.25 to $0.75 per ton. All told, the federal government gave up $44 million in annual revenue.[72]

Note the partisan logic at work here. The voting record reveals that Midwestern opposition to the more severe protectionist tariffs intensified as time went by. Sectional divisions hurt the Republican Party more than its rival. Faced with a budget surplus and internal dissension in 1872, the party therefore struck a compromise: the tariff would be reduced, but a certain level of protectionism would be maintained. A glance at the congressional voting record for 1872 shows that many Northeastern Republicans embraced this compromise, which preserved the essence of the protectionist tariff while avoiding a sectional split in the party.

In 1875, in the middle of an economic crisis and in the wake of a crushing defeat at the polls, the outgoing Republican majority took another look at the 1872 tariff bill and rescinded the 10 percent reduction it had accepted only three years earlier. What followed would only confirm the rule that the party had set for itself in the aftermath of the war: on economic issues, it was essential to avoid any step that might lead to fragmentation of the party along sectional lines, given that the sections tended to conceive of their interests as antagonistic. There was no consensus around the ideology of economic development.

THE TARIFF DEBATE revealed the influence of sectionalism on economic policy. Despite the complexity and technical nature of the issue, which made tariff bills difficult to understand and favored cloakroom wheeling and dealing and political lobbying, the tariff question, like the money question, lent itself to simplification by way of a geographical interpretation that pitted the free-trade agricultural Midwest against the protectionist industrial Northeast. This simplified image only partially reflected reality, but it made political sense and thus made the sections the focal point of the debate. The tariff issue divided the parties, and the need to avoid a party breakdown was the primary reason for the reduction of the tariff in 1872. Clearly, the sectionalization of certain political issues caught the parties off-balance. The party system in place during Reconstruction had been born in the 1850s, mainly in response to the slavery question. The geographical divide over economic issues posed a challenge to the primary ideological divisions between Democrats and Republicans.

The sectional prism illuminates the way that political pragmatism reshaped the Republicans' ideology of economic development. From the standpoint of intellectual history, free trade and a specie-based currency, advocated by classical economists, went together and stood in opposition to protectionism and greenbacks, championed by the proponents of "the American system" (Henry C. Carey and his disciples). For the former, the only path to prosperity was to allow the natural laws of economics free play. Gold and silver coin, the only form of money with intrinsic value, allowed the laws of supply and demand to operate without distortion. Free trade was the best way to maximize the effects of the market's invisible hand. Where the "economic laws" were in command, any interference with the market was seen as harmful. Free trade was therefore logically associated with hard-money principles. By contrast, the opposing school argued that the United States ought to practice economic patriotism: domestic industry should be sheltered from foreign competition and allowed to develop. Paper money was good for two reasons: it helped to isolate the United States from international monetary exchanges, and if gold was worth more than greenbacks on the market, the exchange rate differential only added to the protection of domestic industry (a form of competitive devaluation, to use a modern term).[73]

However cogent these economic theories may be, they are of no use when it comes to understanding the political dynamics of Reconstruction. Carey, for instance, was more influential on the tariff issue than on the money question (except perhaps on Pennsylvania Republicans, such as William D. Kelley and Thaddeus Stevens). Broadly speaking, individual exceptions aside, the voting record shows that congressmen and senators who voted for protectionism also favored a return to the gold standard, while those who preferred low tariffs also favored the use of greenbacks. Consistency on these issues was not intellectual but political. Some, like James A. Garfield, were aware of this:

> If I may say it without being absurd, I should claim to be theoretically a Free-Trader but practically a Protectionist. Free-trade (a doctrine of Political Science) is in most of its positions unanswerable. But our industries

have seventy or eighty years of growth on the basis of some measures of protection, and our policy should be guided not only by scientific [illegible], but also with constant reference to the conditions which the policy of three quarters of a Century have produced.

We see how eminently pragmatic Garfield was, despite his readiness to engage in moral exhortation on the money question. His colleague Rutherford B. Hayes, two times governor of Ohio, also found that "the practical question & the theoretical may be & usually are very different. My leanings are to the free trade side. But in this country the protective policy was adopted in the first legislation of Congress in Washington's time & has been generally adhered to ever since. Large investments of capital, & the employment of a great number of people depend on it. We can not, and probably ought not to suddenly abandon it." Hayes's history is inaccurate, confusing the mere existence of a tariff with protectionism, but his argument shows that the basis of his reasoning was political, not intellectual or theoretical.[74]

It comes as no surprise, moreover, that these two Ohio politicians, who defended positions often associated with the Northeast even though they represented a Midwestern state, were especially sensitive to the contradiction. In the end, what these two political positions have in common is sectionalism, which made it possible to reconcile theoretically opposed stands. The transmutation of economic interests into sectional interests conferred political consistency on intellectually contradictory combinations.

AFTER THE CIVIL WAR, Americans faced a complex and radically new political landscape. Reconstruction politics dealt with the consequences of enforced national unity and the abolition of slavery after four years of bloody combat. The war also had financial consequences and affected the economic role of the federal government. Two issues in particular aroused political passions: the money question, which involved the federal debt and the gold standard, and the tariff question. Despite the prominence of other issues associated with the reintegration of the South and the reform of race relations, these issues were not relegated to the background. Indeed, they took on growing importance. Their political impact cannot be understood without attention to the structure of the debates. Neither of the two major parties had a sufficiently consistent position to make sense of these postwar economic issues. Hence it was the section as political category that enabled people to frame the debates in ways that made sense to them.

Sectional conflict between the Midwest and the Northeast was a central political phenomenon of Reconstruction. Its importance is an argument in favor of a spatial approach to American political history. The section was a social construct that lent a geographic dimension to economic issues. It functioned as a political category whose rich connotations helped to make sense of things. Like the parties, the sections served as rallying points for people who shared, or were supposed to share, similar outlooks and interests. They also served to *identify* a group with a range of political positions. The absence of unanimity and the vagueness and variability of the ideas thus shared were not a handicap. On the contrary, they facilitated the formation of broad coalitions. That is why the sections became such a convenient and "natural" tool for dealing with the economic issues that arose during Reconstruction.

These mechanisms were clearly at work in Congress. The parties, which constituted the most legitimate basis for the formation of coalitions, proved inadequate when it came to setting monetary and tariff policies. In many cases, sectional coalitions made up for the shortcomings of the parties. In this respect, the sections were authentic and potent competitors of the parties. In the minds of postbellum politicians, the sections posed a constant threat of party fragmentation or reconfiguration. This complex reality partly explains the political course of Reconstruction: it was through the competition between the parties and the sections that political economy became mixed up with the social and institutional reform of the South.

PART II

Reconstruction

4

Closing the Books on the War

REPUBLICANISM, CIVIL RIGHTS, FINANCE

————— · —————

The Union of these States, one & inseparable—upon the basis of equal
rights to every loyal man North and South—is the item of great moment
now. . . . After this is accomplished, there is one thing which seems to
me, more than another to demand the earnest attention of Congress, to
wit—the National finances—& the laws governing distribution.
—George Locey to Andrew Johnson, February 25, 1866

WHEN CONFEDERATE FORCES surrendered in April 1865, there was no hint
that the money question would become so contentious or that the Midwest and
Northeast would clash so directly over the economy. After four years of bloody
war, Americans had one concern: to ensure a lasting peace. But the task was
arduous, the problems thorny. What did the Union victory really mean? What
consequences should the Confederate states suffer for having seceded? What reforms were needed to make sure no such thing would ever happen again? And
above all, what should be the place of the 4 million blacks made free by the abolition of slavery?

The great issue of the day was thus: what kind of society did Americans want
to build in the wake of the Civil War? And this hinged on a newly important
concept—national citizenship. Defining national citizenship, deciding who
would participate in it, and assigning it concrete legal and political content would
prove to be among the major legacies of the postwar debates. Surreptitiously,
almost illegitimately, economic issues influenced these debates. What connection was there between civil rights and paper money? What role did the tariff
play in the reform of the South? At first glance, the answer is none. And yet, the
convertibility of greenbacks into gold, the system of taxation, and protectionism
would turn out to have an immense impact on the course of Reconstruction.[1]

Exacerbating sectional tensions within the North, these issues would disrupt the Republican-led reintegration of the South into the Union, a policy already facing opposition from the Democrats and the new president, Andrew Johnson.

The linkage of these issues might seem improbable, and for a time no sign of it was evident. Before long, however, it played a role in the impeachment of a president of the United States, in the election of a general to succeed him, and even in the adoption of an amendment to the Constitution.

Sectionalism Disrupts Reconstruction

In December 1865, the vehement debates that would break out over the contraction of paper currency just a few weeks later were still in the future. The report sent to Congress by the new secretary of the treasury, Hugh McCulloch, was well-received. It presented one primary objective: a rapid return to specie payments in order to put an end to the coexistence of two legal forms of currency with different values. Everyone applauded—Congress as well as newspapers, Republicans as well as Democrats.[2] In February, a bill was introduced to authorize the gradual withdrawal of greenbacks from circulation. This contraction would make paper money more expensive, thereby bringing its value to par with gold coin. In the midst of this consensus, however, objections suddenly erupted on all sides.

For politicians, the problem was not the bill itself but the man it would empower. John M. Broomall, a Pennsylvania Republican, summed up this sentiment quite well: "The people [expect] a return to specie payments at no distant day," and McCulloch was certainly "as competent for the difficult and embarrassing situation he holds as any other financier in the country." But many Republicans "entertain a profound dislike of his political opinion." A former Democrat like Andrew Johnson, McCulloch supported the president's approach to the South, which he saw as "pursuing the only course which he feels at liberty to pursue under the Constitution." He shared Johnson's reluctance to see the federal government intervene in the defeated Southern states, including in the realm of race relations. In McCulloch's view, "the labor question," to which he reduced the problem in the South, "is quite likely to be a self-adjusting one," provided that "there was no outside interference."[3]

None of this concerned the currency. But two days before the debate began, Johnson shocked Republicans by vetoing their first Reconstruction bill. They were taken by surprise, and their confidence in the president's willingness to cooperate was shaken. Some now asked whether it was wise "to place the whole

Government currency of the country and the $1,200,000,000 of Government obligations at the beck, not, be it remembered, of Hugh McCulloch, but of a Secretary of the Treasury" responsible to this president. Some asked whether the "power conferred by this bill" was not "greater in its way" than the delegation of "powers over the Army for the pacification of a large section of the Union and the protection of the right of labor," to which Johnson had so strenuously objected. Even the Radical leader Thaddeus Stevens, who favored a stronger federal government, refused to "confide such discretion in a single man."[4] In the end, Congress only agreed to authorize the secretary of the treasury to withdraw greenbacks after imposing strict limits on his actions.

The money question did not originate with Reconstruction. The transformation of the technical details of fiscal policy into a moral clash between two sections, which was only just beginning in the debates of February–March 1866, followed a different logic (see chapter 2). But the first discordant notes were able to emerge in the midst of consensus because the political context was favorable. By choosing to confront Republicans directly over Reconstruction, Andrew Johnson sowed institutional distrust between the legislative and executive branches. The monetary debates of the spring of 1866 illustrate the suspicion about how the secretary of the treasury, under the authority of the president, would make use of his power. Even before the money question became a major public issue, it had seriously damaged McCulloch's political authority.

The President versus Congress

The consequences of the clash between the president and congressional Republicans transcended the matter of Reconstruction. The abnormal political situation stemmed from a personal initiative of Andrew Johnson's. After coming to power unexpectedly in April 1865, in the wake of Lincoln's assassination, he found himself in sole charge of setting the terms of peace during a period when Congress was not in session. Consulting few people, he followed two convictions: that the large slave-owning planters were responsible for the war and that the secession of the Southern states had been illegal. From these he drew two practical conclusions: that only rich and prominent Confederates should be punished and that to restore the secessionist states to the Union it would be enough to restore governments that recognized its indissoluble nature. The Presidential Proclamations of May 29, 1865, mapped out this program: amnesty for Confederates who swore allegiance to the Union with the exception of large landowners and leaders of the Confederacy, elections to write new constitutions, repudiation of secession, and ratification of the Thirteenth Amendment.[5]

Within a few months, the eleven secessionist states had accepted this plan. This was a remarkable outcome, in itself an index of the transformations wrought by the war. Who would have wagered in 1860 that "the legislature of South Carolina [would] meekly mak[e] haste to ratify a Constitutional Amendment abolishing slavery" just five years later? As the New York Republican lawyer and diarist George T. Strong observed, "Anyone who should have predicted the political status of today, would have been held to be without foresight, judgment, and common sense, and laughed at as a madman, by North and South alike." Satisfied, Johnson announced in December the complete restoration of the Union.[6]

The president had acted alone, however, without consulting the Republican majority in Congress. His policy restored to power the same elite that had ruled before and during the war, whereas loyal Unionists found themselves marginalized. Significantly, ten former Confederate generals were elected to represent the South in Congress. Signs of distrust, such as Mississippi's refusal to ratify the Thirteenth Amendment, proliferated. Southern states passed black codes, which restored "slavery in everything but the name." Despite expressions of outrage in the North and occasional interventions by the Freedmen's Bureau, these codes limited blacks' freedom to work and freedom of movement, subjected them to arbitrary laws, criminalized their "insulting gestures," and went so far as to reinstate certain antebellum laws pertaining to slaves.[7] This determination to impose white supremacy and put freedmen "in their place" was at the root of endemic violence in the region. In white eyes, any number of offenses, such as the refusal by a black man to doff his hat or surrender his whiskey flask, or his presumption to greet a white man in the street without being asked, could justify his being beaten or killed.[8] In a report based on an extensive three-month tour of the South, the German liberal Carl Schurz found that "a *spirit of persecution* has shown itself so strong as to make the protection of the freedman by the military arm of the government in many localities necessary."[9]

As the Republicans saw it, these facts made it all too plain that the Confederate states had refused to draw the lessons of their defeat. "What scares them is the idea that the rebels are all to be let back . . . and made a power in the government again, just as though there had been no rebellion."[10] Not all Republicans agreed as to the proper course to take, however. The most radical, men such as Charles Sumner, Thaddeus Stevens, and John A. Bingham, advocated a lengthy period of federal supervision in order to establish civil and political equality between whites and blacks and even an egalitarian redistribution of land. Moderates such as Lyman Trumbull, William Pitt Fessenden, and John Sherman preferred a rapid return to the "normal" constitutional order and wanted nothing to do with extending the suffrage to former slaves. Nevertheless, they were concerned with protecting the fruits of victory, which included enforcing a modicum of rights for blacks and making room for Union loyalists in the Southern power structure.[11]

When Congress met in December 1865, the political situation was therefore quite fluid. Reintegrating the South was debated, at times quite vigorously, but the arguments were no different from those that Lincoln had known. Although Radicals had concluded by the summer of 1865 that they needed to "arrest the government in its ruinous career," set by a president dedicated to restoring political and social control to whites, the moderates remained optimistic about the possibility of cooperating with Johnson. For them, his policy of clemency was "simply an experiment to evaluate whether former rebels can be trusted," and "the perpetual distrust of the President which appears in some quarters [was] wholly unjustifiable."[12] The Democrats, very much in the minority, were pleasantly surprised by the favorable terms that Johnson had offered to the South but divided as to the lessons to draw from the war.[13] In short, no clear picture of Reconstruction was quick to emerge, although the president tried to forestall congressional action by declaring that the South's civil institutions had been totally restored and that "sectional animosity is surely and rapidly merging itself into a spirit of nationality."[14]

During the winter of 1865–66, however, what had previously been only a vigorous debate with many participants about the future of the South and its institutions and inhabitants turned into a bitter confrontation between the president and Congress with wide repercussions. This came about when Johnson, on February 19 and March 27, 1866, vetoed the first two Republican Reconstruction bills. These vetoes were a veritable slap in the face to all who had actively collaborated with him, who were taken by surprise.[15] A political tempest ensued. "Since the assassination of President Lincoln, no public event has more deeply saddened the hearts and called forth the condemnation of the Union men . . . than the recent veto," one Republican newspaper wrote. Another remarked that "the news of the Veto Message has awakened throughout the North a feeling of indignation in every loyal breast, only equaled by the joy manifested by every Copperhead."[16]

Yet the proposed new laws left intact the Southern state governments that had been installed under presidential authority. These bills were aimed only at preventing those governments from challenging the results of the war. The Freedman's Bureau Act reinforced the authority of that agency of the army to protect blacks from the worst abuses. The Civil Rights Act substantially invalidated the black codes by guaranteeing the civil rights of all Americans, without distinction as to race, and placing those rights under federal jurisdiction. This *national* definition of citizenship was a historic first. A product of the new patriotism, it was aimed primarily at ensuring that the new Thirteenth Amendment would not be empty verbiage. As the moderate Lyman Trumbull explained, "The freedman . . . will by tyrannized over, abused, and virtually reënslaved without some legislation by the nation for his protection."[17]

The vetoes transformed the political chessboard because they closed the door to any negotiation between the president and Congress. Johnson embraced Confederate arguments that Republicans deemed unacceptable. He rejected citizenship for "the entire race designated as blacks, people of color, negroes, mulattoes, and persons of African blood," who in his view had not demonstrated "their fitness to receive and exercise the rights of citizens." More than that, he linked this racism to a narrow view of federalism: the federal government must not "interfere with the municipal legislation of the States, with the relations existing exclusively between a State and its citizens, or between inhabitants of the same State." Otherwise, the central government would "sap and destroy our federative system of limited powers and break down the barriers which preserve the rights of the States." With this statement, the president was repeating virtually word for word statements made by the defenders of slavery before the war.[18]

Above all, Johnson denied that Congress could legitimately legislate with respect to Reconstruction as long as the Southern states were not represented. He thereby set himself up as the sole true representative of the people as a whole. For the Republicans, this was a "monstrous and arrogant assumption," especially "for a man chosen to preside over the Senate, and made President by an assassin."[19] Johnson thus foreclosed the possibility of any future cooperation with Congress, and in so doing, drastically altered the political landscape.

The Republicans, who held a two-thirds majority in both houses, quickly overrode the president's vetoes, but mutual suspicion between the executive and Congress was now established, with important implications for future legislation. In particular, the permanent veto threat forced Republicans to seek a much wider consensus than usual on all new bills. This damaged their capacity for action, because it meant that any dissension in the ranks, even by a small group, had the potential to paralyze Congress.

In this altered political landscape, it became possible for sectionalism to emerge in the North in the months that followed. One immediate consequence was that Republicans were forced to choose a constitutional path in order to protect the fruits of victory from the whims of one man or a change of majority. The Fourteenth Amendment, which was submitted to the country for ratification on June 18, 1866, arose out of an institutional analysis of the political situation.[20] It was now an imperative of Reconstruction that a policy be imposed on the president, that the Southern states be compelled to respect that policy, and that the Supreme Court, which in *Dred Scott v. Sandford* had ruled in 1857 that descendants of Africans were not citizens, be prevented from interfering.[21] Ironically, it was no doubt Johnson's pugnacious hostility that enabled the Republicans to forge a compromise that, in view of the bitterness of the debate, might have been impossible to achieve otherwise.[22] The proposed amendment, calculated to draw maximum possible support, avoided all controversial measures, such as granting blacks the right to vote. It nevertheless permanently altered the constitutional balance of powers. By seeking to block congressional initiatives, the president forced Republicans to take steps that few would have envisioned just a few months earlier.

The amendment had two goals: to incorporate the outcome of the war into the Constitution and to create political conditions favorable to Reconstruction. The first objective was reflected in Article 1. "All persons born or naturalized in the United States" were guaranteed the rights of national citizenship, and federal law was granted priority over state law in this respect. Citizens were also entitled to "equal protection of the laws." Articles 2 and 3 were designed to make possible a veritable reconstruction of the South by redefining the local electorate. Those who had served the Confederacy as representatives or officials were barred from elective office, a move to sideline the traditional elite and create new opportunities for Union loyalists. The representation of the states could be reduced in proportion to the number of adult males deprived of the right to vote. Here, the hope was that Southern whites would either grant blacks the right to vote or suffer a substantial reduction in national representation.

The Fourteenth Amendment was thus a constitutional response to the political reconfiguration precipitated by Johnson's vetoes. For Republicans, this was a way to circumvent two hostile institutions: the federal executive and the Southern state governments. Of course, the new situation affected the whole dynamic of the political system, going well beyond the dispute over Reconstruction from which it stemmed originally. In particular, it would encourage the emergence and crystallization of economic sectionalism in the North.

The Emergence of Sectionalism in the North

One eventual effect of the Fourteenth Amendment was to create a link between Reconstruction and the currency debates. No one anticipated this, however, when an article on the public debt was included in the text, declaring that the Union debt "shall not be questioned" while repudiating debts incurred by the Confederacy. The Republicans reacted directly to episodes which, though sporadic, signaled to them that the Southern states might be refusing to accept the verdict of the armed conflict. For instance, in November 1865, Governor Benjamin Perry of South Carolina offered a lengthy plea for repayment of "the debt contracted by South Carolina during the Rebellion." It was "very inconsiderable," he averred, and had nothing to do with "Expenditures for War purposes . . . paid by the confederate Government." In the North, the Democratic Party called for taxes on Treasury bonds. In Ohio, it denounced the creation of "an odious and privileged moneyed aristocracy" and of a policy "attempting to exonerate the holders [of Government debt] from all obligations to pay their just proportion of taxes." In these positions, the Republicans saw a determination to weaken the nation's credit, which called for a response.[23]

Thus the inclusion of the debt in the Fourteenth Amendment was a consequence of the political context. Some Southern leaders proposed to reimburse those who had financed the war against the Union. We see how the institutional configuration—the president and Southern state governments versus the Republican majority in Congress—helped to create a link between the financial legacy of the war and Reconstruction. It also contributed to the emergence of certain differences on economic issues between the Midwest and Northeast. A good example of this is the Bankruptcy Act. The bill introduced in the spring of 1866 traced its origins to Southern moratoria on debt recovery. Republicans saw the influence of "the owners of this land . . . who control the State legislation and the State courts."[24] In view of the decisions taken by local governments established under President Johnson's policies, a federal law was needed to authorize the seizure of landed property for debt. Such a law would allow creditors, many of whom were in the North, to recover money they had lent to planters. If the seized plantations were then subdivided, the pattern of Southern landholding could be reshaped without sweeping redistribution, which the majority of Republicans rejected.[25] In that sense, it was a Reconstruction measure.

By invoking federal law, however, the Republicans were legislating for the entire country. By authorizing the seizure of land for debt, the bill posed a threat to Midwestern homesteads, which enjoyed certain legal guarantees. In a region where agriculture depended essentially on small farms, mortgages were the only basis of credit, and foreclosure was always a threat, Midwestern politicians were determined to protect the homesteaders whom they had brought into the region with the Homestead Act of 1862.[26] The bankruptcy bill aimed at the South therefore gave rise to a sectional conflict that divided the North (see chapter 1).

The bankruptcy debate presaged a spatial contradiction at the heart of Reconstruction: confronted with hostile Southern governments, the Republicans sought to reinforce federal powers of intervention, but this brought them face to face with local economic interests in the North. The transformation of those interests into sectional conflict in the North was not due to Reconstruction. But in 1866, Reconstruction created a context favorable to the crystallization of the opposition between the Midwest and Northeast. A temporary solution to that contradiction would be achieved in the spring of 1867, when the secessionist states were again placed under military supervision. This gave the Republicans additional levers of local control in the South, making drastic revisions of bankruptcy law unnecessary. The Bankruptcy Act that was finally passed in 1867 can be understood as a sectional compromise that preserved the state exemption against seizure of homesteads.[27] Functionally, direct federal control of the South made it possible to detach Reconstruction from the issues that provoked sectionalism in the North.

Tensions between the Midwest and Northeast had only begun to emerge in 1866, but within a year, they had grown considerably. Meanwhile, an attempt to raise the tariff in June 1866 deepened the sectional split. Congressional debates and votes revealed a geographical polarization among Republicans sufficient to scuttle the bill, but also sufficient to justify a sectional interpretation of political economy that would soon spill over to the money question (see chapter 3).

The prominent role of sectionalism in these tariff debates owed a great deal to the Reconstruction context, because protectionists defended the bill by availing themselves of patriotic rhetoric that came out of the Civil War. Their position derived directly from the wartime strategy of advocating progressive tariff increases in order to pay for military operations. Now, however, the argument was that a higher tariff was needed to defend the United States' "position against foreign competition" and protect American workers. The use of this military metaphor hinted that anyone who opposed the measure was guilty of treason. "Whatever else the secessionists took with them," argued Thaddeus Stevens, "I am very sorry they did not take all their relics of free-trade doctrine." Stevens's identification of his adversaries—the majority of Midwestern Republicans—with those who had started the war was a shameless attempt to avoid debate on the substance of the issue. As James A. Garfield pointed out, however, the argument was relevant to the new political situation. In Garfield's view, Republicans who opposed protectionism took the risk of "now precipitat[ing] a division" by joining "with our political enemies."[28] In a situation in which broader majorities were needed to pass Reconstruction bills over the president's veto, the disruptive potential of sectionalism jeopardized the future of the Republican Party.

The patriotism argument could cut two ways, however. John B. Henderson, a Missouri Republican, expressed outrage at "eastern gentlemen [who] manufactured and sold to the Government at extravagant prices" clothing worn by "our people [who] went to the war and spent four years in the service . . . for the paltry sum of thirteen, fourteen, or fifteen dollars per month."[29] In reality, Reconstruction issues were too remote, and the tariff issue too longstanding and well-established, so that patriotic rhetoric could not move Midwestern Republicans to embrace protectionism. The failure of this maneuver had a number of implications for the future. It stirred up sectional tensions it could not resolve. It showed that the political situation weakened the party's ideological cohesion; since each faction needed the other to win on Reconstruction issues against the President, no version of patriotism could achieve dominance, and this made it difficult to exploit patriotic themes when dealing with unrelated issues. Paradoxically, in other words, the political situation made expanded majorities necessary but at the same time complicated the task of enforcing party discipline. The Republican Party's vulnerability to geographical divisions became obvious.

Because the Democrats were only a small minority in Congress, they were better able to remain united.[30] Some of them drew a partisan lesson from the sectional tensions on the Republican side. The influential *Cincinnati Enquirer*, which denounced a "gigantic robbery of the whole people for the benefit of a few interested monopolists in New England and Pennsylvania," judged that if the South had been better represented, "this abominable scheme of plunder would have been defeated" in the House (where it survived an early vote before going down to eventual defeat). The paper concluded that it was "vitally important . . . for the protection of the West that the Southern members should be in their seats."[31] This prefigured the strategy of using economic sectionalism *against* Reconstruction that Ohio Democrats would try out a few months later.

Sectional Issues versus Reconstruction?

The distinctive alignment of political forces concerning Reconstruction allowed sectional oppositions to emerge between the Midwest and the Northeast. It was not the cause of sectional differences but provided a favorable context for them. This was particularly true during debates on the tariff, which divided the dominant party and therefore accentuated geographic differences regarding economic issues. For the time being, however, these differences remained relatively subdued, because the broader public was not yet aroused.

Many things conspired to make Reconstruction the sole issue of the 1866 midterm elections, which in most states took place in October and November. This was the first federal election since the end of the war, and it would decide which of two visions of the South's future in the Union would prevail: the president's, which left a good deal of autonomy to the white majority in the South, or the Republicans', set forth in the Fourteenth Amendment, which sought to impose political reforms on the secessionist states. With issues such as these in a climate so dramatic, the election inevitably became a referendum on Reconstruction.

Andrew Johnson would even turn it into a plebiscite by attempting to rearrange the political landscape in his favor. Since 1865 he had been working to build an electoral base made up of moderate Republicans, Southern conservatives, and War Democrats while isolating Radicals on one side and the more extreme Democrats on the other. This project took shape in August 1866, when the brand new National Union Party held its convention in Philadelphia. It brought together Republicans and Democrats from both the North and South. In a powerful symbol of national reconciliation, the delegations from South Carolina and Massachusetts made their entrance arm in arm. The former enemies, secessionists and abolitionists, had found harmony thanks to Johnson's policies.[32]

The media coup hid the failure of the convention for only a short time, however. Few Republicans were present, whereas Democrats were very much in evidence, including some whose notorious opposition to the war made their participation embarrassing. The National Union Party did not lead to the party realignment that Johnson had hoped for. Republicans, for their part, reminded him in their platform "that the President himself, as well as the people, should bow to [Congress's] decision." Democrats, meanwhile, supported Johnson's Reconstruction policy but refused to be defined by it, and in Ohio reiterated that they would "adhere in the present and in the future, as in the past, with unfaltering fidelity and firmness, to the organization of the Democratic party."[33] The Philadelphia convention nevertheless ensured that the election of 1866 would be exclusively about Reconstruction, because the only reason for holding it was to defend the president's policy. The other issues that had emerged in 1866, and in particular economic issues such as the currency and tariff questions, vanished from party platforms, although the national debt, mentioned in the Fourteenth Amendment, was discussed here and there.[34]

Andrew Johnson reinforced this shift of focus by entering the arena personally. Convinced that voters shared both his wish that the South quickly resume its place in the Union and his racism, he made a campaign tour through the North. This "swing around the circle" proved disastrous. The press decried "the mortifying spectacle of the President going about from town to town, accompanied by the prominent members of the Cabinet, on an electioneering raid, denouncing his opponents, bandying epithets with men in the crowd, and praising himself and his policies."[35] But it was the news from the South that gripped the public mind. Two events especially galvanized opinion. During the first three days of May, Memphis was rocked by a murderous race riot. A collision between two wagons degenerated into a confrontation between black war veterans and police, and then into riots and attacks on black families and homes.[36] Northern newspapers were aghast at "the demoniac spirit of the Southern whites toward the freedmen," which was "made more malignant in the late Slave States by the fact of [their] unswerving loyalty during the war."[37] On July 30, a riot in New Orleans left an even stronger impression. In a tense political climate, a demonstration by blacks led by veterans in support of the governor was attacked by the local police. Charged with investigating the incident, General Philip Sheridan described "an absolute massacre by the police . . . without the shadow of a necessity. Furthermore I believe it was premeditated, and every indication points to this."[38]

To many Northerners, these episodes of extreme violence proved that Southern whites refused the consequences of their defeat. What is more, Southern states rejected the Fourteenth Amendment one after another. For Republicans, "the sinful ten has . . . with contempt and scorn, flung back into our teeth the magnanimous offer of a generous nation." Even the taciturn General Ulysses S. Grant allowed his impatience to show through in a rare press interview: "A year ago, [the southern states] were willing to do anything; now they regard themselves as master of the situation."[39]

The verdict of the ballot box left no room for doubt. The Republican victory was overwhelming. The party won three-quarters of the seats in the House and all seats in more than half the states, and they won all the governorships and state assemblies that were up for election that fall.[40] Johnson was repudiated, and Republicans held on to a majority sufficient to override any veto. They concluded that "the President has no power to control or influence anybody and legislation will be carried on entirely regardless of his opinions or wishes." In their eyes, the time for real change had come: the South needed "*government*, the strong arm of power, outstretched from the central authority here in Washington."[41] With a popular mandate in hand, they set out to overhaul Reconstruction completely.

The magnitude of the electoral victory strengthened the Republicans' political hand. The institutional situation remained unchanged, however. Johnson was still president, and the veto threat meant that a broad majority was still needed. The party remained vulnerable to dissent within its ranks. Because of the focus on Reconstruction, the election failed to settle other key issues, such as the money question and the tariff, which retained their destructive potential, especially among Republicans. In search of an alternative electoral strategy, Ohio Democrats understood this and decided to exploit it.

Revising Reconstruction

To Republicans, political Reconstruction in the South meant establishing state governments there on new foundations. Once again, the need for a broad majority to counter the threat of a presidential veto led to bitter negotiations. Many different views on Reconstruction coexisted among Republicans, and they evolved rapidly in the face of events in the South. The legislation of 1867 was the fruit of a compromise between Moderates and Radicals. The strategy they hammered together was to place the South under federal supervision and set a course for full reinstatement in the Union. The Military Reconstruction Act divided the South into five districts, each headed by a general. The army was assigned the task of overseeing the establishment of civil institutions compatible with the requirements of the North: elections were to be held, new constitutions drafted (including the right to vote for black men), and the Fourteenth Amendment was to be ratified. After that, there were to be new elections to choose local and federal representatives. If these conditions were met, the Southern states could be readmitted to the Union.[42]

Military supervision was a noteworthy condition for a democracy. The Democrats were quick to denounce "government by bayonet."[43] In fact, this was a conservative choice. It was a way of leaving federalism intact. Rather than reinforce federal power at the expense of the states, it merely imposed temporary oversight on the defeated section of the country. In other words, the Republicans chose a *regional* strategy. The Military Reconstruction Act applied only to the South, unlike the Civil Rights Act of 1866 or the Fourteenth Amendment. By granting the army a relatively free hand in the South, Congress was able to push for extensive local reforms without changing anything in the North. Politically, this made it possible to separate Reconstruction from other issues, such as those having to do with the economy. As one result, a compromise on the Bankruptcy Act became possible.

To make this approach work, however, the Republicans needed the cooperation of two key groups: the federal executive (since the army would be in charge of Reconstruction in the South) and Southern voters. The first problem they faced was therefore the hostility of the president, which the elections of 1866 did nothing to restrain. Congress set out to neutralize him as much as possible by passing the Tenure of Office Act, which forbade the chief executive from removing Cabinet members without the consent of the Senate. The Republicans soon extended this protection to Grant, through whom all military orders were henceforth expected to flow. Their goal was to secure the positions of officials who agreed with the aims of Reconstruction, but in so doing, they upset the equilibrium between two separate and equal branches of government with a law of dubious constitutionality.[44]

Above all, the Republican plan could not succeed without the active cooperation of the Southern electorate. In 1865, a majority of whites showed that they still supported the same elite that had led the war against the Union. Congress accordingly set out to redefine the electorate, following the same logic as the Fourteenth Amendment. It excluded the men it deemed most hostile to Reconstruction, namely, all elected and other officials who had collaborated in secession. Even more striking was the decision to grant the vote to all adult black males. In so doing, Congress sought to give blacks the political means to defend their rights and interests. They also hoped that these new black voters, together with white Unionists, would establish a regional political base favorable to Reconstruction and to the expansion of the Republican Party (which was still mainly confined to the North).

Allowing blacks to vote in the South represented a major social and political upheaval. In the space of two years, 4 million slaves became citizens, and the adult males among them became voters. Ironically, it was Johnson's obstructionism and the intransigence of the South that drove the Republicans to take a step that only a minority among them had championed previously. To carry out Reconstruction without modifying federalism—that is, the balance between the states and the federal government—required the cooperation of a political majority in the South. Giving blacks the vote made this possible.

By adopting a regional strategy, the Republicans separated Reconstruction, which applied only to the South, from legislative issues that also concerned the North. The enormous advantage of this approach was that it separated certain policy domains from others: economic issues no longer impinged on reform in the secessionist states. Yet sectionalism within the North did not disappear. Revived by the tariff debate of the summer of 1866, it spilled over into monetary debates as early as 1867. By severing these issues politically, the Republicans were able to deal separately with internal divisions between Moderates and Radicals on the South and between the Northeast and Midwest on currency. The party nevertheless remained vulnerable to sectional tensions, and some Democrats would soon be tempted to take advantage of this.

The Lessons of an Election: The Pendleton Plan

An elegant lawyer, George H. Pendleton was one of the Democratic Party's lead-ing spokesmen. As a representative from Cincinnati and candidate for the vice presidency in 1864, he had been one of Lincoln's most prominent opponents during the war, a champion of strict interpretation of the Constitution. In 1867, with the Democrats seemingly caught in a political impasse, he took up the money question as an electoral weapon.[45] As a result of this decision, sectionalism soon took on greater political importance than anyone had expected.

After suffering a crushing defeat in 1866, Democrats understood that Johnson, the accidental president, had no political coattails. The more pragmatic politi-cians among them also recognized that Reconstruction would be a political hand-icap as long as their position was considered unpatriotic, as it had been during the war.[46] In November 1866, these politicians began casting about for more favorable political ground. The influential *Chicago Times* suggested accepting the main consequences of Reconstruction. "Is it not inevitable that blacks will have the right to vote?" the newspaper asked. Was it not time that Democrats accepted this inexorable outcome of the war and moved on to other things? Republican diarist George T. Strong immediately saw how "this move would be risky, *periculosae plenum opus aleae*. It would alienate many Southern swashbucklers, and many of the nigger-haters whose votes swell the anti-national majorities." Indeed, hostile reactions were not long in coming. "We are forced to conclude that the Chicago Times, heretofore considered sound, has gone over to the enemy," opined the *Jonesboro Gazette*, a rural Illinois paper. "The Democracy never barter principle for expediency," admonished the *Cincinnati Enquirer.*[47] To preempt Reconstruc-tion in order to neutralize it was clearly a premature tactic for Democrats mobi-lized in favor of "white government."

A more promising tactic emerged in Ohio. Persuaded by the arguments of Washington McLean, editor of the *Cincinnati Enquirer,* George H. Pendleton seized on the money question in the spring of 1867. A cautious man, he experi-mented with a narrow issue, demanding that the series of U.S. bonds known as five-twenties be reimbursed in greenbacks rather than gold (see chapter 2). He portrayed this as a matter of justice. The bondholders could not but agree to be reimbursed in the same legal tender with which they had purchased the wartime issue in the first place, and in any case, this was the rule in regard to all other transactions. In Pendleton's view, this would save the government money and allow it to pay down the debt more quickly.[48]

In the local election campaign of 1867, Pendleton did not ignore Reconstruction issues, especially black suffrage. But at the same time, he slyly introduced the money question to capitalize on the perceptibly swelling discontent. The United States faced economic difficulties. Midwestern farmers, suffering from two successive bad harvests, also found themselves short of cash every autumn, and this hindered the marketing of their crop. Yet "it was easy to see . . . that as each month the degree of contraction was made public, the people more and more attributed their financial troubles to its operation."[49] In Congress, the repercussions were palpable. From December 1866 on, Midwestern congressmen tried on several occasions to bring contraction to stop. In votes and speeches, heightened sectionalism was increasingly apparent.[50] Revived by the previous summer's debates on the tariff, this now affected the money question.

Pendleton thus scored a real political success on an unexpected issue.[51] Downplaying the more traditional tariff issue, he saw greater promise in the money question, which could be couched in simple terms tailored to appeal to voters. It was an attempt to turn sectional feeling to his party's advantage. "If there be one political measure . . . which the people of the entire West are a solid unit in opposition thereto," the influential Republican paper the *Chicago Tribune* averred, "it is the scheme of currency contraction which Secretary McCulloch is forcing upon the country." As the idea that the secretary's policy was harmful spread throughout the Midwest, accompanied by the notion that Republicans, owing to their sectional divisions, could not put a stop to it, it became tempting for Ohio Democrats to depict their adversaries as sellouts to Northeastern interests, "aristocratic, bondholding, tax-exempted *leaders*."[52]

It was no accident that the strategy of taking advantage of sectional tensions for the benefit of the party originated in Ohio. The issue had potential throughout the Midwest, and it divided the Republican Party, as congressional debates showed. Furthermore, this potentially fertile political terrain was distinct from Reconstruction, where Democrats were handicapped. The gamble seemed promising, but it was not without risk. Democrats had been hostile to paper money since the time of Andrew Jackson, because they associated it with the power of the banks. During the war, Pendleton himself had opposed the issue of greenbacks. His new position could have been characterized as an ideological reversal. To parry this charge, he pursued two separate tactics. The first was direct: Pendleton argued that he was not defending paper money as such. By focusing on reimbursement of the five-twenties in greenbacks, he made the issue one of treating bondholders the same as ordinary citizens. The second tactic was to test the issue in a local election in Ohio, where the electorate was more circumscribed and probably more favorable to the proposal than elsewhere. With the help of the *Cincinnati Enquirer*, the issue became a fixture of the campaign within a few weeks. Even Pendleton's chief rival, Clement L. Vallandigham, explained that "if legal tender is good enough to pay for a bushel of corn, it is good enough to pay these bonds."[53] If the popularity of the money question could be demonstrated in a local election, then it might be possible to persuade the national Democratic Party of its usefulness and at the same time improve Pendleton's chance of winning the presidential nomination. By testing the money question locally, he played his section off against the Republicans while protecting himself, at least initially, from a possible sectional division within his own party.

The Pendleton Plan was not the only issue in the 1867 election in Ohio. Reconstruction was a major concern, especially because of the referendum on granting blacks the right to vote in the state. Ohio was seen as a key state in national politics, so the whole country paid attention to its local races.[54] By introducing the money question at this juncture, Pendleton unwittingly linked finance and suffrage. The consequences of the election would alter the course of Reconstruction.

Local Election, National Impact

"The White Man Victorious! . . . Radicalism Played Out! Hurrah!" The headline in the *Jonesboro Gazette*, a southern Illinois paper, like those in other Democratic papers in November 1867, exhibited a triumphal tone that few would have anticipated after the previous year's rout. The 1867 elections were local and not held in all states, but the Republicans suffered a significant setback in the North. This was in striking contrast to the South, where delegates were elected to the constitutional conventions established by Reconstruction legislation. Blacks, who were voting for the first time, turned out in large numbers, and Republicans won landslide victories in all the former secessionist states. In the North, the result was the reverse: The Democrats took Ohio (except for the governorship), New Jersey, and the New York State Assembly. They consolidated their majority in California and the border states, and made progress wherever elections were held, even in New England.[55]

"We went in on principle and got whipped" was the way Benjamin F. Wade summed up the results. An Ohio Radical and president *pro tempore* of the Senate, Wade lost all hope of being reelected when his term ended the following year. Observers throughout the North shared his analysis and that of his colleague John Sherman: "The chief trouble is the suffrage question."[56] All Northern commentators agreed that the Radicals' signature issue had suffered a serious defeat. It failed to win a majority in any of the three states that put it to a referendum—Kansas, Minnesota, and Ohio. Had the Republicans moved too quickly in attempting to grant the right to vote to blacks not only in the South but also in the territories and the capital?[57] Not all Republicans bemoaned the loss, however. Conservative Nathaniel P. Banks was pleased by what he considered "a crusher for the wild men." Although these local elections had only a limited impact on the Republicans at the national level, many Moderates believed that their psychological effect "will be good discipline in many ways and will I am sure be 'blessed to us in the edification and building up of the true faith.'"[58]

Everyone agreed that the Republican setback in the North was due largely to the issue of the suffrage. Those who paid attention to Ohio, however, acknowledged that the money question accounted for the exceptionally good showing by the Democrats. One of these, William Henry Smith, a strategist for Republican governor Rutherford B. Hayes, argued that "the impolitic and unsound theories of Mr. McCulloch . . . [divided] the dominant party," and that the Democrats' "promise [of] a millennium of wealth and plenty" cost his party the support of the masses even though "our folks discussed finances intelligently, showing that if the Democratic theory were carried out it would impoverish everybody."[59] Thus, the 1867 election granted the sanction of the ballot box to what would come to be known as "the Ohio Idea." This Democratic success worried Republicans. Reconstruction was no longer enough to win elections. The Midwest wanted some concession on financial issues, and without one, it would be impossible "to prevent the Copperheads from carrying the next Presidential election." Robert C. Schenck and John Sherman, both from Ohio, who were in charge of financial issues in the House and Senate, were urged to take quick action.[60] On December 7, the House voted by an overwhelming majority to end the contraction by forbidding the secretary of the treasury to withdraw greenbacks from circulation. The Suspension Act became law in February 1868.[61]

This response shows that Pendleton's wager was successful. By taking a subject that divided Republicans sectionally and making it an issue in a state election, he gave it political legitimacy and lifted it to national prominence. Republicans now realized that the money question—reduced in this instance to the use of paper money to reimburse a portion of the debt—had become a political handicap, and with presidential elections just a year away, they put a halt to contraction, something they had been unable to do a few months earlier. But even the passage of this emergency legislation could not paper over the deep divisions within Republican ranks. Schenck, the floor manager for the bill, had great difficulty

TABLE 4. Comparison between vote on impeachment and vote on suspending contraction in the House, December 7, 1867

		Vote on suspension bill			
		Yea	Nay	Abstention	Total
Vote on impeachment	**Yea**	54	3	2	59
	Northeast	15	2	2	19
	West	25	1	0	26
	South	14	0	0	14
	Nay	72	29	9	110
	Northeast	30	21	6	57
	West	32	5	1	38
	South	10	3	2	15
	Abstention	1	0	17	18
	Northeast	1	0	10	11
	West	0	0	6	6
	South	0	0	1	1
	Total	127	32	28	187
	Northeast	46	23	18	87
	West	57	6	7	70
	South	24	3	3	30

Source: Globe, 40th Cong., 2nd sess., 68, 70 (Dec. 7, 1867).

preventing his colleagues from broaching the issue more broadly. Imploring them not to endanger the bill, he promised that the time for further debate would come soon.[62] An overwhelming majority of Republicans voted for the bill, convinced that it was essential for the sake of the party. Ironically, it was now the Democrats who found themselves divided along sectional lines. Pendleton would soon encounter signs of resistance in his own camp.

A small number of politicians found the situation worrisome, however. Those hard-money men were afraid that halting contraction would trigger "a financial earthquake." For them, the elections proved that "this is a question on which the West cannot be trusted," yet debate in Congress had shown that "its voice will be decisive."[63] Faced with this new danger, a small group composed mainly of Northeastern hard-money Moderate Republicans reacted by linking the fate of the South to the resumption of specie payments. We can see this in voting on two bills before the House on December 7, 1867. As table 4 shows, only one group took a consistent position on both issues. This group rejected the suspension bill and on the same day also voted against a bill to impeach Andrew Johnson. As prominent

Republican James G. Blaine observed, this small group, consisting almost entirely of representatives from the Northeast, thus introduced a "geographically . . . traceable division" in a Reconstruction vote.[64]

This linkage was new. George H. Pendleton had hit upon his plan to emphasize the money question precisely because it was *distinct* from Reconstruction and therefore, he believed, more favorable politically to his side. His success convinced some of his Republican adversaries, such as Senator James W. Grimes of Iowa, that "the great question . . . today is the financial question and must, ought to override the reconstruction and impeachment questions." Such a feeling could have arisen only among the more conservative Republicans, whose idea of Reconstruction was narrower than the Radicals'. Politically, they reflexively opposed an impeachment that, they believed, would destabilize institutions. They were also convinced that "all the great Northern capitalists are afraid of the consequences of impeachment." For them, Hugh McCulloch was the best rampart against the rising opposition to contraction. As long as Johnson remained in the White House, he would keep McCulloch as secretary of the treasury. It was for that reason that William Pitt Fessenden, for instance, continued to defend the president, virtually alone in the Senate.[65]

In other words, the connection between the future of Reconstruction and the speedy return to specie payments was not intellectual but political. It had to do not with the substance of the issues but rather with the balance of power within the federal government. For these congressmen and senators, given the conditions of the day, protecting the currency made it necessary to defend a decision with potentially negative consequences for the reform of the South. At this point, they constituted a small minority faction, but the stand they took would introduce sectional issues into the Reconstruction debate.

Constitution, Reconstruction, Currency: The Stakes of an Impeachment

The linkage between the money question and Reconstruction resulted from the confluence of two political dynamics: the electoral success of the Pendleton Plan (which capitalized on sectionalism at the expense of party) and the attempt to impeach Andrew Johnson. The initiative first came from Radicals exasperated by the president's systematic obstruction over a period of several months. He did more than just veto bills passed by Congress. In the spring, Johnson asked the attorney general for a constitutional interpretation granting him the discretion to limit, even nullify, enforcement of the Reconstruction Acts. During the summer, he took advantage of the congressional recess to dismiss Secretary of War Edwin M. Stanton, whom he deemed too favorable to Republican policies. He also relieved Generals Philip Sheridan and Daniel Sickles of command of their military districts in the South, over the objections of Ulysses S. Grant, because Johnson found them too zealous in their endeavors. In his annual message to Congress in December, he defended his right not to enforce measures with which he disagreed, openly asking "how far the duty of the President to 'preserve, protect, and defend the Constitution' requires him to go in opposing an unconstitutional act of Congress."[66]

In the eyes of the Radicals, this was proof that there could be no Reconstruction without getting rid of Johnson. "Are we to leave this officer, if we judge him to be guilty of high crimes and misdemeanors, in control of the Army and the Navy, with his declaration upon the record that under certain circumstances he will not execute the laws?"[67] Nevertheless, in December 1867, a majority of Republicans, their ardor cooled by the elections, felt that impeachment would be too extreme and politically dangerous.[68] It was on this occasion that a small group of Republicans, led by Northeastern conservatives, linked the fate of the president to that of the currency. The consequences of this move would become clear two months later, when the impeachment issue arose once again in much more spectacular fashion. The question of contraction would then help to save Johnson.

The failure of Radicals encouraged the president in his obstructionism, which went unpunished. He gave free rein to everyone in the South who opposed the Reconstruction Acts. In most Southern states, constitutional conventions dominated by Republicans had been elected. While they went about their work, however, the civil authorities installed by Johnson remained in place. The army was the only instrument available for enforcing congressional policy, but, one by one, Johnson replaced overly zealous generals with others hostile to Reconstruction. For instance, John Pope was dismissed after he took action against the governor of Georgia for refusing to fund the constitutional convention in his state, as required by law. In Louisiana, Winfield Scott Hancock, appointed to replace Sheridan, allowed former Confederates to register illegally to vote. The Freedmen's Bureau was one of Johnson's favorite targets: General Oliver O. Howard testified that "the President . . . musters out all my officers. . . . Measures are on foot . . . which are doubtless intended to utterly defeat reconstruction."[69]

By acting as he did, Johnson encouraged white Southerners to resist while depriving their victims of the means to defend themselves from "the intense bitter hatred that is manifested towards [Southern Republicans]." In Tennessee, the Ku Klux Klan, a secret society founded in Pulaski in 1866, spread rapidly throughout the state, attacking freedmen arbitrarily. Within a few months, the Klan had become a fearsome political force. Texas, located beyond the reach of central government power, experienced an unprecedented wave of homicides, and violent beatings were common everywhere. Only the army could intervene, but according to one Alabama Republican, "unfriendly military management has killed us."[70]

The future of Reconstruction was clearly in danger. Radicals were enraged, as the following tirade in the *New York Independent* shows: "If the great culprit had robbed a till; if he fired a barn; if had had forged a check; he would have been indicted, prosecuted, condemned, sentenced, and punished. But the evidence shows that he only oppressed the Negro; that he only conspired with the rebel; that he only betrayed the Union party; that he only attempted to overthrow the Republic—of course, he goes unwhipped of justice." Yet Moderates also worried about the rapid deterioration of the situation. In December, the *Chicago Tribune* had opposed impeachment, but now it anxiously wondered whether Congress could not "devise some means of checkmating the villainous conspiracy of Johnson and Co."[71]

The president himself would provide the opportunity, when he once again dismissed the secretary of war, Edwin M. Stanton, on February 21, 1868. The provocation was deliberate. A month earlier, the Senate had refused to approve Johnson's first dismissal of Stanton under the Tenure of Office Act. By seeking confrontation, Johnson hoped to regain control and widen the split between Moderates and Radicals, perhaps even to win a Supreme Court decision striking down the law that prevented him from firing members of his Cabinet.[72] Sowing the wind, he reaped only the whirlwind. In a moment of high drama, Stanton locked himself in his office, the Senate censured the president's decision, and the House initiated impeachment proceedings, which it had refused to do only two months earlier.[73] For the first time in U.S. history, a president was impeached by the House and sent before the Senate for trial. On this occasion, the connection between monetary orthodoxy and political conservatism, forged earlier by a small group of Republicans, would turn out to be crucial.

By late February, Republicans harbored few doubts as to Johnson's guilt. His obstructionism was plain for all to see, and it was impossible to deny that he neither respected nor enforced duly approved acts of Congress. Impeachment had an immediate and dramatic effect. The Republicans were once again united, though not so much in regard to Reconstruction as in their desire to strip Johnson of power. The president immediately understood that if he wished to serve out his term, he would have to demonstrate conciliatory talents not previously in evidence. He offered any number of tokens of good will and assurances that he would behave well in the future. "Andrew Johnson has been a changed man," the *Chicago Tribune* marveled ironically. "The country has been at peace. The obstruction to the law has been virtually suspended."[74]

The new regime of humility worked, and after a two-month trial in the Senate, Johnson was acquitted by one vote. The voting on May 16 and 26 generally followed party lines, but seven Republicans joined the Democrats, and Johnson was not removed from office. Many Republicans felt betrayed. The newspapers attacked those who sided with the Democrats as "recusants" and "renegades." Some were accused of having been bought or acting out of disappointed ambition.[75] The vehemence of the attacks reflected the widespread belief that the future of Reconstruction hinged on the outcome of the impeachment process. The anger dissipated fairly quickly, however. As George T. Strong observed, "This acquittal is worth many thousand votes to the Republican Party, for it excludes A. Johnson from the prestige of martyrdom."[76] The president lost his political influence, and while he continued to oppose Congress, he kept his promise to end his obstructionism. Although Republicans failed to remove him from office, they ultimately succeeded in neutralizing him for the remainder of his term.

There were many reasons why these seven senators chose to break with their party on impeachment. The charges against the president were poorly formulated and rested on a fragile legal basis (the Tenure of Office Act). Taking a conservative view of the Constitution, they felt that the procedure itself threatened to undermine the balance of powers. Insofar as it is possible to judge, however, their motives were also political, as symbolized by one name: Benjamin F. Wade. In the absence of a vice president, the senator from Ohio and president pro tempore of the Senate would succeed the president if the latter were removed from office. Wade was a controversial figure, however. Many Moderates saw him as "a man of violent passions, extreme opinions, and narrow views."[77] Their objections were political as well as personal. His brusque radicalism repelled those who hoped that after three years, Reconstruction could be ended as quickly as possible. On other issues he held equally clear-cut views. He was a thoroughgoing protectionist and an ardent defender of the greenback. During the Senate trial, the House had once again taken up the money question, confirming the importance of the issue and deepening divisions within the Republican Party. Those who had argued after the previous fall that monetary orthodoxy depended on a "sound" chief executive were afraid of a president who "says that our greenbacks are the best currency in the world," and that there are not enough of them. For them, "the removal of Mr. Johnson [would be] a great misfortune in its ultimate effects."

Here, the opposition to Wade's radicalism and greenbackism converged. In the end, Wade's position on the greenback was as persuasive to the defectors as his position on Johnson himself.[78]

Following Johnson's acquittal, a group of hard-money public men organized a dinner to honor William Pitt Fessenden, who was widely seen as the leader of the seven dissident Republican conservatives. The senator declined the invitation, but the gesture symbolized the political importance the money question had assumed since Pendleton took it up during the campaign. It played a role during the two attempts to impeach the president because a small group had begun to draw a political connection between monetary orthodoxy and Reconstruction. The issue was not so much the substance of policy as the personalities in charge of the nation's finances. At a time when the election of 1867 had strengthened the hand of those who wished to suspend contraction, when the Republican Party seemed disposed to give in to popular pressure on this point, and when Wade, a fervent champion of the greenback, was in line to become president, Johnson and his secretary of the treasury, Hugh McCulloch, may have seemed like the last ramparts against monetary anarchy. At first, only a small number of people made this connection, but in the political situation of the time, even a small dissenting group could have a large impact. As sectionalism was becoming increasingly apparent in debates in the House, Republicans realized that their economic differences were more than minor disagreements: they threatened the future of both the party and Reconstruction.

Forging a Compromise

Eighteen sixty-eight was a presidential election year, the first since the war ended. In many respects, this election would mark a political turning point. If the Republicans won with their record and their candidate, Ulysses S. Grant, the achievements of Reconstruction would be validated, and the Democratic Party would have to find another battleground. By contrast, if the Republicans lost, it would be seen as a disavowal of their program and would mark the beginning of a withdrawal of federal power from the South and of harsher race relations in the region. The end of Andrew Johnson's presidency promised to simplify the political picture and improve the functioning of federal institutions. But sectional tensions complicated the work of the parties, both of which were divided, because the Ohio idea had heightened the salience of the money question. Although the election would explicitly be a referendum on Reconstruction, the solidity of the parties would henceforth depend on their ability to find common ground on this major economic issue. The Republicans faced this challenge more successfully than the Democrats, managing to achieve a compromise, whereas the Democrats fell victim to the money question that they themselves had sought to make an issue in the election.

Divided Parties

By voting to halt contraction in early 1868, the Republicans reduced the sectional pressure that the success of the Pendleton Plan had intensified. But the Suspension Act, an emergency measure, did nothing to resolve the underlying issue. Thus began a long and testy period of debate on the funding of the debt, on the currency, and on the national banking system. Unfolding in parallel with the impeachment proceedings against Johnson, the new debate revealed two things: the intensity of sectional conflict between the Midwest and Northeast, and the temptation for Republicans to use Reconstruction to strengthen the internal cohesion of the party and impose a financial line across the factions.

In congressional debates, the sectional interpretation of the money question had taken hold. No one denied it. Indeed, everyone harped on it.[79] But an attempt was made to use party loyalty to enforce one position to the detriment of others. It all began with Pendleton's proposal to repay the principal of the five-twenties in greenbacks. Its success in Ohio in October 1867 identified this position with the Democratic Party. Hard-money Republicans seized this opportunity to delegitimize the position of their fellow Republicans who shared Pendleton's views. They pointed to the contradictions in his position, since he had condemned the creation of greenbacks in 1862 but was now proposing to use them to pay off the debt: "Mr. Pendleton, now the champion of irredeemable paper money, declared in 1862, on the floor of the House, that the legal-tender notes were sent into the world stamped with irredeemability; that we put on them the mark of Cain, and like Cain they would go forth to be vagabonds and fugitives on the face of the earth." In response, however, it was easy enough for Democrats to point out that the paper currency was a Republican creation, and that the debt had been "contracted with the understanding, with the knowledge of the creditors of the Government, that the Government had made 'greenbacks' a legal tender for such debts as we propose so to pay." Republicans who now renounced paper money were condemning their own handiwork.[80] The internal contradictions regarding the money question were all too glaring. They made it impossible for either party to insist that any given line was obviously ideologically correct. They also made it impossible to accuse adversaries within the party of sharing the enemy's position.

The attempt to play the patriotism card failed for similar reasons. It may have seemed promising to Republicans as a way of dealing with the war debt, which the Fourteenth Amendment had declared inviolable. Wouldn't paying off the debt with devalued currency be tantamount to "repudiation"? "It was not unnatural that a State mad with slavery should dishonor its bonds. Rejecting all obligations of humanity and justice, it easily rejected the obligations of Public Faith," Charles Sumner moralized (in bad faith, since it was the victorious North that had declared the Confederate debt null). "Such an example is not fit for our nation at this great period of its history." But the appeal to patriotism could be parsed in more ways than one and easily stood on its head. "It was right to pay the soldier in currency," John B. Henderson pointed out. "It is now right to pay his bounty and pension in currency . . . but to apply the same rule to-day to the bondholder is sacrilege."[81] Did not the nation have a duty to treat well its soldiers, who had given their blood for their country? It is revealing to see how patriotism mingled with sectionalism in these debates: everyone could chime in with their own position on the money question.[82] Reconstruction proved no more effective as an argument. Although the former secessionist states could be invoked for purposes of ideological contrast, the new situation in the South could also be used to justify an increase in the money supply. "Rebellion has been crushed. The supremacy of the Government is again established, and instead of 25,000,000 people we have not less than 37,000,000 to-day using the currency issued by the Government," Henderson noted. "Nor is it now as it was before the war or during the war. Then the slaves had no use for money. They are now freemen, and take their places in all business operations."[83] Since reintegrating the southern states in the Union was the order of the day, it was only logical to recalculate the amount of circulating currency needed by the economy of the entire nation and not just the North, as was the case before.

By bringing in Reconstruction issues, Republicans were trying to use their party's ideological basis to shore up their position on the money question. Both patriotism and the situation of the South could be used to justify opposing views on financial issues, however, and the only way to find common ground was to invoke principle: "How vain it is to expect financial reconstruction until political reconstruction has been completed, I have already shown," Charles Sumner summed up on the Senate floor. "So long as a great party, called Democratic, better now called Rebel, wars on that political reconstruction, which Congress has organized, there can be no specie payments."[84] In other words, Republicans saw that the only way to achieve reconciliation among themselves on the money question was to emphasize their opposition to the Democrats and their determination to reform the South.

The parties, still internally divided with a new presidential campaign looming, tried to agree on coherent positions. The ultimate decision would be made at each party's national convention, where a presidential candidate would be chosen and a platform drafted. In Chicago, Republicans managed to find a formula around which they could come together. In New York, by contrast, the Democrats became mired in contradiction. As a result, the money question vanished from the campaign.

The Republican national convention opened in Chicago on May 20, 1868. Finding a consensus on the money question was not easy, as the issue was being debated simultaneously in Congress, revealing many differences of opinion. These differences were also apparent in the contradictory instructions that delegates brought to Chicago. All of the Republican state conventions had formulated positions on the Ohio idea. Most stated the necessity of paying the debt in good faith, but the language was fairly vague. Although New York Republicans claimed to "regard any attempt at repudiating these contracts, or evading their payment, as dishonoring us in the eyes of mankind, and a crime against the national honor, only surpassed by the crime of treason itself," the Michigan convention simply noted that "the preservation of the public credit and the national faith are all dependent upon the triumph of the national Republican party at the coming presidential election." The federal structure of the party facilitated the expression of geographical differences. In each state, Republicans had to reconcile two imperatives: addressing local public opinion (as they saw it, at any rate[85]) while emphasizing their differences from the Democrats. In some cases, this attention to local conditions led them to take positions that widened the sectional rift within the party. In Ohio, where the Pendleton Plan was one of the reasons for the party's 1867 defeat, the convention did not hesitate to affirm that the "bonds should be paid in the currency of the country which may be a legal tender when the Government shall be prepared to redeem such bonds." A hard-money man like Garfield could hardly help thinking that such a statement was "ambiguous and cowardly."[86]

It was precisely this ambiguity, however, that allowed the party to remain unified and organized during the campaign. The process was facilitated by the unanimous choice of a candidate. The very popular Ulysses S. Grant became the "natural" choice of the Republicans, capable of uniting them all. The main business of the Chicago convention was thus to draft the party platform, a task essentially assigned to committees. Behind the scenes, hard-money men got the upper hand, and the platform ended up stating that Republicans "denounce all forms of repudiation as a national crime, and the national honor requires the payment of the public indebtedness in the utmost good faith to all creditors at home and abroad; not only according to the letter, but the spirit of the law under which it was contracted."[87]

The alternative on this issue faced two handicaps. First, the Republicans needed to set themselves apart from the Democrats. Second, to have proposed debt repayment in greenbacks would have left the Republicans needing to explain the countless oaths they had sworn, including in the Fourteenth Amendment, to pay back a loan that had made possible the salvation of the Union. Proponents of financial orthodoxy rejoiced: "What a heavy blow the Chicago Convention has dealt to the whole herd of Repudiators and Inflationists!" Being good politicians, however, the Republicans had kept room to maneuver. By avoiding all mention of specie and gold, they left an opening for those who believed that the spirit and letter of the 1862 law allowed the five-twenties to be repaid in greenbacks. As prominent a Republican leader as Thaddeus Stevens, for one, had no problem declaring that he "[held] to the Chicago platform" with such a position.[88] While the need to put distance between themselves and the Democrats gave monetary orthodoxy the advantage in the party platform, the differences were too deep to permit any clearer formulation of policy.

Ironically, the Democrats found themselves more divided than their adversaries, even though they came up with the Ohio idea to capitalize on Republican divisions. While Republicans managed to find common ground (or at least paper over their differences on the issue), Democrats barely achieved a weak compromise that would prove to be a handicap in the presidential campaign.

At the Democratic Convention held in New York in July 1868, George H. Pendleton started off as the favorite for the nomination. Clearly, the success of his plan in 1867 had earned him broad support among Midwestern Democrats. But it had also earned him the hostility of New York party leaders, including prominent financiers and bankers such as August Belmont. Although Pendleton enjoyed the support of a majority of the delegates, this determined opposition would prevent him from gathering the two-thirds of the votes he needed to win the nomination. With no other obvious candidate, it took twenty-two rounds of voting and numerous backroom dealings before a candidate was finally chosen. The winner was Horatio Seymour, a former governor of New York who long resisted the nomination. Once it became clear that Pendleton could not win, Seymour, who during the war had hewed to a narrow line between support for the Union and opposition to Lincoln, became the compromise candidate acceptable to both vehement opponents of Reconstruction and others who were prepared to move on.[89]

Pendleton's failure to win the Democratic nomination is instructive. Clearly, his strategy of confronting the money question head on had made him the favorite, giving him a leg up on his rivals and rallying the Midwest behind him. Nevertheless, convention rules allowed a fairly small group of delegates to block his nomination. A candidacy that was designed to capitalize on sectional divisions among Republicans ultimately created a similar sectional division among Democrats. Pendleton's defeat soon transformed what should have been an advantage for Democrats into a handicap. Although the Ohio idea was included in the platform, the party chose a hard-money candidate. Seymour thus found himself in an awkward position. Initially, in his letter of acceptance, he described the platform planks on the money question as being "in accordance with my wish, and I stand upon them in the contest into which we are now entering," but soon thereafter he disavowed them.[90] Democrats were thus deprived of a campaign issue on which they had been able to capitalize a year earlier. Worse still, the situation fostered resentment within the party. "Western Democrats are much disgusted by it," George T. Strong reported, "and think themselves out-manoeuvred and swindled by the Manhattan Club and by New Yorkers generally."[91] The influential *Cincinnati Enquirer* had to eat its hat and support the candidate. "We do not hesitate to pledge him [our] cordial support," the paper concluded, even though "he was not originally the choice of the West."[92]

Choosing Seymour meant to campaign on Reconstruction. Those who believed, with Clement L. Vallandigham, that they could win on "principles" were satisfied. Republicans could only be pleased: although they were divided on the money question, they were in a position of strength on the issue of Reconstruction. In both conventions, therefore, political infighting led to the avoidance of economic themes for the duration of the presidential campaign.[93] Fractured by sectional tensions, the parties were able to achieve unity only by focusing on Reconstruction, an issue on which the opposition between them was clear.

First Results of Reconstruction

The front page of *Harper's Weekly* for August 15, 1868, featured a full-page cartoon by Thomas Nast that succinctly summed up the Republican presidential campaign (see figure 6). The cartoon depicts a woman, representing the United States, putting South Carolina back into the fasces of states representing the Union. Only Virginia, Texas, and Mississippi remain, awaiting their turn under the aegis of Justice and Liberty on either side of the central figure, while above the scene floats a quotation from Lincoln concerning equal rights. The peace branch is ready, bearing the words that became the slogan of Ulysses S. Grant's campaign: "Let us have peace."[94]

FIGURE 6. "Reconstruction," Thomas Nast, *Harper's Weekly*,
August 15, 1868. (Special Collections, University of Virginia)

In 1866, Republicans had proposed a program of Reconstruction. Two years
later, they presented the results. Despite Andrew Johnson's obstructionism and
the failure to remove him from office, Congress had managed to get seven southern states to hold constitutional conventions elected by loyal white and black men,
leading to the adoption of constitutions including equal voting rights, the ratification of the Fourteenth Amendment, and the holding of elections. In the summer
of 1868, those seven states were readmitted to Congress over Johnson's veto. For
the first time since 1860, they would participate in a presidential election. In June,
moreover, the secretary of state announced that the Fourteenth Amendment had
been ratified.[95]

Republicans thus had a record on which to run and a candidate to run on it.
Grant was popular, being widely seen as the victor of the Civil War. As General of
the Army after the war (a rank created for him), he had managed to enforce acts of

Congress without entering into open conflict with Johnson, even if the break between the two men in January 1868 clearly placed Grant in the Republican camp.
A man of few words, few of his opinions were known enough to be criticized.
His letter accepting the Republican nomination ended with the felicitous phrase
"Let us have peace." Coming from the military man, these words reassured the
public as to his peaceful intentions; coming from the candidate, they emphasized
his desire for national reconciliation while at the same time suggesting that he
would make sure that peace was restored. Grant offered Americans a way to turn
the page after three years of Reconstruction, which many who did not look too
closely thought was ending in any case. Grant's phrasing was as vague as it was
firm, intended to reassure people about Grant the man rather than define any
specific policy. Two generals with positions on Reconstruction as different as
Philip Sheridan's and John Schofield's came to believe that Grant's election would
indeed bring about a definitive peace.[96]

By contrast, the Democratic choice for presidential and vice-presidential candidates proved much less inspired. Horatio Seymour had been chosen by a divided convention, accompanied by rumors of backroom wheeling and dealing.
Western Democrats were forced to support a candidate they did not want. Worst
of all, Seymour's wartime role made him vulnerable to attacks on his patriotism.
Republicans pointed out that as governor, he had opposed Lincoln. They loudly
denounced his actions during the draft riots in New York City in the summer of
1863, when he had reportedly addressed the crowd as "my friends" and acknowledged the justice of their angry rejection of conscription.[97]

Francis P. Blair, Jr., the party's vice-presidential candidate, might have been
expected to balance the ticket. The scion of a conservative but Unionist Missouri
family, he had served as a general in the Union Army. But he had become a
vehement opponent of Reconstruction, and this worked against the Democratic
ticket. In an incendiary letter, he called for "a President who will execute the will
of the people by trampling into dust the usurpations of Congress, known as the
Reconstruction Acts." He also seemed to argue that violent resistance to federal
policies was justified. He thus made easier the work of Republicans, who had a
field day proclaiming that "Seymour was opposed to the late war, and Blair is
in favor of the next one." Between Grant, who promised peace, and Blair, who
seemed ready once again to take up arms, even some Democrats favored Grant.
"As a Democrat who supported the war," Edwards Pierrepont stated publicly, "I
can not conceive how any intelligent man, who does not wish the rebels returned
to power, the nation's faith violated, its debt repudiated, its name dishonored, its

prosperity destroyed, its patriots insulted, and the 'lost cause' restored, can vote against Grant."[98]

By blocking the Pendleton nomination, sectional division in the Democratic Party deprived the party of a potentially important campaign issue. With the campaign limited to a debate about Reconstruction, the Democrats were vulnerable to attacks on their patriotism and their identification with the Confederates. Their choice of candidates only compounded this handicap. Unsurprisingly, they lost the election. This time, however, they drew the right lesson from their defeat. For the first time, those who wanted to move beyond Reconstruction would gain the upper hand and begin to change the party's strategy.

End Reconstruction? The Fifteenth Amendment

The Republicans won by a landslide: Grant carried twenty-five of thirty-three states, and the party held on to more than two-thirds of the seats in the House. The victory was not without worrisome signs for the future, however. Grant captured less than 53 percent of the popular vote. His majority was narrow in some states such as Indiana and California. In the congressional elections, Democrats came close to winning a majority in Ohio and Pennsylvania. And Republican control in the South was uncertain in the medium term. At least six of the eight readmitted states excluded former Confederates from voting—a temporary situation. The black vote was not a sure thing for Republicans: Democrats, it was reported, had successfully courted black votes in some districts. More troubling, many blacks had been kept away from the polls by a mixture of chicanery and violence. In Louisiana, Seymour won 70 percent of the computed vote in a state where nearly half the population was black. In short, many Republicans believed that the "future of the Republican party in the South is by no means secure," owing to "the disloyalty, the obstinacy and the blind folly of the Southern whites; the ignorance, inexperience and the changeableness of the negroes."[99]

As analyzed by Republican leaders, the situation called for two simultaneous responses: one was to shore up the party's electoral base, while the other was to remedy the sectional division that threatened party unity. In December 1868, they set to work forging the twofold compromise needed to secure the party's future.

"Victory is nothing unless you secure its fruits," opined the *Philadelphia Press.* To that end, the paper suggested "an amendment to the Constitution conferring the power to vote for national purposes and officers on colored men, under equal conditions with white men. . . . Where the colored men vote, there the cause of

Republicanism is entirely safe, and will be."[100] Such a change would protect the achievements of Reconstruction from a change of majority. The Republicans also hoped to forestall any such change by broadening their electoral base at a time when it was becoming dangerously fragile.

The idea was already afoot, particularly among Radicals. In 1867, Thaddeus Stevens had sought to "establish the doctrine of National jurisdiction . . . of the Franchise, or we shall finally be ruined—We must thus bridle Penna. Ohio Ind et cetera, or the South, *being in*, we shall drift into democracy." The moment for action seemed to have arrived. The results of the election, together with the readmission of the Southern states (which would no longer be governed by the Acts of Reconstruction Acts), pushed Republicans to amend the Constitution to grant blacks the right to vote, which they had refused to do two years earlier. This idea was made credible by the success of two referenda on the issue in Iowa and Minnesota in November 1868.[101]

Thus "party expediency and exact justice coincide for once," as William D. Kelley happily noted. Justice meant granting all blacks the right to vote, thus crowning the longstanding Radical insistence on equal civil rights for all. With the vote, it was assumed, blacks would be able to influence political decision-making and defend their own interests. Party expediency meant broadening the electoral base of the Republican Party. "You need votes in Connecticut, do you not?" Charles Sumner asked his colleagues. "There are three thousand fellow-citizens in that State ready at the call of Congress to take their place at the ballot-box. You need them also in Pennsylvania, do you not? There are at least fifteen thousand in that great State waiting for your summons. Wherever you most need them, there they are; and be assured they will all vote for those who stand by them in the assertion of Equal Rights." Indeed, blacks were excluded from voting only in certain Northern and border states, as they had been voting since 1867 in the former secessionist states. Their numbers were small but large enough to strengthen narrow Republican majorities in certain key states such as Connecticut and Ohio, and perhaps sufficient to allow the Republicans to take still other states from the Democrats, most notably New Jersey and New York. In the border states, where blacks made up from 15 to 30 percent of the electorate, they could put the Republican Party over the top in states that had never voted Republican before.[102]

This difficult agreement on the franchise for black men was new among Republicans, and testifies to the speed at which political opinions evolved in those years. Yet Republicans divided sharply on the means to that end. Should the suffrage issue be nationalized or left to the states? Should universal male suffrage be enacted, or should racial discrimination only be banned? Should the right to hold office be explicitly protected, or should the amendment only mention voting rights? While Republicans agreed on the necessity of an amendment, debate on the wording revived tensions between Radicals and Moderates. They were obliged to forge a compromise, however, since an amendment to the Constitution required a two-thirds majority in both houses of Congress and ratification by three-quarters of the states.

The Democrats, holding only a small minority of congressional seats but determined to block the amendment, took advantage of divisions among the Republicans. Local issues complicated the situation. In California, any move to grant Chinese immigrants the right to vote stood no chance of approval. In the Northeast, Republicans were attached to property qualifications and literacy tests that allowed them to prevent many people of Irish descent from voting.[103] The Republicans were also victims of their own sectional divisions: concurrent debates about appropriations and a money and banking bill created such tension that for a time the House and Senate were unable to cooperate.[104] Here was proof of the need to strike a lasting compromise on the issues of Reconstruction and currency.

The Republican leadership, having grasped the significance of the 1867 and 1868 elections, evinced determination to forge a compromise that would hold the party together. The constitutional amendment granting blacks the right to vote was the centerpiece of their strategy. The urgency of acting before the session ended, the need to draft a text that would be sufficiently moderate to have a chance of being approved and ratified, and the clever use of a conference committee[105] made it possible to draft an amendment that all Republicans found acceptable: "The right of citizens of the United States to vote shall not be denied or abridged by the United States or by any State on account of race, color, or previous condition of servitude. The Congress shall have the power to enforce this article by appropriate legislation."

The Fifteenth Amendment was the product of remarkable political pragmatism for a party with a wide variety of opinions on the issue. Choosing to end Reconstruction by way of a constitutional amendment, more difficult to achieve than merely passing a bill through Congress, made it possible to force a compromise, which might have seemed less necessary for an ordinary bill. The negative formulation of the amendment, which left it up to the states to set conditions on voting and said nothing explicit about eligibility for office, made it a restrained measure that left little for critics to attack, since the vast majority of black Americans had already voted in two elections. But the enforcement clause left the door open to further legislation. Radicals, despite their disappointment, recognized the importance of the amendment and decided, in the words of Indiana Senator Oliver P. Morton, to take "half a loaf when I cannot get a whole one."[106]

After weeks of stormy debate, the Republicans thus managed to forge what they hoped would be a lasting compromise. Although it did not establish universal suffrage, it did propose impartial suffrage. Although it did not guarantee that the achievements of Reconstruction could not be undone, it did increase the Republicans' electoral base in the hope of extending their control of the federal government, essential to ensure that the process would not be reversed. With Grant in the White House, eight of eleven secessionist states restored to the Union, and an amendment to the Constitution intended to guarantee blacks the right to vote, the Republicans hoped to bring Reconstruction to a successful close.

The Public Credit Act: A Sectional Compromise

The Republicans understood, however, that no compromise could last without a resolution of the money question, whose disruptive consequences had been demonstrated numerous times. The Chicago convention had hit on a temporary formula for the sake of maintaining party unity for the duration of the presidential campaign. The promise to repay the loan "not only according to the letter, but the spirit of the law" gave the advantage to those who preferred a speedy resumption of specie payments. Still, the terms remained vague, and the five-twenties were only a small part, made visible by Pendleton, of a much larger set of unresolved financial issues.[107]

Republican leaders sought to take advantage of the momentum created by their electoral victory to resolve the problem. But when a bill proposing a modest geographical redistribution of the capital allocated to the national banking system was introduced in Congress, the debate took a passionate sectional turn. The voting revealed an unprecedented level of Midwest-Northeast polarization. Tensions ran so high that a conference committee could not agree on a common wording: of the three House members on the committee, two were from the West, and of the three senators, two were from the Northeast. Indeed, this sectional representation provoked a quarrel between the two houses of Congresses that threatened to jeopardize the Fifteenth Amendment.[108]

This failure revealed the full extent of the sectional split in the party and underscored the urgency of the need for compromise. Republican leaders required no convincing, especially Senator John Sherman of Ohio. Chair of the Senate Finance Committee since 1867 and a recognized expert on financial issues, Sherman was also a shrewd politician. From the beginning he had taken a middle-of-the-road position on the five-twenties, arguing that the notion that the government could pay back the principal of the bonds in greenbacks was correct in law but counterproductive in practice. In short, the government could take this course but it would be a serious mistake to do so.

The political context in the winter of 1869 favored a compromise. On the one hand, Pendleton's formulation of the problem offered three advantages: it forced the Republicans to differentiate themselves from the Democrats; it linked the greenback question to the debt issue, on which the Republicans already had a position; and, last but not least, it focused attention on a narrow issue, the five-twenties. Resolving this specific issue was easier than finding a comprehensive solution to the money question. Furthermore, resolution of the five-twenty issue would mark a major step toward consolidation of the Republican Party, which was divided by conflict between the Northeast and Midwest on the money question and between Radicals and Moderates on Reconstruction.

The Republican compromise was facilitated by two presidential declarations. The first was a final provocation from Andrew Johnson, whose December 9, 1868, annual message was a remarkable turnabout in which he suggested that a partial repudiation of the debt would soon be necessary. Since the United States paid interest on its debt in gold, and greenbacks were worth less than the precious metal, the president argued that "the holders of our securities have already received upon their bonds a larger amount than their original investment. . . . It would seem but just and equitable that the six per cent interest now paid by the Government should be applied to the reduction of the principal." This provocation inevitably drew criticism, and it was formally censured by the House several days later.[109]

By contrast, in his inaugural address on March 4, 1869, Ulysses S. Grant unequivocally stated that "to protect the national honor every dollar of Government indebtedness should be paid in gold."[110] This clear statement allowed things to move forward. The Public Credit Act of 1869, the first bill signed into law by the new president, contained only a single article. Although the act is often described today as a victory for hard money, it was actually a compromise measure. On the one hand, the United States promised to pay its debt in gold dollars, ending the ambiguity of previous legislation. But the government pledged not to redeem the five-twenties before convertibility was restored, making the distinction between payment in greenbacks and payment in gold meaningless.[111] This was a narrow compromise, which did not settle the money question but held the Republican Party together.

Grant's inaugural address was a distillation of the Republican pact, based on granting blacks the constitutional right to vote and striking a sectional compro-

mise on the money question. The new president's speech began with a rebuke
to his predecessor: "All laws will be faithfully executed." The good relations between the executive branch and Congress were the token of a unified Reconstruction policy, which Grant promised to approach "calmly, without prejudice,
hate or sectional pride," while nevertheless guaranteeing the "security of person, property, and free religious and political opinion . . . without regard to local
prejudice."[112]

This careful, firm statement of the principles of Reconstruction was also presented as the basis for a settlement of financial questions, to which Grant re-
vealingly devoted the major part of his speech. He stated that the debt would be
repaid in full and in gold, and insisted on the need to restore the convertibility of
greenbacks. He expressed pleasure at the discovery of new deposits of precious
metal in the Rocky Mountains and hoped that this would lead to a resolution of
these issues. For him, the goal was "to protect the national honor," an objective
in which "All divisions—geographical, political, and religious—can join in this
common sentiment."[113]

The conclusion of Grant's first inaugural address deserves to be quoted at
length because it epitomizes the compromise the Republicans had just forged:

> How the public debt is to be paid, or specie payments resumed, is not so
> important as that a plan should be adopted, and acquiesced in. A united
> determination to do is worth more than divided counsils upon the method
> of doing. Legislation on this subject may not be necessary now, nor even
> advisable, but it will be when the civil law is more fully restored in all parts
> of the country, and trade resumes its wanted channels.
>
> The question of suffrage is one which is likely to agitate the public so long
> as a portion of the citizens of the nation are excluded from its privileges in
> any state. It seems to me very desirable that the question should be settled
> now, and I entertain the hope and express the desire that it may be by the
> ratification of the fifteenth article of amendment to the Constitution.[114]

Reconstruction, the debt, and the money question were now clearly intertwined. Closing the books on the war meant both restoring law and order in the
South and reimbursing the debt in gold. Restoring the convertibility of greenbacks also meant restoring national unity and pride while paving the way for
the economic development promised by the reintegration of the South and the
discovery of silver in the West. Grant's speech made the full restoration of civilian
rule in the South a precondition for resolution of the financial issues bequeathed
by the war. That was why the question of suffrage had to be resolved once and

for all. The Fifteenth Amendment was thus the cornerstone of the Republican compromise: its ratification, intended to give the former slaves the institutional means to defend their liberty and property, was the final pillar of Reconstruction.

IN THE FIRST FEW YEARS after the end of the Civil War, Reconstruction was at the heart of political debate. From the beginning, it set the new president, Andrew Johnson, against Republicans in Congress. But another political dynamic emerged around the money question. In the wake of the 1866 tariff debates, it stirred up sectional feeling between the Midwest and Northeast.

At first, Reconstruction and the money question were fairly distinct issues. This changed, however, when Midwestern Democrats seized on the money question as a campaign issue. From that point on, the money question (aligned with sectionalism) and Reconstruction (organized around party conflict) were increasingly linked. One issue pitted the parties against each other, while the other divided both.

In this context, the Fifteenth Amendment, adopted in early 1869, marked not just the culmination of Republican Reconstruction policy following Ulysses S. Grant's election as president. It was also the centerpiece of a compromise whose other pillar was the Public Credit Act. Although the Republicans won in 1868, they recognized the fragility of their political coalition. The purpose of the constitutional amendment was to strengthen their majority while unifying the party around a single objective. The Public Credit Act, for its part, was meant to put an end to the sectional disputes that jeopardized party unity.

When sectional divisions on economic issues threatened to split the party, Republicans experimented with a strategy of recentering their approach around basic ideological principles. They would remember this lesson when the compromise of 1869 proved insufficient in the months that followed Grant's accession to the presidency.

5

For the Good of the Country and the Party

———— • ————

Terrific battle of the Bulls and Bears in the Gold Room Friday. A Bedlam, it's said. Gold actually fluctuated during two or three hours of the wildest frenzy between 135 and 170. At last the Secretary of the Treasury appeared with heavy artillery ($4,000,000) on the flank of the Bulls, and the Ring broke and collapsed and ran (as we did at Bull Run). Gold closed at about 135. We do not yet know the killed and wounded, because the combatants were *too much prostrated* yesterday to write up their accounts, and there was an armistice by mutual consent.
—George Templeton Strong, diary entry, September 26, 1869

ON SEPTEMBER 24, 1869, a small group of speculators on the New York Stock Exchange, led by Jay Gould and James Fisk, dropped on the gold market a net they had patiently woven over several weeks. Using a variety of subterfuges, they had managed surreptitiously to take control of a large quantity of gold certificates, thereby causing the price of the precious metal to rise. That Friday, the battle for control of the gold market turned to panic. The speculative maneuver was thwarted only when the Treasury that afternoon injected a large quantity of specie.[1]

The "Gold Corner" made the front page of every newspaper in the country and abruptly put the money question back in the spotlight. The episode was possible only because two legal currencies coexisted, neither convertible into the other and both necessary—gold for international commerce and paying customs duties and greenbacks for local and national transactions. The panic underscored the danger due to the shortage of money in the Midwest, which induced financial stress at harvest time (see chapter 2). The episode—notorious, complex, and morally suspect—lent credence to two contradictory opinions. For some, "the panic in New York, though disastrous to a few, will do good," because "it will prove the absolute necessity of getting upon a specie basis," and thus enforce

a return to convertibility.[2] For others, however, especially in the Midwest, the
episode proved that money was too scarce: had there been enough of it, the speculators could not have cornered the market.

The Gold Corner destroyed the fragile compromise enshrined in the Public
Credit Act. Sectional conflict intensified in the months that followed. Congress
could no longer avoid economic issues. Worse, the upcoming census transformed
those economic issues into a raw struggle for power that threatened the cohesiveness
—and some feared the very existence—of the Republican Party. To counter this
danger, party leaders decided to build on the strategy they had embarked on early
in 1869, when they coupled the Fifteenth Amendment with the Public Credit Act.
They would use Reconstruction to maintain party unity and impose a sectional
compromise on the tariff and the money question. A single policy thus embodied
two distinct but convergent goals: the good of the country and the future of the
party. As effective as this strategy proved to be, however, it would ultimately work
against the party, when Liberal Republicans bolted from it in 1872.[3]

The Exacerbation of Sectional Tensions

"There are two very strong forces at work, antagonistic to each other, in regard
to our financial policy," observed James A. Garfield, the new chair of the House
Banking and Currency Committee, in December 1869. The effects of the Gold
Corner made themselves felt: "The same cry comes in from the West for more
currency."[4] The spring compromise was already teetering. The Public Credit Act
had resolved only the narrow issue of whether five-twenties could be redeemed
in greenbacks. But Republicans had also agreed on another measure to relieve
the Midwest (and South) of its money shortage. The bill was modest and ingenious. It did not touch the greenbacks but redistributed a small amount of the
national banking capital among the states. It should therefore have satisfied all
Republicans: Midwesterners would have obtained needed circulation, while the
financially orthodox would have been pleased that not a single dollar would be
added to the money supply. But the bill succumbed to sectional opposition from
the Northeast, which Garfield derided as "the short-sighted selfishness of the Puritan Members . . . [even though it] would have been a concession in the interest
of manifest justice."[5] Thus this pragmatic compromise failed.

This failure might have been little more than a temporary setback, a hitch
in the patient elaboration of a solution acceptable to all Republicans. In fact,
however, the missed opportunity transformed the money question into a test of
strength between sections. Principles fell away, and all that remained was naked

defense of economic interests. The reason for this was that a new census was in the offing, and with it a reapportionment of the House of Representatives. By failing to strike a durable compromise on the money question, the Republicans ensured that the impending shift in representation due to the census would bring sectional economic differences to the fore. Relations between Midwesterners and Northeasterners became so tense that they endangered the future of the Republican Party.

The Census and the Geography of Power

The constitutional requirement to conduct a census every ten years means that the representation of each state in the House, which must be proportional to its population, is adjusted at the same interval. Ever since the inception of the United States, the decennial headcount has had the effect of altering the nation's political geography.[6] Each census changes the balance of power among the states. But "balance of power" is an abstract concept, which in each instance has to be translated according to the issues of the day. In 1870, the money and tariff questions, which were already geographical in nature, implied that the reapportionment would inevitably have economic significance. The process, therefore, exacerbated sectional tensions between the Midwest and Northeast to the point of threatening the unity of both parties, but especially Republicans.

In December 1869, Norman B. Judd of Chicago introduced a bill proposing that the results of the census be immediately applied to the 1870 midterm elections. It was a departure from previous censuses in which the process had taken two years. Counting the population, compiling the results, discussing and passing a reapportionment bill, and redrawing election districts were all operations that took time. Although Judd's bill might seem to have been a purely technical measure, its import was far from insignificant. For Judd, waiting until 1872 was out of the question: "Two years at the present time, with the questions now pending and to be acted upon during that time, may fix the fate . . . of many communities." The stakes were explicitly economic, including "tariffs and internal taxation, banking, and the regulation of the currency and its proper distribution, the mode and terms for arranging and settling our great indebtedness." And all of these were sectional issues, whose resolution would inevitably depend on how representation was reapportioned between the Midwest and Northeast. Hence "the West, whose business interests are as great as those of any other portion of the Union . . . demands that this apportionment should be made at the earliest day possible."[7]

In this context, Judd analyzed the census in terms not of states (the only

geographical entities recognized by the Constitution) but of sections. This was
an indication of how much the importance of sectionalism in the North had increased since 1866. It was also a direct response to the failure in the spring of "a
redistribution of the banking capital, which all acknowledge is unjust and unequal, and that has been refused us." A fair compromise might have satisfied
Midwestern Republicans, at least initially. In its absence, they were now convinced that their Northeastern colleagues would not cede an inch, and that their
best hope was to take advantage of their region's demographic growth.

It was obvious to everyone that the center of gravity of the American population was shifting westward. Judd was the only representative from Chicago, a
city with "a larger population than the entire State of Vermont, which has three
Representatives upon this floor."[8] The election results showed that many Midwestern congressional districts had far more voters in them than the districts of
New England. All signs pointed to what the Ninth Census would confirm: the
extraordinary growth of the West (+43%) compared with the smaller though
still substantial growth of the Northeast (+16%). Leaving aside the states of the
Pacific Coast, the Midwest by itself had a larger population than the group of
states stretching from Pennsylvania to Maine. The conclusion was inevitable:
"The political power of this Union is surely settling and centralizing in the West,"
Maine Republican Eugene Hale acknowledged, "and we in the East may as well
admit it." George W. McCrary of Iowa put it more bluntly: "The West will gain
and the East will lose power in this House."[9]

It was not inevitable, however, that the consequences of the census would be
interpreted in sectional terms. After all, American politics was organized primarily around the two major parties. Republicans might have found it advantageous
to accelerate the reapportionment of House seats, since demographic growth
was concentrated in states that were Republican bastions (see table 5). Several
congressmen pointed out that "the Northwest will roll up large Republican majorities."[10] Democrats knew this and therefore opposed speeding up reapportionment. Once again we see the great importance of "technical" details: states
would not have time to redraw districts before holding elections in 1870, making
it necessary to elect all their additional representatives as "at-large" statewide
candidates. Under single-round, majority voting rules, that would mean that the
party that eked out even a small majority of the vote would take all the new seats.
It is then hardly surprising that Midwestern Democrats, though not unmoved
by Judd's sectional argument, preferred "to forgo their numerical rights in Congress" for the next two years "rather than Jacobinism should any longer wield that
power."[11]

TABLE 5. Population growth by state, 1860–1870

Section	State	Population, 1860	Population, 1870	Population growth (%)	Republican majority in 1868 election (% of vote)
Northeast	Connecticut	460,147	537,454	14	3.0
	Maine	628,279	626,915	0	24.8
	Massachusetts	1,231,066	1,457,351	16	39.5
	New Hampshire	326,073	318,300	-2	10.5
	New Jersey	672,035	906,096	26	-1.8
	New York	3,880,735	4,382,759	11	-1.2
	Pennsylvania	2,906,215	3,521,951	17	4.4
	Rhode Island	174,620	217,353	20	33.0
	Vermont	315,098	330,551	5	57.1
West	California	379,994	560,247	32	0.5
	Illinois	1,711,951	2,539,891	33	11.4
	Indiana	1,350,428	1,680,637	20	2.8
	Iowa	674,913	1,194,020	43	23.8
	Kansas*	107,206	364,399	71	37.7
	Michigan	749,113	1,184,059	37	14.0
	Minnesota	172,023	439,706	61	21.8
	Missouri	1,182,012	1,721,295	31	13.9
	Nebraska*	28,841	122,993	77	27.8
	Nevada*	6,857	42,491	84	10.8
	Ohio	2,339,511	2,665,260	12	8.0
	Oregon	52,465	90,923	42	-0.7
	Wisconsin	775,881	1,054,670	26	12.5
South	Alabama	964,201	996,992	3	2.5
	Arkansas	435,450	484,471	10	7.4
	Delaware	112,216	125,015	10	-18.0
	Florida	140,424	187,748	25	—‡
	Georgia	1,057,286	1,184,109	11	-28.5
	Kentucky	1,155,684	1,321,011	13	-49.1
	Louisiana	708,002	726,915	3	-41.4
	Maryland	687,049	780,894	12	-34.4
	Mississippi	791,305	827,922	4	—‡
	North Carolina	992,622	1,071,361	7	6.8
	South Carolina	703,708	705,606	0	15.9
	Tennessee	1,109,801	1,258,520	12	36.9
	Texas	604,215	818,579	26	—‡
	Virginia	1,596,318	1,225,163	4	—‡
	West Virginia†	n/a	442,014	n/a	17.7

* Federal territory in 1860.

† West Virginia separated from Virginia in 1863; the figure for population growth is for the total Virginia + West Virginia.

‡ No federal election held in these states in 1868.

Having been in the minority for years, Democrats united to defend the interests of their party. By contrast, Republicans, who enjoyed a substantial majority and who had been in power for nearly ten years, divided along sectional lines. Northeastern Republicans found themselves on the defensive. They worried about the balance of power within their own states: urbanization had increased and with it the likely influence of Democrats, who were stronger in the cities than in the countryside. Many also believed that the next local elections would put them in a better position to control the delicate process of electoral redistricting.[12] But their primary motive was economic and set them at odds with the Midwest. The tariff was a recurrent theme in debates about the census. John A. Logan, a senator from Illinois, was not wrong to say that "if all these States would only send men here who would vote taxes upon our people for the benefit of the iron-mongers of Pennsylvania, you would vote to let them come."[13]

This bias was evident in the debates. The weakness of the arguments used shows clearly that the issue was not the constitutionality of the measure or the practical obstacles to its application. Judd's avowed goal in introducing his bill was to shift the balance of power between the sections before decisions were made on pending economic issues. The resistance of Northeastern Republicans stemmed from similar concerns. And it succeeded thanks to an objective alliance with Democrats — some denounced a "strange combination" for depriving "the West [of] its just representation." By exacerbating sectional tensions, these debates threatened the unity of the Republican Party. Republican papers in the Midwest were quick to attack the "twelve apostates," Midwestern representatives who "voted to defeat the apportionment bill," that is, "to deprive the Northwest of one-quarter of its rightful representation and voice in the next Congress." They did not hesitate to hint at corruption, denouncing "the invisible but potent influence" of the "Bessemer-steelers," an "infamous ring" of steel manufacturers determined to defend "their plunder."[14] This wrenching division within the Republican Party was all the more dangerous because it threatened the party's ideological ballast: Reconstruction.

The three constitutional amendments ratified after the war all affected the way in which the nation was represented. The Thirteenth, by abolishing slavery, nullified the infamous "three-fifths clause," which included three of every five slaves in the calculation of each state's representation. Henceforth, all blacks were free, but since the composition of the House reflected the census of 1860, "more than a million and a half of people . . . are excluded," McCrary noted. "We have no right to postpone at our pleasure . . . the legislation by which this provision of the Constitution is to be enforced."[15] This invocation of one of the key issues of

Reconstruction was more important than it might seem at first glance. Granting blacks citizenship and the right to vote had become central Republican policies as Reconstruction evolved. At the time, the Fifteenth Amendment was still working its way toward ratification (which was achieved in February 1870). The census issue and its impact on the House thus meant that the political consequences of the constitutional changes sought by Republicans could no longer be avoided. Suddenly, Northern economic sectionalism intersected with Reconstruction not in electoral or partisan terms but in a substantive way.

The debate around the application of the Fourteenth Amendment is enlightening in this regard. Section Two, which reduced the representation of each state in proportion to the number of adult males deprived of the vote, was a real puzzler. Its original purpose was to force the South to grant blacks the right to vote or suffer a reduction of influence in Washington. But the Reconstruction Acts and the Fifteenth Amendment settled that question. Ironically, in 1870, only the New England states restricted the right to vote by way of literacy tests—a device aimed primarily at immigrants.[16] Democrats were not displeased to see the Fourteenth Amendment turned against its authors. "You made this constitutional amendment," Samuel S. Cox exclaimed with glee, "to hold it *in terrorem* over the southern States. . . . You did not know that it would apply to Ohio or Massachusetts. Oh, no!" In other words, it was the Northeast that had the most to lose if Section Two of the Fourteenth Amendment were enforced—which explains why it never was.[17] This clause of the Constitution became a dead letter and has to this day never been applied. By the end of the century, the South was thus able to deprive most blacks of the right to vote with total impunity. In short, the sectional interpretation of the census undermined one of the achievements of Reconstruction, though no one yet realized just how much.[18]

The 1870 census raised a number of specific issues. The reapportionment of the House might have been a symbol of the success of Reconstruction, translating the consequences of the war and of subsequent constitutional reforms into a new political equilibrium. But by bringing Northern sectional opposition into the equation, Republicans transformed its political significance. The census became an instrument for altering the balance of power between Midwest and Northeast. For more than two years, until the new apportionment was enacted in May 1872, the issue would continue to fuel sectional rivalry.[19]

The New Sectional Balance

With the readmission of Virginia, Georgia, Mississippi, and Texas in early 1870, all the states of the Union were represented in Congress for the first time since

TABLE 6. Partisan and sectional makeup of the House of Representatives

Congress	39th (1865–67)	40th (1867–69)	41st (1869–71)	42nd (1871–73)	43rd (1873–75)	44th (1875–77)
Total representatives	193	192	219	243	292	292
Representatives from each section (%)						
Northeast	87 (45)	87 (45)	87 (40)	87 (36)	95 (33)	95(33)
West	80 (41)	80 (42)	80 (37)	80 (33)	104 (36)	104 (36)
South	26 (13)	25 (13)	52 (24)	76 (31)	93 (32)	93 (32)
Representatives from each party (%)						
Republican	154 (80)	147 (77)	157 (72)	141 (58)	203 (70)	107 (37)
Democrat	39 (20)	45 (23)	62 (28)	102 (42)	89 (30)	185 (63)
Representatives from each party within each section (%)						
Northeast						
Republican	66 (76)	66 (76)	65 (75)	54 (62)	78 (82)	46 (48)
Democrat	21 (24)	21 (24)	22 (25)	33 (38)	17 (18)	49 (52)
West						
Republican	71 (89)	68 (85)	59 (74)	55 (69)	77 (74)	45 (43)
Democrat	9 (11)	12 (15)	21 (26)	25 (31)	27 (26)	59 (57)
South						
Republican	17 (65)	13 (52)	33 (63)	32 (42)	48 (52)	16 (17)
Democrat	9 (35)	12 (48)	19 (37)	44 (58)	45 (48)	77 (83)

Note: This table shows the number of representatives at the start of each Congress. Southern states that were readmitted during a session are thus not included until the next Congress. Party affiliation is shown as of the day of election. The table does not show occasional party changes between elections. Percentages are rounded and thus do not always add up to one hundred.

Source: Martis et al., *The Historical Atlas of Political Parties.*

the Civil War.[20] The return of these states to the fold radically altered the political balance. First, it became impossible to pass bills aimed specifically at secessionist states, because the Constitution required Congress to legislate for the entire country uniformly. Any further laws had to be placed on a new legal footing, and Southern lawmakers had to be included in the deliberations. Furthermore, the addition of new representatives and senators to the mix altered the balance of power. In the short run, the impact on the parties was minimal: the South sent a large Republican delegation to Congress in 1868 (see table 6), and the party was thus able to preserve its two-thirds majority. In sectional terms, however, the change was significant: the House was henceforth divided into three more or less equal factions—Northeast, West, and South. The new institutional equilibrium—based on an altered role for the federal government and a new sectional balance in Congress—meant that the fate of Reconstruction would be tied to economic issues in unprecedented ways.

Partisan and sectional considerations converged to create this new context. At the national level, the return of the South as a sectional force in Congress created a three-way game out of the Midwest-Northeast faceoff. On the tariff issue, the antebellum South had been strongly identified with the free-trade position. This continued to be the case after the South began to elect Republicans, despite the variation of local interests. For example, sugar and rice growers were more protectionist than cotton growers. Virginia and Alabama were iron producers, and Southern iron manufacturers, like their counterparts in the North, demanded high tariffs. As in the other sections, however, and as a result of similar mechanisms (see chapter 3), this local diversity was subsumed in a broad sectional position, and overall, the South continued to be seen as pro–free trade. Congressional voting confirms this. "The pet idea of all Southern statesmen, the main political principle upon which the Southern people of all political shades have ever been a unit . . . is that of unrestricted trade," as one New Orleans newspaper summed things up. This continuity between the ante- and postbellum South made a rapprochement with the Midwest difficult, because some Republicans viewed the free-trade position as being of a piece with slavery: "The suspicion of free trade sounded to the ears as terrible a charge as that of having worn a rebel uniform or having been out with the Ku-klux clan."[21]

This was not the case with the money question, however, which had emerged too recently to carry so much baggage from the past. Like the Midwest, the South faced real economic difficulties for which soft money was seen as a remedy. The region badly needed banking capital. Most Southern banks had gone under during the war, and the national banks created by the Union during the conflict existed only in the North. Like the Midwest, the South regularly suffered from a shortage of money at harvest time. The need was so acute that even conservative Democrats, traditionally attached to specie and hostile to banks, nevertheless made expanding the money supply a top priority. In principle they favored a return to convertibility, but that meant contraction, and meanwhile the need for more greenbacks was urgent. They were also wary of the national banking system, which was alien to the Jacksonian ideology they had inherited. These views did not prevent them from fighting in Congress for a geographical redistribution of national banking capital aimed at bringing more banknotes into the South. On this issue, all Southern representatives, be they Republican or Democrat, agreed.[22]

This sectionalization of the South's monetary position made a rapprochement with the Midwest possible. It came about slowly, however, as party logic and memories of the war stood in the way. On the Democratic side, the shared economic interests of the two "agrarian" sections were mobilized initially as an argument against Reconstruction.[23] For symmetrical reasons, Republicans refused to identify with "rebels." In 1866, the *Chicago Tribune* issued this blast against New England: "Had the Representatives of the rebel States never proved traitors; had not the people of these States withdrawn their members of Congress, and had they remained faithfully in allegiance to the Union, the peculiar high tariff notions of New England could have been checked and restrained. . . . We will have no policies but National policies, no interests but National interests."[24] This initial reflex gradually succumbed to the growing sectionalization of economic issues, however (see chapter 4), so that by the end of the decade, the common interests of both regions were frequently mentioned. One voice denounced the proposed scheme of debt funding as "a gross injustice to the South and West." Another declared that unequal representation in the House was "a just cause of complaint on the part of the people of the West and South." Tensions associated with the reapportionment of the House linked the legacy of Reconstruction to sectional conflict in the North and encouraged this rhetorical rapprochement.[25]

Paradoxically, the success of Reconstruction legitimized a geographical alliance, because the South was now represented by Republicans who could hardly be suspected of disloyalty. Furthermore, the fact that politicians in both the Northeast and Midwest continued to defend the interests of their respective sections justified Southerners in doing the same. In this respect, secession did not delegitimize all expression of sectional interests, because sectionalism in the North coexisted with pro-Union nationalism. At the local level, moreover, Republicans throughout the South made the defense of economic interests the keystone of their political program. The party bet its future on its economic development policy, the only policy capable of consolidating an electoral base of blacks and whites in the face of the Democrats' racial rhetoric.

State by state, Southern Republicans preached a local version of the "gospel of prosperity" that their Northern colleagues had formulated during the war. With the abolition of slavery, the Southern economy would be able to rebuild on the sound foundation of free labor and thus achieve a prosperity as impressive as that of the North. With quasi-religious fervor, Republicans proclaimed progress toward "a higher order of growth, development, and civilization."[26] The Southern states committed themselves to a program of public investment and assistance, including elimination of taxes, homestead exemptions, and so on. Railroad construction was at the heart of this program. Following the lead of local "boost-ers" in the West, Southern towns fought to obtain railroads, which promised to spur the local economy. In order to attract investors (from the North and Europe), local governments offered to guarantee bonds issued by private companies.[27]

Within a few years, these debts would plunge some states into bankruptcy after the stock market crash of 1873. In the meantime, however, Republican strategy in the South hitched its wagon to a national investment policy that yielded some gen-uinely impressive results, such as the completion of the transcontinental railway in 1869.[28] This drew the support of white Southerners (especially former Whigs) on policies unrelated to race, on the grounds that Republicans were in a better position to obtain federal subsidies and attract Northern investors. Southern con-gressmen (like their colleagues) defended the economic interests of their section, seeking federal subsidies for railway construction and waterway improvements along with increased circulation and loans to finance economic development. On these issues Democrats and Republicans took the same approach. Economic de-velopment offered a way out of direct confrontation over racial issues, although the South had too little influence in Congress to obtain many concessions.[29]

The Southern Republican focus on economic issues yielded paradoxical re-sults. Although it achieved some success in the South, it remained vulnerable to the unshakable determination of many Southern whites to restore white su-premacy. At the national level, however, it fueled sectional tension on economic issues and weakened both major parties. Thus, the return of Southern states to the Union, portrayed in the 1868 campaign as an indicator of Reconstruction's success, indirectly threatened the Republicans' postwar legacy.

On the Fragility of the Parties

By 1870 the feeling was widespread that the parties were increasingly obsolete. "New parties and new divisions in which I shall take no prominent part are in plain view ahead," Ohio governor Rutherford B. Hayes prophesied.[30] Senator Lyman Trumbull of Illinois observed that "the war pressure is off, and there is now no great principle to hold [the Republican Party] together," while one of his constituents reported that "the democrats about here consider their party *politi-cally dead.*" James A. Garfield believed that "we are rapidly reaching that period when the two great political parties must dissolve their present organization; must die from exactly opposite causes. The Democratic Party, because every substan-tial idea it has advanced for the last twelve years is now utterly and hopelessly dead. The Republican Party, because every substantial idea it has advanced has been completed, realized. The fate of one is likely to end by failure, the other by having finished its work."[31]

Some applauded the prospect; others feared it. But it is striking to see how widespread the feeling of party fragility was. In part this reflected the notion that Reconstruction was over. The Republican Party was born in the 1850s out of opposition to slavery and defense of "free labor" as the basis of American society.[32] It was the Republican Party that waged war on behalf of the Union and promoted Reconstruction. Now that the Southern states were fully reintegrated into the nation's political institutions and three constitutional amendments had made equal rights the centerpiece of the system, many people became convinced that their work to complete the American Revolution had come to an end. Celebrating the ratification of the Fifteenth Amendment, the *New York Times* could applaud "the final crowning of the edifice of American republicanism."[33]

Similarly, many saw the Democratic Party as a relic of the past. The victory of the Union also marked the defeat of a party torn by the war between its Southern and Northern wings, as well as torn in the North between those who opposed the war and those who supported it. The systematic reverses suffered by the party in national elections since the end of the war, its support of Andrew Johnson, the electoral stigma of its identification with anti-patriotism—all of these were reasons for pessimism about its future. The Pendleton Plan showed that the party was aware of this handicap. The plan's failure bolstered the notion that the Democrats had no future.

This sense of party obsolescence was reinforced by the failure of the parties to come to terms with the economic issues of the day: the money question and the tariff. On these issues they divided along sectional lines. Some people felt that economic issues would dominate in the future and that the parties should therefore be reorganized around them. The *Chicago Republican* explained that "free-traders and protectionists are like oil and water, they cannot be forced to mix, they will and must separate."[34] Such a sweeping transformation of the political landscape was not out of the question. The Whig Party had collapsed and the Republican Party had been born only twenty years earlier, within the living memory of all voters.[35] Furthermore, the reapportionment debate had shown how destructive to the parties white-hot sectional tensions might become. As early as 1867, a few politicians had demonstrated that they were ready to grant the money question priority over Reconstruction. For the many who wanted to save their parties, the situation was alarming. Resolving economic problems was no longer merely the duty of an elected representative; it was also an urgent partisan need.

Rebuilding Party Unity

As one Ohio judge put it, "the Republican Party is too valuable an organization to crumble because no longer held together by the bonds that created it."[36] John Sherman agreed, and joined with other Republican leaders to save his party from collapse. By early 1869 they had settled on a two-pronged strategy: on the one hand, they sought a compromise on economic issues, especially the money question, while on the other hand, they tried to unite the party around Reconstruction, the only issue that was an effective tool for both ideological mobilization and differentiation of Republican and Democratic positions.

Thus it was to save their party that Republicans brought together issues that stemmed from the war but had previously been treated separately. It was not clear, however, how the achievements of Reconstruction could be preserved and economic problems resolved at the same time. Although Reconstruction held Republicans together, despite sometimes sharp disagreements, it was difficult to pass any new measures now that the Southern states were once again represented in Congress. On the economic front, financial exigencies made it imperative to make decisions that threatened to exacerbate intraparty divisions. This conundrum is the key to understanding the course of federal policy toward the South. On the one hand, Reconstruction enabled Republicans to remain united and strike a real if fragile compromise on economic policy. On the other, sectional tensions pushed them to forge ahead with Reconstruction, the party's sole *raison d'être*, and prevented them from washing their hands of worrisome developments in the South on the grounds that "normal" federal relations had been restored.

In such a process, it is pointless for the historian to try to parse out the degree to which Republicans were sincere as opposed to cynical or motivated by "pure" intentions as opposed to "self-interested" ones.[37] Such value judgments, which led in the 1930s to seeing Reconstruction as a way of dividing the agrarian majority in order to impose industrial capitalism on the country,[38] or more recently, to seeing politics as having taken an "organizational" turn in 1870, with party leaders suddenly more interested in perpetuating their power than in great causes,[39] obscure the mechanisms that made the years 1870–72 a turning point in the history of Reconstruction. This was a time when the money question was prominent in public debate and violence and fraud in the South could not be ignored. Finding a response to both problems was essential for the survival and legacy of the Republican Party. This is the best way to understand the course chosen for the continuation of Reconstruction.

A Pragmatic Compromise

The congressional session that began in December 1869 was remarkable in many respects. Within the space of eight months, Republicans managed to forge a genuine if imperfect compromise on the economic issues of the day while at the same time charting a political and institutional course for the continuation of Reconstruction. It was a political tour de force. In the longer term, this compromise set the Republican Party on a course of economic conservatism and withdrawal from the South, but this should not be allowed to hide the far more radical potential implicit in the party's choices.

The economic aspect of the Republican compromise was essentially the work of two men. The first was George S. Boutwell, who was appointed secretary of the treasury in March 1869. Hailing from Massachusetts, he was one of the founders of the Republican Party and the first commissioner of internal revenue, an office created during the war to collect the new taxes (except customs duties).[40] A Radical, he led the fight to impeach Andrew Johnson and actively participated in drafting the three Reconstruction amendments. Although hesitant to accept the Treasury post, he took up his duties determined to reduce the federal debt. He used the substantial revenue generated by taxes and customs duties to buy back Treasury bonds.[41] "Two months of the new Administration and the public debt reduced six million dollars!" one newspaper exclaimed.[42] Although his interventionism alarmed some financiers, it successfully broke the Gold Corner in September 1869.[43]

In Congress, the key man on financial issues was John Sherman. A Moderate on Reconstruction, Sherman, as the Republican chair of the Senate Finance Committee, was "a politician with 'conservative' financial views, rather than . . . a financial 'conservative' in politics; the politics had to come first, and govern his tactics."[44] It was Sherman, along with Robert C. Schenck in the House, who guided the Public Credit Act through Congress in March 1869. Sherman then worked to find a compromise on the money question that could hold the sectionally divided Republican Party together without losing sight of the resumption of specie payments. He steered a middle-of-the-road course: neither inflation nor contraction.

Pressure increased when the new Congress convened in December 1869. The Midwestern offensive on reapportionment threatened the unity of the Republican side. The Gold Corner three months earlier had made resolution of the money question seem more urgent. And something had to be done about the exorbitant cost of the public debt, a substantial part of which was due soon. Reconstruction was left to President Grant, while Congress seemed totally preoccupied with

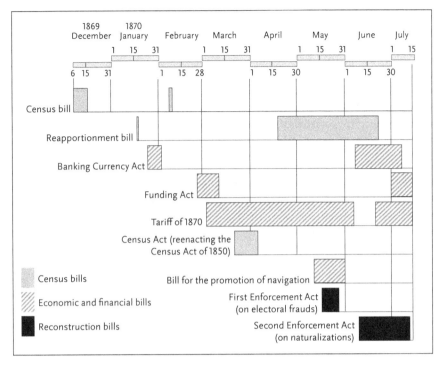

FIGURE 7. Chronology of major congressional debates, 1869–70

economic issues (see figure 7). Given the tensions that divided his party, Sherman's tactic was to split his proposed legislation into several distinct pieces "so as to confine this debate, if possible," to one thing at a time. "There are a great multitude of financial questions now agitating the public mind that are somewhat kindred, connected with these two. The enlargement of the discussion by introducing them would, I think, rather obscure the argument than make it plain."[45] He introduced two bills in succession: the first, resurrecting the proposal defeated the previous session, effected a geographic redistribution of national banking capital; the second set forth a plan for funding the debt and reducing interest. He thus hoped to satisfy Midwestern representatives, who were demanding increased access to monetary instruments, but without increasing the circulation of greenbacks, thereby reassuring the Northeast. The second bill would decrease the Treasury's payments in gold (as interest on its bonds), thereby increasing its gold reserves in anticipation of a return to convertibility.

Sherman's call for a pragmatic approach went largely unheeded, however. His colleagues stuck to principled positions that had hardened over five years of controversy. The sectional confrontation was harsher than ever, especially because the issue was now being debated all across the country. Senator Timothy O. Howe of Wisconsin complained that "a popular lecturer has recently assured the South and West that they need no more circulation. But, sir, it takes a very ingenious physician to persuade a man who is fainting from exhaustion that there is nothing the matter with him." The presence of Southerners in Congress strengthened the position of the Midwest. Frederick A. Sawyer, a Republican from South Carolina, castigated his colleagues from the Northeast for defending their section's virtual monopoly on national banks, a business that had "proved one of the most profitable" in the country and thus placed "the rest of the country in a condition where every single transaction which occurs must pay tribute to the monetary power centered there."[46] The voting on the bill to reallocate national banking capital reflected a particularly acute sectional polarization, which divided both parties.[47] The different political complexions of the Senate and House—the former more conservative than the latter—made compromise difficult. It took two conference committees to achieve a very modest result. The Northeast made only minor concessions: some $25 million in national banking capital was reallocated to the Midwest and South (out of a total of $318 million), and a new issue of $54 million was approved.[48] Norman B. Judd, the Chicago representative who initiated the fight over reapportionment in the House, judged "half a loaf [better] than no bread" and was happy "that Congress shall declare now, without further agitation, that they will proceed in the direction of justice and equity."[49]

The same logic governed the adoption of the second measure, which dealt with funding the debt. Seventy-five percent of it consisted of five-twenties on which the government paid six percent annual interest. Since these bonds could be called after five years, the idea was to exchange them for new Treasury bonds paying a lower rate of interest, which would reduce the amount the government had to pay out in gold. Boutwell and Sherman proposed to authorize the issue of bonds of 10, 15, and 30 years yielding, respectively, 5, 4.5, and 4 percent. Although this move seemed advantageous to the government, it touched the hard-earned compromise on Public Credit Act. Benjamin F. Butler rose to denounce the attempt in the House: "Against the people you promised, a year ago last March, to pay these five-twenty bonds in coin, when the contract did not call for coin. But you said you would not pay them in coin until you could also pay the people's currency, the greenbacks, in coin." The Public Credit Act had confirmed the link between the public debt and paper money. The proposal to amend it instantly revived sectional tensions. "I say here, in behalf of my constituents, in behalf of the Northwest, that there is no finality on this subject except obedience to the contract as it was made," Daniel W. Voorhees of Indiana insisted. A Democrat, Voorhees was nevertheless openly supported by numerous Midwestern Republicans.[50] Roll-call votes reflected this sectional polarization.

Once again, compromise was difficult to achieve and required two conference committees. Republicans ultimately found common ground by presenting the bill as a money-saving measure. By reducing the interest paid on the debt, it would alleviate the fiscal pressure. Republicans from the Midwest and South, whose primary goal was to obtain more money for their regions, also won an easing of the rules governing the creation of new national banks along with the new bond issue.[51] The Funding Act of July 1870 was the culmination of the Sherman-Boutwell strategy: it stabilized the monetary situation and thus alleviated sectional tensions within the Republican Party while maintaining the ultimate goal of specie payments. In short, the political move succeeded. But the choice of a middle course, predicated on achieving contraction through economic growth instead of retiring greenbacks, was not without danger. It required the Treasury to intervene visibly in financial markets by regularly injecting gold to buy its outstanding debt, stabilize the value of the greenback, and ensure that specie circulation remained adequate.[52] Nevertheless, it established a sectional *modus vivendi* among Republicans, although it remained a precarious compromise made possible only by the need to hold the party together.

In order to preserve this equilibrium, essential to the future of both the party and the country, Republicans had to respond quickly to the danger posed by a Supreme Court decision handed down in February 1870. In *Hepburn v. Griswold*, the Court held that greenbacks were not legal tender for the payment of debts contracted before they were created in 1862. Ironically, the majority opinion was written by Chief Justice Salmon P. Chase, who had overseen the creation of the greenback as secretary of the treasury. In itself, the case had only a limited impact, but it contained the implicit threat that the Court might soon declare greenbacks unconstitutional. Although the most intransigent hard-money men applauded "the single step . . . towards the restoration . . . of a solid basis to the currency," most people worried about the devastating implications for commerce. Grant's reaction prevented panic, however. On the day the decision came down, he announced the nomination of two judges to fill the vacant seats on the Court. William Strong and Joseph P. Bradley were both solid Republicans, and it was expected that the change in the political complexion of the Court would alter its position on the law. In May 1871, *Knox v. Lee* confirmed that greenbacks enjoyed full constitutional legitimacy.[53] The Republicans' quick reaction preserved the hard-won compromise, an important result for both the unity of the party and the financial future of the country. This laid the groundwork for the political consolidation of a party that was still threatened by sectional divisions.

The tariff was the other issue that threatened the unity of the Republican Party. It was the concern that had initially triggered sectionalism in 1866, but since then, it had remained on the backburner. In the winter of 1869–70, however, Republicans found it much more difficult to strike a viable compromise on the tariff issue than on the money question. Several factors conspired to place the tariff high on the political agenda and at the heart of Midwestern political demands. The reduction of federal spending (primarily on the military) and the good health of the economy[54] created a record budget surplus of nearly $50 million in June 1869, with $102 million projected for 1871.[55] This made it hard to justify the continuation of a tax system designed for wartime and left largely untouched since the end of that war. Furthermore, it emerged that tariff protections had allowed salt and coal producers, among others, to earn scandalously high profits. Even the most fervent protectionist newspapers, such as the *Chicago Republican*, denounced "the combination of coal-owners" made possible by the tariff and warned "the coal engrossers and forestallers that they are menaced not only by the free-traders, but by the protectionists," who had joined forces to ask Congress "in the name of common justice [for] an abrogation of the tariff, as regards coal."[56]

All this came about in a transformed political context. The election of a president whose views were largely unknown encouraged active lobbying of the new administration.[57] The return of the Southern states to Congress was also seen by free-traders as a positive development, because the South before the war had traditionally favored a low-tariff regime. Seizing the moment, the American Free Trade League, founded in New York in 1865, published a number of pamphlets, "a magazine of hand grenades" against "the most popular arguments in favor of protection."[58] The budget surplus, the salt and coal scandals, and the South's return to Congress all encouraged such an initiative. When it failed to produce much in the way of legislative results in 1870, many free-traders were impelled to turn against the Republican Party in the name of "liberal" principles.

While the thinkers came mainly from the intellectual elite of New York and New England, the political troops were recruited in the Midwest. From the first skirmishes in December 1869 to the adoption of a new tariff in July 1870, the sectional dimension was a regular fixture in the bitter debates over a long, technical bill that occasioned "a fight on every paragraph and on almost every single line." There was bargaining over every item subject to duty, bargaining in which defense of local interests was combined with ideological jockeying. Broadly speaking, the protectionists were on the defensive, which marked a difference from 1866. Their primary goal was to prevent a lowering of the tariff barrier, and to that end, they tried to persuade Midwesterners that it was in their interests to maintain high duties. "The charcoal furnaces of the West and Southwest are already feeling the increased importation of Scotch pig consequent upon the decline of the premium on gold," one of them warned. "I love to talk of the great West," another added, but "it is difficult to understand why more than three fourths of the laboring men of the western States should even now be engaged exclusively in agriculture, to the neglect of mining and manufacturing." A third pleaded for an end to sectional confrontation on the grounds that "protective legislation is not a sectional boon but a national demand."[59]

To judge by the voting, these calls fell on deaf ears.[60] Nevertheless, Republicans did manage to strike a compromise, once again under pressure of the calendar. The end of the session was drawing near, and it would have been disastrous to go to the polls with nothing accomplished after many months of debate (see figure 7). The bill that finally passed combined a sharp decrease in direct taxes with a modest reduction of the tariff. Cutting taxes was a tangible and therefore politically attractive result, and most Midwestern Republicans were satisfied.[61] The tax cut also reduced the size of the fiscal cushion available for lowering the tariff, and the technical complexity of the bill buried the actual changes in a myriad of details. The items on which import duties were reduced were mainly those not produced in the United States: tea, coffee, wine, sugar and molasses, and spices. On other goods the results varied: the tariff on cast iron was reduced significantly, but on steel rails the shift from an *ad valorem* duty to a fixed duty in effect raised the protectionist barrier higher at a time when the price of rails in Europe was falling.[62]

In the end, this lame compromise failed to satisfy either camp. Given the inflated rhetoric of the debate, the end result inevitably proved disappointing. The new tariff, along with the Funding Act and the Currency Act of 1870, were hardly of a nature to put an end to sectional antagonism. But they did forge a political *modus vivendi:* however little they contributed to resolving the fundamental issues, they gave every Republican representative, whether in the Northeast or the Midwest, a record he could run on. This alone counted as a success. But it would have been impossible to reach a compromise without the pressure of a threatened explosion that worried party leaders at a time when the reapportionment issue was exacerbating tensions between the Midwest (and, increasingly, the South) and the Northeast. In view of this danger, compromise was possible only if

Republicans could agree on a common purpose. In 1870, that common purpose was Reconstruction, which remained as necessary to the party as it was to the country, given the situation in the South.

Safeguarding the Elections and the Unity of the Party: The Enforcement Acts

It was while these economic debates were raging in the midst of rising sectional tensions that the Fifteenth Amendment was ratified. The proclamation of March 30, 1870, was accompanied by a solemn message from the president: "The adoption of the 15th Amendment to the Constitution completes the greatest civil change, and constitutes the most important event that has occurred, since the nation came into life."[63] In the view of Republicans, it "confers upon the African race the care of its own destiny. It places their fortunes in their own hands."[64] The federal government was now liberated from the task of overseeing Southern affairs. Congress had readmitted the last of the secessionist states, and equality before the law was now enshrined in the Constitution. With these objectives achieved, Reconstruction, it seemed, had come to an end.

In fact, the opposite was the case. By making the Fifteenth Amendment the crowning achievement of their postwar settlement, Republicans identified Reconstruction with the right to vote—something it was not when it began. Although they disagreed in the particulars, they recognized the suffrage as part of the legacy they now had to defend. Moreover, any attack on the electoral process, and especially on Southern blacks' access to the polls, endangered their own hold on federal power. This is why political violence across the South, but also election fraud elsewhere, were identified as threats to Reconstruction. In response, between 1870 and 1872, Republicans would pass five laws known collectively as the Enforcement Acts. These laws, based on the new Fifteenth Amendment, were intended to ensure that the rights of all citizens to vote would be respected. The Enforcement Acts, which applied to the country as a whole, "nationalized" Reconstruction and substantially strengthened the federal government's ability to intervene at the local level. Reconstruction, far from over, was in fact just entering a new stage.

Several factors converged to push the Republicans in this direction. The decisive element was the threat that violence in the South posed to the political reforms Republicans had introduced there. This was reinforced by concerns about the future of the party and its ability to remain in power. Reconstruction was the only thing that held it together, while violence in the South and voting fraud in

New York City benefited Democrats, so partisan self-interest bolstered Republican commitment to reform. The Enforcement Acts were necessary both to save Reconstruction and to preserve Republican party unity. But by using the acts to counter divisive sectionalism, the Republicans brought tensions between the Midwest and Northeast into the heart of Reconstruction—and provoked, as we see below, the revolt of Liberals in 1872. Thus, in order to prevent a split along sectional lines, they unwittingly encouraged another, this one ideological rather than geographical.

The first Enforcement Act was introduced in Congress only a few days after ratification of the Fifteenth Amendment, on which it was explicitly based. The act was a response to the political violence afflicting the South, which continued "unchecked and unrestrained." One congressman described the situation in Alabama: "To be a Republican, an advocate of liberty, and a supporter of the Administration and its policy, is a heinous crime. It sets a mark upon the brow and a price upon the head."[65] Although violence was not prevalent everywhere, it took on an ostensibly political dimension wherever it occurred. The more or less clandestine groups known collectively as the Ku Klux Klan proliferated as Republicans began to take control of local governments. The Klan's actions, which initially sought to restore an allegedly "natural" social order, were increasingly aimed at wrenching power from the Republicans. This became clear during the 1868 campaigns, which witnessed numerous attempts to keep voters away from the polls through intimidation or aggression.[66] "If elections take place this fall," black legislators from Alabama warned in a petition, "violence and bloodshed will mark the course of such elections, and a fair expression of the will of the people cannot be had. We shall be driven from the polls, as in the Presidential election, by armed and organized bands of rebels, and our state given over to the guidance and control of the most extreme men of the Democratic party."[67]

By attacking the right to vote, this political violence struck at the principle that Republicans had made the cornerstone of Reconstruction with the Fifteenth Amendment: enfranchisement as the guarantee of each citizen's liberty and equal rights for all. "All we have is the ballot," New York Republican Hamilton Ward explained to the House. "The ballot stands between the rich man and the poor, and between the poor man and the rich. The ballot stands between the oppressed and the oppressor. The ballot stands between the ignorant and the wise, between the designing and the simple."[68] The first Enforcement Act was therefore intended to give the federal government the means to punish voting fraud. It established a long list of possible offenses covering the entire voting process from registration to counting, and imposed heavy penalties on local officials who violated the law. Exclusive jurisdiction over these crimes was given to the federal courts, and federal marshals were authorized to call on the army for support. Procedures were established for federal officials to intervene on the day of the vote rather than take the politically difficult course of appealing to the courts to invalidate a certified election result.[69]

Superficially, this first Enforcement Act might seem to be no more than a continuation of the Reconstruction program that the Republicans had been pursuing for the previous four years. In fact, it went much further: it made the federal government the arbiter of relations between states and their own citizens, a sharp change from prewar practice.[70] Once the Southern states were readmitted to the Union with all their rights and prerogatives restored, direct intervention became impossible. Continuing Reconstruction required new legal means. If local authorities could not or would not protect the rights of blacks to vote, Republicans would have to take a new approach. The response was cautious and narrowed to voting rights alone.[71] Nevertheless, the significance of the first Enforcement Act should not be underestimated: it placed the states' treatment of their own citizens, as far as elections were concerned, under federal supervision and transformed Reconstruction into a national policy.

A new phase of Reconstruction thus began. Previously, Reconstruction had been a national problem in the sense that it concerned the entire country, but the geographical focus of reform was the South. Only the Civil Rights Act of 1866 and the three postwar constitutional amendments applied to the whole country. Now Congress was required to pass laws that applied uniformly to the entire country. Republicans therefore set about reconceiving Reconstruction for the whole United States and not just a single region. This national conception became apparent in the second Enforcement Act, which followed soon after the first and aimed at voting fraud in the large cities of the North. One consequence of the new act was to encourage a new round of sectional demands. The tensions between the Northeast and Midwest over economic issues thus directly affected Reconstruction policy.

"In the presidential election of 1868 at least four States of this Union were carried by fraud for the Democratic candidate—New York, New Jersey, Georgia, and Louisiana," William M. Stewart denounced in May 1870. By comparing election fraud in the South to that in the North, the Nevada senator treated protecting the voting process as an issue for the entire country. And by emphasizing fraud by Democrats, he linked this nationalization of Reconstruction to the future of the Republican Party.[72]

In this perspective, it was perfectly logical to pay attention to what was happening in New York City. Because of its large population, election fraud there had national repercussions. For some years the city had been under the control of "Boss" William M. Tweed, the head of what was probably the first modern political machine in American history. Tweed's system was built on three pillars: a comprehensive political network, patronage, and election fraud. Every neighborhood in the city had a Democratic club, a meeting place that welcomed all comers. The clubs shared information and offered assistance and even work in exchange for political support. This grassroots outreach touched everyone from poor day laborers fresh off the boat to the well-to-do. The Americus Club, for instance, was a gathering place for influential people: politicians, judges, public officials, and businessmen. City contracts greased the palm of the businessman and provided work for the laborer, and they could also be used to purchase social peace, a welcome relief after the riots of 1863. In order to keep the machine going, however, elections had to be won. And there, nothing was left to chance. Patronage and get-out-the-vote efforts were complemented by a range of less legal practices. "Repeaters" were recruited to vote in several different wards, the police prevented opposition voters from going to the polls, election officials stuffed ballot boxes, and so on.[73]

These practices were exposed by a congressional investigation in the winter of 1869. Their existence was not as surprising as their scale. Frauds were perpetrated by both parties in many places other than New York in this period.[74] But New York City achieved industrial efficiency, as a cartoonist suggested in *Harper's Weekly* in October 1868 (figure 8). In 1802, the federal government had assigned state courts the task of naturalizing immigrants. In New York City, judges working hand-in-glove with Boss Tweed handed out citizenship papers at a superhuman pace: eight per minute for a Judge McCunn according to the *New York Tribune;* a daily average of 711 in October 1868 for a Judge Barnard, who nevertheless "did not occupy [the bench] over three and a half hours a day," according to the committee report.[75] By naturalizing en masse, the courts created hosts of new voters out of the immigrants (mostly Irish Catholics, who made up nearly one-quarter of the city's population[76]) of whom the Democratic machine had taken care from the moment of their arrival, providing social contacts and jobs in return for political loyalty. This system served as an important social safety net and helped to integrate the newcomers into American society, but its national political impact attracted hostility.[77] In October 1868 alone, the New York courts had naturalized 68,000 immigrants by procedures that the congressional inquiry deemed illegal. This number was substantially greater than the 10,000-vote difference between Grant and Seymour in the presidential election.[78]

FIGURE 8. "'M'Cunn Manufactures Citizens at the Rate of
8 a Minute, or 480 an Hour'—*N.Y. Tribune*," *Harper's Weekly*,
Oct. 24, 1868. (Special Collections, University of Virginia)

Republicans had good reasons for thinking that this was one of the reasons why
they lost New York.

Noah Davis and Roscoe Conkling, both New York Republicans, proposed a
drastic remedy to Congress: assign exclusive responsibility for naturalizations to
the federal courts and tighten the procedure. The bill they introduced proposed
to allow any citizen to challenge a naturalization for a period of six months. It
also proposed to reexamine all naturalizations awarded in large cities after July 4,
1868. After a stormy debate, however, the bill was rejected.[79] The law that was
finally passed in July 1870, the second Enforcement Act, was far more moderate.
It left the naturalization process in the hands of the state courts but placed it

under the supervision of the federal courts, which were given jurisdiction over related offenses such as making a false declaration, making or using false citizenship documents, identity theft, and bribery of judges and other officials. This was undeniably a Reconstruction law in that it included a principle of racial equality: access to American citizenship was explicitly open to "aliens of African nativity and to persons of African descent," and there was also provision for supervision of elections by federal observers.[80]

The second Enforcement Act, or Naturalization Act, was thus a mixture of boldness and timidity, and in that respect, typical of the Reconstruction legislation of 1870–72. Constitutionally, Congress was well within its rights to nationalize the naturalization process under Article I, Section 8, and to enact federal election supervision under the Fifteenth Amendment. But the law left the existing institutional balance largely intact, apart from authorizing the federal courts to deal with election fraud. Still, there was political audacity in a measure that for the first time explicitly applied a Reconstruction principle to a problem that originated in the North. The actual content of the second Enforcement Act may not seem very impressive, but it paved the way for the more radical measures that would be enacted in 1871.

This mixture of conservatism and audacity was a consequence of the sectional implications of the bill and the party's need to see it passed. Midwestern opposition to the measure emerged early in the debate, even though the subject was far removed from the economic issues that usually triggered sectional tensions. Warnings were sounded against a bill aimed at "the evils which afflict or are said to afflict the great cities of the East" but inevitably threatening to "almost all the northwestern and western States."[81] Voting on the measure exhibited a pronounced sectionalism.[82] Negotiations were initiated to respond to Midwestern objections without compromising the Republican Party's need to do something about election fraud in New York. The latter agenda was widely acknowledged: for example, Gustavus A. Finkelnburg, a German-born Missouri Republican, who had fought hard against the original version of the bill, stated flatly that "as to the object itself, as purifying the elections in New York or in any other State, I say that I do fully sympathize with the gentlemen. I will cooperate toward the passage of any law which I do not consider burdensome to immigrants from foreign lands."[83]

The sectional interpretation of the second Enforcement Act was fueled by the tensions of the summer of 1870. Debates about the census and reapportionment had made congressmen acutely aware of how demographics affected the balance of political power. The simultaneous discussion of the money question and the tariff heightened these tensions (see figure 7). Differences were formulated in sectional terms, just as they had been on economic issues. Underlying the discussion were real geographic differences, but these were interpreted according to a preexisting category that was politically more effective. There was no intrinsic reason why these differences had to be seen through a sectional lens, but once they were, political consequences followed immediately.

Many Midwestern congressmen rejected any attempt to "restrict the means of obtaining naturalization, to complicate the machinery and render the process of naturalization expensive, burdensome, and oppressive." They came from states with rapidly growing populations, many of which were actively involved in promoting European immigration with stands at world fairs (as in Paris in 1867), use of European recruiting agents, and so on. There were also civic considerations: for example, "the constitutions of Missouri, Alabama, Arkansas, Florida, Georgia, Indiana, Kansas, Michigan, Minnesota, Nebraska, and Wisconsin provide that a man shall be admitted to vote when he has simply declared his intention to become a citizen." The original bill would have voided these provisions while restricting access to citizenship in a region where federal courts were few and far apart.[84]

The danger of the new law was above all political. Oliver P. Morton, a senator from Indiana, denounced what he saw as a Know-Nothing measure, reminding his colleagues that the nativist party of the 1850s had given the impression that "the people of the United States were becoming hostile to men of foreign birth." James Howell of Iowa asked his fellow Republicans whether they ought to give Democrats a golden opportunity "to arouse the prejudices and passions of the foreign population in our country against us." In the Midwest, one-fifth of the population was foreign-born, and those people voted. In many states, Germans were a key group for winning elections. In short, many Republicans saw the initial version of the second Enforcement Act as suicidal.[85] The final bill was more tepid politically and more conservative constitutionally, but it held the Republican Party together around an issue that stemmed directly from Reconstruction.

The congressional debates of the spring of 1870 contained two lessons for Republicans. First, Reconstruction would henceforth be national in scope: continued reform in the South would necessarily have an impact on the North. For that reason, and in a context of heightened sectional tensions, the clash between the Northeast and Midwest had for the first time a direct influence on the Reconstruction debate. The second lesson, a corollary of the first, was that Reconstruction policy could help to unify the Republican Party in two ways: first, by mobilizing support for voting rights protections as the party's central ideology, and, second, by protecting the party from election fraud by Democrats. In other words, the intersection of debate on economic issues with debate on the Enforcement Acts ensured that sectional tensions would spill over onto Reconstruction. It also revealed that Republican unity depended on Reconstruction, which trumped geographical divisions. This session of Congress thus served as a crucible in which a political strategy was forged under pressure of events, a strategy that would remain serviceable well after 1871 and work so well that eventually it would trigger a reaction from within the Republicans' own ranks.

Radicalization

The 1870 fall elections demonstrated incontrovertibly that the Enforcement Acts did not go far enough in either New York City or the South. In New York, the clash between the city and federal governments nearly led to bloodshed, yet large-scale fraud continued despite some progress.[86] In the South, the campaign was marred by repeated violence. In Eutaw, Alabama, a group of armed whites attacked a Republican rally in October, killing four blacks and wounding fifty-four others. In the same month, in Laurensville, South Carolina, a savage assault on blacks left 13 dead and 150 homeless. Churches and schools were singled out as targets, as well as white teachers who taught black students, as in Cross Plains, Alabama. Through acts of terror like these, Democrats were able to regain control of Georgia and of some parts of the governments of Alabama, North Carolina, and Florida.[87]

These developments threatened to undermine Reconstruction, pervert the electoral process on which the country's political institutions were built, and deprive Republicans of control of the federal government. The party lost votes everywhere, perhaps not surprisingly after ten years in power. But the loss of 12 percent of House seats could be traced to two regions in particular: the South (which now sent more Democrats than Republicans to Congress) and the Mid-Atlantic states of Pennsylvania and New York (see table 6). Together, Boss Tweed and the Ku Klux Klan made their power felt on Capitol Hill.

Congress responded in 1871 with two additional Enforcement Acts. The third, also known as the Federal Elections Act, established a comprehensive system for overseeing national elections in large cities. The fourth, known as the Ku Klux Act, gave the federal government the means to intervene to prevent or punish acts of political violence. These two laws were similar in conception to the two previous Enforcement Acts, passed in 1870. But they went a good deal further by authorizing direct federal intervention to protect the ballot box.

The third Enforcement Act reinforced the federal government's power to oversee elections. The text enumerated various types of election fraud and granted exclusive jurisdiction to the federal courts. It also prohibited election by voice vote. But the real novelty was the authorization of *direct* intervention in the electoral process: District judges were given the power to appoint two supervisors (one for each party) at each polling place. Supervisors were empowered to examine and countersign voting registers, compile lists of dubious voters, and prepare their own vote tallies. At the same time, U.S. marshals and their deputies were authorized to make arrests. This unprecedented federal intervention into the electoral process was limited to cities with populations greater than twenty thousand and could be undertaken only at the express request of at least two citizens. A year later, the law was extended in a more limited way to the rest of the country by a fifth Enforcement Act.[88]

Republicans went even further with the fourth Enforcement Act, which specifically targeted Ku Klux Klan violence. Whereas the first Enforcement Act had been limited to the electoral process itself, the fourth made it a federal crime for any group of two or more persons to violate the Constitution (or any of its amendments) or to impede the actions of the federal courts (by intimidating witnesses, for example). If, moreover, state authorities proved unable or unwilling to stop violent attacks, the president could declare martial law, suspend habeas corpus, and use the army to put down the criminal activity.[89]

Republicans were aware that their new law marked a dramatic departure from the past. It was the first time that the federal government attempted to regulate relations among citizens of the same state and proposed to stand in for local authorities without being called upon to do so.[90] "We are working at the very verge of the Constitution," James A. Garfield suggested, "exposing us to the double danger of having our work overthrown by the Supreme Court, and of giving the Democrats new material for injuring us on the stump." Congress therefore limited the provision on the suspension of habeas corpus to one year, hoping that the exceptional nature of the case would make it acceptable. There was something paradoxical in Republican behavior: although many held a conservative view of federal powers (as if they failed to draw the consequences of the changes they themselves had introduced into the Constitution), they passed a law that went far beyond anything that had been attempted previously. Republicans were divided between their reluctance to tamper with institutional balances and their political and partisan need to protect the achievements of Reconstruction and the safety of countless black and white Southerners.[91]

For some Republicans, however, the new law went too far. Many "independent" urban newspapers felt this way. The *Chicago Tribune* expressed fear that "the bill just passed proposes, for the first time in the history of the United States, to destroy this fundamental constitutional boundary between the jurisdiction of the States and of the General Government." The *Nation* was alarmed at these "momentous changes. . . . They not only increase the power of the central government, but they arm it with jurisdiction over a class of cases of which it has never hitherto had, and never pretended to have, any jurisdiction whatever."[92]

Interestingly, these constitutional doubts were often expressed in sectional terms. The Ku Klux Act "conferred upon the President powers equal to those possessed by the Czar of Russia," the *Chicago Tribune* protested. "It gives the President the same powers in Ohio and Illinois as in Alabama and Texas."[93] In other words, the states of the Midwest were as vulnerable to Washington-led military intervention as the states of the South. Similar arguments were raised against the Federal Elections Act, which primarily targeted the North: of the seventy-one cities with populations greater than twenty thousand covered by the law, only ten were located in the South.[94] "While there may be great frauds in a single city of the Union—in New York, in Philadelphia, perhaps, and one or two other cities—I am satisfied that that is not the general condition of things throughout the country. I do not suppose this law would have any effect whatever in my own State," Senator Lyman Trumbull of Illinois maintained. "We have several cities to which it could be made applicable; and if administered by bad men, . . . they might use this very law and the machinery under it for practicing the grossest frauds and accomplishing the very object which the law itself is now designed to prevent." In fact, none of the votes on these bills revealed any identifiable sectional cleavage. But the mere fact that Republican opponents employed sectional rhetoric in their attacks attests to its political importance: "Do the Republicans of Chicago," the *Chicago Tribune* asked, "or of any part of the West or South, want to surrender their right to hold their election under State laws, and local officers, to irresponsible Deputy Marshalls [under the control of] the Democratic party?"[95]

Most Republicans in Congress looked at the matter differently. Their votes and speeches reveal that they were responding to a double threat: to Reconstruction and to their party. Black congressmen, for example, had little patience for conservative pettifoggery. "Tell me nothing of a constitution which fails to shelter beneath its rightful power the people of a country!" exclaimed Joseph H. Rainey of South Carolina. Henry L. Dawes of Massachusetts spoke for the majority of the party when he asked rhetorically, "Am I to abandon the attempt to secure to the American citizen these rights, given to him by the Constitution?"[96] Although some newspapers minimized the extent of the violence in the South, Republicans faced a simple alternative—abandon Reconstruction or give the government the means to intervene.[97]

The decision to ignore the objections to the new Enforcement Acts and pass laws reinforcing the power of the federal government over previously understood constitutional limits reflected the Republicans' belief that the future of their party depended on the future of Reconstruction. For one thing, the party's strength in the South reinforced its hold at the federal level. For another, as Rutherford B. Hayes wrote in congratulating John Sherman on his speech "on the Ku Klux outrages," "Nothing unites and harmonises the Republican party like the conviction that Democratic victories strengthen the reactionary and brutal tendencies of the late rebel States. It is altogether the most effective thing that has lately been done." The move was all the more necessary because sectional divisions remained threatening. For several weeks, President Grant, who "greatly desire[d] legislation" that would allow him to act against southern violence, "hesitate[d] to recommend it, for fear the Session will be prolonged and the high tariff men will be offended by assault on their pet interests." Instead, the Enforcement Acts allowed the Republicans to refocus their policy on Reconstruction and solidify the party. The newspapers focused on the South, the violence, and the federal government's response, whether to support it or criticize it. The *Chicago Republican* complained that "members were altogether too deeply absorbed in considerations affecting Carolina ruffianism, to waste time in thinking about the rights of decent people in Illinois. In that way our State and the entire West are to be swindled out of their proper representation and just influence in the settlement of questions of taxation and other important matters."[98]

The objective of the Enforcement Acts was thus achieved in 1871. Threatened by strong sectional tensions over economic issues, the Republican Party succeeded in rallying around issues at the heart of its ideological history. The risk of fragmentation became palpable when those issues seemed to be dying out. This should not hide the fact that federal intervention came to be seen as necessary in the eyes of all who did not wish to see the achievements of Reconstruction undone. Republicans did not invent Southern Democrats' resorting to social intimidation and violence to regain power in the region. Nevertheless, Republicans had an obvious interest in continuing Reconstruction and faced clear difficulties in striking a truly satisfactory economic compromise at a time when sectional tensions were being heightened by reapportionment. These two factors undermined the effectiveness of the Republican strategy, because they allowed opponents to cast doubt on the true motivations behind it. Although Reconstruction enabled Republicans to solidify the party in the face of sectional tensions, those same tensions came to undermine Reconstruction policy in the South.

Backlash: The Liberal Bolt

"What I seek is not a sham break-up of parties, such as the Greeley movement promises, but a real break-up, involving something more than the construction of a new party machine out of the pieces of the old ones."[99] This, in the words of the *Nation* editor E. L. Godkin, was the goal of the national convention that "Liberal Republicans," as they called themselves, held in May 1872 in Cincinnati. After months of denouncing the real and imagined corruption of the Grant administration and attempting to impose their political views on the larger Republican Party, Liberals ultimately decided that the best way to achieve their goal was to create a new movement and thus force a transformation of the political landscape.

A cartoon by John Cameron (figure 9) denounced the maneuver. It shows Horace Greeley, the Liberal candidate in the 1872 presidential election, as a wedge being used to smash the bedrock of the Republican Party. The fact that Greeley, a longtime protectionist, was the candidate of a movement initiated by free-traders, was personally wrenching to the candidate but presented as an effective weapon for dividing Republicans. The cartoonist attacked an initiative that he deemed hypocritical and selfish. Two groups stood ready to profit from it: the Democrats, here represented by Boss Tweed and his acolytes, to discredit the sincerity of the anticorruption rhetoric, and Liberals themselves, depicted as self-interested Republicans motivated by hatred of Grant. Political commentary aside, the diagnosis was fairly astute. Among the key issues pushed by the Liberals, free trade was one of the most important. In 1872, they concluded that the Republican Party was an obstacle to tariff reform. They felt that they had no choice but to split the party they had failed to transform from within.

The Liberal challenge in 1872 is evidence of the political efficacy of the Enforcement Acts, which mobilized Republicans ideologically and held the party together in the face of sectional divisions on economic issues. But the compromises on the money question and even more on tariff reform inevitably failed to satisfy those for whom these issues were a priority. The Republican strategy, therefore, boomeranged: intended to strengthen party unity, Reconstruction became an obstacle to those who hoped to see the party's positions on economic issues evolve. Liberals concluded that the party had to be destroyed in order to

FIGURE 9. "Splitting the Party; The Entering Wedge," John Cameron, published in
New York in 1872 by Currier & Ives. (© American Antiquarian Society)

bring about a political realignment. They wanted to create a new Republican Party
under their leadership. That was the significance of the 1872 Liberal convention
in Cincinnati.

The irony is palpable: Republicans, with the Enforcement Acts, overcame sectional divisions in order to rally around the party's ideological core, but in so
doing, they provoked an ideological split in their ranks. Liberals in turn would
meet with difficulty when it came to quelling the same sectional divisions. Like
Democrats in 1868, they were soon forced to campaign on Reconstruction, bringing to Republicans the largest election victory in the party's brief history.

Did the Enforcement Acts Work Too Well?

As the 1872 elections drew near, Republicans had every reason to believe that
the Enforcement Acts were a success. Although the two acts passed in 1870 had
not yielded the desired results, the additional laws passed in the spring of 1871
made it easier to go after the most visible instances of election tampering, both
of which were associated with the Democrats: the political machine in New York
City and the Ku Klux Klan in the South. The advantage for the Republicans was
twofold: refocusing on Reconstruction would strengthen a party threatened with

fragmentation, and enforcing the law would allow more Republican voters to go to the polls in many Southern states in 1872 while at the same time countering the influence of the Tweed machine in New York City.

The Ku Klux Act produced an immediate effect in the South by making the prospect of federal intervention more tangible. Enforcement of the law was difficult, however. Accused by his adversaries of being a military despot, President Grant moved cautiously. The newly created Department of Justice had only a small operational staff, and after years of demobilization, there were too few federal troops in the South. But the repeated failure to negotiate a compromise, together with multiple acts of violence in the South, forced Grant to intervene. Charges were brought in Mississippi, Tennessee, and the two Carolinas. The effort was concentrated above all in South Carolina, where a number of violent incidents were already under investigation. In October 1871, the president suspended habeas corpus in nine counties and dispatched troops to assist in the arrest of numerous suspects. Thanks to evidence amassed by local authorities and to the decisive action of the federal government, numerous convictions were obtained in federal court. This halted the momentum of the Ku Klux Klan.[100]

This success should not be overestimated, however. Despite the undeniable success of the federal effort, the interventions showed the degree to which Republican governments in the South were dependent on federal support. The shortage of federal resources and the conservatism of the courts suggested that political violence would remain a potential danger. Furthermore, many politicians came to believe that the public was growing tired of repeated interventions in the South. Taken together, these signs did not augur well for the future of Reconstruction.[101] In the short run, however, federal action proved (or at any rate seemed) effective. The return of a safer environment undoubtedly helped to secure a good Republican turnout in 1872; except in Georgia, the elections that year were the calmest the South had known since Reconstruction began.[102]

The impact of the Enforcement Acts on the situation in New York City, though less direct, was nevertheless undeniable. With an investigation underway in Congress, the new laws helped to change the political climate, cutting the ground out from under the Tweed machine. "There are signs that the rural democracy begins to find the Ring a burthen too heavy to be borne," Republican lawyer George T. Strong noticed. "They say the unexpected Republican victory in California is due to the discredit brought on the Democratic party by these colossal frauds in New York." Under pressure, the system was beginning to break down. In 1871, three events occurred in quick succession that made Tweed and his gang suddenly dispensable: press reports of budgetary malfeasance alarmed creditors, depriving the city of the means to finance its program of public works; the building trades withdrew their support from Tweed's machine, which could no longer supply them with work or negotiate with contractors; and, finally, on July 12, a demonstration of Orangemen triggered street fighting between Irish Protestants and Catholics, ending the fragile truce that Tweed had engineered after the riots of July 1863. If the machine could no longer guarantee social peace, why should it be allowed to continue?[103]

These developments were good for Republicans. The end of the Tweed system and the new federal election oversight made New York State competitive again. Grant would carry the state in November 1872, and a Republican would be elected governor. But Liberals were emboldened most of all, because they had played a key role in Tweed's downfall. The major newspapers had been attacking his system for months, and the bourgeois elite led the final charge. Bankers and businessmen who had long profited from a system that guaranteed social peace and public contracts lost all interest in perpetuating it owing to a concatenation of factors: Tweed's apparent complicity in the Gold Corner of 1869; heightened tensions between workers and bosses in the wake of several strikes; fear of "the dangerous classes" aroused by the Paris Commune in an elite whose rapid enrichment had quickly estranged it from the rest of the population. Their method was by no means anodyne. After forming a patrician "Committee of Seventy," they staged a veritable municipal coup in September 1871 to finish off the tottering machine.[104] This political success, supported by both Republicans and Democrats among the elite, including Samuel J. Tilden, a business attorney who would run for president as a Democrat in 1876 and who gained a reputation as a reformer at this time, emboldened Liberals.[105] The time seemed to have come to strike a major blow against political corruption and set things back on a proper course.

Political Opportunity

Liberals saw Tweed's downfall in New York as confirmation that the tide was turning in their favor. Their decision a few weeks later to hold a national convention in Cincinnati was based on the conviction that the parties were fragile and the political game was wide open. Their analysis combined an assessment of the state of the two major parties with an analysis of the potential for sectional mobilization on the tariff issue. Republicans had used Reconstruction to combat sectional divisions within the party, and now Liberals would try to break the link between the Republican Party and Reconstruction in order to liberate forces in favor of free trade.

Liberals formed a rather amorphous group but exhibited certain common characteristics. To begin with, they shared an ideology, or more precisely elements of an ideology, that combined classic American republicanism with European liberalism (imported in particular by German refugees after 1848). For them, the economy, like the universe, was governed by immutable laws, and ignoring those laws led to moral and political corruption. They also believed that the government was likely to become tyrannical if captured by "special interests." This ideology, which varied from individual to individual, was a fairly strong incentive to engage in political action.

Socially, Liberals drew on a fairly narrow stratum of society, an elite that included many college-educated individuals. Among them were economists such as Edward Atkinson and David A. Wells; independent journalists such as E. L. Godkin, Murat Halstead, and Horace White; and politicians such as Jacob D. Cox, Lyman Trumbull, and the liberal German immigrant Carl Schurz. Most were Republicans who had initially supported Reconstruction (Trumbull was one of the drafters of the legislation). Individual differences aside, all shared a few fundamental ideas: opposition to corruption, the need for civil service reform, the desirability of free trade, a return to specie payments, and a fairly conservative understanding of the constitutional order.[106]

Politically, they began to part company with other Republicans on economic issues after the war. Some of them had joined the American Free Trade League in New York in 1865. The tariff debates had convinced them that Republicans served the interests of lobbyists to the detriment of the public good. Similarly, they were alarmed by the strength of greenbackism, which for them represented a dangerous and immoral inflationism. The debates caused them to harden their position. They were among those who linked the money question to impeachment in December 1867 (see chapter 4).

Until 1870, however, those who would ultimately dub themselves Liberal Republicans did not form a distinct or coherent group. It was on November 22, 1870, that the nucleus of a group determined to take control of the Republican Party formed in New York at a meeting organized by the American Free Trade League with liberal Missouri Republicans who had managed to beat the Radicals in their party by forming an alliance with Democrats. This local success persuaded them that they could pursue the same strategy at the national level and thus "be recognized as the true leaders of the Republican party."[107]

As it happens, the Missouri success came about because a certain partisan logic reinforced the sectional dynamic. The 1870 election in Missouri witnessed a confrontation between two Republican senators, Charles D. Drake and Carl Schurz. Many issues divided the two men, but the tariff question and loyalty to Grant proved decisive. To win the election and thus take control of the party, Liberals courted Democratic votes. Their candidate won the race for governor. Schurz was not yet aware that this maneuvering would cost him his seat as senator: in 1874, the new Democratic majority in the state legislature naturally chose one of its own rather than send Schurz back to Washington for another term. In the meantime, however, Schurz saw only that he could take control of the state Republican Party by leveraging Democratic support.[108] Soon thereafter, he and others would try to extend this method to the entire country.

Geographically speaking, it made sense that the Liberal experiment began in Missouri. The state occupied the middle ground between the South (for slavery had existed there) and the Midwest (of which it shared many of the characteristics, including a substantial German population). Two distinct political logics therefore converged: a Midwestern sectional logic, which made the tariff question a major issue, and a Southern partisan logic based on a Democratic centrist strategy, soon to be known as the "New Departure." The conjunction of these two dynamics was the crucial factor that allowed Liberals to emerge as a political force, but it would also doom them to failure in 1872.

The Democratic parties of the former Confederacy adopted a centrist line in response to Grant's election in 1868, which confirmed the Republican policy of Reconstruction and strengthened Republican governments across the South. Many Southern whites responded with violence, as the spread of the Ku Klux Klan model throughout the region attests. Democratic officials often turned a blind eye to these acts of violence when they did not actively abet them. But the balance of power within the Democratic Party shifted, and proponents of a more centrist strategy took control. They realized that incendiary racist rhetoric would only spur the federal government to intervene in their affairs, and that the Republican program of economic development was attractive to part of the white elite. These Democrats decided to gain power by courting the center, downplaying "white supremacy" in favor of social and institutional conservatism. In order to reassure both Northerners and local Republicans, they even went so far as to change the name of their party: in Virginia, for example, they called themselves "Conservatives." And in the several states, this strategy paid off. In Virginia and Tennessee, Democrats took advantage of dissension in Republican ranks to form (temporary) alliances with the more conservative Republican faction, enabling them to win in 1869 elections only rarely marred by violence.[109]

Missouri Democrats took advantage of this new tactic in the fall of 1870. Their success did not go unnoticed, because it enabled them both to win a majority in the legislature and to foment division in Republican ranks. It was then adopted in Ohio, which turned it into a national strategy with the slogan "New Departure." In Dayton in May 1871, Clement L. Vallandigham announced that it was time to turn the page on Reconstruction. This was a noteworthy reversal for a man who had previously refused to make the slightest concession on the war and its consequences. Under his leadership, the delegates to the Democratic county convention proclaimed that "we accept the natural and legitimate results of the war . . . and acquiesce in the same as no longer issues before the country. . . . Now that reconstruction is complete . . . the Democratic party pledges itself to the full, faithful, and absolute execution and enforcement of the Constitution as it is. . . . The absolute equality of each and every State within the Union is a fundamental principle." They then went on to list the issues that remained to be resolved: universal amnesty, tax reform, civil service reform, and a move to a revenue-only tariff.[110] This was very close to the platform of Liberal Republicans.

In proclaiming this "New Departure," the Ohio Democratic Party signaled a tactical shift at the national level. It adopted a centrist line born in the South and adapted it to conditions in the North. The goal was to help Liberals in order to divide the Republican Party and gain power. That is why the powerful *Cincinnati Enquirer* decided in March to throw its support behind Ohio Liberals to elect Jacob D. Cox, Grant's estranged former secretary of the interior, to John Sherman's Senate seat. The attempt failed, but not by much.[111]

Throughout the country, Liberals were encouraged by these developments, which set the stage for them to take control of the Republican Party and "cleanse" it of what they saw as its corrupt elements. This partisan analysis of the situation was coupled with a second line of thinking, which took note of the sectional dimension of a key part of the Liberal program, namely, free trade. Liberals knew that support for free trade came mainly from the Midwest and South, and they understood from the debates around the Enforcement Acts that Reconstruction impeded open support for free trade by these sections for the sake of maintaining Republican Party unity, which Liberals regarded as artificial. They also believed that Southern Republicans, who were committed to a policy of economic development and railway investment, were more protectionist than traditional Democratic elites. Persuading themselves that the latter had sincerely embraced the results of Reconstruction, and unwilling to push constitutional strictures (conservatively understood) for further legislation—many were critical of the

Enforcement Acts on that ground—Liberals decided to move beyond Reconstruction to hasten a political realignment that would make free trade possible.[112]

In using the Enforcement Acts to unify a party divided over economic issues, Republicans had succeeded only too well. Those who believed, whether by conviction or out of personal ambition, that the tariff ought to be a priority concluded that Reconstruction had become an obstacle that would have to be eliminated. A favorable political situation, together with Grant's looming candidacy, persuaded Liberals to split off from the Republican Party. They held their national convention in Cincinnati on May 1, 1872. The gauntlet had been thrown.

The Liberal Challenge

The Liberal convention aroused mixed emotions, from enthusiasm to anxiety. In Congress, then in session, members followed the proceedings at a distance. The "excitement" caused by every "telegram from Cincinnati" spurred irony in some, who mocked the "running to and fro" of colleagues too busy to legislate.[113] Within three days, the convention produced a surprising result: Horace Greeley, the eccentric editor of the *New York Tribune*, was chosen to represent the movement. For George T. Strong, it was "the most preposterous and ludicrous nomination to the Presidency ever made on the continent." Strong was not the only flabbergasted commentator. "Was there ever so strange a freak in the history of politics!" Garfield wondered. "The nomination is so at variance with the spirit of the platform. The movement was a revolution but the revolution has revolted." For many Liberals, the disappointment was palpable. Some, like Godkin, refused to support Greeley. In June, a small group met behind closed doors in a chic New York hotel to replace him—but to no avail.[114]

The Cincinnati convention was significant because it was riven by the same contradiction—between party logic and sectional forces—that plagued Republicans and Democrats. Those tensions had allowed the Liberal movement to blossom. But the same tensions were also partly responsible for the platform and candidate that emerged from the Cincinnati convention, culminating in fatal defeat. Although both major parties survived the Liberal challenge, Reconstruction suffered a setback.

Why was the Cincinnati convention vulnerable to sectional factions? Because Liberals, once they gave up on working within the Republican Party, needed to expand their base and create a broader coalition. They therefore needed to look beyond the small, ideologically homogeneous nucleus of founding members. Consequently, the delegates who converged on Cincinnati were an eclectic mix of anticorruption reformers, independent journalists, more or less marginalized

Republicans, and Democrats seeking to capitalize on the new movement. What did August Belmont, the New York financier who had long headed the Democratic National Committee, have in common with Charles Sumner, the abolitionist senator and champion of equal rights? The real common denominator was hostility to Grant. In fact, Liberals had decided to create a movement outside the Republican Party when they realized that they would not be able to prevent the nomination of Grant for a second term as president. "Grant will nominate himself," one of them predicted. "The ordinary party machinery" was under "official control," another claimed, so that it was time "to consult the wishes of the unfettered masses."[115] The convention had gathered an army of malcontents whose only shared goal was to defeat Grant.

The convention operated under numerous handicaps. Without a well-lubricated organization to guide the proceedings, state delegations proved difficult to control. The meeting was led by a handful of editors who called themselves "the Quadrilateral," a reference to the fortresses that enabled Austria to maintain control of northern Italy. They sought to pull strings behind the scenes. Horace White of the *Chicago Tribune*, Samuel Bowles of the *Springfield Republican*, Murat Halstead of the *Cincinnati Commercial*, and Henry Watterson of the *Louisville Courier Journal* saw themselves as kingmakers, along with Carl Schurz, who served as convention chair. But they were soon outflanked by other backroom operators, most notably Whitelaw Reid of the *New York Tribune*, who worked on behalf of his boss, Horace Greeley. The crowd dynamics inevitable wherever large delegations are called upon to vote on important questions also interfered with the machinations of the would-be kingmakers. The editors of the Quadrilateral, impressed by their ability to shape public opinion and introduce reform into the national conversation, had failed to grasp how political conventions actually work.[116]

Sectionalism played a key role in determining the final outcome. This is clear from the content of the platform, which reflected the concessions Liberals were forced to make to their new allies. The most striking of these had to do with the tariff, a key issue for a movement that had grown out of the American Free Trade League. Instead of insisting on the need to lower the tariff, the convention proclaimed, in a plank relegated to the end of the platform, that the problem ought to be left to the states, each of which would instruct its congressional representatives as it saw fit. The Quadrilateral were forced to give in to the demands of the influential (and protectionist) *New York Tribune*, whose support they deemed indispensable. On the convention floor, moreover, the delegates from Pennsylvania and New York made the tariff issue a *casus belli*. With such crucial states in the balance, equivocation was the only course possible. But by relegating the question to the states, the Liberal convention failed to resolve its sectional divisions, and this failure would remain a handicap throughout the campaign. The final platform is revealing: by devoting most of its attention to Reconstruction—defense of prior achievements and general amnesty for former Confederates—and downplaying or evading the issues of civil service reform and tax reduction, the platform skirted the strengths of the movement and chose to wage the campaign on Republican ground.[117]

This being the case, the choice of candidate became crucial. This, too, was a consequence of, among other things, sectional differences. Among the contenders, David Davis had certain advantages: a former friend of Abraham Lincoln's, Supreme Court justice, and millionaire, he had been nominated by the new National Labor Reform Party and enjoyed the support of many Democrats. But Liberals wanted no part of him. They believed he would alienate Republican voters, and they viewed unions as "special interests" working against the common good. As Davis's star faded, two darlings of the core group of Liberals remained in contention: Charles Francis Adams, a Boston patrician, the son and grandson of presidents, and former ambassador to England, and Lyman Trumbull, a senator from Illinois, coauthor of much of the Reconstruction legislation, and one of seven "recusants" at Johnson's trial. Support for both of candidates was clearly sectional; New England backed Adams, whereas the Midwest backed Trumbull. Trumbull was too clearly pro–free trade for many delegates from New York and Pennsylvania, while Adams was too much a symbol of New England to attract support in the West. Ironically, both men were early Liberals and perhaps too liberal for a convention as heterogeneous as the one that met in Cincinnati.[118]

Sectional interests coupled with backroom machinations thus enabled Horace Greeley to win the nomination. At the time, the choice of the noted editor seemed a good one. "He is popular from Maine to California and will receive more votes than any other candidate in already contested States such as New York, Pennsylvania, New Hampshire and Connecticut," one delegate suggested, alluding to the candidate's support for protectionism. Furthermore, "he will be acceptable to the Democrats and will receive liberal support in the South from both the white and colored voters," having been an ardent abolitionist in the past but more recently a vociferous campaigner for amnesty for former Confederates, which made him "acceptable to the Democrats."[119] Could Greeley, on his name alone, transcend sectional differences?

In the event, the choice proved disastrous. The editor of the *New York Tribune* had a long career behind him. He had written too much for too long in a newspaper too widely read not to have accumulated many enemies. The cartoonist

Thomas Nast scored a bull's-eye when he depicted Greeley being forced to eat his own words. Greeley's belligerence and pugnacity served him well as a crusader on behalf of blacks and workers, but his eccentric appearance and opinions alienated many voters. Over the course of his career he had flirted with prohibition, spiritualism, Fourierism, and even vegetarianism.[120] As a Liberal candidate, he suffered from two major handicaps. First, his protectionism, and more generally his position on tax reform, prevented him from campaigning for a lower tariff and reduced taxes. Second, many Democrats hated him. Despite this, they decided at their Baltimore convention to support his candidacy. This shows how much the Democrats were committed to the New Departure strategy as their best hope of dislodging the Republicans. But the pill proved too bitter for Democratic voters to swallow, and many chose to stay home on election day.[121]

The internal dynamics of the Cincinnati convention produced a candidate and a platform that were handicaps for the new Liberal-Republican Party, which forfeited its political strengths in making the transition from a small, ideologically coherent nucleus to a national movement. One problem was the failure to master convention politics. Beyond that, Liberals fell victim to the same sectional turmoil that divided their rivals. Deprived of their original issues (free trade and civil service reform), they were forced to campaign essentially on Reconstruction. Hence their alliance with the Democrats became a handicap, because it allowed Republicans to identify them with the "rebels." One Liberal admitted that "the great difficulty in the way of reforming the present state of things is the persistence of the Democratic party in not dying." The goal was to isolate the "old element in the Democratic party which has to be lost or got rid of" by forming "new combinations over new issues." Forced to fall back on old issues, Liberals became prisoners of Democrats of many stripes.[122] Accordingly, many early Liberal sympathizers refused to join the movement and preferred to vote Republican.

On election day, the Liberal-Democrat tandem was completely routed. Grant took more than 55 percent of the vote and captured 62 percent of the counties and 31 of 37 states — the Republicans' best score to date. They also took 70 percent of the seats in the House, regaining the two-thirds majority they had lost two years earlier.[123] The Liberal movement did not survive as a party: some of its leaders returned to the Republican fold, while others joined the Democrats. In this respect, the whole episode was a tempest in a teapot. Grant compared it to "the deceptive noise made in the West by prairie wolves," adding that "he once estimated at 100 the noise made by two of them when he was an officer in Western Texas."[124]

The 1872 campaign actually had a much greater impact than the president's anecdote might suggest: it pushed Republicans toward disengagement from Reconstruction. To counter the Liberal challenge, they tried to preempt part of the Liberal program. Two new laws signaled that the Republicans were also ready to put Reconstruction behind them. In May, the Amnesty Act restored political rights to those who had been deprived of them by the Fourteenth Amendment, except for the principal leaders of the Confederacy. The measure was mainly symbolic. Few individuals were concerned, but the North sent a message of reconciliation to the South. At the same time, however, white Southerners could once again look to those who had led the secession. The achievements of Reconstruction were weakened further when Congress at about the same time abolished the Freedmen's Bureau and refused to extend the law authorizing the president to suspend habeas corpus and declare martial law in case of serious political violence, thus weakening the federal government's ability to intervene.[125]

With Liberals harnessed to Democrats, Republicans might have seen Reconstruction as an advantage for their side. But the defections from their camp and newspaper reports of Southern reactions to federal interventions worried them, and they began to pull back. Although Reconstruction remained an important campaign theme, necessary for ensuring party unity, it had increasingly little to do with any actual policy initiatives to protect the reforms achieved previously.

Paradoxically, the need for Reconstruction for party's sake receded because Liberal pressure forced Republicans to strike a compromise on the tariff—a compromise that had previously eluded them. The Cincinnati convention "greatly unsettled the opinions of men in regard to the tariff," one Republican admitted. Another ironically observed in the House,

> It is barely possible that, with the next clicking of that little instrument which brings news from Cincinnati . . . we may change sides on this subject; and that my Democratic friends, under the lead of the heroic Greeley, may be marching forth with "high protection" inscribed upon their banners . . . ; and I warn my Republican friends not to be too high protective tariff just now, for to-night or to-morrow we may be outstripped by the Democracy.[126]

In fact, the Liberal nomination ensured that the tariff question would not be a campaign issue. But the fact that a number of major Republicans had defected to the Liberals increased the pressure on the remainder of the party to come to an agreement on the highly divisive tariff question. The act of 1870 had satisfied no one, the federal budget was in substantial surplus, and demand for reform was increasing. After tense and lengthy negotiations, Congress eliminated duties on coffee and tea and approved a reduction of 10 percent on all other goods.[127] Liberal pressure had forced Republicans to reach a compromise that internal party dynamics alone had been unable to achieve.

In the end, the 1872 election strengthened both major parties as organizations. The Republican landslide reinforced the power of both the president and the party leadership. Many shared John Sherman's sentiment: "The chief interest I feel in the canvass is the preservation of the Republican party, which I think is essential to secure the fair enforcement of the results of the war."[128] The efficacy of the Republicans stemmed primarily from their organization. Unlike Liberals, they had election committees in every state and campaign workers who had been rewarded with public patronage for more than a decade. Democrats, for their part, remained the only organized alternative to Republicans after the collapse of the Greeley candidacy, and stung by the failed alliance, they would soon choose to regroup.[129]

Thus, the failure of Liberals to alter the partisan landscape gave both major parties a new lease on life. The 1872 campaign also had two other long-term consequences: first, it made the active interventionism in the South by a Republican-dominated federal government more difficult both legally and politically, and, second, it persuaded Democrats that a centrist strategy was doomed. In this respect, 1872 marked a turning point in Reconstruction—the Liberal revolt had created an unfavorable political context. Ironically, it was at the intersection of sectional tensions over economic issues and Reconstruction, the only issue that unified Republicans, that the Liberal movement was born. At a time when Republican leaders were trying to strengthen their party by striking a sectional compromise on the money question and the tariff, and by intervening vigorously in the South, the unanticipated consequence of their actions was to divide the party by spurring the departure of the Liberals. Despite this, the Republican Party emerged stronger in the end, with a tighter lock on the federal government and greater party unity than before. But the consequences for Reconstruction were less positive, because Northern Republicans would subsequently have to be more cautious about federal intervention, while Southern Democrats, drawing a lesson from the failure of their centrist strategy, would now prepare for head-on racial confrontation.

6

The Republican Retreat to the North

———— · ————

The political *Mare Putridum* is heaving vaguely in the calm that has followed the last grand presidential typhoon. . . . There seems to be a prevalent feeling that a new party is wanted. Republicanism has grown immoral in its old age and survived much of its usefulness. But there are many thousand disgusted Republicans who remember the war times, and would as soon vote for the Devil as with the Democracy. . . . There are signs, also, . . . that a certain considerable number of "Democrats" would like to change the name of their party. Not that they are ashamed of it, as they ought to be, but because it is a "Scarlet Letter," and a badge of disloyalty, *incivisme,* and infamy, which keeps them out of office and profit.
— George Templeton Strong, diary entry, June 25, 1873

THE ELECTION OF 1872 reinforced the status quo, as Liberals failed to trigger the redrawing of the political landscape they sought. Yet the issues at the root of their challenge remained unresolved, and the electoral landslide actually hid a growing dissatisfaction with Republicans, as Democrats repeatedly proved unable to establish themselves as an attractive alternative.

The increasing fragility of the Republican Party would soon become apparent, however. Liberals, and their allies in the independent press, had started campaigning on the corruption within government—an outgrowth of their free-trade, hard-money ideology that gained only a little traction in 1872 but would soon find ample justification with the multiplication of scandals. These revelations would permanently damage the Republican Party's image just at the time when Southern Democrats, relinquishing their failed centrist strategy, decided to take a hard line on race. As 1873 wore on, Republicans found themselves with less room to maneuver on Reconstruction, and this made the party all the more vulnerable to its internal sectional divisions. When the stock market crashed in

September 1873, unleashing a new economic crisis, this new fragility brought the Republican Party to a breaking point—and with it, Reconstruction.

This chapter explores how monetary sectionalism played a key role in reshaping the political landscape between 1873 and 1876, and ultimately led to a historic electoral crisis. The victory of the Republican candidate in the 1876 presidential election completed the North's abandonment of reform in the South, which was well on its way to becoming a one-party region. The breakdown of the Republican sectional compromise in 1873 set the stage for the end of Reconstruction and a political reconfiguration that would persist until the end of the century.

The Weakening of the Republican Party

The Republican victory in 1872 was impressive, but it bore within it the seeds of worrying trends. First, it put on the political agenda the corruption issue that, fed with a growing list of scandals, would undermine the Republicans' moral standing and, with it, much political legitimacy. All this came at a time when Democrats in the South, taking a much more radical line on race, challenged Reconstruction head-on. Republicans, finding themselves on the defensive on corruption accusations, would find it much more difficult to defend their policies, and their own members and voters, in the South.

A Barrage of Scandals

Associated with Liberals, the self-styled independent press had started to denounce the corruption, alleged or real, within the Grant administration and among Republicans more generally. During the 1872 campaign, those accusations had achieved, all in all, little traction. But that soon changed, tarring the Republican Party with the broad brush of dishonesty.

This moral crusade grew out of the fight against Boss Tweed in New York City and drew on two sources: classical republican ideology, with its perpetual worries about the fragility of institutions, and the revelation of actual mismanagement of government budgets that were now much larger than they had been in the antebellum era. It was also associated with a particular vision of the economy. Shocked by the direction the debates on money and the tariff had taken, many Liberals had concluded that free trade and specie payments resumption were essential in order to eliminate what they saw as sources of government profligacy. To remedy these ills, Liberals advocated civil service reform, which they hoped would deprive politicians of the patronage they saw as the root of all evil. From this standpoint, too, the 1872 election was a failure. Many representatives, especially in the West, opposed the idea of civil service examinations, which in their view would benefit the large cities of the Northeast close to the capital.[1]

Nevertheless, the issue of corruption did not disappear from the news. The major independent newspapers thrived on scandal. Although they often invented or embellished the facts, they turned up enough actual scandals to do lasting damage to the reputation of the Republican Party and President Grant.[2] The Crédit Mobilier affair, uncovered by the *New York Sun* in September 1872, proved to be a decisive turning point. A congressional investigation quickly uncovered embezzlement and possible influence-peddling. Crédit Mobilier was a company created by officials of the Union Pacific Railroad to build the transcontinental railway, which enjoyed generous government subsidies (in the form of public lands and bond guarantees). The Union Pacific signed a number of juicy contracts with Crédit Mobilier, which was owned by the same people who controlled the Union Pacific. They thus lined their own pockets on the construction contracts while the railroad lost money on its operations. It emerged that a congressman named Oakes Ames had arranged for a number of important Republicans to receive shares of Crédit Mobilier stock at preferential prices. Although bribery was never proven, it became clear that a dozen leading Republicans had accepted those gifts. Most of them, including Vice President Schuyler Colfax, were brought down by the scandal. Only James A. Garfield and Henry L. Dawes were able to salvage their political careers.[3]

The Crédit Mobilier affair was only one in a long line of corruption scandals that filled the pages of the newspapers for nearly three years. At times, the Republicans' political instincts seemed to fail them. In March 1873, senators and representatives approved a 50 percent increase in their own pay, as well as the pay of the president and justices of the Supreme Court. Even more, they made it retroactive to two years earlier. The measure was not unprecedented and may have been justified by economies in other areas such as travel expenses and the franking privilege. At a time of corruption scandals, however, the bill was naturally seen as an attempt by congressmen to enrich themselves at the taxpayers' expense. Whipped up in the press, the controversy raged throughout the summer, nearly eclipsing the Crédit Mobilier scandal. Its political effect was so devastating that Congress quickly repealed the pay raise when it reconvened in December.[4]

These corruption scandals weakened the Republican Party in the North, its historic base. Already in 1872 the Republican vote had declined in some states as a result of Liberal attacks, including party bastion Massachusetts where it fell by as much as 10 percent. Although the Republicans still won nationally by a landslide, these signs of weakness worried some party leaders.[5] More troubling, the corruption issue put wind in the sails of Southern opponents of Reconstruction, as it cast permanent suspicion on the motives behind federal interventions. Each new scandal lent plausibility to Democratic charges against Republican governments in the South. The public in the North judged the situation in the South in the light of developments closer to home. Was it not plausible to believe that the so-called terror in the South had been exaggerated, since Northern Republicans mostly confined their attacks on the alleged violence to election season? Was it not possible that the real reason for Grant's interventions was to prop up corrupt but friendly Southern governments under attack by righteous reformers outraged by abuses of power, at a time when Liberals were expressing similar outrage in the North? Moreover, Southern Democrats were clever enough to take advantage of this new context. They organized "taxpayer conventions" to disguise their racial counterrevolution. At a time when northern newspapers had to rely on Southern correspondents for news about the South, it was all the easier to minimize the violence and exaggerate the corruption and despotism of the Republicans.[6]

Thus corruption scandals undermined Reconstruction by lending credibility to attacks by Southern leaders on the incompetence and wastefulness of Republican governments in the South. Some of the allegations were accurate; many were exaggerated. The scandals also impeded federal intervention. For one thing, the retrenchment of federal spending, which campaign pressure accentuated in 1872, meant that the federal government had fewer and fewer means to intervene.[7] For another, the Liberals' focus on Grant as the target of their investigations and denunciations encouraged and legitimized Democratic charges that the president was a military despot prepared to trespass constitutional limits in order to impose martial rule on the South.

The accumulation of corruption scandals fed paranoid attacks on Grant's alleged "Caesarism." The "third-term" affair was symptomatic of this. The idea that the just-reelected president was already contemplating a third term in the White House sprang from the fertile imagination of James Gordon Bennett, Jr., the owner of the sensationalist *New York Herald*. In an editorial published on July 7, 1873, he denounced Grant's "Caesarist" ambitions without a shred of evidence. The fantasy of one editor was quickly taken up by newspapers across the country. Democrats saw the rumors as confirmation that Republicans had seized on Reconstruction as a way to use illiterate blacks and corrupt Northerners as shock troops in order to impose tyranny on the South. Liberals, already convinced of Grant's outsized ambitions, saw corroboration of their fear that corruption had infected all the institutions of the Republic. The affair lasted nearly two years, until the president finally swallowed his pride and agreed to sign an open letter solemnly forswearing any intention to run for a third term.[8]

All of this might be dismissed as typical journalistic excess. But the accusations of Caesarism against the general who became president made any federal intervention in the South, no matter how legitimate, a more complicated matter. The expulsion of five Democrats from the Louisiana legislature in January 1875 is the most striking example of this. Following the election of 1874, which was marred by numerous incidents of fraud and violence, Democrats tried to force the state legislature to seat five members of their party, which would have given them a majority. This was tantamount to a coup and ended only when a detachment of federal troops was dispatched to expel the five Democrats. When the news reached Washington, Democrats accused Grant of staging a putsch and protested the fact that federal troops had entered a civilian legislature. What is revealing about this incident is that Republicans, before any details of what had actually happened were available, accepted the initial reports as true. Garfield professed himself "shocked and distressed" and contemplated a break with the president. Only after General Philip Sheridan's report arrived, "putting his conduct in Louisiana in a new light," did Republicans rally in support of Grant. But the fact that even experienced political veterans, accustomed to the partiality of the press, of which they themselves were often victims, nevertheless believed the first dispatches to arrive from Louisiana says a great deal about the discredit into which the Grant administration had fallen.[9]

The president was partly responsible for this situation. In response to the resurgence of Southern violence, he failed to offer a clear line, and one historian has referred to his policy as a "study in incongruities." He dispatched troops often enough to expose himself to charges of military despotism but failed to use them systematically enough to prevent the violence from achieving its intended effects. The corruption scandals that engulfed people close to the president deprived him of indispensable legitimacy. All too often, the charges that his interventions favored the corrupt governments of personal friends seemed credible to people in the North. More and more Republicans began to think "that we are injuring the party by doing justice to the Negro."[10] The corruption scandals sapped Northern support for Reconstruction—and with it the ideological cohesiveness of the Republican Party.

Racial Division and White Terror

The weakening of the Republicans' moral standing made any federal intervention in Southern affairs increasingly difficult, allowing a true counterrevolutionary movement to emerge. Once again, this was a paradoxical consequence of Grant's and the Republicans' clear victory in much of the South in 1872. For one thing, the defeat delegitimized the centrist strategy within the Democratic Party, which quickly moved to a more radical line on race. For another, it led to a resumption of political violence and the use of paramilitary tactics in a bid to regain power. These two phenomena fed on each other, and the consequences were all the more dreadful because the weakening of the Republican Party in both the North and the South made any firm or sustained action by federal authorities impossible. The geographically diverse consequences of the 1872 election converged to imperil Reconstruction.

Until then, the centrist strategy had proved more or less successful for Democrats in states where conservative Republicans had broken with other factions of the party, for example, Virginia in 1869 and North Carolina in 1870. But the crushing defeat that Democrats suffered in 1872, partly because many Southerners could not bring themselves to vote for Horace Greeley, discredited the centrist strategy. Among Southern Democrats, those who favored a radical line—sometimes called "Bourbons," in allusion to the French dynasty and its hopes for a restoration of the ancien régime—gained the upper hand.[11] Backed by secessionist elites recently amnestied by Congress, the Bourbons focused entirely on one issue: was government for whites or blacks? For them, the only thing that mattered was to take a racial side. They drew the color line relentlessly—and violently.[12]

The Bourbon strategy proved all the more effective because Southern Republicans were too divided to offer a coherent response. Factionalism, which existed in all parties, became dangerous in such a context. In some states, such as Mississippi, Southern-born white conservatives had quit the Republican Party, leaving whites from the North vulnerable to charges of being "carpetbaggers" who had come South to profit from Southern woes, and putting blacks who had at last gained access to public office in an even more exposed position.[13] This lent credence to Democratic rhetoric, which distinguished between "true" white sons of the South and blacks manipulated by Northern adventurers, initiating a vicious circle that made it even more difficult for Republicans to attract a wider white membership.

Even worse, Republicans were beginning to lose their best weapon: economic policy. The Liberal anticorruption campaign had cast suspicion on the investments made by Republican governments, especially in railroads. North Carolina's semi-bankruptcy in 1872 raised doubts about whether it was wise to use taxpayer money to enrich railway companies.[14] Democrats seized on the fiscally conservative language of Northern Liberals to accuse Republicans representing poor blacks of imposing excessive taxes on honest white men who happened to be in the minority. This rhetoric echoed that of upper-class New Yorkers who sought to limit the suffrage at about the same time for similar reasons.

The radicalization of Democrats and deep factional divisions among Republicans encouraged the emergence of a terrorist strategy for regaining power. In 1873, Louisiana served as a laboratory of counterrevolution. Having been reconquered relatively early in the war, the state had become the focal point of early hopes for Reconstruction under Abraham Lincoln. The large community of free colored people in New Orleans might have served as a seedbed for the successful transformation of Southern society. In fact, however, power struggles in the state led to chronic political instability. Several attempted coups had to be put down by federal forces. The 1872 elections saw a clash between an alliance of Democrats and dissident Republicans and another Republican faction. The voting was marred by fraud and intimidation of all kinds, leading one historian to note that "there are no means short of necromancy to determine who won the election of 1872 in Louisiana."[15] The commission charged with counting and certifying the votes proclaimed the Republicans the winners, but the Democrats refused to accept the verdict. Two rival governments set up shop until the police and the army thwarted an attempted Democratic putsch on March 5, 1873.[16]

Although federal troops were present in New Orleans, they were nowhere to be found in remote corners of Louisiana. In Colfax, the capital of Grant Parish, there were two sheriffs and two judges—two rival "governments" having named one of each. This powder keg exploded on Easter Sunday, April 13, 1873. The Democratic "sheriff," after recruiting reinforcements from neighboring parishes, laid siege to the local courthouse and the black militiamen gathered there to defend it, many of whom had fought for the Union. The day ended with more than a hundred blacks slain, most of them killed at night by their drunken jailers.[17]

The repercussions of this episode, one of the bloodiest of the Reconstruction era, reached far beyond Grant Parish. A detachment of federal troops arrested the perpetrators, but the case led in October 1875, in a transformed political climate, to a Supreme Court decision in *United States v. Cruikshank*, which set the guilty parties free and emptied the first Enforcement Act of much of its content by severely constraining the federal government's power to regulate individual behavior. The Court thus reinforced a restrictive interpretation of the Reconstruction amendments it had adumbrated a year earlier in another decision involving Louisiana, the Slaughterhouse cases.[18]

In the days that followed, local Democrats drew a tactical lesson from the events.

The presence of federal troops in New Orleans made the use of force unlikely to succeed there, but in remote rural areas, Republicans were vulnerable. "White Leagues" quickly organized. These paramilitary groups hunted down officials appointed by the Republican governor and terrorized blacks and Republican officials with the goal of isolating the Republican authorities in New Orleans. To be sure, Louisiana had seen considerable violence since the end of the war but never of such a systematic and concerted kind. Local militias were no match for these paramilitary units. On September 14, 1874, another attempted coup was thwarted only after the army intervened once again. The Democrats thus proved that the Republican government in Louisiana could not survive without federal support. Other Southern states—especially those with substantial numbers of black voters—quickly took a page out of Louisiana's new book. In Mississippi, a systematic terror campaign enabled Democrats to regain power in 1875 after Grant refused to use the army to stop them. And in 1876, the Red Shirts played a crucial role in putting the former Confederate general Wade Hampton in the governor's seat in South Carolina.[19]

In 1873, all these developments in the South, as well as the effects of corruption scandals nationally, were only at their inception. In a way, they all had been made possible by the Liberal revolt in 1872. Paradoxically, the decisive Republican victory that year weakened the winner. Yet those events and their consequences were not ineluctable. Republicans had already overcome many obstacles and managed to make substantial reforms in the South. But now they were weakened internally and found it difficult to respond to the new outbreaks of violence there. Admittedly, their ideological commitment was on the wane. But more crucial was the Panic of 1873 and the shock waves it sent through the country. Weakened ideologically, divided sectionally on economic issues, Republicans would turn against one another and fail to respond to the new situation. Their abandonment of Reconstruction was thus due in large part to the internal threat of party collapse.

The Shattering of the Republican Sectional Compromise

On September 18, 1873, Jay Cooke & Co. collapsed when it could not sell bonds of the Northern Pacific Railroad, the new transcontinental enterprise in which it had invested heavily. A speculative bubble in railroads had been threatening to burst for several months. A series of corruption scandals had undermined investor confidence. European investors, daunted by the crash of the Vienna stock market in May, turned cautious. In September, the Bank of England raised its rates, and this, together with seasonal demand for money to move the crops in

the Midwest, drained the New York money markets. Unable to roll over its short
term paper, Jay Cooke & Co. declared bankruptcy. Wall Street panicked. The
stock exchange closed for ten days. Banks partially suspended payments and consolidated their obligations in the New York Clearinghouse. The Treasury was
forced to inject liquidity into the market (by buying bonds) to restore calm. Only
by November did a relative calm return to the money markets.[20]

But the financial panic had initiated a deep economic crisis. The railroads were
the first to be affected: over the next three years, half of them would be liquidated. Their collapse led to the bankruptcy of many banks that had lent too much
during the postwar railway construction boom. The iron and steel industries
were hard-hit by the loss of their best customers, and production fell by 45 percent in one year. Commerce, construction, and the service industry also suffered.
Agricultural prices fell as did farmers' income. Industrial wages collapsed, and
unemployment skyrocketed: a quarter of the population of New York City could
not find work during "the hard, blue winter" of 1873–74. Soup kitchens sprang up
everywhere. Tensions rose, and things sometimes got out of hand, as in New York
on January 13, 1874, when demonstrators in Tompkins Square shouting "Work or
bread!" met with bloody repression by the police.[21]

The panics in Vienna and New York triggered a "long depression," which
would endure until the end of the century, with global repercussions.[22] As usually
happens, the party in power suffered immediately at the ballot box. In local elections that fall and the following spring, Republicans lost Connecticut, New York,
Ohio, Wisconsin, and Oregon. The crisis suddenly put economic issues back at the
top of the agenda. "The political field for this Winter is dismal enough," James A.
Garfield wrote in November. "The panic is the all-absorbing theme. . . . Congress
will be a babel of confusion on the questions of finance."[23]

The Political Consequences of the Financial Panic

Politics would transform the response to the crisis into a pitched battle on the
money question, with troops from the Northeast arrayed on one side of the issue
and those of the Midwest and South on the other. Once the panic subsided,
Americans began to analyze events in terms familiar from the debates that had
raged since the end of the war. *Bankers' Magazine*, a monthly professional journal
read by bankers, reflected this transformation. The October issue, blindsided by
the crash (the stock market report was dated September 25), blamed the overex-
tension of credit and sudden cancellation of loans for the suspension of payments
by many banks and the shuttering of certain factories for lack of credit. The next
issue indicated two different causes for the crash: the policy of New York banks

to pay interest on reserves deposited with them by other banks, and their rash decision to lower their reserve rate. In December, however, *Bankers' Magazine* changed its tune again. Now the Treasury was to blame for the crisis because of its decision to reduce the public debt by buying back Treasury bonds rather than withdrawing greenbacks from circulation.[24]

In the weeks between the panic and the beginning of the new congressional session, the crisis, reduced to the money question, had thus been politicized. The Black Friday of 1873 reminded some observers of 1869: speculators, abetted by the existence of a paper currency that could not be converted into specie, were said to be the culprits. For these observers, convinced that the economy was self-regulating, it was clear that returning to a coin-based currency would by itself ensure an adequate money supply. But others saw the crash as the result of a notorious shortage of liquidity. If the money market had not been so tight because of the harvest, short-term loans would have been available, and businesses that were solvent but illiquid would have been able to avoid bankruptcy. In other words, the problem was not a surfeit of greenbacks but a shortage.[25]

The crisis therefore failed to inspire a fresh look at the money question and the way in which it had been framed since 1866. Instead, it hardened the position of the two camps. The economic and social difficulties of the moment added a sense of urgency to the deliberations that began when Congress reconvened in December 1873. Members were convinced that the country's future depended on their ability to react to the crisis. The frenzy was palpable. Financial issues dominated the congressional session. In less than two months, more than two thousand bills were introduced. The debates, including some 125 prepared speeches, fill more than 1,700 columns of the *Congressional Record*. The proceedings were soon dubbed "the inflation session."[26]

In the event, party leaders lost all control of the situation as sectionalism undermined party unity on both sides of the aisle. The economic crisis had brought with it political disarray. Here we see the delayed effects of two laws passed in 1872, one of which reapportioned seats in the House as required by the census of 1870, while the other granted amnesty to former Confederates. "It would be difficult to tell you how complicated and diverse are the various political forces which have been at work in this city during the last two days," Garfield wrote. "So much depends upon the new members that no one can say what the outcome will be."[27] There were fifty additional representatives in the House (see table 6, p. 158), all new men unfamiliar with the ways of the institution and unknown to their colleagues. The sectional balance had changed in unpredictable ways: with twenty-three new seats, the Midwest now outnumbered the Northeast. Although the Republicans had an overwhelming majority (70 percent), the breakdown of the compromise on the money question split the party along sectional lines.

On the Democratic side, the destabilization was no less profound. The party had lost ground in the North but withstood the Republican onslaught fairly well in the border states, Texas, and Georgia. This shifted the geographical balance. Southerners alone now made up half of the Democratic delegation. Thanks to the Amnesty Act, many former Confederate leaders found themselves back in Washington, including Alexander Stephens, the former vice president of the Confederacy. All these changes made it hard to predict how the voting on economic issues would go and complicated the always difficult business of managing congressional coalitions.

With political uncertainty rampant, sectional polarization proved inevitable. The urgent need to act and the interpretation of the crisis through the money question shattered the Republicans' sectional compromise. But the Democrats were also divided. This was new. Previously, Democrats in Congress (unlike outside of it) had managed to preserve some semblance of party unity. The renewed influence of the South was just as important as the increased representation of the Midwest. Representatives of both sections voted together, regardless of party. This was one of the most visible consequences of the inflation session.[28]

Debate focused on greenbacks and national banking capital. At the height of the panic, Secretary of the Treasury William A. Richardson had injected greenbacks back into the economy. Some members wanted to maintain this expanded money supply or even restore the original ceiling of $400 million on greenbacks in circulation. The banks were the second front in this battle. The Currency Act of 1870 had provided for an increase of $54 million in authorized circulation of national banknotes, of which $25 million was to be reallocated from the Northeastern states to the Midwest and South. But the comptroller of the currency, John Jay Knox, failed to enforce this law, de facto nullifying one of the terms of the Republican compromise. Congress took up the matter again, considering proposals to increase the authorized banking capital in states that needed it and even to abolish the ceiling altogether and move to free banking.[29]

After debating various proposals for weeks, the "inflationists" finally gained the upper hand and pushed through a simple bill. It restored the ceiling on greenbacks in circulation to $400 million and added $46 million in banking capital for states that had yet to reach their quota. The bill passed both houses on a strictly sectional vote in which Northeastern and West Coast representatives voted against the bill while Southerners and Midwesterners voted for it. The new role of the South is noteworthy: the final draft of the bill was based on language suggested by Augustus S. Merrimon, a Democratic senator from North Carolina, one of the former Confederates amnestied in 1872. The voting pattern reflected the breakdown of the Reconstruction coalition and party discipline.[30] The money question, revived by the crisis, exacerbated sectional tensions between the Northeast and Midwest to an unprecedented degree.

Nevertheless, the final bill was quite moderate, adding only $64 million to the existing circulation. In the impassioned climate of the spring of 1874, however, opposing views of financial issues resembled religious convictions more than rational analyses. Supporters and opponents of the bill inevitably viewed it in the starkest light. For some, it was the wellspring from which parched throats would drink, while for others, it was the breach in the dike that foretold the flood to come. Such millennial expectations explain the devastating effect of Grant's veto on April 22, 1874, which took everyone by surprise.

An Explosive Veto

"The President's veto of the inflation bill is the most important event of his administration," *Harper's Weekly* approvingly judged. "It saves the national honor, it redeems the pledge of the great popular majority which elected him, it renews the hope of the Republican party, and it restores the old regard of the country for the citizen whom it had so gladly honored for his great service in the field." This ode to the president may be taken as an index of the polarization that existed on the money question. It also hints at the political confusion the veto caused. Liberals, who had attacked Grant without letup for three years, now applauded him: "One of the great and good things of his administration." And many shared Garfield's sentiment: "I feel like forgiving him for a multitude of blunders in view of this veto."[31]

In the Midwest, the reaction was much less enthusiastic. For the Democratic papers, Grant's action was incontrovertible proof that the president was working on behalf of "a privileged class located mainly at one little portion of the Union." But, they warned, henceforth "the west and south have the means to ultimately command the situation by their overwhelming majority of voting population, and when the question comes to a decision by the people, they will scatter the dry bones of the Shylocks and sophists like chaff before an autumnal gale." Republican newspapers were all the more embarrassed to share this view of Grant's motives because they were convinced that it was correct. Some nevertheless tried to defend the president against the charge that he favored the financiers, noting, for instance, that a delegation of bankers to the White House had reportedly met with a chilly reception. Still, even as Midwestern Republicans tried to put the best face on the president's veto, they were nonetheless dismayed. "What does Grant Mean," one asked. "Has he gone over to the enemy does he wish to break up the Republican party by his infernal Veto of your Bill & recomending aditional *Taxes?*" "No danger of Grant ever becoming 'Dictator' now," another wrote, referring ironically to the charges of Caesarism. "All our papers are a unite in the expressions of surprise and indignation."[32]

Grant described his veto as a reluctant decision: he wanted to sign the bill but failed to find the arguments he needed to justify his signature. He had rarely involved himself in financial matters, leaving economic policy to his secretaries of the treasury, but his veto message reflected his longstanding adherence to a sort of hard-money "common sense." He may not have fully anticipated, however, the hostility that his veto would arouse in large segments of the Republican faithful, especially in the Midwest and South. In Washington, too, tensions erupted. Some Republican leaders, such as Senators Oliver P. Morton of Indiana, John A. Logan of Illinois, Thomas W. Ferry of Michigan, and Simon Cameron of Pennsylvania, took the veto as a personal slap in the face, and for a while considered a public rebuke of the president. The party was on the brink of disintegration, and a good deal of maneuvering, cajolery, and intimidation was needed to prevent a total collapse. The bill was definitively buried when it failed to gather the two-thirds vote in the Senate needed to override the veto—a vote that was revealing not only for its very strong sectional polarization but also because a clear majority of Republicans opposed the president. The veto had precipitated a crisis in the Republican Party.[33]

Moderate leaders such as James G. Blaine in the House and John Sherman in the Senate sought to glue the pieces back together. In regard to the substance of the controversy, they were glad to see the prospect of an increase in the circulation of greenbacks eliminated. Nevertheless, they recognized the disastrous consequences of the veto. They seized on another bill on banknote circulation to forge a compromise between the president and the various factions of congressional Republicans. Anti-Grant feeling ran so high that the task was difficult, but the bill, which the president signed on June 20, succeeded in keeping the party from breaking apart. Its content was ridiculously meager for the conclusion of such an epic battle, however: the Banking Act confirmed the $18 million in additional greenbacks issued by the Treasury at the height of the panic but prohibited any further injection; it also authorized a reallocation of $55 million in banknotes from New York and New England to other states. In short, the new law hewed so close to the status quo that it accomplished nothing.[34]

Republicans avoided a public breakup by the skin of their teeth, but the damage had already been done. Although they held a majority in Congress, they had wasted six months in futile debate that ended in a highly publicized veto. In the end, they accomplished nothing tangible to end the crisis. Hence they found themselves headed into the midterm election in very difficult straits. In the Midwest, the Democratic Party, which had been campaigning on the money question since 1867, was handed a huge gift on a silver platter. In the South, Republicans found themselves even more handicapped. Their economic policy had been their best hope for attracting white Southerners and countering the racial logic of their adversaries. The crisis had wiped out the investments made by Republican governments in any number of Southern states, and now Grant's veto had undermined their political stance as well. In short, with a stroke of the pen, Grant had aggravated the sectional divisions of his party in the North and undermined Reconstruction in the South.

Confusion was the most prominent feature of the campaign. As one observer noted,

> Everything political is in a sort of jelly-fish condition, moving round upon the waters without form or substance, and melting into nothingness when the hand is closed upon it. . . . What may pass current for correct doctrine in Tennessee and Indiana, finds no echo in Massachusetts or in New Hampshire. . . . Political cohesiveness has become almost an impossibility. . . . The day is fast approaching when there will be no politics in the country undisturbed by local measures and unfettered by the clamors of section. . . . No party announces any "fixed" principles—fixed principles being at present unpopular and dangerous.[35]

The result of the election was a "Waterloo or Sedan to the Republicans. Total rout, North and South." The reversal of fortune was spectacular: Democrats came close to a two-thirds majority in the House and dominated twenty-five of thirty-seven states. Only in New England did Republicans withstand the onslaught. They suffered a spectacular defeat in the South, where the only delegation they still controlled was South Carolina's (see table 6). In the Midwest, they lost the key states of Illinois, Indiana, and Ohio. The Democrats also took the governorships of California, Missouri, New Jersey, New York, and even Massachusetts, the Republicans' bastion.[36]

Although sectional differences on the money question were not the only cause of the Republican defeat, they did play a large part, albeit in different ways in different sections. The most direct impact of the money question was probably in the Midwest, where many saw the veto as taking away what they believed was the

ideal remedy for their economic distress. To be sure, any economic crisis makes
the party in power vulnerable at the polls, but the fact that Republicans spent a
year on the money question without doing anything to resolve it left them at the
mercy of Democrats. The most careful studies of the voting, in Indiana in particular, suggest that economic issues had a major impact. The results show not that
Republicans switched parties but that many of them stayed home, while fervent
Democrats turned out in large numbers.[37] Contemporary political observers offered the same analysis. Ohio Republicans pointed to "the [temperance] 'crusade'
and the inflation nonsense" as "the chief factors in our disaster." The conclusion
was obvious: "The financial settlement cannot be postponed until after another
Presidential election, neither party will be in shape to then win the battle." Survival would henceforth be the Republican Party's watchword.[38]

In the Northeast, the money question also worked against the Republicans, but
in a paradoxical way. Grant's veto met with a favorable welcome there, especially
among Liberals, who were outspoken in their approval. Yet they continued to
denounce "stories (half true, at least) of corruption and extravagance at Washington" and remained "nervous about a 'third term' and 'Caesarism.'" In a cartoon
that has remained famous for depicting for the first time the Republican Party as
an elephant and the Democratic Party as a donkey, Thomas Nast alluded to the
power of these accusations, which forced the mighty elephant over the edge of a
cliff (see figure 10). For those who saw specie as the only "honest money," the timid
Republican bill was hardly a moral affirmation, and in any case, there was too
much immorality among Republicans. We see this in Massachusetts, where Republicans waged a bitter campaign against reelecting Congressman Benjamin F.
Butler, whom they had made a symbol of public corruption.[39]

For Republicans, however, the most desperate situation was in the South. The
presidential veto meant that they could not campaign on economic issues, leaving
them with no alternative to counter their adversaries' strategy of "endeavoring to
force the issue of a war of races, the white man against the black, and *vice-versa*."
For Democrats, the Senate's passage of a new civil rights bill was ideal for sowing
fear in the South. In Alabama, the Democratic platform was entirely devoted to
the question of whether "the American people . . . will or will not be coerced to
absolute, social as well as political, equality of the negro race with themselves."
The Republican Party was accused of having "influenced the passions and prejudices of the negroes, as a race, against the white people," thereby making "it
necessary for the white people to unite and act together in self-defense, and for
the preservation of civilization."[40]

FIGURE 10. "The Third-Term Panic; 'An Ass, having put on the Lion's skin, roamed about in the Forest, and amused himself by frightening all the foolish animals he met with in his wanderings'—Shakespeare or Bacon," Thomas Nast, *Harper's Weekly*, November 7, 1874. (Library of Congress, Prints and Photographs Division, LC-DIG-ppmsca-15785)

The civil rights bill in question was an old warhorse long ridden by Charles Sumner, the abolitionist senator from Massachusetts, who died in March 1874. It proposed to ban all segregation in public places: in transportation, hotels, theaters, and even schools and cemeteries. Republicans passed the bill in the Senate in homage to Sumner but also as a calculated political move to attract more black votes in the South and above all to unify a party deeply divided over the money question. The idea was once again to unify the party around its core ideology, a tactic that had worked well in 1870–71 but that required pushing Reconstruction even farther at a troubled time. The gesture was not altogether sincere, however, since many senators thought that the House would never pass the bill, but it served the purpose of reaffirming the Republican commitment to equal rights. This time, though, the maneuver proved to be a miscalculation. Across the South, the bill only played into the hands of Democrats and their strategy of racial polarization. The crisis and ensuing economic distress had swollen the ranks of paramilitary groups, especially in Alabama and Arkansas, where violence and intimidation largely determined the outcome of the elections, and the Senate bill only fed the racial paranoia of white Southerners. Democrats won a crushing victory: only sixteen of ninety-three Southern House seats escaped their control.[41]

The 1874 election thus set up a triangular contest unfavorable to Republicans. In the North, heightened tensions over the money question divided them along sectional lines. In the Midwest, the party was vulnerable to Democrats, who had favored increased circulation of greenbacks for some time, while the president's veto identified the Republicans with contraction. The Reconstruction issue had lost its power to mobilize and had even taken on a negative coloration by association with corruption. Support for Reconstruction in the North diminished, depriving Republicans of an electoral advantage. Meanwhile, in the South, Republican economic policy was discredited, laying the groundwork for the return of radical racist rhetoric. In 1874, to put it in a nutshell, threats that had hung over the Republican Party for years finally came together: sectional divisions over monetary issues, exacerbated by the economic crisis, took Reconstruction out of the political equation in the North and confined it to the South, where Republicans found themselves disarmed in the face of a counterrevolutionary insurgency.

Saving the Party: A Sectional Strategy

The 1874 election debacle proved to Republicans beyond a shadow of a doubt that sectional differences threatened the survival of their party. Furthermore, Reconstruction had proved to be of no further use in overcoming those differences; indeed, it had become a handicap. They therefore availed themselves of the lame-duck session of the 43rd Congress to restore the unity of their party. Threatened by sectionalism, Republicans conceived a sectional response: a compromise between the Northeast and the Midwest on the money question and a disengagement from the South, which the Democrats had all but completely recaptured. Their ability to manage such a political tour de force attests to their resilience, if not to their convictions. The resolution of the tension between sections and party largely explains how the Republicans managed in under two years to make up most of the ground they lost in 1874.[42] The party's survival depended on reaching a sectional compromise on the currency issue together with retreat from Reconstruction.

A Compromise for Survival

The Republican solution was made possible by a peculiarity of the American political system: the lame-duck session.[43] The Congress elected in 1874 did not convene until March 4 of the following year. Meanwhile, the Congress elected in

1872 reconvened in December 1874. Republicans, who still held a large majority in both houses, would take advantage of those three months to forge a legislative compromise that they hoped would save their party. Once again, the winning combination involved a sectional compromise on currency and a new law concerning the South. But the dynamic was now the opposite of what it had been in 1870. It was not Reconstruction that made it possible to strike a compromise on the economy but the identification of common ground on monetary policy that permitted a strategic and orderly withdrawal from Reconstruction.

"The necessity of an agreement was so absolute that a failure to agree was a disruption of the Republican party," John Sherman recalled in his memoirs. In view of the danger, party leaders preferred to avoid public controversy and negotiate behind closed doors. A committee of eleven senators was formed to do so, representing the gamut of opinions on the money question, from inflationists such as Oliver P. Morton of Indiana and John A. Logan of Illinois to contractionists such as George F. Edmunds of Vermont and Roscoe Conkling of New York. The sectional breakdown was familiar: the four senators from the Northeast were the most hard money; of the seven others, six from the Midwest and one from the West, three favored an expansion of the money supply, while the four others held intermediate positions. The senators from the Midwest represented the center of the party, aware that political survival demanded that they set themselves apart not only from inflationist Democrats in their section but also from orthodox bullionists in the Northeast. Tellingly, no Southern senators were invited to join the discussions.[44]

John Sherman, the Senate's leading figure on financial issues, chaired the committee. He discreetly sounded out the new secretary of the treasury, Benjamin H. Bristow, but very discreetly: hostility to the president still ran high among Republicans, as the reactions to his hard-money annual message made clear. The bill that emerged from the committee, which was mainly Sherman's work, offered something to everyone while remaining vague on divisive issues. To the hard-money men, it offered to replace worn-out small bills with silver coins, the abolition of seignorage on gold coin, a pledge to resume specie payments on January 1, 1879, and the title of the bill—the Specie Resumption Act. To those who wanted a larger money supply, the bill offered free banking, that is, it abolished the ceiling on circulating national banknotes but proposed to withdraw $80 in greenbacks for every $100 issued in national banknotes until the amount of greenbacks in circulation was reduced to $300 million. Finally, the Treasury was authorized to purchase gold on the open market as long as it did not increase the debt, in order to increase its gold reserves.[45]

Free banking now became the linchpin of the Republican position, particularly in the Midwest. The theory of free banking is that, as long as banknotes are based on specie reserves, the invisible hand of the money market will automatically adjust the amount of money in circulation to the needs of the economy. By abolishing the ceiling on the issue of national banknotes in exchange for a return to convertibility, it became possible to satisfy hard-money men in the Northeast while promising the Midwest that the banks would be able to meet the need for liquidity. Although the law did not really establish the technical conditions necessary for free banking, it did provide Republicans with a politically defensible position and allowed the two sections to find limited but real common ground.[46]

The bill passed both houses on largely party-line votes after severely limited debate. Its many ambiguities were the price to pay for an agreement and, if all went well, for depoliticizing the issue. Neither the Liberals' embarrassing demands for clarification nor the attacks of the Democrats derailed the vote on a bill that was economically lame but politically indispensable for the Republicans. Every amendment that might have jeopardized the fragile equilibrium was rejected by a party-line vote. Final passage followed the same logic. As Blaine put it, "Public necessity and party interest combined to induce a sacrifice of financial theories in order that practical results might be achieved."[47]

Relief was apparent when the bill was signed into law on January 14, 1875. "The Finance bill is a compromise," Sherman acknowledged, "and although not what I considered the *best* yet is a *good* measure and the only one that could unite Republican Senators. I hope it will pass the House without amendments and thus leave us to consider the much more difficult problem presented by the state of affairs in the South."[48] In other words, the partisan logic was now stood on its head: Reconstruction could no longer unite a party divided on the money question; on the contrary, a sectional compromise had to be achieved before Reconstruction issues could be dealt with.

Reconstruction was thus deferred to a second phase. House Republicans now took up the civil rights bill that had passed the Senate in the previous session. It is perhaps surprising that instead of burying a bill that had lost the Republican Party so many votes in the South, they revived it. But since the damage was already done, the decision was made to capitalize on an issue that was sure to enrage Democrats, who did everything they could to block the measure. In the event, the Democrats' obstructionist tactics and vehement rhetoric went a long way toward unifying the Republicans. After a long fight, the Civil Rights Act of 1875 was finally signed into law on March 1.[49]

In its final version, the law prohibited racial segregation in public transportation, hotels, recreational spaces, and juries. It did not include schools or cemeteries, which had aroused the most vigorous opposition.[50] On paper, this federal law was probably the most radical of all Reconstruction laws, since it regulated *social* relations between individuals. It was a political assertion of the commitment to equal civil rights that had become a staple of postwar Republicanism, but it affected the balance of power between the federal government and the states at a time when the Supreme Court was beginning to adopt a restrictive interpretation of the Fourteenth Amendment. Indeed, the Court would strike the law down barely eight years later.[51]

In fact, the Civil Rights Act of 1875 marked the Republicans' disengagement from Reconstruction and strategic withdrawal to the North. The law did not need to be enforced to be useful to the Republican Party. The majority of Southern states were in the hands of the Democrats, and the federal government's ability to act on its own was limited. Furthermore, the majority of congressional Republicans had no intention of strengthening the federal means to intervene in the South. This became clear when Republicans refused to pass a sixth Enforcement Act, introduced by the Radical Benjamin F. Butler after the failure of the attempted coup in New Orleans in September 1874 followed by the events of January 1875. This draconian bill, which would have restored the president's power to suspend habeas corpus (as the Ku Klux Act had done in 1871) was probably the only bill in Congress that would have empowered the government to respond to systematic violence in the South. Southern Republicans certainly thought so. There is "no hope in the future except . . . in such laws as Congress may pass before the fourth of March Next," one Alabama lawmaker wrote. But many in the North were reluctant to take this step. "Our chances of winning the next Presidential election are *slim* enough Lord knows without willfully decreasing them," warned Joseph Medill of the *Chicago Tribune*. Such a law would "do our party infinite mischief and arm the Democrats with a club to knock out our brains." Speaker of the House James G. Blaine buried the bill. The Republicans were prepared to use Reconstruction for electoral purposes but did not want to meddle in Southern affairs.[52] Words were still possible, but action much less so.

Other measures completed the compromise the Republicans forged during this session of Congress. The tariff was increased by 10 percent as a fiscal measure required by the state of public finances. Colorado was admitted to the Union as of 1876, a step that favored Republicans, although the partisan aspect of the decision was obscured by the sectional overtones of the debates.[53] At the heart of the action was a coupling of two changes: Republicans withdrew from the South, although they reaffirmed the principles of Reconstruction, while the sections of the North reached a compromise on the currency. This new political alignment was put to the test in local elections in the fall of 1875.

Testing a New Strategy: Ohio, 1875

When the 43rd Congress ended on March 3, 1875, the political situation was highly uncertain. For the first time since the war, Democrats stood a real chance of winning the White House in 1876 following their impressive showing in the midterm election of 1874. But the Republicans had made shrewd use of the final session of the 43rd Congress. Would this be enough to save them? Looking for signs of the country's mood, political observers scrutinized state elections that fall. "This [in Ohio] is a *National Canvass*," Rutherford B. Hayes, the Republican candidate for governor, was warned. "The Republicans of Ohio are already on the advanced skirmish line in the great battle about to be fought on the national field."[54]

Of all the states, Ohio occupied a place of special importance in the eyes of politicians. The two parties were closely matched there. For example, Democrats won the state elections in 1867 and 1873. Ohio politicians were among the most prominent leaders of both parties, such as George H. Pendleton, Clement L. Vallandigham, and Allen G. Thurman on the Democratic side, and Robert C. Schenck, James A. Garfield, and John Sherman on the Republican. Ohio Democrats were influential in the national party, and the Pendleton Plan had been tested in 1867. In 1875, Republicans would try out their new compromise in the state. Ohio was situated at the crossroads of Midwest and Northeast. Greenbacks were popular there, but some leaders of both parties favored hard money. The farmers' movement was active, but industry was also well-established, including protectionist iron and steel manufactures. In short, contemporaries saw Ohio as a good place to observe what the new political equilibrium might be after the whirlwind of the previous two years.

The Ohio campaign witnessed a bit of successful political sleight of hand on the part of Republicans, who knew that they were vulnerable on the money question. By choosing incumbent governor William Allen as their candidate, Democrats put greenbacks at the center of their campaign. Rutherford B. Hayes, the Republican candidate, recognized that "our position on currency will be damaging." The Republican position was further complicated by the action of Secretary of the Treasury Benjamin H. Bristow, who turned the 1875 law into a contraction instrument (which it was not intended to be) by withdrawing greenbacks from circulation without issuing national banknotes in compensation. Recognizing the political danger, the Republicans did not repudiate their winter compromise. They defended a return to convertibility as the ultimate goal, but at the same

FIGURE 11. "The American River Ganges," Thomas Nast, *Harper's Weekly*, May 8, 1875 (first published September 30, 1871). (Special Collections, University of Virginia)

time, they whipped up a recent controversy about the Catholic vote and the Democratic Party to campaign against the public financing of confessional schools and denounce the Democrats "for subserviency to Roman Catholic demands."[55]

There was a precedent in New York, which for a time authorized public assistance to parochial schools. The Republican press seized on this law, which had originally gone unnoticed, in order to attack the Catholic Church for preying on American children. Thomas Nast lent his talents to the attack in cartoons that remain famous, such as one showing bishops as crocodiles threatening children in their public schools (see figure 11). Protestant anti-Catholicism, revived by the Vatican council of 1869 (which denounced "modern errors" and declared the pope infallible on matters of doctrine) and mingled with anti-Irish sentiment, ensured that these attacks in the press would receive a wide audience.[56]

In Ohio, no parochial schools in the state were financed with taxpayer money, but recently the Democrat-led legislature had passed a law allowing Catholic priests, like their Protestant counterparts, to serve as chaplains in prisons and mental hospitals. Catholic newspapers had put pressure on the Democrats to pass the bill, on account of the strength of the Catholic vote. In response, Republicans raised the specter of Democrats under the thumb of a church obedient to a foreign prince. They also alleged that their next target would be the public schools, and made it the centerpiece of their electoral strategy. "We must not let them [the Democrats] select the topics [of the campaign]," Hayes wrote. "We must not let the Catholic question drop out of sight. If they do not speak of it we must attack them for their silence. If they discuss it, or refer to it, they can't help getting into trouble."[57]

Hayes did not conceal his position on the money question: he favored the resumption of specie payments. This won him the support of Liberals—and Carl Schurz's backing was precious in the German community, which had been turning against the Republicans because of the temperance agitation. But Hayes's position on currency was unpopular, whereas his attacks on parochial schools enabled him to mobilize Republican voters. So as the money question played a prominent part in the campaign, the school issue was used to deflect its effects. For example, Garfield did not mention the money question in his stump speeches, but if a newspaper wished to publish the text of one of them, he would add a paragraph or two at the end. Even some loyal Republican editors sometimes had trouble convincing themselves that the school issue was relevant.[58]

The Democrats were not dupes. Senator Allen G. Thurman accused Republicans of seeking to "divert public attention to some other theme." The Democratic platform expressly supported "complete separation of Church and state . . . and purely secular education," but to no avail. By accentuating ethnocultural differences in the population, Republicans turned out their voters and won the October election. But the margin of victory was narrow. "We came out of the late election in Ohio triumphant," the veteran Benjamin F. Wade concluded, "but not without experiencing how popular inflation is among the classes named, and had it not been for the attack of the Roman Catholic church upon our free school system, I have reason to fear that we might have been defeated."[59]

The Ohio election had considerable national impact. It showed that the money question was not an insurmountable handicap for Republicans: the Midwest could be won despite support for hard money. Ohio suggested a campaign strategy that might just work at the national level. President Grant saw this clearly and in December urged Congress to pass a constitutional amendment to protect the public schools from "sectarianism."[60] Conversely, Ohio Democrats were weakened at the national level relative to their colleagues from the Northeast, who were not unhappy to see the Ohioans' "shameful inflation platform" go down to defeat. The *Cincinnati Enquirer* did not shrink from accusing "wealthy Democrats of New York" of contributing "large sums in behalf of Hayes" and of acknowledging a sectional "pit as wide and impassable as that which separates Dives from Lazarus."[61]

For Republicans, by contrast, the 1875 Ohio state election showed that if they campaigned on "values," they could overcome their sectional divisions. But it also made plain that the North would be their priority. Grant's refusal to dispatch federal troops to put down the wave of violence that was sweeping Mississippi at the time was the clearest sign of this. Despite the massacres in Yazoo City and Clinton, despite the systematic intimidation of Republican voters during the campaign and the deployment of artillery near polling stations, Grant refused to answer the repeated calls for intervention from Governor Adelbert Ames. "The whole public are tired out with these annual, autumnal outbreaks in the South," Grant laconically replied, and "the great majority are ready now to condemn any interference on the part of the Government." The priority was to do nothing that might endanger the Republicans' chances in the close Ohio race. "I was sacrificed last fall that Mr. Hayes might be made Gov of Ohio," Ames bitterly reflected. More broadly, it was Reconstruction that was sacrificed: the Republicans abandoned the South to save themselves in the North.[62]

This marked a major turning point. Severely beaten in the 1874 elections on two fronts—Reconstruction in the South and the economy and currency in the North—Republicans in the winter of 1875 adopted a sectional strategy for political survival. On the one hand, they forged a compromise between the Midwest and Northeast on currency, while on the other hand, they concentrated their efforts on the North, reinforcing their symbolic attachment to Reconstruction (with the Civil Rights Act of 1875) while disengaging from the South (with the rejection of the sixth Enforcement Act). Republicans did not abandon Reconstruction wholesale; they would periodically attempt to enforce election laws, deploying troops at polling places in 1876 and stepping up prosecutions for more than a decade after that. Yet in the fall of 1875, their national focus on the Ohio race (in a sort of synecdoche, the part standing for the whole) made clear that they would give higher priority to their consolidation in the North over intervention in the South. The success of their new strategy, however tenuous, set the two parties on a course toward a new political equilibrium between sections and parties that would endure for the remainder of the century—but not before plunging the country into a major electoral crisis.

Realignment in Crisis: The End of Reconstruction

In 1876, Americans made ready to celebrate the hundredth anniversary of their independence with the Centennial Exhibition in Philadelphia, the first world fair to be held in the United States. By the time the country was ready to display its newfound power in this international showcase, however, the circumstances had become dire.[63] The economic crisis continued unabated. The political situation was highly uncertain, tainted by scandal and marred by eruptions of violence in the South. When November came, the results of the presidential election were so close that both the Republican and Democratic candidates claimed victory. Barely eleven years after the end of a bloody Civil War, the United States once again found itself in turmoil.

The nation's predicament could be traced to the upheavals triggered by the financial panic of 1873. The near-breakup of the Republican Party along sectional lines in 1874, its crushing defeat that year, and its new electoral strategy, forged in the winter of 1875 and tested in Ohio, had created great political uncertainty. Hence the 1876 presidential election promised to be one of the most wide-open contests since the end of the war. The parties went into the race not knowing whether the 1874 election signaled a new balance of power. Sectional tensions within both major parties encouraged the formation of third parties, which further obscured the political landscape. In this context, Reconstruction once again came to the fore, both during the campaign and again in the dénouement of the electoral crisis—even though it was nearly moribund: the Republicans had practically abandoned it, and the Democratic majority in the House blocked any new initiatives on that front. Once again, sectionalism put Reconstruction back at the center of the political stage. But this time, instead of ensuring the continuation of Republican domination, it crystallized a new national equilibrium between the parties.

Reform: A Partisan Weapon?

For the first time since the war, Democrats had an issue that offered them a way out of the impossible alternative between Reconstruction (unfavorable terrain for them) and the money question (which divided them geographically). Thanks to the Liberals, "reform" had been placed on the national political agenda. The corruption scandals that haunted the Republicans were manna from heaven for the Democrats. Here was an issue that could bring them together, put their adversaries on the defensive, and win over new voters. It established a clear distinction between the parties without activating sectional tensions. Because they had previously been associated with election fraud in New York, the Democrats found the situation all the more to their liking.

Availing themselves of a majority in the House when Congress convened in December 1875, the Democrats launched a series of investigations. They planned to use powerful House investigating committees to punish Republicans and uncover new scandals.[64] The strategy was to attack "the opposition, expose their corruption, *investigate*, shake out their dirty linen before the people, keep them defending, keep them at it constantly." While depicting Republicans as corrupt politicians, Democrats sought to cloak themselves in the mantle of reform, to eliminate "useless offices, show the immense increase of officials, . . . institute measures of economy, show a *determination* to reform." They hoped this would be a winning strategy in 1876 and enable them at last to put Reconstruction behind them—provided they could make sure that "every Southerner votes readily for pensions to Northern soldiers" while "breath[ing] no word about rebel debt or pay for slaves."[65]

The choice of the austere Michael C. Kerr to lead the House was the first political signal, and the proliferation of investigations was the second. The Democrats succeeded in uncovering new scandals. One involved the wife of the secretary of war, William W. Belknap, and the supply of military bases in the West. Another concerned the award of Navy contracts, although it turned out to be less damning than Democrats had hoped. Former Speaker James G. Blaine himself was investigated for taking bribes in exchange for his help in passing legislation desired by several railroad companies. The charges were probably true, but the clever Blaine managed to deflect them, while accusing his adversaries of seeking partisan advantage.[66]

The nomination of Samuel J. Tilden as the Democratic candidate for president in 1876 marked the logical culmination of this strategy. Tilden had all "the Democratic qualifications," having been a member of the party for quite some time. He was governor of New York, whose thirty-five electoral votes were essential if a Democrat was to win the White House. But Tilden's greatest advantage was his reputation as a reformer. He had worked to bring down Boss Tweed's machine in 1871, using his expertise to ferret out secrets hidden in the city's accounts. As governor, he enjoyed abundant good press for his fight against the "Canal Ring," another political machine linked to the management of the Erie Canal. Ironically, virulent opposition to his candidacy by New York City Democrats served him as a badge of morality. As his advisor John Bigelow put it, this gave "the Gov[r] the benefit of not being regarded as having sold out to Tammany." At the Democratic Convention in St. Louis in late June 1876, Tilden easily won the nomination. The platform heavy-handedly insisted on "the urgent need for immediate reform" and proposed a straightforward line of attack: end corruption and drastically reduce the size of the federal government.[67]

Republicans were aware of the danger that corruption scandals posed for them. Grant had already taken the initiative. A shrewder politician than he is generally credited with being, he appointed two reformers to key Cabinet positions in the summer of 1874: Marshall Jewell became postmaster general and Benjamin H. Bristow, secretary of the treasury, giving the two men control of the vast majority of federal jobs. In 1875, he replaced a suspect secretary of the interior with Zachariah Chandler, who, though opposed to civil service reform, managed his department honestly and competently. Above all, the government set out to fight corruption and did so much more effectively than all the Democrats' investigations in the House. With Grant's very public backing, Bristow went after the Whiskey Ring, a conspiracy of tax collectors and distillers based in St. Louis, which had been siphoning off part of the receipts from the excise on alcohol. The president's uncompromising instruction to Bristow — "Let no guilty man escape if it can be avoided" — quickly made the front pages of newspapers. Grant's enthusiasm waned when his private secretary, Orville E. Babcock, was implicated in the scandal, and in 1876, he sacked Bristow. But if this affair, probably the most serious of his term in office, severely tested Grant's presidency and established Bristow's reputation as "incorruptible," it nevertheless served Republican interests: the party showed that it could reform itself if necessary.[68]

By choosing Rutherford B. Hayes as their presidential candidate, moreover, the Republicans effectively undermined the Democrats' strategy. Hayes was a "new" man, who had remained aloof from Washington after serving a brief stint in the House just after the war. He nevertheless managed to be elected governor of Ohio twice against well-known Democrats, and the 1875 campaign thrust him into the national spotlight. In a letter dated January 1876, John Sherman remarked that Hayes was "unblemished in name, character, and conduct." His remoteness from Washington and its intrigues was his greatest asset. He was "free from the personal enmities and antagonisms that would weaken some of his competitors."[69]

This was the main reason why the Republican Convention, which met in Cincinnati in mid-June, chose Hayes to represent the party. The great favorite was James G. Blaine, a congressman from Maine and former Speaker of the House. But Blaine was vulnerable to charges of corruption, and he had made enemies, most notably Roscoe Conkling, a senator from New York, and Oliver P. Morton, a Radical senator from Indiana. Hayes won as the heavies canceled each other out, and the choice gave the Republicans a candidate who could credibly campaign on a reform platform. In his letter of acceptance, Hayes explained that he intended to end the spoils system and promised not to run for a second term. He was also shrewd enough to seek the support of Carl Schurz by including verbatim a paragraph Schurz authored on civil service reform. The result was as desired: although some Liberals, such as Charles Francis Adams, found

Tilden more convincing, most wanted to believe that Hayes's nomination showed that Republicans had come around to their view and therefore supported his candidacy.[70]

Republicans thus parried the Democrats' campaign strategy by promising that they, too, would bring back limited and honest government. Liberals took this to be an ideological victory: both parties now embraced the principles that Liberals had placed on the agenda in 1872. But there were limits to their success. Both major parties courted Liberal votes but rejected Liberal influence. On the Democratic side, Tilden won the nomination with the support of Southern delegates, whose primary concern was that the federal government cease to intervene in Southern affairs. "Triumph to us is *salvation*, defeat *worse than death*," one Virginian wrote to Tilden, "hence we cannot and do not permit any questions to enter our local or State canvasses but the one great issue: old Conservatism against Radicalism." The Southern vote was therefore a wager: Tilden seemed to be the likely winner. Reform was hardly the primary concern.[71]

On the Republican side, the Liberal candidate was Secretary of the Treasury Bristow, who carried too much baggage to have any real chance of victory. His crackdown on patronage had alienated some influential Republicans, and his firm hard-money positions ran the risk of reviving the party's internal divisions. During the campaign, Hayes paid attention to the advice of certain Liberals, but he also listened to other voices. Schurz's insistence that Republicans cease to solicit contributions from federal officeholders fell on deaf ears. Hayes reassured Schurz with soothing words, but Zachariah Chandler, who managed his campaign, continued to seek money from federal employees.[72]

Indeed, the emphasis on "reform" confirmed Liberal influence in some ways but weakened it in others. Once both parties embraced (vague) promises to end corruption and reduce the size of the federal government, these issues lost their electoral potency, especially since many of the independent editors who mercilessly attacked Grant supported Hayes. More important than this, however, was the continued devastation wreaked by the economic crisis. This made the money question more urgent than ever. The issue, whose salience had only increased since 1873, remained unresolved. On this point, Liberals had less reason to be satisfied with the party platforms, even though both candidates favored hard money. The two parties, especially Democrats, were too deeply divided to take a clear stand. Reform had failed to establish an obvious difference between Democrats and Republicans. Hence the outcome of the election inevitably hinged on the tension between two by now familiar issues: Reconstruction and the currency. Once again, sectionalism interfered with the strategies of both parties.

The Persistence of Monetary Sectionalism

The money question could not be avoided, with the economic situation still dire and the consequences of the 1874 election. But it also continued to severely divide both Republicans and Democrats sectionally—although the former had reached a compromise in early 1875. The money question was therefore a major campaign issue in 1876, but with two complicating developments: the emergence of the silver issue and the creation of the Greenback Party.

The Greenback Party came into being on May 17, 1876, in Indianapolis, where delegates convened to consider "the necessities of the people, whose industries are prostrated, whose labor is deprived of its just reward, as the result of serious mismanagement of the national finances, which errors both the Republican and Democratic neglect to correct." Selecting Peter Cooper of New York, a former iron industrialist and philanthropist, as their candidate, and running a soft-money platform, they strove to break out of the paralyzing effect of the two-party system on the issue. The Greenback Party marked the culmination of a lengthy process that began with the ephemeral Labor Reform Party of 1872. At the state level, independent coalitions blossomed, especially after the Panic of 1873. Their target was monopoly and their primary goal was to regulate the railroads. Farmers and workers joined in the movement but sought to broaden their appeal by invoking the common interests of "producers." The protest was particularly strong in Illinois and Indiana, where the flourishing Grange movement took up the defense of the greenback. With the two major parties paralyzed by sectional division on the money question, a national party emerged from the protest movement and nominated a presidential candidate, disrupting an already complicated contest between Democrats and Republicans and ensuring that the issue of the currency would figure on the agenda. The "greenbackers" were influential in some Midwestern states, worrying Republican and Democratic leaders that the greenbackers could damage their own champion's chances, especially in Illinois, Ohio, and Indiana. It would prove true in that last state: while less than 1 percent of the vote separated Tilden and Hayes, Cooper took nearly 4 percent.[73]

The sectional divisions that fractured the two major parties were responsible for the growth of third parties, particularly in the Midwest. The money question became a touchstone for debate about the country's economic future, bringing together workers, farmers, businessmen, and industrialists convinced of the benefits of the greenback. This militancy forced the parties to confront the issue. Republicans remained reasonably united. The Ohio election of 1875 had taught them that their compromise was viable as long as they did not discuss it in too much detail and focused instead on more favorable issues. By contrast, differences among Democrats had only deepened since the Pendleton Plan of 1867. Ohio Democrats accused their colleagues in the Northeast of having sabotaged their candidate's chances in 1875. There was in fact some basis to the allegation, in that Republicans had seized on the hard-money editorials of the influential *New York World* for use as campaign propaganda. In the House, where Democrats held the majority, they ripped each other apart. Although hard-money Democrats were few in number, they held key positions, and thanks to Republican support, were able to block attacks by Midwestern and Southern Democrats on the Resumption Act of 1875. In congressional voting on this bill, the sectional polarization of the Democrats stands out with particular clarity.[74]

This intraparty division complicated Samuel J. Tilden's task, first in winning the nomination and then in waging his campaign. In the Midwest, he suffered from having been both an attorney for major railroad companies and an opponent of greenbacks. His career, which had made him a millionaire, did not make him popular with farmers, who for years had fought for regulation of the railroads. His position on the money question also aroused strong opposition among Midwestern Democrats, especially in the crucial states of Indiana and Ohio. These weaknesses worried Tilden's supporters: "The theory is that the result in the October States [Ohio and Indiana] will determine the result, and that you are weak in both on account of 'Wall St.' and your pronounced views for sound money."[75]

Although the New York governor easily won the Democratic nomination, he was obliged to accept Thomas A. Hendricks as his running mate. The governor of Indiana was known as a soft-money man. It took weeks of negotiations to narrow the gap between the two men on the issue, and they never reached a common understanding. Their letters of acceptance reflect their uneasiness on this score. Although Tilden was running as a reform candidate, he devoted most of his letter to a point-by-point account of his plan to return to convertibility. Hendricks, for his part, agreed that "gold and silver are the real standard of value" but warned that "a return to specie payments" could not "be reached in harmony with the interests of the people by artificial measures for the contraction of the currency." This was grist for the mill of pro-Republican (and hard-money) cartoonist Thomas Nast, who depicted the Democratic tandem as a two-headed tiger with the two heads pulling in opposite directions (see figure 12).[76]

In the House, Midwestern Democrats were determined to repeal the provision of the 1875 law that provided for specie payments on January 1, 1879. They did not want to go to the voters without having done anything about the issue now that they were in the majority. Tilden's backers did all they could to prevent

FIGURE 12. "The Elastic (Deformed) Democratic Tiger; They pull together so very nicely,"
Thomas Nast, *Harper's Weekly,* August 9, 1876. (Special Collections, University of Virginia)

passage of a bill that would be awkward to explain on the campaign trail, but in
the end they had to give in. They did so knowing that the bill would be blocked
by the Republican-controlled Senate. In any case, the wording of the measure
was sufficiently ambiguous that the issue could be temporarily sidestepped. In the
Midwest, Democrats could campaign on their intention to stop the contraction of
the currency that they attacked the Republicans for backing—not unreasonably
with Bristow at the Treasury. In the Northeast, they could defend their attempt
as a matter of sound financial management. If the government was not capable of
exchanging greenbacks for specie by January 1, 1879, was there not a risk of a run
on Treasury gold? This protective measure did not stand in the way of a return
to the gold standard. Abram S. Hewitt, chairman of the Democratic National
Campaign Committee, expressed his relief in a letter to Tilden: "The hard money
men have made their record & the soft money men have got the repeal, and no
longer any excuse for not carrying their States. I think that the matter is in the
best possible shape."[77]

Congressional Republicans were much less divided. They clung to their compromise of the winter of 1875. In the Northeast, they could stress the party's firm
commitment to an eventual return to convertibility, though without specifying
the means of achieving that goal. In the Midwest, they could argue that they
had courageously decided to resume specie payments while ensuring an adequate
money supply through the issue of national banknotes. But they remained cautious. Their candidate, Hayes, knew the strength of pro-greenback sentiment.

The idea of "inflating our irredeemable paper currency is bad enough. But there are debtors and speculators in large numbers in Ohio who want it," he acknowledged, adding pragmatically that "they are not all Democrats." His view was "pronounced and well known," since he had spoken out publicly on the question, but he preferred to say no more about it during the campaign. For a time he even considered not mentioning the issue in his letter of acceptance, although ultimately he changed his mind.[78]

The money question remained explosive. Delegates to the Ohio Republican convention spoke very cautiously of a return to convertibility but refused to grant explicit support to the law sponsored by their own senator John Sherman in 1875. Illinois Republicans insisted that "the Republican party has given to the people the best system of paper currency ever devised." In Indiana, Republicans called for repeal of the January 1, 1879, deadline, declaring, "any attempt to hasten this period [of redemption in gold and silver] . . . inexpedient." The national convention in Cincinnati responded to the question in the most lukewarm of terms, but even that tepid formula was not obtained without a fight. The Republican *modus vivendi* remained fragile.[79]

An unforeseen development further undermined the basis of the Republican compromise: the emergence of the silver issue. In the spring of 1876, Congress suddenly awakened to the fact that it had demonetized the silver dollar three years earlier. The Coinage Act of 1873 limited the use of silver to fractional coins (less than $1) and small transactions (less than $5). This provision had passed unnoticed by most. Even Grant, who had signed the bill into law, had not realized its effect. Yet the United States had transitioned from a bimetallic system to a de facto gold standard.[80]

In 1876, Bristow refused to issue those silver fractional coins, as mandated by the Resumption Act of 1875. Since silver ore was flooding the market, thus pushing its market value down, he was afraid that bad money would drive out the good. When he asked Congress for permission to issue fractional paper instead, Midwestern and Southern Democrats, frustrated at their inability to repeal the resumption clause, seized on this request as an opportunity to expand the money supply. In so doing, they provoked a split on silver, which strongly echoed that which already existed on greenbacks.[81] The controversy would continue to rock the United States down to the end of the century, despite a temporary truce effected by passage of the Bland-Allison Act in 1878.[82]

The "Crime of '73" blurred political lines on the money question.[83] Confusion reigned as Congress tried to answer two questions: Should the silver dollar (now redubbed "the dollar of our fathers") once again be made legal tender? And should the use of silver coin be allowed for all transactions, no matter how large? Silver had tradition going for it: the United States began its existence as an independent nation on a monometallic silver standard before moving to bimetallism. Furthermore, silver was a precious metal and therefore covered by the doctrine of "intrinsic value" that hard-money apologists had been defending since the end of the war. The lower price of silver made it attractive to mint silver coin, and this idea appealed to those who believed that the country suffered from a shortage of liquidity. On the other hand, European countries had been abandoning the silver standard of late. The German Reich had done so, and France and the Latin Union had (partially) followed suit. Hence silver was less and less useful as a medium of international exchange, although it was used in India and China. Finally, greenbackers, who insisted that the money supply should be controlled entirely by the government, were as hostile to the circulation of silver as they were to a return to gold.[84]

In the spring of 1876, the silver question upset even the most firmly established positions on the currency. For example, some hard-money men were quite happy to see the return of silver, while others worried that it might drive gold out of circulation. Similarly, among those who insisted on more liquidity, some were pleased that silver might increase the amount of specie in circulation, while others preferred to retain a paper currency controlled by the government. Even congressmen well-versed in financial matters became lost in the maze of issues. The initial votes on silver reproduced the divisions associated with greenbacks, but positions subsequently evolved in a chaotic way, cutting across both party and sectional lines. It took Congress two years to come to a (temporary) compromise with the Bland-Allison Act of 1878, which established a new sectional alignment: Representatives of the Pacific Coast and Western mining states voted as a bloc in favor of the remonetization of silver. Northeastern Democrats ultimately joined Republicans from their section in opposing remonetization, while growing numbers of Midwestern Republicans moved toward bimetallism, which allowed them to tell voters that they were working toward a solution of the money shortage while continuing to defend the Resumption Act.[85]

In 1876, however, the silver debate was still too new to have much of an impact on the presidential campaign. Since it came up as debate on the greenback was raging, however, it took on the characteristic features and alignments associated with that controversy, and these would have quite significant political implications when the issue emerged again at the end of the century. That is why the return to convertibility on January 1, 1879, did not resolve the money question. More immediately, the silver issue undermined the Republican compromise on the currency and weakened the cohesiveness of the party, which had already been damaged by the economic crisis and the emergence of the Greenback Party. Both Republicans and Democrats remained divided on the money question, but to different degrees. Neither party could see an obvious political advantage to campaigning on the issue; the election promised to be too close to risk alienating even the smallest group of voters. Hence both candidates stuck to declarations of principle. Everyone took John Sherman's words to heart: "Still, the expression should be clear & strong . . . [but] the measures proper to accomplish that object and the time when are properly within the discretion of Congress."[86] Although they could not avoid the money issue, neither party could properly campaign on it.

More of the Same? Reconstruction without Substance

The combined effect of interparty competition (which largely neutralized reform as a campaign issue) and sectional division (which did the same on the money question) put Reconstruction back at the top of the agenda. The Reconstruction issue was no longer the same as in previous elections, however. Republicans stopped pursuing reform in the South. In speeches they no longer offered any proposal to change the situation in the South, but they steadfastly denounced the dangers of returning "rebels" to power.

There was a sectional dimension to the return of Reconstruction. The new House had only a handful of Southern Republicans, but Southerners made up 42 percent of the Democratic delegation. Of 107 Southern congressmen, 80 had served in the Confederate Army, with no fewer than 35 former generals among them. They were all the more visible in that they chaired 21 of 34 House committees.[87] The Republican Party had become a party of the Northeast and Midwest (with only 16 congressmen from the South), while the Democrats were once again present in all three sections, with Southerners exerting considerable influence.

After more than ten years of Reconstruction, one might think that Democrats would have grasped the fact that the memory of secession was their greatest political liability. Yet they immediately proposed a bill to give amnesty to the handful of high Confederate officials still deprived of the right to vote and hold office under the Fourteenth Amendment. This was a bold move considering that Republicans held a majority in the Senate. The calculation was astute: if the law passed, the amnesty of former Confederates would be complete; if it failed, Democrats could argue during the campaign that the Republicans were resisting the final restoration of peace between North and South. But it required of them a self-control they did not have, and they got caught in their own trap. Offering a simple amendment excluding Jefferson Davis from the amnesty on the grounds that the former Confederate president was responsible for the atrocities at the Anderson-ville Prison, James Blaine provoked Southern Democrats, who responded with anti-Union invective. One extolled white Southern soldiers and disparaged the blacks who had fought for the Union; another sang the praises of Jefferson Davis while attacking Grant. By taking the bait, those Southerners handed Republi-cans a useful election issue. They could argue that the Democrats' idea of reform scarcely concealed the vehemence of anti-Union sentiment in the South. "The debate has done great good," Garfield reported, "in arousing the people to [the] real spirit of the South." It was an ideal issue for Republicans to campaign on.[88]

In order to repeat on the national level the success they had scored in Ohio in 1875, Republicans needed a good issue, one that could deflect the effects of both the money question and the corruption scandals and mobilize voters around the core of the party. An attempt to nationalize the school issue fizzled. Although it figured in the Republican platform, Hayes was forced to fend off accusations of nativism and anti-immigrant bias lest he lose the support of key groups such as the German community, an important voting bloc in several states.[89] Republicans, therefore, ran on Reconstruction. "Our main issue must be *It is not safe to allow the Rebellion to come into power*," the candidate wrote during the summer before the election. "These positions give us the prestige of the attack, and are in the line of a decided and growing public sentiment."[90]

The goal was no longer to intervene directly in the South but to warn against the Southerners who controlled Washington before the war. "The election of a Democratic president means a restoration to a full power in the Government of the worst elements of the rebel confederacy," John Sherman warned. "The Southern States are to be organized by violence and intimidation into a com-pact political power only needing a small fragment of Northern States to give it absolute control. . . . The constitutional amendments would be disregarded; the freedmen would be nominally citizens but really slaves; . . . and the honors won by our people in subduing rebellion would be subjects of reproach rather than of pride."[91]

One event in particular would serve the Republican campaign: the massacre that occurred in Hamburg, South Carolina, on July 8, 1876. It all began with the Fourth of July parade, when the black local militia refused to give way to two white farmers in a wagon. Two days later, Matthew Butler, a former Confederate general, appeared on the scene and, without legal authority, ordered the militia to lay down their arms. When they refused, he set out for nearby Georgia in search of a cannon and a troop of nearly a hundred men. In the ensuing attack, seven people were killed (six of them black), and the town was sacked. This was

FIGURE 13. "The 'Bloody Shirt' Reformed; Governor Tilden: 'It is not I, but the Idea of Reform which I represent,'" Thomas Nast, *Harper's Weekly*, August 12, 1876. (Special Collections, University of Virginia)

to serve as a lesson to a Republican bastion: South Carolina, where blacks were in the majority, had imported the counterrevolutionary tactics of Mississippi.[92]

To Republicans, this bloody incident illustrated the grave danger of a Democratic victory. Thomas Nast captured the feeling (see figure 13). His cartoon shows Tilden pontificating on "reform" while standing over the bodies of blacks slain at Hamburg. He was right about Democrats, at least in the South, who thought that violence was justified in order to regain political power. But Republicans had no intention of taking concrete steps to end the terror—although Grant did dispatch troops, he only did so to keep the peace at the polls on election day. Hayes himself took it for granted that the South was "gone (as it is all but one or two states)." Campaign calculations focused solely on the North, and above all on "the doubtful states [of] Indiana, Ohio, California, New York, and Wisconsin."[93]

Reconstruction had been drained of its substance. Republicans campaigned to save it, and the federal government, from Democrats—the Trojan horse of unrepentant Confederates—but not to pursue it further. There was genuine feeling in this: Hayes was convinced that "if we lose, the South will be the greatest sufferer."[94] But to a large extent, the strategy was calculated to mobilize the

Republican electorate in the North. And it paid off, to judge by the very high rate of participation in the presidential election—the highest in the history of the United States. The determination of white Southerners to regain power, together with the closeness of the race, which for the first time since the war gave them a real chance of victory, encouraged Democratic voters to go to the polls. When compared with 1874, however, it was the Republicans who made the more spectacular comeback. Their strategy of coopting the rhetoric of reform, striking a sectional compromise on the money question (even if it was an uneasy compromise), and attacking their adversaries on Reconstruction, paid off, but at the cost of a retreat from the South. It was therefore all the more ironic that the outcome of the election was ultimately determined in the Southern states.

Electoral Crisis and Realignment

When they went to bed on the night of Tuesday, November 7, 1876, both candidates were convinced that the election was over and that Tilden had won. "From that time, I never supposed there was a chance for Republican success," Hayes wrote in his diary.[95] The next morning, however, the vote turned out to be closer than predicted. At Republican campaign headquarters in New York City, the results when tallied showed that Tilden one vote short of the majority in the Electoral College: Hayes could still win if Louisiana, South Carolina, and Florida went for him. Both parties claimed victory, precipitating one of the most serious electoral crises in the history of the United States. Coming after two years of major changes, the election inaugurated—in spectacular fashion—a new political balance, which would endure until the end of the century.

The final throes of Reconstruction took on national significance. Florida, Louisiana, and South Carolina were the last Southern states still governed by Republicans. Blacks (who constituted a majority in two of the three states) were the target of a veritable campaign of terror, and both camps were guilty of election fraud. Counterrevolutionary tactics that had already proved successful in other states were meant to drive blacks and Northern-born Republicans out of office. But now those tactics, against which Grant's party protested but did little, suddenly took on national importance. The White House hung in the balance. The electoral crisis would end Reconstruction and give birth to a new partisan equilibrium—with the South under Democratic control.

Over the next four months, the political crisis unfolded in two acts. The first act took place in the contested Southern states. As a precautionary measure, President Grant dispatched the army to forestall any attempt at a coup, while both parties sent representatives ostensibly to make sure that there would be no fraud in the counting and certification of the vote. The counts had to be validated by state election boards before being signed and sealed by the governor and sent to Congress. In Louisiana, Florida, and South Carolina, Republicans controlled those bodies, which, after various political and judicial side battles, all declared Rutherford B. Hayes the winner in those states. But the Democrats protested and sent Congress a rival set of certifications in favor of Tilden.[96]

The second act took place in Washington. The Constitution made no provision for resolving such a conflict. It simply stated that "the President of the Senate shall in the Presence of the Senate and House of Representatives, open all the Certificates, and the Votes shall then be counted."[97] In 1876, the Senate was Republican, the House Democratic. As tensions mounted, some feared a new civil war if Congress blocked the election and the United States found itself without a president when Grant's term expired on March 3. After feverish negotiations, Congress agreed on an extra-constitutional solution: a special Electoral Commission would decide which of the controversial certificates were valid. It was to be made up of fifteen members, five from the House (three Democrats and two Republicans), five from the Senate (three Republicans and two Democrats), and five Supreme Court justices. Only four of the latter were to be appointed, two Republicans and two Democrats, who would together choose the fifth—the one who would decide the election. Following a series of improbable episodes, Joseph P. Bradley became the fifth man, and after a period of unbearable suspense—everyone made "a manifest effort to appear unconcerned," Garfield would remember— tilted the balance in favor of Hayes. Despite last-minute Democratic attempts to block the inauguration, Rutherford B. Hayes was sworn in as president of the United States on March 4, 1877.[98]

The electoral crisis pitched the parties into a naked struggle for power: no political principle mattered except winning the election. The last state governments of the Reconstruction era hung in the balance, but this really mattered only to Southerners. The clash reinforced the cohesiveness of both parties, as the congressional voting would show. The votes broke almost perfectly along party lines. But party unity could not be taken for granted. On the contrary, it was the result of considerable effort to reduce dissension and division in the ranks. On the Republican side, for example, some thought that Hayes was too close to the Liberals, including the cordially detested Carl Schurz, and argued that this would cause him to lose "the friendship and support of enough Senators, in the approaching struggle in the Senate, to change the result of the Presidential election, and bring in Mr. Tilden." Ruffled feathers also had to be smoothed. Senator Roscoe Conkling of New York still had not forgiven the obscure Hayes for depriving him of the nomination. His support for Hayes in the campaign had been minimal. Grant took Hayes's promise not to seek a second term as a personal attack. And last but not least, the fate of Southern Republicans was uncertain: they were "afraid they [would] be ignored, as 'carpetbaggers,' or [as] otherwise objectionable under the Hayes policy of conciliation."[99] Yet party unity was essential for victory.

Throughout the negotiations, the candidates remained far from Washington and exerted little control. The decision to create the Electoral Commission was symptomatic: neither Tilden nor Hayes approved. "Nothing but great and certain public danger not to be escaped in any other way could excuse such a measure," the Democratic candidate wrote to his colleagues on Capitol Hill, but too late to make any difference. Similarly, Hayes disliked a compromise that he saw as surrendering his constitutional rights, and that his friend Garfield saw as "singularly attractive to that class of men who think that the truth is always half way between God and the Devil." Despite the opposition of both candidates, Congress created the Electoral Commission: clearly defending the party's interests did not necessarily mean lining up behind the contenders.[100]

Maintaining party unity took a lot of work, especially when it was necessary to mollify strong personalities who had varying views about the good of the party (and their own role in it). On the Republican side, Hayes's supporters were tireless in their efforts. James M. Comly, the editor of the *Ohio State Journal,* was dispatched to assure Grant of Hayes's friendship. In January, "six of Hayes' friends" were sent "to confer with doubtful Senators, and confirm their courage." Garfield, one of the six, did not hesitate to tell Blaine, "who I think is wavering," that "the West would never forgive the East, if they deserted us in this hour." The recourse to sectional rhetoric speaks volumes. Blaine, a senator from Maine with presidential ambitions, knew how dangerous it would be to risk the hostility of an entire section.[101] Expressing the stakes in sectional rather than personal terms served to underscore the danger of breaking ranks.

Thus even in a moment of extreme polarization of the parties, the section remained a relevant and useful category. Certain Republicans even made it the basis of their negotiating strategy, which targeted certain Southern Democrats. "Those who are old whigs are saying that they have seen war enough and do not care to follow the lead of their Northern associates," Garfield reported to Hayes in mid-December 1876. "And they talk a good deal about the old whigs having been forced unwillingly into the Democratic Party. I think one of the worst things in our last management of the South has been the fact that we have not taken into our confidence, and invited to our support, a class of men whose interests are identified with the South and who will help to divide the white people politically." Hayes and his advisors then worked out a strategy to separate these old Whigs from the Democratic Party. The electoral crisis was seen as an opportunity to lay the groundwork for a new Republican Party in the South. "It is so desirable to restore peace and prosperity to the South that I have given a good deal of thought to it," Hayes wrote two days later. "The two things I would be exceptionally liberal about are education and internal improvements of a national character. Nothing I can think of would do more to promote business prosperity, immigration and a change in the sentiments of the Southern people on the unfortunate topic." The idea—the basis of what would be President Hayes's "Southern Strategy"—was to rebuild the party in the South around economic issues, like those that had separated Democrats and Whigs before the war.[102]

In fact, the attempt to bring about a party realignment in the South proved illusory. It was based on a strategy that Southern Republicans had already tried at the beginning of Reconstruction but that had collapsed in the face of racial hostility. Those Democrats who discreetly negotiated with Hayes's supporters raised this hope only to get more from the next president than Tilden was in a position to offer. Their priority was political control at the state level. There would be, however, no recomposition of parties in the South. When Hayes ordered the troops back to their barracks and watched the last Southern Republican governments fall without protection, he did so with the conviction that there was no viable political alternative. His subsequent, sporadic attempts at fostering the rebuilding of the Republican Party in Southern states all failed. The South was now a de facto one-party region.[103]

Hence there was no party realignment in the South. The electoral crisis of 1876 put an end to Reconstruction and sealed the Republicans' withdrawal to the North, despite the persistence of a few enclaves in the South. Ironically, this made the Republicans more vulnerable to sectional differences between the Midwest and Northeast, so that Reconstruction cropped up from time to time as a campaign issue: it was still part of the Republican legacy and identity. The Democratic Party now consisted of three sectional factions, with the Southern faction the largest numerically and in a position to arbitrate between the Northeast and Midwest, which remained deeply divided on economic issues. In this new political system, the two parties were closely matched at the national level. The Democrats controlled the South, while Republicans held a majority in the North, but their margin was such that small variations in the vote sufficed to bring about a change of majority in Congress. The situation made it all the more crucial to maintain party unity. In this respect, the electoral crisis of 1876 marked the triumph of the parties.

DESPITE THE REPUBLICAN victory, the balance of power that had existed between the parties after the war was upset by the election of 1872. The economic crisis, triggered by the stock market crash of September 1873, reshaped the political landscape. Sectional tensions between the Midwest and Northeast reached the boiling point and brought the Republican Party to the brink of disintegration. A crushing defeat at the polls spelled the end of Reconstruction: the Republicans no longer had either the political capital or the will to cope with the rapid deterioration of the situation in the South. Erratic federal interventions to put down violence gradually lost popular support. Party survival became the priority, and it required a withdrawal to the North.

A period of great uncertainty then followed, in which each party sought to win a position of dominance. Here, too, sectionalism played a key role in reshaping the political landscape. As Republicans worked out a difficult compromise on the money question (the tariff issue having virtually disappeared from the scene), the gap between the Midwest and the Northeast widened on the Democratic side. This sectional animosity strengthened the Southern wing of the party, which now had the largest congressional delegation and could play the role of arbiter. These severe sectional differences helped to weaken the Democrats in the North, as did the spectacular revival of the Republicans in the 1876 election, despite the continuing economic depression. The unprecedented electoral crisis altered the balance of power between sections in a strange new way: thanks to their majority in the North, the Republicans were more or less evenly matched with the Democrats, despite their virtual exclusion from fifteen of thirty-eight states. Thus it was at the intersection of partisan and sectional dynamics, of Reconstruction and the money question, that the political configuration that would endure until the end of the nineteenth century came into being.

Epilogue

ON SPACE IN POLITICS

———— · ————

THE ELECTORAL CRISIS of 1876 ended Reconstruction. It marked the close of a political sequence that opened with the election of Abraham Lincoln in 1860 and the subsequent secession of the South. To be sure, in most states, Republican efforts to transform local power relations, particularly in regard to race, had ended much earlier. But Reconstruction, in the sense of federal intervention in and federally imposed reform of the former Confederacy, ended when Rutherford B. Hayes took office. Not that the new president was indifferent to these issues, but the political situation had changed profoundly. Despite several attempts to reinvigorate the Republican Party in the South, despite bouts of enforcement of national election laws against violence, and despite the waving of the bloody shirt during campaigns, it was once again left to local governments to regulate social and racial relations, and the issue ceased to be central at the national level.

What changed in 1876 was the balance of power between parties and between sections. A new (unstable) equilibrium emerged from the electoral crisis. Reconstruction, therefore, is best understood as a national political configuration as much as the policy to restore the Southern states to the Union, which led to redefine citizenship and the suffrage. The very word "reconstruction" has encouraged a polysemic interpretation, especially in view of the many changes that occurred in the United States in this period: the place of freedmen in society among them, of course, but also industrialization, economic relations, the Indian wars and confinement of Indians to reservations, and so on. Recent historiography reflects these plural readings. Initially, however, and in the language of its promoters, Reconstruction referred to political reform of the secessionist states in order to bring them back into the Union on a new basis congruent with the results of the war. It is in this light that the political battles of the era should be seen: equal civil rights, the redefinition of citizenship, and the extension of the franchise —all revolving around the question of race. Reconstruction in this political sense ended in 1877, when the federal government renounced any ambition to enforce its idea of a "republican form of government" in the Southern states. The postwar controversies did not disappear, but from then on, they would be handled differently. The political configuration had changed.

By "political configuration" I mean a particular set of power relations among the more or less institutionalized groups that structure the political field. In the United States in this period, that field included the state governments, and, at the national level, the executive, legislative, and judicial branches. Politics was organized around two major parties, the Republicans and Democrats (in addition to ephemeral third parties), but also—as this book seeks to demonstrate—around geographical blocs known as sections—South, Northeast, and West. These entities overlap, since each political actor belongs to more than one at any given moment. This way of looking at things enables us to understand the special role of sectionalism, and in particular of sectional tension between the Northeast and Midwest, in the aftermath of the Civil War. It also explains why the study of Reconstruction, when viewed in a national context, must take into account political dynamics that might seem irrelevant to it if one were to focus solely on the racial question.

Understanding Reconstruction in terms of the political configuration calls for *a spatial history of politics,* that is, an analysis of political processes that incorporates spatial dynamics and articulates together three notions: spatial categories, scales, and places.

Issues took on a sectional dimension because the sections functioned as *categories.* Like parties, they expressed shared interests and positions in culturally intelligible and politically relevant terms. The spatialization of politics occurred when economic and geographic interests interacted with historically constructed entities known as "sections." These spatial entities encapsulated important economic differences, but they could do so only because they already existed as mental categories endowed with political significance. In short, sections were not mere lines on a map. They conveyed meaning and, therefore, they could serve as an effective shorthand for expressing shared positions on certain political issues, some old (the tariff) and others new (the money question), when parties failed to perform this task effectively.

If the division of the country into sections defined the horizontal dimension of political spatialization, sectionalism in action revealed its vertical dimension, that is, the importance of different spatial *scales,* of the relation of the local to the national, and vice versa. Sections made sense only in the national arena, because they identified economic interests with regions in opposition to other regions. But this economic image of the sections was subject to internal tensions, because at the local level, these economic interests and positions could be in contradiction with one another and subject to vigorous debate. This diversity largely disappeared at the national level, however, where each section was identified with a uniform position. Yet both parties still had to win elections locally, state by state, and at the local level, they were held responsible for the consequences of national policies. They therefore had to differentiate themselves at both levels, defending the section nationally while justifying national policy locally.

The Pendleton Plan of 1867 illustrates how these different scales interacted. After the Civil War, the money question became a national issue, stirring up sectional feeling. Grasping the issue's political potential, Ohio Democrats used it successfully against their Republican opponents at the state level. The Republicans, obliged to set themselves apart from the Democrats, found themselves on the defensive and paid for it locally. But the initiative of Ohio Democrats divided their party nationally. They thus transformed the money question (by focusing on repayment of the public debt) and altered the national political dynamic.

Finally, a spatial history of the political should devote particular attention to the *places* where different political dynamics interact. In the case studied here, it was in the national political arena, and primarily Congress, that economic issues and Reconstruction came together, because they were organized around categories (the sections and parties, respectively) that condensed complicated political positions and set up competition among them. Parties, being national coalitions, had to deal with sectional divisions at the national level. Partisan and sectional logics intersected. Their interaction and confrontation were spatially situated. The national capital, and especially Congress, were the places where this interaction occurred, because the same politicians who waged party battles simultaneously represented sectional interests.[1]

This spatial approach to political history—with its attention to the categories that structure the field, the scales on which debates unfold, and the places where different political dynamics intersect—allows us to view Reconstruction in a national context. Reconstruction was not confined to local politics in the South after the Civil War. Federal policy depended to a great extent on sectionalism, which divided the parties on economic issues. Focusing solely on the reform and reintegration of the South tells only a part of the story. It is because sectionalism was a *national* phenomenon, because regional confrontation could only take place at the national level, that it intersected with the politics of Reconstruction, which had a sectional dimension of its own, because it was the policy of the North to transform the South.

Reinterpreting the history of Reconstruction in light of sectional conflict between the Midwest and Northeast over economic issues thus tells us a great deal about what was possible, what obstacles stood in the way, and what the North hoped to accomplish in its treatment of the South. It is not a matter of confusing two separate things: Reconstruction was not a strategy of capitalists in the Northeast seeking to divide the agrarian majority (South and Midwest) in furtherance of their own economic interests. In fact, there is no correlation among Republicans between their radicalism on Reconstruction and their economic positions.[2] But while the parties expressed fairly consistent views on the reform of the secessionist states, they were deeply divided along sectional lines on economic issues. Basically, it was this political dynamic that transformed Reconstruction. There is no need here to rehash the numerous examples discussed in this book, from the Fourteenth and Fifteenth Amendments to the impeachment of Andrew Johnson, from the census to the Liberal revolt, from the Panic of 1873 to the closely contested election of 1876. It may, however, be useful to identify some of the principal interactions.

Initially, sectionalism served as part of an effort to find a way out of Reconstruction. This was clearly the case among Ohio Democrats, who seized on the issue as a campaign strategy at a time when they were in a position of weakness on all issues affecting the South. This approach failed, not only because it divided the Democratic Party along sectional lines but also because many refused to give up the fight against Reconstruction. Furthermore, a small and fairly conservative group of Republicans concluded that the time had come to put Reconstruction behind them and make economic issues their top priority.

Later, Reconstruction served to unify parties divided along sectional lines. This strategy was especially clear in the passage of the Enforcement Acts, but it can also be seen at work in every national election to the end of our period, if only as rhetoric. Republicans of course had an interest in using Reconstruction this way, but so did Democrats and Liberals in 1872.

In a third phase, sectionalism contributed to the end of Reconstruction rather than to its perpetuation. It was sectionalism that prevented Republicans from finding a political response to the economic crisis in 1874 and led them to defeat. Southerners learned to make use of the issue, justifying their actions by claiming to defend the taxpayer. Similarly, it was a sectional compromise that led the Republican Party to focus its efforts on the North, while division among Northern Democrats made it easier for Southerners to regain control of their party.

Conversely, Reconstruction influenced sectionalism and the economic issues associated with it. For instance, it was difficult for Ohio Republicans to take the same position as Ohio Democrats after having described them throughout the war as traitors. Reconstruction was a powerful ideological weapon for delegitimizing an opponent's position. Midwestern Democrats tried to gain advantage within the party by caricaturing the position of New Englanders as "Radicals," and suggesting that all who ever voted with them (Northeastern Democrats and Midwestern Republicans) were "sellouts." Finally, the reality of Reconstruction affected sectional competition between the Northeast and Midwest, because national economic decisions could be counterproductive or downright harmful to the reform process in the South—as was the case with the Bankruptcy Act of 1867, for example.

These interactions between Reconstruction and sectionalism gave rise to a new political configuration, which would persist until the end of the nineteenth century. It is impossible to understand the United States in this period without understanding how this political landscape originally came about. It featured two major parties closely balanced at the national level, leading to frequent changes of majority. Between 1876 and 1896, control of at least one of the three major federal institutions (presidency, House, and Senate) changed from one party to the other with every election except that of 1886. In other words, the balance of political power in Washington moved back and forth across the political divide every two years. Furthermore, one party controlled all three organs of government during only three congressional terms: 1881–83 and 1889–91 for Republicans and 1893–95 for Democrats. This institutional division and instability favored what historian Keith Ian Polakoff has called "the politics of inertia," ruling out the kind of federal activism the country had witnessed during the Civil War and Reconstruction.[3]

The competitiveness between the parties was a direct result of the reconfiguration of the political field at the end of Reconstruction. The failure of federal policy toward the South turned the region into a Democratic fiefdom: the few Republican officeholders who remained were an endangered species. Republicans successfully retreated to the North, where they remained in the majority. This dominant position was reinforced by the admission of new states in the West, always motivated in part by the hope that they would help Republicans win elections. This was already the case when Nevada was admitted during the war, and then during Reconstruction, with Nebraska in 1867 and Colorado in 1875. It was no accident that the next six territories to become states did so during one of the rare moments when Republicans controlled both houses of Congress as well as the White House, in 1889–90.[4]

Thus, with the end of Reconstruction, a Democratic South was born, and it would remain so until the civil rights movement of the 1950s and 1960s. In the

North, two parties were in contention. Although Republicans often had enough votes to control at least one part of the federal government, this was not always the case. Hence sectional tensions in the North would remain important, because they threatened both parties. The need to preserve a fragile equilibrium in order to avoid any split explains why presidential election strategies remained so constant. For Republicans, the winning combination was to choose a candidate from a key Midwestern state (usually Ohio, sometimes Indiana) with an influential New York Republican as his running mate. In this way, Republicans won the White House in 1880, 1888, and 1896. In 1892, on the other hand, the incumbent president, Benjamin Harrison of Indiana, ran with the reform journalist Whitelaw Reid of New York, who was far too controversial among fellow Republicans to mobilize the necessary votes. In 1884, the choice of James G. Blaine as the candidate proved counterproductive: having been in politics too long, he carried a great deal of baggage, but he also came from Maine, and this lack of geographic centrality proved to be a serious handicap. On the Democratic side, the winning ticket featured a candidate from New York, but not from the city, where the machine was discredited, with a vice-presidential candidate from the Midwest. It was with this configuration that Grover Cleveland, the only Democratic president between 1860 and 1912, won in 1884 and 1892. In 1888, the choice of Senator Allen G. Thurman of Ohio as the vice-presidential candidate was unfortunate. He was not in sync with Midwestern Democrats on the money question and did not help to mobilize voters in his section.[5]

The geographical structure of the political field can also be seen in the delicate balances revealed by presidential elections. As during Reconstruction, campaigns in this period tended to downplay issues that divided the parties internally. Economic issues such as the money question still aroused sectional tensions in the post-Reconstruction political configuration. When the silver question arose in 1876, it blurred the sectional lines at first, but these soon returned to a configuration similar to that which placed champions of an increased money supply in opposition to orthodox financiers, who insisted on the gold standard. This first episode resulted in the Bland-Allison Act of 1878, a compromise measure that remonetized the silver dollar but limited coinage to between $2 and 4 million a month. The following year, resumption of specie payments, orchestrated by John Sherman at the Treasury, eliminated the greenback problem (greenbacks remained in circulation but were now convertible). A second episode began in the late 1880s, when renewed economic difficulties revived the money question. A new compromise, the Sherman Silver Purchase Act of 1890, increased silver purchases by the Treasury for the purpose of minting silver coins. The repeal of the Sherman Act in 1893 made silver the centerpiece of a Populist crusade in the election of 1896.[6]

The same sectional configuration that existed during Reconstruction figured in these later monetary debates. Northeastern politicians from both parties occupied the more orthodox positions. Conversely, Southerners and Midwestern Democrats favored an expansion of the money supply, now in the form of silver coin. They were joined after 1876 by the West Coast congressmen. Midwestern Republicans held the balance of power; they favored a limited issue of silver coin, or, in other words, a controlled expansion of the money supply.[7] This position was a direct consequence of political developments at the end of Reconstruction. The compromise of 1875 and the elections of that year refocused Midwestern Republicans on a less inflationary position yet left them still staunchly opposed to deflation. The appearance of silver in 1876 delivered them from the greenback issue. They could now support an injection of specie, hence of "honest" money. The political byplay of the late Reconstruction era had put them in a key position that allowed them to forge sectional compromises that could then be voted into law.

The distance between Northeastern Democrats on the one hand and Southern and Midwestern Democrats on the other was much larger, however. Neglecting this fact, the Democratic president Grover Cleveland repeated in 1893 the mistake that Grant had made in 1874: worried about the depletion of the Treasury's gold reserves, Cleveland pressured Congress to repeal the Sherman Silver Purchase Act, which it had passed three years earlier. Thanks to party discipline, Congress did as it was asked. This fractured the Democratic Party, much as Grant had fractured the Republican Party in 1874. The Democrats suffered a severe defeat in 1894, and Congress came under Republican control. But the Democrats were unable to strike a sectional compromise to piece the party back together. In the South and West, they were overtaken by the Populist movement, and William Jennings Bryan emerged as the Democratic candidate for president.

The presidential campaign of 1896 was waged on the silver issue, and William McKinley won easily because Midwestern Republicans and many Northeastern Democrats backed him. The result of this sectional reconfiguration was a durable party realignment. Republicans subsequently dominated Congress and the White House until the 1930s (with the exception of the 1910s), and Bryan's two electoral failures (in 1896 and 1900) marked the end of the money question. A new political configuration replaced the old one.

Tariff policy followed a similar trajectory. When the tariff issue reemerged in the 1880s, it revived sectional conflict. Although Republicans were, broadly speaking, more favorable to a high tariff than Democrats, both parties remained divided along geographic lines: the industrial Northeast was protectionist, with the notable exception of New York Democrats linked to mercantile interests; the Midwest and South pushed for lower rates. These coalitions were represented in the tariff debates of 1883 and 1888. The latter year marked a turning point, however, because Grover Cleveland threw all the weight of his presidency behind a reduction of the tariff. Party discipline came into play, and the Democratic Party backed a (moderate) free-trade line, despite the fact that sectional differences had not completely disappeared. They were aided by the fact that Ohio Republicans shifted gradually to the protectionist side, identifying the Republicans with protectionism. One sign of this change is that after 1888, no tariff law could be passed unless both houses of Congress and the presidency were controlled by the same party, as was the case in 1890, 1894, and 1897.[8]

These partisan alignments were possible only if sectional accommodations could be reached. In the Republican Party, this came about, as at the beginning of Reconstruction, when protecting Midwestern wool interests was coupled with the use of tariff revenues ostensibly to pay for the pensions of Civil War veterans.[9] On the Democratic side, a compromise was reached by replacing lost tariff revenues with the proceeds of a federal income tax, the idea being that the latter would weigh mainly on the Northeast (the wealthiest region), while the tariff redistributed wealth to the same Northeast (the most industrialized region). With this configuration, as with the silver issue in 1896, the sectional dynamic ceased to be orthogonal to the party logic. Nevertheless, the tariff question did not disappear from politics and would remain an important issue until World War II.[10]

The political realignment of the late nineteenth century was therefore in large part a sectional realignment. Democrats split over the money question, with many leaving the party when it backed free coinage of silver. The decisive defeats they suffered in 1896 and 1900 ended the distinctive political configuration created during Reconstruction from the intersection of section and party. Ironically, it was this reconfiguration that allowed the South to complete the subjugation of blacks by establishing legal segregation and denying them the right to vote. Republicans went along with this all the more easily because they now had firm control of the North. As long as the parties remained fairly evenly balanced, the handful of Republican representatives from the South held the crucial balance. As late as 1890, a new Enforcement Act was submitted to Congress to strengthen federal oversight of elections. But by the end of the century, the South had a free hand. Ironically, if sectional conflict between the Northeast and Midwest helped to end Reconstruction in the 1870s, it was the end of sectional tensions twenty years later that allowed many of the achievements of Reconstruction to be undone.[11]

The spatial dimension remained an important feature of American politics in the twentieth century and beyond. Sectional categories continue to resonate today. Take, for example, the South's frequent insistence on its southern heritage and defense of the Confederate flag, or the constant reference to the "heartland" in the speeches of Midwestern politicians. A spatial history of American politics remains relevant to the twentieth- and twenty-first-century United States. But the specific configuration born with Reconstruction disappeared in 1896. When L. Frank Baum wrote *The Wizard of Oz* in 1900, his fable spoke to everyone who over the past forty years had followed the heated debates on the money question. By the time the film adaptation appeared in 1939, however, Dorothy's shoes were no longer silver. They had become red, a color that more fully revealed the magic of Technicolor. The political allegory had been lost.

NOTES

Note on Statistical and Geographic Analysis

1. Rosenthal and Poole, *United States Congressional Roll Call.*

2. The Rice Index is the difference between the percentage of yea votes and the percentage of nay votes within a group. John M. Carey, "Party Unity in Legislative Voting," 2000, http://citeseerx.ist.psu.edu/viewdoc/summary?doi=10.1.1.25.720; Carey, "Competing Principals"; Harris, "Right Fork or Left Fork?"

3. Martis, *The Historical Atlas of United States Congressional Districts.*

4. The data was smoothed spatially using Philcarto, a software developed by geographer Philippe Waniez: http://philcarto.free.fr.

Introduction

1. Rockoff, "The 'Wizard of Oz'"; Ritter, *Goldbugs and Greenbacks,* 19–25, 288–90. Not every scholar agrees with this interpretation, citing Baum's later political leanings. Nevertheless, his tale lends itself very easily to such a reading, and this echo to popular cultural tropes no doubt contributed to its extraordinary popularity.

2. There is also evidence that race and money were already linked in American culture, making this pairing all the more powerful; see O'Malley, *Face Value.*

3. Gillette, *Retreat from Reconstruction,* xiii.

4. Foner, *Reconstruction.*

5. On the long and contentious history of Reconstruction before the 1980s, see Foner, "Reconstruction Revisited." For more recent works, see O. Vernon Burton, David Herr, and Matthew Cheney, "Defining Reconstruction," in Ford, ed., *A Companion to the Civil War and Reconstruction,* 299–322; and Brown, ed., *Reconstructions.*

6. Donald et al., *The Civil War and Reconstruction,* 478. Morton Keller also called for a fresh look at the North in *Affairs of State.*

7. A useful historical synthesis of these works can be found in Heather Cox Richardson, "Reconstruction and the Nation," in Ford, ed., *A Companion to the Civil War and Reconstruction,* 447–67; Richardson, "North and West of Reconstruction: Studies in Political Economy," in Brown, ed., *Reconstructions,* 66–90; Balogh, *A Government out of Sight,* 309–51; and Schneirov, "Thoughts on Periodizing the Gilded Age."

8. Richardson, *The Death of Reconstruction;* Richardson, *West from Appomattox;* Foster, *Moral Reconstruction.*

9. Rouberol and Chardonnet, *Les Sudistes,* 9–10.

10. Bensel, *Sectionalism and American Political Development,* 6; Ayers et al., *All over the Map,* 1–10; Cayton and Gray, eds., *The Identity of the American Midwest,* 1–26.

11. Turner, *The Significance of Sections,* 50–51, 41.

12. Beard and Beard, *The Rise of American Civilization,* 2:52–121; Beale, *The Critical Year.*

13. Coben, "Northeastern Business and Radical Reconstruction"; Sharkey, *Money, Class, and Party;* Unger, *The Greenback Era;* Nugent, *The Money Question;* Nugent, *Money and American Society.*

1. Sectionalism

1. The description of the Grand Review is taken mainly from Royster, *The Destructive War,* 406–17. The quotation, from a letter of Frederick Marion to his sister dated May 17, 1865, can be found on p. 415. See also Gallagher, *The Union War,* 7–32.

2. *Cincinnati Commercial,* May 27, 1865, quoted in Royster, *The Destructive War,* 415; Blaine, *Twenty Years of Congress,* 2:19.

3. The black men marching in the parade were former slaves who had fled to the Union Army and worked in it through the war. Yet there was no black soldier parading that day. See Gallagher, *The Union War,* 7–32. On the evolution of the concept of nation in international perspective, see Bender, *A Nation among Nations,* 116–81.

4. Nicolay and Hay, *Abraham Lincoln,* 10:334, quoted in Royster, *The Destructive War,* 417.

5. Ibid., 406.

6. For details of the military history of the Civil War, see Donald et al., *The Civil War and Reconstruction,* 183–224, 347–408, 465–75; and McPherson, *Battle Cry of Freedom,* chap. 11 et seq.

7. Donald et al., *The Civil War and Reconstruction,* 225–34; Paludan, *A People's Contest,* 3–31; Shannon, *The Organization and Administration of the Union Army,* 1:15–50; Nevins, *The War for the Union,* 1:169 (quotation).

8. Royster, *The Destructive War,* 406–17; *New York Herald,* May 25, 1865.

9. U.S. Congress, *Congressional Globe,* 37th Congress, 3rd session, Appendix, 1–5 (Dec. 1, 1862).

10. Donald, *Lincoln,* 230–56; Carwardine, *Lincoln,* 118–19; Harris, *Lincoln's Rise to the Presidency,* 244–45.

11. Kenneth Winkle, "'The Great Body of the Republic': Abraham Lincoln and the Idea of the Middle West," in Cayton and Gray, eds., *The Identity of the American Midwest,* 111–22.

12. M. A. Livermore to George W. Julian, Aug. 15, 1869, Joshua R. Giddings and George W. Julian Papers, box 5, Library of Congress; *Ashtabula Sentinel,* Feb. 20, 1867; unidentified newspaper clipping, June 17, 1868, box 93, and clipping from *The Western Soldier's Friend and Fireside Companion,* Sept. 24, 1870, box 94, John A. Logan Papers, Library of Congress; Blondheim, *News over the Wires,* 143–68; *Jonesboro Gazette,* March 13, 1875; *Chicago Republican,* Sept. 12, 1866, Feb. 19, 1870, and June 4, 1869.

13. William H. Brewer, "The Woodlands and Forest Systems of the United States," in Walker, ed., *Statistical Atlas of the United States,* 1–5.

14. Shortridge, *The Middle West*, 13–26; Meinig, *The Shaping of America*, 3:157.

15. Cronon, *Nature's Metropolis*, xviii–xix.

16. Onuf, *Statehood and Union.*

17. *Globe*, 41th Cong., 2nd sess., Appendix, 272 (April 1, 1870). *The North American* is excerpted in the *Quincy Whig*, Jan. 6, 1874; Shortridge, *The Middle West*, 13–26.

18. Edward L. Ayers and Peter S. Onuf, "Introduction," in Ayers et al., *All over the Map*, 1–10; Anderson, *Imagined Communities*, 170–78; Shortridge, *The Middle West*, 13–21.

19. Ayers and Onuf, "Introduction," 9.

20. Shortridge, *The Middle West*, 27–38.

21. Jeremy Atack, Fred Bateman, and William N. Parker, "Northern Agriculture and the Westward Movement," in Engerman and Gallman, eds., *The Cambridge Economic History of the United States*, 2:285–328; Van Atta, *Securing the West.*

22. Onuf, *Statehood and Union*, 109–32.

23. Foner, *Free Soil, Free Labor, Free Men;* Morrison, *Slavery and the American West.*

24. Etcheson, *The Emerging Midwest*, 108–26; Kathleen Neils Conzen, "Pi-ing the Type: Jane Grey Swisshelm and the Contest of Midwestern Regionality," in Cayton and Gray, eds., *The Identity of the American Midwest*, 91–110.

25. Cayton and Onuf, *The Midwest and the Nation*, 25–30; Richard K. Vedder and Lowell E. Gallaway, "Migration and the Old Northwest," in Klingaman and Vedder, eds., *Essays in Nineteenth Century Economic History*, 159–76 (figures corrected with the Eighth Census).

26. Conzen, *Immigrant Milwaukee;* Gjerde, *From Peasants to Farmers;* Gjerde, *The Minds of the West;* Hine and Faragher, *The American West.*

27. Cayton and Onuf, *The Midwest and the Nation*, 34–39; Clark, *The Grain Trade in the Old Northwest;* Scheiber, *Ohio Canal Era;* Earle, "Regional Economic Development West of the Appalachians"; Meinig, *The Shaping of America*, 2:323–32.

28. Cronon, *Nature's Metropolis;* Heffer, *Le Port de New York.*

29. These observations are based on analysis of figures from the Seventh and Eighth Censuses (1850 and 1860). The ratio of the workforce in the agricultural sector is taken from Robert A. Margo, "The Labor Force in the Nineteenth Century," in Engerman and Gallman, eds., *The Cambridge Economic History of the United States*, 2:207–43.

30. Peter S. Onuf, "Federalism, Republicanism, and the Origins of American Sectionalism," in Ayers et al., *All over the Map*, 11–37; Cayton and Gray, eds., *The Identity of the American Midwest*, 140–96. Frederick Jackson Turner's debt to these cultural conceptions is striking; see Cayton and Onuf, *The Midwest and the Nation*, 125–26.

31. Etcheson, *The Emerging Midwest*, 1–15; Gjerde, *The Minds of the West*, 283–96.

32. Etcheson, *The Emerging Midwest*, 15–26; Onuf, *Statehood and Union*, 67–87.

33. Etcheson, *The Emerging Midwest*, 90–94, 93 (quotation); Onuf, *Statehood and Union*, 21–43; Atack et al., "Northern Agriculture and the Westward Movement"; Rohrbough, *The Land Office Business;* Van Atta, *Securing the West.*

34. Etcheson, *The Emerging Midwest*, 52–62; Irwin, "Antebellum Tariff Politics."

35. Finkelman and Kennon, eds., *Congress and the Emergence of Sectionalism.*

36. Cronon, *Nature's Metropolis,* 31–46.

37. Maizlish, "The Meaning of Nativism"; Anbinder, *Nativism and Slavery.*

38. Etcheson, *The Emerging Midwest,* 108–39.

39. Patricia N. Limerick, "Region and Reason," in Ayers et al., *All over the Map,* 83–104, 83 (quotation).

40. Only roll-call votes lend themselves to statistical analysis, as they provide the individual vote of each congressman or senator. Most votes, however, were taken *viva voce* or by division, and the records only show the aggregate result. On the analysis of roll-call votes, see the note on statistical and geographic analysis.

41. Bogue, *The Earnest Men.* The small number of senators—between fifty and seventy-four during Reconstruction—makes the analysis of their votes less statistically significant than for the House.

42. On the notion of the partisan imperative, see Silbey, *The Partisan Imperative.*

43. In this book, the phrase "sectional vote" will be used for votes opposing the Northeast and the Midwest.

44. This is one possible interpretation of the "sectionalism by abstention" evident in the table. The decision to abstain is hard to analyze: Although prohibited in theory by the rules, it was in fact relatively common. Representatives simply stayed away from the floor during voting. Nevertheless, the frequency of votes in which a majority of representatives of one section chose to abstain rather than vote with the majority of another section suggests that representatives did not regard sectionalism as a minor matter, especially within their own party. Its importance is actually quite remarkable. The rules can be found in Barclay, *Constitution of the United States,* 2:3.

45. *Globe,* 39th Cong., 1st sess., 755 (Feb. 8, 1866).

46. Ibid., 39th Cong., 2nd sess., 949 (Feb. 1, 1867); Sandage, *Born Losers,* 199–218.

47. Richardson, *The Greatest Nation of the Earth.*

48. *Globe,* 39th Cong., 1st sess., 755 (Feb. 8, 1866), 1699 (March 28, 1866).

49. Ibid., 1693–94 (March 27, 1866).

50. Ibid., 1686; 39th Cong., 2nd sess., 954 (Feb. 1, 1867).

51. Ibid., 39th Cong., 1st sess., 1686–91 (March 27, 1866); 39th Cong., 2nd sess., 954 (Feb. 1, 1867).

52. Richardson, *The Greatest Nation of the Earth,* 144–49; Bogue, "Senators, Sectionalism, and the 'Western' Measures."

53. *Globe,* 39th Cong., 1st sess., 1689–90 (March 27, 1866). The Star Chamber was a tribunal in England that secretly judged political offenses from the fourteenth to the seventeenth centuries. It became synonymous with arbitrary power.

54. Bensel, *Yankee Leviathan;* Hyman, *A More Perfect Union.*

55. *Globe,* 39th Cong., 2nd sess., 962 (Feb. 2, 1867).

56. Ibid., 979–80 (Feb. 4, 1867); Sharp, "Stay and Exemption Laws"; Thomas, "Homestead and Exemption Laws"; Foner, *Reconstruction,* 212.

57. Roll-call votes showed strong sectionalism; see *Globe,* 39th Cong., 1st sess., 1699 (March 28, 1866); 39th Cong., 2nd sess., 1708 (March 1, 1867). On how the reality of the

enforcement of the law was advantageous to Southerners, see Thompson, *The Reconstruction of Southern Debtors*.

58. H.R. 836, "A Bill to Equalize the Bounties of Soldiers, Sailors, and Marines Who Served in the Late War for the Union," 39th Cong., 2nd sess. Texts for all bills can be found in U.S. Congress, *Bills and Resolutions of the House and the Senate*, for each session.

59. Skocpol, *Protecting Soldiers and Mothers*, 102–51.

60. *Globe*, 39th Cong., 2nd sess., 1266–67 (Feb. 15, 1867).

61. Ibid., 1268.

62. Ibid., 1270–71. On bounties and the recruitment of soldiers, see Geary, *We Need Men*.

63. *Globe*, 39th Cong., 2nd sess., 1271–72 (Feb. 15, 1867).

64. Ibid., 1272. On "bounty hunters," see Murdock, *Patriotism Limited;* Murdock, *One Million Men;* and Smith, "The Most Desperate Scoundrels Unhung."

65. Foner, *Reconstruction*, 487–88.

66. *Chicago Republican*, March 2, 1869; *Joliet Republican*, March 13, 1869. In fact, the Kansas legislature *did* act too hastily, as it ratified on February 27, 1869, an erroneous wording and had to do it over again on January 19, 1870. Killian et al., *The Constitution of the United States of America*, 33.

67. *Globe*, 41st Cong., 2nd sess., 671–93, 679 (quotation) (Jan. 22, 1870). Press comments on his speech can be found in Logan Papers, box 94.

68. *Joliet Republican*, Oct. 16, 1869; *Chicago Republican*, Nov. 21, 1869; *Cincinnati Enquirer*, Oct. 22, 1870.

69. *Joliet Republican*, Oct. 16, 1869; *Quincy Whig*, June 18, 1868.

70. *Quincy Whig*, June 18, 1868.

71. James A. Garfield to Lionel A. Sheldon, Dec. 17, 1868; Garfield to Colonel [illegible], Jan. 21, 1869, James A. Garfield Papers, series 6A, vols. 1–2, Library of Congress.

72. S. Bassett French to Samuel Tilden, Nov. 21, 1875, Samuel J. Tilden Papers, box 8, New York Public Library; House, "The Speakership Contest of 1875."

73. *Cincinnati Enquirer*, Dec. 14, 1865.

74. *Cincinnati Enquirer*, Dec. 7, 1874.

2. Gold and Paper

1. Samuel Hooper (R, MA), *Globe*, 39th Cong., 1st sess., 975 (Feb. 21, 1866).

2. Ibid., 1500 (March 19, 1866); U.S. Congress, *Journal of the House of Representatives*, 39th Congress, 1st session, 84 (Dec. 18, 1865).

3. *Worcester (MA) Sentinel*, Oct. 17, 1868; William D. Sylvis (1868), quoted in Ritter, *Goldbugs and Greenbacks*, 28; Unger, *The Greenback Era*, 120–26.

4. Nugent, *The Money Question*.

5. Flaherty, *The Revenue Imperative*, 35–79; Taussig, *The Tariff History in the United States*, 158–61, 259; Sexton, *Debtor Diplomacy*, 84–95.

6. Wilson, *The Business of Civil War*.

7. Hammond, *Sovereignty and an Empty Purse;* Edling, *Hercules in the Cradle,* 178–215.

8. Sharkey, *Money, Class, and Party,* 29–50.

9. Redlich, *The Molding of American Banking,* vol. 1.

10. Ritter, *Goldbugs and Greenbacks,* 125.

11. Acts of Feb. 25, 1863, ch. 58, 12 Stat. 665, and of June 3, 1864, ch. 106, 13 Stat. 99; Sharkey, *Money, Class, and Party,* 227–29; Redlich, *The Molding of American Banking,* 1:107.

12. On the persistence of state banks until the creation of the Federal Reserve in 1913, see Hugh Rockoff, "Banking and Finance, 1789–1914," in Engerman and Gallman, eds., *The Cambridge Economic History of the United States,* 2:643–84.

13. Redlich, *The Molding of American Banking,* 1:113; Sharkey, *Money, Class, and Party,* 56–59; Flaherty, *The Revenue Imperative,* 138.

14. Speech in Fort Wayne, Oct. 1865, in McCulloch, *Men and Measures of Half a Century,* 201.

15. Mitchell, *Gold, Prices & Wages.*

16. Sharkey, *Money, Class, and Party,* 81.

17. *Alton Telegraph,* Nov. 24, 1865. See also *Chicago Republican,* Jan. 6, 1866; *Cincinnati Enquirer,* Dec. 13, 1865; *Bankers' Magazine and Statistical Register* 15, no. 6 (Dec. 1865): 433–36; no. 7 (Jan. 1866): 513–22.

18. *Globe,* 39th Cong., 1st sess., 971 (Feb. 21, 1866).

19. Ibid., 1453–54 (March 16, 1866).

20. Ibid., 975 (Feb. 21, 1866); 1496 (March 19, 1866).

21. Ibid., 1456 (March 16, 1866); 1427 (March 15, 1866).

22. Ibid., 1459 (March 16, 1866), 1427–28 (March 15, 1866).

23. Belz, *Reconstructing the Union;* Bensel, *Yankee Leviathan.*

24. *Globe,* 39th Cong., 1st sess., 1846 (April 9, 1866).

25. See, e.g., ibid., 971 (Feb. 21, 1866), 1466 (March 16, 1866), 1848 (April 9, 1866).

26. Act of April 12, 1866, ch. 39, 14 Stat. 31.

27. *Globe,* 39th Cong., 1st sess., 1499 (March 19, 1866).

28. The polarization index on House votes oscillated between .2 and .25 (with one peak at .36), on a scale of 0 to 1 (see the note on statistical and geographic analysis), thus there was sectionalism in the votes, but it was mild. Ibid., 1467 (March 16, 1866), 1496, 1500 (March 19), 1614 (March 23), 1854 (April 9).

29. In the next session (Dec. 1866–March 1867), the polarization index had moved up to .4–.6; see *Globe,* 39th Cong., 2nd sess., 151 (Dec. 17, 1866), 992 (Feb. 4, 1867), 1424, 1426 (Feb. 21), 1666 (Feb. 28), 1735 (March 2).

30. Nugent, *Money and American Society,* 3–6; Sklansky, *The Soul's Economy,* 105–36.

31. *Globe,* 39th Cong., 2nd sess., 1420–23 (Feb. 21, 1867).

32. Ibid., 1870 (Feb. 27, 1867), 1664–65 (Feb. 28, 1867).

33. On the formation of the Republican Party, see Gienapp, *The Origins of the Republican Party;* Holt, *The Political Crisis of the 1850s;* and Foner, *Free Soil, Free Labor, Free Men.*

34. Coben, "Northeastern Business and Radical Reconstruction"; Sharkey, *Money, Class, and Party;* Unger, *The Greenback Era.*

35. *Globe,* 41st Cong., 2nd sess., 4176 (June 7, 1870).

36. Ibid., 40th Cong., 2nd sess., 3962–64 (July 11, 1868).

37. *Cincinnati Enquirer,* April 25, 1871.

38. Simeon Nash to John Sherman, Dec. 26, 1865, John Sherman Papers, vol. 89, Library of Congress.

39. On currency as a social institution suddenly "denaturalized" by greenbacks, see Carruthers and Babb, "The Color of Money and the Nature of Value."

40. Garfield, *Diary,* 2:305 (March 28, 1874); 1874 Massachusetts Republican platform in *Appleton's Annual Cyclopaedia,* 1874, 522.

41. *Bankers' Magazine* 2, no. 8 (Feb. 1868): 628–29; Nugent, *The Money Question,* 67–90; Reti, *Silver and Gold,* 33–60.

42. *Globe,* 39th Cong., 1st sess., 972 (Feb. 21, 1866); 40th Cong., 2nd sess., 3959 (July 11, 1868); "Public Debt of the United States," *Bankers' Magazine* 14, no. 11 (May 1865): 922.

43. *Globe,* 39th Cong., 2nd sess., 1420 (Feb. 21, 1867); 40th Cong., 2nd sess., 1810 (March 11, 1868); 41st Cong., 2nd sess., 702–3 (Jan. 24, 1870). On Cooke's methods of advertisement, see Oberholtzer, *Jay Cooke,* 1:232–53.

44. *Globe,* 40th Cong., 2nd sess., 3992 (July 13, 1868).

45. Unger, *The Greenback Era,* 74.

46. *Globe,* 40th Cong., 2nd sess., 3988 (July 13, 1868); James A. Garfield to David A. Wells, Aug. 14, 1871, Garfield Papers, series 6A, vol. 9. The *Cincinnati Enquirer* especially favored the word "bondocrat," which it coined; see, e.g., June 22, 1867, or July 12, 1875. At the other end of the spectrum, *The Nation* kept denouncing anyone attempting to, in their view, "repudiate" the financial obligations of the government; see, e.g., Aug. 15, 1867, 135.

47. *Globe,* 41st Cong., 2nd sess., 701 (Jan. 14, 1870).

48. *Jonesboro Gazette,* Oct. 5, 1867; *Cincinnati Enquirer,* March 14, 1867.

49. *Chicago Republican,* April 11, 1868.

50. Oberholtzer, *Jay Cooke,* 1:235; Scott Derks, *The Value of a Dollar: Prices and Incomes in the United States, 1860–2004* (Millerton, NY: Grey House, 2004), 9. As an indication, $50 in 1862 corresponded to $1,150 in 2011, according to one index based on consumer's prices (measuringworth.com). Robert Sharkey contends that most of the bonds were bought during the war by middle-class businessmen and professionals. Sharkey, *Money, Class, and Party,* 298.

51. Heather Cox Richardson points out the need for such a study in "North and West of Reconstruction," 76.

52. Stephen Mayham (D, NY), *Globe,* 41st Cong., 2nd sess., 5022 (June 30, 1870); *Cincinnati Enquirer,* July 18, 1868.

53. *Globe,* 41st Cong., 2nd sess., 5024 (June 30, 1870); 40th Cong., 2nd sess., 4224 (July 18, 1868).

54. Ibid., 41st Cong., 2nd sess., 702 (Jan. 24, 1870); 40th Cong., 2nd sess., 3963 (July 11, 1868).

55. Ibid., 41st Cong., 2nd sess., 729 (Jan. 25, 1870); *New York Daily Tribune,* March 19 and 24, 1866, quoted in Unger, *The Greenback Era,* 117.

56. *Globe,* 39th Cong., 1st sess., 1427 (March 15, 1866).

57. Garfield, *Honest Money,* quoted in Ritter, *Goldbugs and Greenbacks,* 79; James A. Garfield to L. E. Holden, Jan. 27, 1873, Garfield Papers, series 6A, vol. 12.

58. In reality, the national banking system probably lacked that elasticity. Selgin and White, "Monetary Reform and the Redemption of National Bank Notes."

59. *Globe,* 40th Cong., 3rd sess., 1272 (Feb. 16, 1869); ibid., 41st Cong., 2nd sess., 4226 (June 8, 1870); *Cincinnati Enquirer,* April 20, 1869.

60. Foner, *Free Soil, Free Labor, Free Men;* Foner, *Reconstruction;* Nugent, *Money and American Society;* Sklansky, *The Soul's Economy,* 73–136; Ritter, *Goldbugs and Greenbacks,* esp. 1–27; Carruthers and Babb, "The Color of Money and the Nature of Value."

61. Historians and political scientists in the 1950s have focused on interest-group politics, including analyzing the money question after the Civil War. Although the following interpretation owes much to them, it differs in its conclusions. Coben, "Northeastern Business and Radical Reconstruction"; Sharkey, *Money, Class, and Party;* Unger, *The Greenback Era;* Nugent, *The Money Question;* Nugent, *Money and American Society.*

62. Unger, *The Greenback Era,* 126–31; Dorfman, *The Economic Mind,* 3:73–77.

63. Francis Bowen, *American Political Economy, Including Strictures on the Management of the Currency and the Finances since 1861, with a Chart Showing the Fluctuations in the Price of Gold* (New York: Charles Scribner, 1870), iv, 342; Perry, *Elements of Political Economy,* 249–63; Lyman Atwater, "The Late Commercial Crisis," *The Presbyterian Quarterly and Princeton Review* 3 (Jan. 1874): 123–24; *Christian Mirror,* Dec. 2, 1873, 68, all quoted in Unger, *The Greenback Era,* 120–40. On the transformation of social sciences at this period, see Ross, *The Origins of American Social Science,* 53–63.

64. *New York Christian Advocate,* Aug. 8, 1868; *Boston Christian Examiner* 86, no. 271 (Jan. 1869): 37; Unger, *The Greenback Era,* 120–26.

65. Ibid.; Nugent, *Money and American Society,* 3–5, 263–65.

66. Unger, *The Greenback Era,* 144–58; Nugent, *Money and American Society,* 44–48; Bensel, *Yankee Leviathan,* 257–58.

67. Speech of R. McChesney in *Proceedings of the National Commercial Convention,* 189. See also *Proceedings at the Mass Meeting of Citizens in the Cooper Institute* and Unger, *The Greenback Era,* 144–58.

68. Sharkey, *Money, Class, and Party,* 238–41.

69. James Gallatin, "Letter on the Financial Economy of the United States, with Suggestions for Restoring Specie Payments," *Hunt's Merchants' Magazine and Commercial Review* 58 (March 1868): 188–202; C. L. Boalt to John Sherman, Jan. 4, 1867, Sherman Papers, vol. 110; "New Views on the Currency Communicated to the *Bankers' Magazine* by a Western Banker," *Bankers' Magazine* 15, no. 12 (March 1866): 680–81; Unger, *The Greenback Era,* 158–62; Sharkey, *Money, Class, and Party,* 241–71; Redlich, *The Molding of American Banking,* 1:99–124.

70. Testimony of George S. Coe, U.S. House Report No. 328, in U.S. Congress, *Congressional Serial Set,* 43rd Cong., 2nd sess., 63, 73; Nugent, *Money and American Society,*

44–48; Sharkey, *Money, Class, and Party*, 255–71. On Coe, see Redlich, *The Molding of American Banking*, 1:424–38.

71. Jay Cooke's quotations are from letters to his brother Henry D., transcribed in Larson, *Jay Cooke, Private Banker*, 204–6; Unger, *The Greenback Era*, 46–48; Sharkey, *Money, Class, and Party*, 245–50.

72. Ibid., 141–73.

73. *Commercial and Financial Chronicle*, Dec. 16, 1865, 784; *Iron Age*, Oct. 31, 1867, both quoted in ibid., 144, 158.

74. Carey, *Monetary Independence;* Sharkey, *Money, Class, and Party*, 153–66; Unger, *The Greenback Era*, 50–54. On currency and sovereignty in the United States, see Barreyre, "Les échelles de la monnaie."

75. One of the most forceful expression of this producerism after the war is Carey, *The Harmony of Interests.*

76. Nugent, *Money and American Society*, 48–60; Sharkey, *Money, Class, and Party*, 141–73; Unger, *The Greenback Era*, 48–60.

77. John Rogers Commons et al., *A Documentary History of American Industrial Society* (Cleveland: A. H. Clark, 1910), 9:178; Ritter, *Goldbugs and Greenbacks*, 126–28.

78. Kellogg, *A New Monetary System;* Campbell, *The True American System of Finance;* Sylvis, *The Life, Speeches, Labors and Essays*, 231–32, 247; Unger, *The Greenback Era*, 95–114; Sharkey, *Money, Class, and Party*, 186–94.

79. *Workingman's Advocate*, Dec. 9, 1868; Unger, *The Greenback Era*, 100–114; Sharkey, *Money, Class, and Party*, 192–99; Nugent, *Money and American Society*, 50–54.

80. *Workingman's Advocate*, Oct. 10, 1868; Unger, *The Greenback Era*, 108; Sharkey, *Money, Class, and Party*, 199–206; Nugent, *Money and American Society*, 50–51; Ritter, *Goldbugs and Greenbacks*, 123–36.

81. Jeremy Atack, Fred Bateman, and William N. Parker, "The Farm, the Farmer, and the Market," in Engerman and Gallman, eds., *The Cambridge Economic History of the United States*, 2:245–84.

82. Ibid.; Ritter, *Goldbugs and Greenbacks*, 128–31; Buck, *The Granger Movement*, 9–16, 34–39; Nordin, *Rich Harvest;* Woods, *Knights of the Plow;* Sanders, *Roots of Reform*, 108–9.

83. Unger, *The Greenback Era*, 195–212, 228–33; Atack et al., "The Farm, the Farmer, and the Market."

84. "The National Bank Circulation," *Bankers' Magazine* 15, no. 12 (June 1866): 945–53; *Globe*, 40th Cong., 2nd sess., 2762–63, 3081, 3184 (June 2–16, 1868); Redlich, *The Molding of American Banking*, 1:118.

85. Reserve cities were, from west to east, San Francisco, New Orleans, Leavenworth (KS), St. Louis, Chicago, Milwaukee, Detroit, Louisville, Cincinnati, Cleveland, Pittsburgh, Albany, Washington, Baltimore, Philadelphia, New York City, and Boston. Sharkey, *Money, Class, and Party*, 227–29; Bensel, *Yankee Leviathan*, 265.

86. Alexander G. Cattell (R, NJ), *Globe*, 40th Cong., 2nd sess., 2146–47 (March 27, 1868).

87. Ibid., 3153 (June 15, 1868); 41st Cong., 2nd sess., 5020 (June 30, 1870); U.S. Comptroller of the Currency, *Annual Report*, 1868; Davis, "The Investment Market."

88. Redlich, *The Molding of American Banking*, 1:117–21. We owe this estimate to the banker James Buell, who gave it in his testimony to the House Banking and Currency Committee in 1874.

89. Some were worried; see, e.g., U.S. Comptroller of the Currency, *Annual Report*, 1868, and *Hunt's Merchants' Magazine and Commercial Review* 58 (Dec. 1868): 453–64. On movements of capital each fall, see U.S. Comptroller of the Currency, *Annual Report*, 1876, 141; and Bensel, *Yankee Leviathan*, 265–74.

90. *Cincinnati Trade List and Commerce Bulletin*, quoted in *Jonesboro Gazette*, May 16, 1874; *Quincy Whig*, Jan. 26, 1874. On the presence of the whole range of positions on the currency question in the Midwest, see Carruthers and Babb, "The Color of Money and the Nature of Value."

91. *Chicago Republican*, Sept. 14, 1866.

92. *Chicago Republican*, July 9, 1866.

93. Ritter, *Goldbugs and Greenbacks*, 123–36.

94. Ibid.; Miller, *Railroads and the Granger Laws*.

95. Thomas T. Davis (R, NY), *Globe*, 39th Cong., 2nd sess., 1257 (Feb. 14, 1867).

96. Ibid., 40th Cong., 2nd sess., 3190 (June 16, 1868).

97. *Cincinnati Enquirer*, July 21, 1866.

3. Economic Policy and Spatial Justice

1. On the development of the central state during the war, see Bensel, *Yankee Leviathan*.

2. *The Free-Trader* 3, no. 8 (Jan. 1870).

3. On the tariff at the end of the century, see Reitano, *The Tariff Question in the Gilded Age*, and Bensel, *The Political Economy of American Industrialization*.

4. *Harper's Weekly*, July 7, 1866, 418. On antifiscal mobilization, see Huret, *American Tax Resisters*.

5. Wilson, *The Business of Civil War*, 191–204; Flaherty, *The Revenue Imperative*, 135–42; U.S. Secretary of the Treasury, *Annual Report*, 1866, 16–17.

6. Brownlee, *Federal Taxation in America*, 14–30; Heffer, "L'âge d'or"; Edling, *A Revolution in Favor of Government;* Onuf and Onuf, *Nations, Markets, and War*.

7. Sherman, *Recollections of Forty Years*, 1:281; Flaherty, "The Exhausted Condition of the Treasury." See also Blaine, *Twenty Years of Congress*, 1:398.

8. John McClernand (R, IL), *Globe*, 37th Cong., 1st sess., 248–49 (July 24, 1861), quoted in Richardson, *The Greatest Nation of the Earth*, 112; Stanley, *Dimensions of Law in the Service of Order*, 29–30.

9. Flaherty, *The Revenue Imperative*, 103–31; Brownlee, *Federal Taxation in America;* Richardson, *The Greatest Nation of the Earth;* Bensel, *Yankee Leviathan*.

10. *Globe*, 39th Cong., 1st sess., 3711 (July 10, 1866); 2nd sess., 1217 (Feb. 13, 1867).

11. Act of July 13, 1866, ch. 189, 14 Stat. 98; Act of March 2, 1867, ch. 169, 14 Stat. 471; Act of March 31, 1868, ch. 41, 15 Stat. 58; Act of July 14, 1870, ch. 255, 16 Stat. 471; Act of June 6, 1872, ch. 315, 17 Stat. 230; Act of Dec. 24, 1872, ch. 13, 17 Stat. 401.

12. Huret, *American Tax Resisters,* 13–44.

13. *Globe,* 39th Cong., 1st sess., 3711 (July 10, 1866); U.S. Secretary of the Treasury, *Annual Report,* 1866; Blaine, *Twenty Years of Congress,* 2:326.

14. Onuf and Onuf, *Nations, Markets, and War;* Holt, *The Political Crisis of the 1850s;* Holt, *The Rise and Fall of the American Whig Party;* Huston, *The Panic of 1857.* There were exceptions to this "revenue-only" approach, however, as duties on iron and woolens, for instance, were raised to much higher levels to attract votes in Pennsylvania and Midwestern states. Taussig, *The Tariff History in the United States,* 159.

15. John Henderson (R, MO), *Globe,* 39th Cong., 2nd sess., 771 (Jan. 26, 1867); Taussig, *The Tariff History in the United States,* 103; Richardson, *The Greatest Nation of the Earth,* 103–38.

16. The Tariff of 1828 was higher, but the ensuing political crisis led to its rapid demise, making it an exceptional rather than typical episode of antebellum tariff policies; see Heffer, "L'âge d'or." The tariff was very complex, putting together different duties for different articles, mixing fixed rates (with amounts expressed in dollars) and *ad valorem* duties (determined as a percentage of commercial value). This effectively prevents any calculation of a theoretical level of protection. The figures given here are the ratio of duties collected out of the total declared value of imports; see Taussig, *The History of the Present Tariff,* 103.

17. Ibid., 155–70; Richardson, *The Greatest Nation of the Earth,* 103–38; Stanley, *Dimensions of Law in the Service of Order,* 17–37.

18. *Globe,* 39th Cong., 2nd sess., 771 (Jan. 26, 1867).

19. Ibid., 39th Cong., 1st sess., 3468, 3515, 3498 (June 28–30, 1866); 3755 (July 12, 1866).

20. Ibid., 3497–99, 3513 (June 29–30, 1866); 3602 (July 5, 1866).

21. On antebellum debates, see Stanwood, *American Tariff Controversies,* and Onuf and Onuf, *Nations, Markets, and War.*

22. *Globe,* 39th Cong., 1st sess., 3604 (July 5, 1866); 3469, 3466 (June 28, 1866); 39th Cong., 2nd sess., 696 (Jan. 24, 1867). On the protectionists' Anglophobic rhetoric, see Tuffnell, "Uncle Sam Is to Be Sacrificed," and Palen, "Foreign Relations in the Gilded Age."

23. *Globe,* 39th Cong., 1st sess., 3466–68 (June 28, 1866).

24. Ibid., 3641, 3754 (July 6–12, 1866).

25. John, "Affairs of Office"; Einhorn, *American Taxation, American Slavery;* Larson, *Internal Improvement.*

26. Irwin, "Antebellum Tariff Politics"; Richardson, *The Greatest Nation of the Earth;* Bensel, "Congress, Sectionalism, and Public-Policy Formation."

27. *Globe,* 39th Cong., 1st sess., 3500, 3468 (June 28–29, 1866); *Cincinnati Enquirer,* Nov. 10, 1866.

28. Walker, ed., *Statistical Atlas of the United States,* 12–14, plates XI–XII.

29. *Chicago Republican,* April 15, 1868.

30. *Quincy Whig,* Jan. 6, March 25, 1874. On Carey, see Sklansky, *The Soul's Economy,* 73–104.

31. *Chicago Republican,* April 5, 1867; James A. Garfield to James Ward & Co., Harris Blackford & Co., and Thomas Carter, Dec. 29, 1869, Garfield Papers, series 6A, vol. 4.

32. Reitano, *The Tariff Question in the Gilded Age,* 59; *American National Biography,* 3:49–50. Examples of the league's publications include Atkinson, *On the Collection of Revenue,* and Lieber, *Notes on the Fallacies Peculiar to American Protectionists.*

33. *Cincinnati Enquirer,* Nov. 7, 1871; *Globe,* 39th Cong., 1st sess., 3515 (June 30, 1866).

34. Edward C. Biddle to Benjamin F. Wade, Jan. 17, 1867, Benjamin F. Wade Papers, vol. 12, Library of Congress; *Globe,* 39th Cong., 1st sess., 3468 (June 28, 1866).

35. Letter of the Bureau of Statistics, Aug. 7, 1871, Garfield Papers, series 11, vol. 17; Garfield, *Diary,* 2:54 (May 15, 1872).

36. James A. Garfield to Thomas W. Sanderson, Aug. 5, 1868, Garfield Papers, series 6A, vol. 1.

37. *Globe,* 39th Cong., 1st sess., 3541, 3544 (July 2, 1866); 39th Cong., 2nd sess., 748 (Jan. 25, 1867).

38. Ibid., 39th Cong., 1st sess., 3521, 3542 (June 30, July 2, 1866).

39. *Louisville Democrat,* quoted in *Cincinnati Enquirer,* June 4, 1866; *Globe,* 41st Cong., 2nd sess., 3621, 3782 (May 19–25, 1870). On the decline of the U.S. merchant marine, Heffer, *Le Port de New York,* 306–12.

40. *Globe,* 39th Cong., 2nd sess., 829 (Jan. 29, 1867).

41. Ibid., 39th Cong., 1st sess., 3472 (June 28, 1866); *Chicago Republican,* Nov. 16–17, 1866; Taussig, *The History of the Present Tariff,* 40–64.

42. Act of March 2, 1867, ch. 197, 15 Stat. 559; Harris, *Memorial of Manufacturers of Woolen Goods;* Taussig, *The History of the Present Tariff,* 40–64.

43. *Globe,* 39th Cong., 2nd sess., 696, 677 (Jan. 23–24, 1867); *New York Evening Post,* quoted in *Cincinnati Enquirer,* July 13, 1866. On the role of lobbying in Congress after the Civil War, see Thompson, *The "Spider Web."*

44. Garfield, *Diary,* 2:33 (March 22, 1872); Summers, *The Era of Good Stealings;* Summers, *The Press Gang;* White, *Railroaded;* Bensel, *Yankee Leviathan;* Taussig, *The History of the Present Tariff;* Taussig, *The Tariff History in the United States.*

45. *Globe,* 39th Cong., 1st sess., 3717, 3754 (July 10–12, 1866); 39th Cong., 2nd sess., 705 (Jan. 24, 1867).

46. Atkinson, *On the Collection of Revenue,* 27–28.

47. Bensel also insists on this point in *Yankee Leviathan,* 329–41.

48. *Alton Telegraph,* May 12, 1871; Atack et al., "The Farm, the Farmer, and the Market"; Heffer, *Le Port de New York,* 184–202; Nelson, "A Storm of Cheap Goods." The phrase "granary of the world" can often be found in editorials; see, e.g., *Cincinnati Enquirer,* Sept. 4, 1873.

49. Nelson Taylor (D, NY), *Globe,* 39th Cong., 1st sess., 3685 (July 9, 1866); Hubbard, *The Burden of Confederate Diplomacy.*

50. *Joliet Signal,* Oct. 23, 1866; *Chicago Tribune,* Aug. 30, 1867.

51. *Chicago Republican,* Jan. 5, 1868, Feb. 2, 1867; letter of D. J. Morrell, of Cambria Iron Works, read in the Senate by Alexander G. Cattell (R, NJ), *Globe,* 39th Cong., 2nd sess., 638–39 (Jan. 22, 1867).

52. Taussig, *The History of the Present Tariff,* 26–27; Atack and Passell, *A New Economic View of American History,* 402–26.

53. Burchard, *Tariff Reduction—Should Able-Bodied Men Be Pensioned?; Globe,* 39th Cong., 2nd sess., 772 (Jan. 26, 1867); Thornton and Ekelund, *Tariffs, Blockades, and Inflation,* xxiv–xxvii.

54. *Joliet Signal,* Aug. 12, 1873. On the role of gender in political discourse in those years, see Edwards, *Angels in the Machinery.*

55. Irwin, "Tariff Incidence in America's Gilded Age."

56. *Globe,* 39th Cong., 2nd sess., 772 (Jan. 26, 1867); 39th Cong., 1st sess., 3685 (July 9, 1866).

57. *Cincinnati Enquirer,* April 3, 1873; Ritter, *Goldbugs and Greenbacks;* Nordin, *Rich Harvest,* 197–204.

58. Ron, "Developing the Country."

59. Atack and Passell, *A New Economic View of American History,* 402–26; Margo, "The Labor Force in the Nineteenth Century."

60. Bogue, "Senators, Sectionalism, and the 'Western' Measures"; Richardson, *The Greatest Nation of the Earth,* 103–69.

61. *Chicago Republican,* Jan. 5 and March 17, 1868.

62. *Chicago Republican,* Nov. 16, 1866. On free trade in Britain, see Trentmann, *Free Trade Nation.*

63. *Chicago Republican,* Nov. 16, 1866, and Jan. 11, 1867.

64. *Chicago Republican,* June 13, 1867.

65. Gienapp, *The Origins of the Republican Party;* Holt, *The Political Crisis of the 1850s;* Holt, *The Rise and Fall of the American Whig Party.*

66. James A. Garfield to Charles E. Henry, Feb. 12, 1870, Garfield Papers, series 17M; M. E. Force to John Sherman, June 9, 1870, Sherman Papers, vol. 126; *Chicago Republican,* Oct. 11, 1870.

67. *Chicago Republican,* July 14, 1866.

68. James A. Garfield to Harmon Austin, Jan. 31, 1870, Garfield Papers, series 17M; Garfield to "Mr. Morgan," March 22, 1871, Garfield Papers, series 6A, vol. 7.

69. *New York Post,* quoted in *Cincinnati Enquirer,* Feb. 9, 1867; James A. Garfield to Brown, Bonnel & Co., Dec. 22, 1869, and Garfield to James Ward & Co., Harris Blackford & Co., and Thomas Carter, Dec. 29, 1869, Garfield Papers, series 6A, vol. 4; *Alton Telegraph,* March 10, 1871; Act of June 6, 1872, ch. 315, 17 Stat. 230.

70. *Chicago Republican,* Jan. 26, 1871; *Ashtabula Sentinel,* Feb. 1, 1872.

71. *Globe,* 42nd Cong., 2nd sess., 3200 (May 8, 1872); Stanley, *Dimensions of Law in the Service of Order,* 54–56.

72. *Bulletin of the Wool Manufacturers* 3, no. 3 (1873): 283–90; Blaine, *Twenty Years of Congress,* 2:560–61; Taussig, *The History of the Present Tariff,* 29–36; Taussig, *The Tariff History in the United States,* 185–91.

73. Nugent, *Money and American Society,* 33–43.

74. James A. Garfield to R. Hawley, Nov. 12, 1869, Garfield Papers, series 6A, vol. 3; Rutherford B. Hayes to Birchard Hayes, Jan. 23, 1873, Rutherford B. Hayes Papers, Hayes Presidential Center.

4. Closing the Books on the War

1. There were precedents, however, in the close relationship between taxation and slavery; see Einhorn, *American Taxation, American Slavery.*

2. U.S. Secretary of the Treasury, *Annual Report,* 1865; McCulloch, *Men and Measures of Half a Century,* 219; *House Journal,* 39th Cong., 1st sess., 84 (Dec. 18, 1865).

3. *Globe,* 39th Cong., 1st sess., 1496 (March 19, 1866); Hugh McCulloch to Charles Sumner, Aug. 22, 1865, quoted in Rhodes, *History of the United States from the Compromise of 1850,* 5:532; McCulloch, *Men and Measures of Half a Century,* 203.

4. *Globe,* 39th Cong., 1st sess., 1428, 1453, 1459 (March 15–16, 1866).

5. Proclamations 37 and 38, 13 Stat. 758–60 (May 29, 1865). On Johnson and his view of Reconstruction, see Trefousse, *Andrew Johnson;* McKitrick, *Andrew Johnson and Reconstruction;* and Simpson, *The Reconstruction Presidents,* 67–130.

6. Strong, *Diary,* 4:56 (Dec. 7, 1865); *Globe,* 39th Cong., 1st sess., Appendix, 1–5 (Dec. 4, 1866).

7. Atkinson, *On Cotton,* 40; Foner, *Reconstruction,* 198–216; Carter, *When the War Was Over,* 176–92; Zuczek, *State of Rebellion,* 10–27.

8. Foner, *Reconstruction,* 78–88; Cimbala, *Under the Guardianship of the Nation,* 204–8; Rable, *But There Was No Peace,* 1–15.

9. Schurz, *Report on the Condition of the South;* Trefousse, *Carl Schurz,* 152–60. On the political controversy around this report, see Simpson, "Grant's Tour of the South Revisited."

10. Charles A. Dana to Isaac Sherman, Sept. 17, 1865, quoted in Foner, *Reconstruction,* 225.

11. Radicals and Moderates were polarities within the Republican Party, rather than well-defined groups. Republicans moved in and out of these broad groupings, depending on the rapid evolution of the political situation, even though those polarities were a constant, at least until the early 1870s. For attempts at classification, see Gambill, "Who Were the Senate Radicals?"; Linden, "'Radicals' and Economic Policies"; and Benedict, *A Compromise of Principle,* 339–77.

12. Thaddeus Stevens to Charles Sumner, June 3, 1868, Charles Sumner Papers, Library of Congress; Trefousse, *Andrew Johnson,* 217–18; *Harper's Weekly,* Dec. 2, 1865, 754; William P. Fessenden to George Harrington, Feb. 3, 1866, quoted in Jellison, *Fessenden of Maine,* 198–99; *Harper's Weekly,* Jan. 20, 1866, 34.

13. Silbey, *A Respectable Minority,* 177–89.

14. *Globe,* 39th Cong., 1st sess., 78 (Dec. 19, 1865).

15. Lyman Trumbull confessed it unadornedly to the Senate. Ibid., 943 (Feb. 20, 1866).

16. *Delaware State Journal* and *Cleveland Leader,* quoted in *New York Tribune,* March 3, 1866; McKitrick, *Andrew Johnson and Reconstruction,* 291–92.

17. *Globe,* 39th Cong., 1st sess., 943 (Feb. 20, 1866); Foner, *Reconstruction,* 243–46; Maltz, *Civil Rights, the Constitution and Congress,* 61–78.

18. *Globe,* 39th Cong., 1st sess., 1679–81 (March 27, 1866).

19. Ibid., 39th Cong., 1st sess., 915–17 (Feb. 19, 1866); John Lynch to Israel Washburn, Feb. 21, 1866, quoted in Hunt, *Israel, Elihu and Cadwallader Washburn,* 119.

20. There have been many studies of that major constitutional amendment, both on its use to protect corporations and on the incorporation of the Bill of Rights. The following analysis on the Fourteenth Amendment essentially follows Foner, *Reconstruction,* 251–61; Benedict, *A Compromise of Principle,* 162–87; Hyman, *A More Perfect Union,* 433–41; James, *The Framing of the Fourteenth Amendment;* Maltz, *Civil Rights, the Constitution and Congress,* 79–120; McKitrick, *Andrew Johnson and Reconstruction,* 326–63; and Nelson, *The Fourteenth Amendment.*

21. Valelly, "Deflecting the Ex-Post Veto Player."

22. See, e.g., Thaddeus Stevens quipping that "I accept so imperfect a proposition . . . because I live among men and not among angels." *Globe,* 39th Cong., 1st sess., 3148 (June 13, 1866).

23. Benjamin F. Perry to Andrew Johnson, telegram, Nov. 1, 1865, in Johnson, *Papers,* 9:324–25 (see also Perry's telegram to William H. Seward, Nov. 27, 1865, quoted in James, *The Framing of the Fourteenth Amendment,* 27); *Appleton's Annual Cyclopaedia,* 1865, 685 (see also Massachusetts, Minnesota, New Jersey, and Wisconsin entries); James, *The Framing of the Fourteenth Amendment,* 24–27, 92–95.

24. *Globe,* 39th Cong., 2nd sess., 984 (Feb. 4, 1867); Foner, *Reconstruction,* 212; Thompson, *The Reconstruction of Southern Debtors,* 13–30.

25. See, at the same time, the debates on the Southern Homestead Act. Michael L. Lanza, "'One of the Most Appreciated Labors of the Bureau': The Freedmen's Bureau and the Southern Homestead Act," in Cimbala and Miller, eds., *The Freedmen's Bureau and Reconstruction,* 67–92.

26. Foreclosures were in fact not numerous but happened often enough to be a tangible threat to farmers. Atack et al., "The Farm, the Farmer, and the Market."

27. Act of March 2, 1867, ch. 176, 14 Stat. 517.

28. *Globe,* 39th Cong., 1st sess., 3466, 3517 (June 28–30, 1866); 39th Cong., 2nd sess., 1657 (Feb. 28, 1867).

29. Ibid., 39th Cong., 1st sess., 3514 (June 30, 1866).

30. Democrats only made up 22 percent of the House. They divided on two of the fourteen sectional votes on this bill. See also Seip, *The South Returns to Congress,* 282–83.

31. *Cincinnati Enquirer,* July 12, 1866.

32. *Appleton's Annual Cyclopaedia,* 1866, 755–57; McKitrick, *Andrew Johnson and Reconstruction,* 394–420; Perman, *Reunion without Compromise,* 194–228; Trefousse, *Andrew Johnson,* 258–62.

33. *Appleton's Annual Cyclopaedia,* 1866, 399, 603; Silbey, *A Respectable Minority,* 181–89.

34. *Appleton's Annual Cyclopaedia,* 1866, 400, 508, 613.

35. *New York Independent,* Sept. 13, 1866, quoted in Trefousse, *Andrew Johnson,* 266. See also Ulysses S. Grant to Julia Dent Grant, Sept. 9, 1866, Grant, *Papers,* 16:308; and McKitrick, *Andrew Johnson and Reconstruction,* 428–38.

36. Hardwick, "Your Old Father Abe Lincoln Is Dead and Damned"; Ryan, "The Memphis Riots of 1866"; Waller, "Community, Class and Race in the Memphis Riot of 1866."

37. *Cleveland Leader,* June 4, 1866; *Harper's Weekly,* June 2, 1866, 339.

38. Philip H. Sheridan to Ulysses S. Grant, telegram, Aug. 2, 1866, Grant, *Papers,* 16:289. The official count (largely underestimated) was 38 dead, 184 wounded, almost all of them blacks. Rable, *But There Was No Peace,* 43–58; Hogue, *Uncivil War,* 31–52.

39. James A. Garfield to Burke A. Hinsdale, Jan. 1, 1867, in Garfield, *Works,* 1:249; Peskin, *Garfield,* 278; Grant, *Papers,* 16:257–59.

40. Martis et al., *The Historical Atlas of Political Parties,* 102; Burnham et al., "State-Level Congressional, Gubernatorial and Senatorial Election Data"; McKitrick, *Andrew Johnson and Reconstruction,* 447.

41. James W. Grimes to Charles H. Ray, Dec. 2, 1866, quoted in Foner, *Reconstruction,* 271; *Globe,* 39th Cong., 2nd sess., Appendix, 78 (Jan. 28, 1867).

42. McKitrick, *Andrew Johnson and Reconstruction,* 448–85; Benedict, *A Compromise of Principle,* 216–43; Foner, *Reconstruction,* 271–80.

43. Blair, "The Use of Military Force."

44. Act of March 2, 1867, ch. 153, 14 Stat. 428; Act of March 23, 1867, ch. 6, 15 Stat. 2; Act of March 2, 1867, ch. 154, 14 Stat. 430; Act of March 2, 1867, ch. 170, 14 Stat. 485.

45. Bloss, *Life and Speeches of George H. Pendleton;* Mach, *"Gentleman George" Hunt Pendleton,* 1–110.

46. *Joliet Signal,* Aug. 15, 1865; Silbey, *A Respectable Minority,* 177–210; Sawrey, *Dubious Victory,* 26–70.

47. *Chicago Times,* Nov. 17, 1866; Strong, *Diary,* 4:113–14 (Nov. 18, 1866); *Jonesboro Gazette,* Nov. 24, 1866; *Cincinnati Enquirer,* Dec. 1, 1866.

48. Pendleton, *Payment of the Public Debt.*

49. Blaine, *Twenty Years of Congress,* 2:328.

50. The polarization index went from .4 to .6 during the session.

51. It is revealing that copies of his Nov. 2, 1867 Milwaukee speech (see note 48, above) can be found in the papers of many Republican leaders; see, e.g., Garfield Papers, series 11, vol. 20; and Robert C. Schenck Papers, Hayes Presidential Center.

52. *Chicago Tribune,* Jan. 11, 1867; *Cincinnati Enquirer,* Sept. 9, 1867. The *Enquirer* made it a campaign issue throughout the year.

53. *Cincinnati Commercial,* Aug. 12, 1867.

54. Ohio was a competitive state between the parties. It was also the third largest in population, giving to its local politics national significance.

55. *Jonesboro Gazette,* Nov. 9, 1867; Foner, *Reconstruction,* 314–15; Benedict, "The Rout of Radicalism"; Gillette, *The Right to Vote,* 33; Burnham et al., "State-Level Congressional, Gubernatorial and Senatorial Election Data."

56. *New York Times,* Nov. 8, 1867; John Sherman to Schuyler Colfax, Oct. 20, 1867, quoted in Benedict, "The Rout of Radicalism."

57. Dykstra and Hahn, "Northern Voters and Negro Suffrage"; Berwanger, *The West and Reconstruction,* 163–73; Bonadio, *North of Reconstruction,* 94–106.

58. Nathaniel P. Banks to Mrs. Banks, Nov. 13, 1867, quoted in Benedict, *The Impeachment and Trial of Andrew Johnson*, 70; James G. Blaine to Israel Washburn, Sept. 12, 1867, quoted in Hunt, *Israel, Elihu and Cadwallader Washburn*, 121.

59. William H. Smith to R. D. Mussey, Oct. 21, 1867, William H. Smith Papers, box 10, vol. 23, Ohio Historical Society.

60. See letters of T. J. McLain, Dec. 18, 1867, and of J. Medill, Nov. 22, 1867, to John Sherman, Sherman Papers, vols. 123–24; *Globe*, 40th Cong., 2nd sess., 69–70 (Dec. 7, 1866); Henry C. Carey to Robert Schenck, Nov. 26, 1867, and the many bills sent to the Ways and Means Committee, Schenck Papers; Moore, "Ohio in National Politics"; Unger, *The Greenback Era*, 84; Thomas Stuart Mach, "'Gentleman George' Hunt Pendleton: A Study in Political Continuity" (Ph.D. dissertation, University of Akron, 1996), 231–33.

61. Act of Feb. 4, 1868, ch. 6, 15 Stat. 34.

62. *Globe*, 40th Cong., 2nd sess., 69–70 (Dec. 7, 1867).

63. Strong, *Diary*, 4:160 (Nov. 5, 1867).

64. Blaine, *Twenty Years of Congress*, 2:347; Benedict, *The Impeachment and Trial of Andrew Johnson*, 81–88; Benedict, *A Compromise of Principle*, 262–65.

65. James W. Grimes to Edward Atkinson, Oct. 14, 1867, quoted in Trefousse, *Andrew Johnson*, 302–3; T. W. Egan to Andrew Johnson, Oct. 7, 1867, Johnson, *Papers*, 13:141; Fessenden, *Life and Public Service of William Pitt Fessenden*, 2:118.

66. *Globe*, 40th Cong., 2nd sess., Appendix, 3–4 (Dec. 3, 1867); Trefousse, *Andrew Johnson*, 288–98; Sefton, *The United States Army and Reconstruction*, 153–64; Simpson, *The Reconstruction Presidents*, 116–20.

67. George S. Boutwell (R, MA), *Globe*, 40th Cong., 2nd sess., Appendix, 61 (Dec. 4, 1867).

68. Many newspapers predicted that the electoral results had killed any chance of impeachment; see, e.g., *Baltimore Sun*, Oct. 11, 1867. Benedict, *The Impeachment and Trial of Andrew Johnson*, 61–88.

69. Oliver O. Howard to Edgar Ketchum, Dec. 30, 1867, quoted in ibid., 90; Dawson, *Army Generals and Reconstruction*, 63–75; Sefton, *The United States Army and Reconstruction*, 165–78.

70. Foster Blodgett to John Sherman, Dec. 30, 1867; John C. Underwood to Elihu B. Washburn, Dec. 9, 1867; and George Ely to Washburn, Feb. 9, 1868, all quoted in Benedict, *The Impeachment and Trial of Andrew Johnson*, 91; McKitrick, *Andrew Johnson and Reconstruction*, 500; Trelease, *White Terror*, 25–46; Crouch, "A Spirit of Lawlessness."

71. *New York Independent*, Dec. 12, 1867; *Chicago Tribune*, Dec. 30, 1867.

72. Several recent decisions led many to think that the Supreme Court was hostile to Reconstruction. *Ex parte Milligan*, 71 U.S. (4 Wall.) 2 (1866), overturned a military tribunal sentence made during the war because civil courts were in operation at the place of the trial; *Cummings v. Missouri*, 71 U.S. (4 Wall.) 277 (1866), and *Ex parte Garland*, 71 U.S. (4. Wall.) 333 (1867), struck down laws requiring priests, teachers, and lawyers to take loyalty oaths. See Keller, *Affairs of State*, and Kutler, *Judicial Power and Reconstruction Politics*.

73. U.S. Congress, *Journal of the Executive Proceedings of the Senate,* 40th Cong., 2nd sess., 172 (Feb. 21, 1868); *House Journal,* 40th Cong., 2nd sess., 392–97 (Feb. 24, 1868); Trefousse, *Andrew Johnson,* 313–16.

74. *Chicago Tribune,* May 14, 1868; Benedict, *The Impeachment and Trial of Andrew Johnson,* 137–39; Trefousse, *Andrew Johnson,* 316–25.

75. See, e.g., *Quincy Whig,* June 5, 1868; *Alton Telegraph,* May 19, 1868.

76. Strong, *Diary,* 4:209 (May 17, 1868); Roske, "The Seven Martyrs?"

77. James A. Garfield to James Harry Rhodes, May 7, 1868, Smith, *The Life and Letters of James Abram Garfield,* 1:425.

78. Richardson, *The Death of Reconstruction,* 70. The quotation is from Edward Atkinson, quoted in Trefousse, *Andrew Johnson,* 330. Financiers in New York watched the impeachment trial with trepidation; see Henry H. Van Dyck to Andrew Johnson, Feb. 29, 1868, Johnson, *Papers,* 13:597–98, and Benedict, *A Compromise of Principle,* 300–314.

79. Such self-evidence is transparent in *Globe,* 40th Cong., 2nd sess., 3190 (June 16, 1868).

80. Ibid., 3187, 4194 (June 16, July 17, 1868).

81. Ibid., 3963, 1651 (July 11, March 4, 1868).

82. For example, see ibid., 1811 (March 11, 1868).

83. Ibid., 1653 (March 4, 1868).

84. Ibid., 3965 (July 11, 1868).

85. On the perception of public opinion, see Barreyre, "Lire l'opinion publique."

86. *Appleton's Annual Cyclopaedia,* 1868, 549, 494, 604; James A. Garfield to George S. Coe, May 23, 1868, Garfield Papers, series 6A, vol. 1.

87. *Appleton's Annual Cyclopaedia,* 1868, 744; John Hope Franklin, "Election of 1868," in Schlesinger and Israel, eds., *History of American Presidential Elections, 1789–1968,* 2:1247–66.

88. James A. Garfield to Edward Atkinson, May 25, 1868, Garfield Papers, series 6A, vol. 1; *Globe,* 40th Cong., 2nd sess., 4177–78 (July 17, 1868).

89. Coleman, *The Election of 1868;* Franklin, "Election of 1868"; Silbey, *A Respectable Minority,* 203–8.

90. *Cincinnati Enquirer,* July 13, 1868; Merrill, *Bourbon Democracy of the Middle West,* 55; Bonadio, *North of Reconstruction,* 162.

91. Strong, *Diary,* 4:223 (July 10, 1868).

92. *Cincinnati Enquirer,* July 10, 1868.

93. Foner, *Reconstruction,* 340; Mach, *"Gentleman George" Hunt Pendleton,* 134.

94. *Harper's Weekly,* Aug. 15, 1868, 513. On Thomas Nast, see Keller, *The Art and Politics of Thomas Nast;* Fischer, *Them Damned Pictures,* 1–49; Jarman, "The Graphic Art of Thomas Nast."

95. James, *The Ratification of the Fourteenth Amendment,* 289–304; Benedict, *A Compromise of Principle,* 315–25; Foner, *Reconstruction,* 316–38.

96. Philip H. Sheridan to Ulysses S. Grant, May 22, 1868; John M. Schofield to Ulysses S. Grant, May 25, 1868, both Grant, *Papers,* 18:266; Simpson, *Let Us Have Peace,* 205–49.

97. See, e.g., *Harper's Weekly*, July 25, 1868, 466. On the 1863 riots, see Bernstein, *The New York City Draft Riots*.

98. McCabe, *The Life and Public Services of Horatio Seymour*, 464; Foner, *Reconstruction*, 340–41; *Harper's Weekly*, Oct. 24, 1868, 675.

99. J. M. Forney to William E. Chandler, Dec. 27, 1868, quoted in Gillette, *The Right to Vote*, 42; Burnham et al., "State-Level Congressional, Gubernatorial and Senatorial Election Data."

100. *Philadelphia Press*, Nov. 6, 1868, quoted in Gillette, *The Right to Vote*, 43.

101. Thaddeus Stevens to Edward McPherson, Aug. 16, 1867, quoted in Current, *Old Thad Stevens*, 288; Gillette, *The Right to Vote*, 26; Dykstra and Hahn, "Northern Voters and Negro Suffrage."

102. *National Anti-Slavery Standard*, Nov. 14, 1868; *Globe*, 39th Cong., 2nd sess., 252 (Jan. 3, 1869); 40th Cong., 3rd sess., 904, 559 (Feb. 5, Jan. 23, 1869) (the estimates are George S. Boutwell's); Benedict, *A Compromise of Principle*, 325–36; Foner, *Reconstruction*, 444–49.

103. Gillette, *The Right to Vote*, 46–78; Keyssar, *The Right to Vote*, 93–104 and *passim;* Wang, *The Trial of Democracy*, 1–48.

104. *New York Times*, Feb. 15, 1869.

105. Conference committees, made up of three senators and three representatives, meet when both houses of Congress disagree on a bill, to hammer out their differences and find, if possible, a solution. See Barclay, *Constitution of the United States*, 2:77–79.

106. *Globe*, 40th Cong., 3rd sess., 1627–28 (Feb. 26, 1869); Gillette, *The Right to Vote*, 75–78; Belz, *Emancipation and Equal Rights*, 126, 139, and *passim*.

107. *Appleton's Annual Cyclopaedia*, 1868, 744.

108. The index of polarization oscillates between .58 and .86. *Globe*, 40th Cong., 3rd sess., 1183–86, 1270–74, 1320–27, 1331–33, 1897 (Feb. 13–March 3, 1869).

109. Ibid. 2–3, 71–73 (Dec. 9–14, 1868).

110. Grant, *Papers*, 19:140.

111. Act of March 18, 1869, ch. 1, 16 Stat. 1.

112. Grant, *Papers*, 19:139–42.

113. Ibid. On the rising production of silver in the Rocky Mountains, see Weinstein, *Prelude to Populism*, 18.

114. Grant, *Papers*, 19:139–42.

5. For the Good of the Country and the Party

1. Klein, *The Life and Legend of Jay Gould*, 99–115.

2. John Sherman to William T. Sherman, Oct. 10, 1869, Sherman and Sherman, *Letters*, 329.

3. Parts of the following analysis were first developed in Barreyre, "Réunifier l'union."

4. James A. Garfield to J. D. Ensign, Dec. 9, 1869, Garfield Papers, series 6A, vol. 4.

5. James A. Garfield to Thomas J. Wood, April 12, 1869, Garfield Papers, series 6A, vol. 2.

6. Anderson, *The American Census*, 7–32; Schor, *Compter et classer*, 27–30.

7. *Globe*, 41st Cong., 2nd Sess., 525 (Jan. 17, 1870).

8. Ibid., 105 (Dec. 13, 1869).

9. Ibid., 532, 527 (Jan. 17, 1870). Figures are from the Eighth and Ninth Censuses.

10. Ibid., 4747 (June 23, 1870).

11. *Chicago Times*, June 25, 1870. Midwestern Democratic newspapers were, however, sensitive to the sectional call in the debates (e.g., *Cincinnati Enquirer*, Jan. 19, 1870).

12. Letter of James A. Garfield to Reuben P. Cannon, Jan. 27, 1871, Garfield Papers, series 6A, vol. 8; *Chicago Tribune*, Feb. 14, 1871.

13. *Globe*, 41st Cong., 2nd sess., 4747 (June 23, 1870).

14. Ibid., 4746–47; James A. Garfield to Joseph Medill, Jan. 11, 1870, Garfield Papers, series 6A, vol. 4; *Chicago Tribune*, July 7, June 25, 1870.

15. *Globe*, 41st Cong., 2nd sess., 535 (Jan. 17, 1870).

16. Keyssar, *The Right to Vote*, 101, 374–79.

17. *Globe*, 42nd Cong., 2nd sess., 82 (Dec. 12, 1871). This problem had already created a brief moment of sectional tension during the debates in Congress on the Fourteenth Amendment in 1866. As the male/female ratio was unfavorable to the Northeast, representatives from this part of the country had opposed basing the representation of the states on their male adult population, and imposed the solution of basing representation on the whole population, while only reducing it by the same proportion of the adult male population that was deprived of the suffrage. Both methods restricted the suffrage to males, but one counted women and children while the other did not. Kromkowski, *Re-creating the American Republic*, 413–18.

18. Anderson, *The American Census*, 72–82; Schor, *Compter et classer*, 135–44. The only attempt to enforce the new constitutional provision failed. *Globe*, 41st Cong., 2nd sess., 142–43 (Dec. 14, 1871).

19. Act of Feb. 2, 1872, ch. 11, 17 Stat. 28; Act of May 30, 1872, ch. 239, 17 Stat. 192. On the various possible statistical methods used for reapportionment, see Balinski and Young, *Fair Representation*.

20. Georgia was among the states that were to be readmitted in 1868, but following renewed political violence (including the forceful expulsion of black elected members of the legislature and the assassination of a Republican judge), Congress decided to impose new Reconstruction measures. Donald et al., *The Civil War and Reconstruction*, 597.

21. *New Orleans Times*, March 4, 1869; Adams, "The Session"; Seip, *The South Returns to Congress*, 136–70.

22. Ibid., 171–218.

23. See, e.g., *Cincinnati Enquirer*, July 12, 1866.

24. *Chicago Tribune*, Oct. 1, 1866. It is on this contradiction between interests and ideology that the Beards and Howard Beale built their interpretation of Reconstruction. See also Bowersox, "The Reconstruction of the Republican Party in the West."

25. *Globe*, 41st Cong., 2nd sess., 5465 (July 12, 1870), 532 (Jan. 17, 1870). The evolution of the *Chicago Tribune* editorials is a striking example; see, e.g., Feb. 16, 1871.

26. Summers, *Railroads, Reconstruction, and the Gospel of Prosperity*, esp. 14–21, 16

(quotation; from *Little Rock Republican,* July 11, 1868). On the Republicans' economic program during the Civil War, see Richardson, *The Greatest Nation of the Earth.* On free-labor ideology, see Foner, *Free Soil, Free Labor, Free Men,* and Tuchinsky, *Horace Greeley's New-York Tribune.*

27. Foner, *Reconstruction,* 379–92; Seip, *The South Returns to Congress,* 37–68, 219–68; Summers, *Railroads, Reconstruction, and the Gospel of Prosperity,* 3–210.

28. See, e.g., *Harper's Weekly,* May 25, 1869; Klein, *Union Pacific,* 1:212–28.

29. Seip, *The South Returns to Congress,* 220–68; Summers, *Railroads, Reconstruction, and the Gospel of Prosperity,* 163–74; Perman, *The Road to Redemption,* 87–107.

30. Rutherford B. Hayes to Guy M. Bryan, Dec. 24, 1871, Hayes Papers.

31. Letter of Lyman Trumbull to William Jayne, Aug. 5, 1870, quoted in Roske, *His Own Counsel,* 156; William B. Tyfe to Lyman Trumbull, Dec. 1, 1871, Lyman Trumbull Papers, vol. 72, Library of Congress; James A. Garfield to Lyman W. Hall, April 6, 1872, Garfield Papers, series 6A, vol. 10.

32. Foner, *Free Soil, Free Labor, Free Men;* Gienapp, *The Origins of the Republican Party.*

33. *New York Times,* March 31, 1870; Gillette, *The Right to Vote,* 159–65.

34. *Chicago Republican,* May 16, 1870.

35. Holt, "Change and Continuity in the Party Period."

36. M. F. Force to John Sherman, June 9, 1870, Sherman Papers, vol. 126.

37. Gillette, *Retreat from Reconstruction,* ix–xiv, 19–20.

38. Beard and Beard, *The Rise of American Civilization;* Beale, *The Critical Year.*

39. Keller, *Affairs of State,* 238–83.

40. As commissioner he had several guides published on the new taxes: Boutwell, *A Manual of the Direct and Excise Tax System of the United States,* and Boutwell, *The Tax-Payer's Manual.*

41. Unger, *The Greenback Era,* 163–65.

42. *Joliet Republican,* May 15, 1869.

43. Henry D. Cooke to John Sherman, June 8, 1869, Sherman Papers, vol. 126; Boutwell, *Reminiscences of Sixty Years,* 2:164–82.

44. Nugent, *Money and American Society,* 77.

45. *Globe,* 41st Cong., 2nd sess., 698 (Jan. 24, 1870).

46. Ibid., 704 (Jan. 24, 1870), 812 (Jan. 27, 1870).

47. The polarization index was .7–.8 for the votes in the Senate.

48. Act of July 12, 1870, ch. 252, 16 Stat. 251.

49. *Globe,* 41st Cong., 2nd sess., 5303 (July 7, 1870).

50. Ibid., 5058–60 (July 1, 1870); Unger, *The Greenback Era,* 179–80; Seip, *The South Returns to Congress,* 153–54.

51. Act of July 14, 1870, ch. 256, 16 Stat. 272.

52. Unger, *The Greenback Era,* 163–70; Boutwell, *Reminiscences of Sixty Years,* 2:137–44. The funding strategy also had an international relations aspect linked to the *Alabama* affair; see Sexton, *Debtor Diplomacy,* 193–229.

53. *Hepburn v. Griswold,* 75 U.S. (8 Wall.) 603 (1870); *Knox v. Lee* and *Parker v. Davis,*

79 U.S. (12 Wall.) 457 (1871); Adams, "The Session"; Boutwell, *Reminiscences of Sixty Years*, 2:208–10; Unger, *The Greenback Era*, 172–78; Keller, *Affairs of State*, 78–81.

54. Irwin Unger saw in 1869 the beginning of a phase of strong economic growth. Unger, *The Greenback Era*, 165. More recent economic studies identified a mild downward phase in the economic cycle from June 1869 to December 1870, followed by a phase of rapid growth until October 1873. Moore, "Business Cycles, Panics, and Depressions."

55. U.S. Secretary of the Treasury, *Annual Report*, 1869, xx–xxi.

56. *Chicago Republican*, July 31, 1869.

57. *Chicago Republican*, May 9, 1869.

58. *Harper's Weekly*, Aug. 21, 1869, 531.

59. James A. Garfield to William C. Howells, April 21, 1870, Garfield Papers, series 6A, vol. 5; *Globe*, 41st Cong., 2nd sess., 2042–43 (March 17, 1870), 2117 (March 21, 1870).

60. See, e.g., *House Journal*, 41st Cong., 2nd sess., 828–29 (May 23, 1870), 877–79 (May 31, 1870).

61. See, e.g., *Globe*, 41st Cong., 2nd sess., 2049 (March 17, 1870).

62. Act of July 14, 1870, ch. 255, 16 Stat. 256; Unger, *The Greenback Era*, 178–79.

63. Grant, *Papers*, 20:130–31; Gillette, *The Right to Vote*, 161.

64. James A. Garfield to Robert Folger, April 16, 1870, quoted in Foner, *Reconstruction*, 449.

65. *Globe*, 41st Cong., 2nd sess., 3668 (May 20, 1870).

66. Trelease, *White Terror*, 113–85; Zuczek, *State of Rebellion*, 47–70; Michael Perman, "Counter Reconstruction: The Role of Violence in Southern Redemption," in Anderson and Moss, eds., *The Facts of Reconstruction*, 121–40.

67. Wang, "The Making of Federal Enforcement Laws," 1013–59, 1019 (quotation).

68. *Globe*, 41st Cong., 2nd sess., 4270 (June 9, 1870).

69. Act of May 31, 1870, ch. 114, 16 Stat. 140.

70. On citizenship before the Civil War, see Novak, "The Legal Transformation of Citizenship."

71. Some scholars have argued that the new amendments, especially the Thirteenth, allowed for much more, even though the Supreme Court would later take a conservative view on this. Hyman and Wiecek, *Equal Justice under Law;* Benedict, "Preserving the Constitution."

72. *Globe*, 41st Cong., 2nd sess., 3808 (May 25, 1870).

73. Callow, *The Tweed Ring;* Beckert, *The Monied Metropolis*, 173–75; Bernstein, *The New York City Draft Riots*, 195–219; Shefter, "The Emergence of the Political Machine."

74. Summers, *Party Games*, 91–106; Bensel, *The American Ballot Box*, 26–85.

75. *Globe*, 41st Cong., 2nd sess., 4269 (June 9, 1870).

76. Thernstrom, *Harvard Encyclopedia of American Ethnic Groups*, 531.

77. Erie, *Rainbow's End*.

78. Davenport, *The Elections and Naturalization Frauds in New York City*. Historians have since lowered this estimate to 50,000. Burke, "Federal Regulation of Congressional Elections in Northern Cities."

79. *Globe,* 41st Cong., 2nd sess., 4266–84 (June 9, 1870), 5114–77 (July 2–4, 1870).

80. Act of July 14, 1870, ch. 254, 16 Stat. 254. The wording is designed to make sure Chinese immigrants would not gain access to citizenship through this law. Wang, *The Trial of Democracy.*

81. *Globe,* 41st Cong., 2nd sess., 4281 (June 9, 1870).

82. Polarization index between .34 and .63.

83. *Globe,* 41st Cong., 2nd sess., 4280 (June 9, 1870).

84. Ibid., 4280–81 (June 9, 1870), 5115 (July 2, 1870); *Chicago Republican,* Aug. 24, 1866.

85. *Globe,* 41st Cong., 2nd sess., 5115–18 (July 2, 1870); Kleppner, *The Cross of Culture,* 92–129. Population figures are from the Ninth Census.

86. *New York Times,* Nov. 11, 1870; Burke, "Federal Regulation of Congressional Elections in Northern Cities."

87. Foner, *Reconstruction,* 427–28; Trelease, *White Terror,* 189–284; Zuczek, *State of Rebellion,* 71–87.

88. Act of Feb. 21, 1871, ch. 99, 17 Stat. 433; Act of June 10, 1872, ch. 415, 17 Stat. 847.

89. Act of April 21, 1871, ch. 22, 17 Stat. 13.

90. Foner, *Reconstruction,* 454–59; Belz, *Emancipation and Equal Rights,* 127–28.

91. James A. Garfield to Burke Hinsdale, March 30, 1871, Garfield Papers, series 6A, vol. 7; Hyman and Wiecek, *Equal Justice under Law,* 459–72; Belz, *Emancipation and Equal Rights,* 127–29.

92. *Chicago Tribune,* April 10, 1871; *The Nation,* March 23, 1871; Foner, *Reconstruction,* 455.

93. *Chicago Tribune,* April 2, 10, 1871. See also *Chicago Republican,* April 17, 1871.

94. Ninth Census; Gillette, *Retreat from Reconstruction,* 48–49.

95. *Globe,* 41st Cong., 3rd sess., 1640 (Feb. 24, 1871); *Chicago Tribune,* Feb. 28, 1871.

96. *Globe,* 42nd Cong., 1st sess., 394–395 (April 1, 1871), 477 (April 5, 1871).

97. See, e.g., *Chicago Republican,* Jan. 25, 1871; *New York Times,* March 16, 1871; *Cincinnati Enquirer,* April 3, 1871. For an answer to this trend, see *Harper's Weekly,* April 15, 1871, 330. Seip, *The South Returns to Congress,* 77–79; Summers, *The Press Gang,* 207–22.

98. Rutherford B. Hayes to John Sherman, April 1, 1871, Sherman Papers, vol. 126; James A. Garfield to Burke Hinsdale, March 23, 1871, Garfield Papers, series 6A, vol. 7; *Chicago Republican,* April 4, 1871.

99. E. L. Godkin to Carl Schurz, June 28, 1872, quoted in Hoogenboom, *Outlawing the Spoils,* 116.

100. Trelease, *White Terror,* 399–418; Williams, *The Great South Carolina Ku Klux Klan Trials;* Simpson, *The Reconstruction Presidents,* 155–57; Sefton, The *United States Army and Reconstruction,* 220–29.

101. Gillette, *Retreat from Reconstruction;* Williams, *The Great South Carolina Ku Klux Klan Trials;* Zuczek, *State of Rebellion.*

102. Donald et al., *The Civil War and Reconstruction,* 603; Hogue, *Uncivil War,* 95.

103. Strong, *Diary,* 4:383 (Sept. 8, 1871); Bernstein, *The New York City Draft Riots,* 228–36.

104. Beckert, *The Monied Metropolis,* 172–95.

105. Holt, *By One Vote,* 98–99.

106. Michael Les Benedict, "Reform Republicans and the Retreat from Reconstruction," in Anderson and Moss, eds., *The Facts of Reconstruction,* 53–77; Hoogenboom, *Outlawing the Spoils;* Richardson, *West from Appomattox;* Slap, *The Doom of Reconstruction;* Sproat, *The "Best Men."*

107. Charles Nordhoff to Carl Schurz, Dec. 21, 1870, quoted in Slap, *The Doom of Reconstruction,* 23.

108. Trefousse, *Carl Schurz;* Simpson, *The Reconstruction Presidents;* Hoogenboom, *Outlawing the Spoils,* 83–84; Slap, *The Doom of Reconstruction,* 1–24.

109. Perman, *The Road to Redemption,* 3–131.

110. *Appleton's Annual Cyclopaedia,* 1871, 609–11; Moore, "Ohio in National Politics."

111. Ibid., 266–73.

112. Benedict, "Reform Republicans."

113. *Globe,* 42nd Cong., 2nd sess., 3046 (May 3, 1872).

114. Strong, *Diary,* 4:424 (May 3, 1872); Garfield, *Diary,* 2:48–49 (April 27, 1872); J. A. Hendricks to David Davis, May 4, 1872, David Davis Papers, box 18, Chicago Historical Society; Hoogenboom, *Rutherford B. Hayes,* 114–6; Slap, *The Doom of Reconstruction,* 158–59.

115. Joseph S. Fowler to Lyman Trumbull, Feb. 1, 1872, Trumbull Papers, vol. 73; B. Gratz Brown to George W. Julian, Feb. 28, 1872, Giddings and Julian Papers, box 6; Sproat, *The "Best Men,"* 74–78.

116. Summers, *The Press Gang,* 237–45.

117. *Appleton's Annual Cyclopaedia,* 1872, 777; Sproat, *The "Best Men,"* 81; Hoogenboom, *Rutherford B. Hayes,* 113; Slap, *The Doom of Reconstruction,* 158–59.

118. John Wentworth to David Davis, telegrams, April 26 and 30, 1872, David Davis Papers, box 17; Lyman Trumbull to Horace White, April 29, 1872, and O. Follett to Lyman Trumbull, May 11, 1872, both Trumbull Papers, vol. 75; *Cincinnati Enquirer,* April 29, 1872; William Gillette, "Election of 1872," in Schlesinger and Israel, eds., *History of American Presidential Elections, 1789–1968,* 2:1303–30.

119. Walter M. O'Dwyers to Lyman Trumbull, April 29, 1872, Trumbull Papers, vol. 75.

120. *Harper's Weekly,* July 13, 1872, 560; Gillette, "Election of 1872"; Summers, *The Press Gang,* 237–55.

121. Holt, *By One Vote,* 1–5, 250–57.

122. W. C. Stagg to Lyman Trumbull, July 15, 1872, Trumbull Papers, vol. 76; Joshua Brown to Trumbull, Dec. 2, 1871, Trumbull Papers, vol. 72.

123. Gillette, "Election of 1872"; Martis et al., *The Historical Atlas of Political Parties.*

124. Garfield, *Diary,* 2:104 (Oct. 19, 1872); McGerr, "The Meaning of Liberal Republicanism."

125. Act of May 22, 1872, ch. 193, 17 Stat. 142; Act of June 10, 1872, ch. 415, 17 Stat. 347; Foner, *Reconstruction,* 504–5.

126. Garfield, *Diary,* 2:54 (May 15, 1872); *Globe,* 42nd Cong., 2nd sess., 3046 (May 3, 1872).

127. Taussig, *The Tariff History in the United States,* 180–89; Foner, *Reconstruction,* 504. For a more detailed analysis, see chapter 3.

128. John Sherman to William T. Sherman, Aug. 4, 1872, Sherman and Sherman, *Letters,* 338–39.

129. On the organization and practice of parties, see Summers, *Party Games.*

6. The Republican Retreat to the North

1. Hoogenboom, *Outlawing the Spoils;* Slap, *The Doom of Reconstruction;* Summers, *The Era of Good Stealings.*

2. Summers, *The Press Gang,* 171–88. On Grant's reputation, see Waugh, *U.S. Grant.*

3. Klein, *Union Pacific,* 1:285–305; Summers, *The Era of Good Stealings,* 236–37; White, *Railroaded,* 62–66.

4. "Simmer" (?) to John Sherman, June 23, 1873, Sherman Papers, vol. 127; Summers, *The Era of Good Stealings,* 238–42; Alston et al., "Who Should Govern Congress?"

5. Holt, *By One Vote,* 11.

6. Richardson, *The Death of Reconstruction,* 111–21; Summers, *The Press Gang,* 207–22.

7. For instance, the number of troops garrisoned in the South kept declining. Sefton, *The United States Army and Reconstruction;* Holt, *By One Vote,* 7–12.

8. Summers, *The Press Gang,* 266–78. On paranoia as a force in Reconstruction, see Summers, *A Dangerous Stir.*

9. Garfield, *Diary,* 3:4–8 (Jan. 5–9, 1875); Hogue, *Uncivil War,* 144–59; Gillette, *Retreat from Reconstruction,* 123–31.

10. Garfield, *Diary,* 3:21 (Feb. 5, 1875).

11. *Cincinnati Enquirer,* Dec. 1, 1866.

12. Perman, *The Road to Redemption,* chap. 7.

13. Foner, *Reconstruction,* 537–41.

14. Ibid., 383.

15. Rable, *But There Was No Peace,* 123.

16. Hogue, *Uncivil War,* 91–106.

17. Ibid., 109–12; Rable, *But There Was No Peace,* 126–29; Keith, *The Colfax Massacre,* 82–110; Lane, *The Day Freedom Died,* 9–22.

18. *United States v. Cruikshank,* 92 U.S. 542 (1875). The decision was reached in October 1875 but the opinions made public only the following March. Fairman, *Reconstruction and Reunion,* 2:225–89; Brandwein, *Rethinking the Judicial Settlement of Reconstruction,* 93–108. On the Slaughterhouse cases, 83 U.S. (16 Wall.) 36, see Labbé and Lurie, *The Slaughterhouse Cases.*

19. Rable, *But There Was No Peace,* 112–85; Hogue, *Uncivil War,* 116–43; Gillette, *Retreat from Reconstruction,* 150–65; Perman, "Counter Reconstruction"; Zuczek, *State of Rebellion,* 159–87.

20. *Harper's Weekly,* Oct. 11, 1873, 891; *Bankers' Magazine* 8, no. 4 (Oct. 1873): 324–28; Barreyre, "The Politics of Economic Crises"; David Glasner, "Crisis of 1873" in Glasner

and Cooley, *Business Cycles and Depressions,* 132–34; Nelson, "A Storm of Cheap Goods"; White, *Railroaded,* 47–87; Wicker, *Banking Panics of the Gilded Age,* 16–33.

21. Strong, *Diary,* 4:498 (Oct. 27, 1873); *Jonesboro Gazette,* Oct. 30, 1875; Margo, "The Labor Force in the Nineteenth Century"; Atack et al., "The Farm, the Farmer, and the Market"; Unger, *The Greenback Era,* 220–26; Gutman, "The Tompkins Square 'Riot'."

22. Fels, "The Long-Wave Depression."

23. McPherson, *A Hand-Book of Politics,* 1874, 228; James A. Garfield to William C. Howells, Nov. 15, 1873, Garfield Papers, series 6A, vol. 14.

24. *Bankers' Magazine* 8, no. 4 (Oct. 1873): 324–28; no. 5 (Nov. 1873): 329–34, 404; no. 6 (Dec. 1873): 418–23.

25. Barreyre, "The Politics of Economic Crises."

26. Garfield, *Diary,* 2:288 (Feb. 9, 1874); Adams, "The Currency Debate of 1873–1874."

27. James A. Garfield to Burke Hinsdale, Dec. 4, 1873, and to Harmon Austin, Nov. 19, 1873, Garfield Papers, series 6A, vol. 14.

28. The polarization index averaged .4 in the House and .5 in the Senate on currency. On Southerners' actions in Congress on this issue, see Seip, *The South Returns to Congress,* 171–218.

29. Ibid., 189–93; Unger, *The Greenback Era,* 213–48.

30. The polarization index was .69. U.S. Congress, *Congressional Record,* 43rd Congress, 1st session, 3078 (April 14, 1874); Seip, *The South Returns to Congress,* 192–93; Unger, *The Greenback Era,* 233–45.

31. *Harper's Weekly,* May 9, 1874, 390; *Springfield Republican,* April 23, 1874; James A. Garfield to Burke Hinsdale, April 23, 1874, Garfield Papers, series 6A, vol. 16; Unger, *The Greenback Era,* 241–45.

32. *Cincinnati Enquirer,* April 25, 1874; *Cincinnati Trade List and Commerce Bulletin,* quoted in *Jonesboro Gazette,* May 16, 1874; *Quincy Whig,* April 23, 1874; John T. Deweese and Daniel G. Mark to John A. Logan, April 24, 1874, Logan Papers, box 2.

33. *U.S. Record and Gazette* 1, no. 6 (May 1874): 44; *Congressional Record,* 43rd Cong., 1st sess., 3425–26 (April 28, 1874); Seip, *The South Returns to Congress,* 189–94; Unger, *The Greenback Era,* 244–48.

34. Garfield, *Diary,* 2:327, 336 (May 27, June 13, 1874); Act of June 20, 1874, ch. 343, 18 Stat. 123.

35. *U.S. Record and Gazette* 1, no. 10 (Sept. 1874): 76.

36. Strong, *Diary,* 4:541 (Nov. 4, 1874); McPherson, *A Hand-Book of Politics,* 1876, 255; Holt, *By One Vote,* 17.

37. Nugent, *Money and American Society,* 221–28; DeCanio, "Religion and Nineteenth-Century Voting Behavior"; Kleppner, *The Third Electoral System,* 126–28.

38. J. I. Smith to John Sherman, Oct. 22, 1874, Sherman Papers, vol. 128; *Utica Herald,* quoted in *Alton Telegraph,* Nov. 19, 1874.

39. Strong, *Diary,* 4:541 (Nov. 4, 1874); *Harper's Weekly,* Nov. 7, 1874, 912; Summers, *The Era of Good Stealings,* 244–58.

40. *U.S. Record and Gazette* 1, no. 10 (Sept. 1874): 76; *Appleton's Annual Cyclopaedia,* 1874, 15.

41. Gillette, *Retreat from Reconstruction,* 196–258.

42. Michael Holt sees the Republican recovery after their landslide defeat of 1874 as one of the central historical problems of the years 1874–76. Holt, *By One Vote,* xiii.

43. On the political effects of this peculiar American institution, see Jenkins and Nokken, "Partisanship, the Electoral Connection, and Lame-Duck Sessions of Congress."

44. Sherman, *Recollections of Forty Years,* 1:507–19, 509 (quotation); Unger, *The Greenback Era,* 249–63; Weinstein, *Prelude to Populism,* 33–52.

45. Act of Jan. 14, 1875, ch. 15, 18 Stat. 296.

46. Unger, *The Greenback Era,* 254–59; Holt, *By One Vote,* 23–25.

47. *Congressional Record,* 43rd Cong., 2nd sess., 195–206, 318 (Dec. 22, 1873; Jan. 7, 1874); Blaine, *Twenty Years of Congress,* 2:563.

48. John Sherman to James H. Stingens, Dec. 28, 1874, Sherman Papers, vol. 128.

49. Gillette, *Retreat from Reconstruction,* 259–79.

50. Act of March 1, 1875, ch. 114, 18 Stat. 335.

51. *Civil Rights Cases,* 190 U.S. 3 (1883); Hyman and Wiecek, *Equal Justice under Law,* 496–500; Brandwein, *Rethinking the Judicial Settlement of Reconstruction,* 161–83.

52. D. E. Leoon to Philip H. Sheridan, Jan. 15, 1875, and Joseph Medill to James G. Blaine, Feb. 14, 1875, both quoted in Gillette, *Retreat from Reconstruction,* 281–88; Holt, *By One Vote,* 21–22; Simpson, *The Reconstruction Presidents,* 180–81.

53. Blaine, *Twenty Years of Congress,* 2:564; Holt, *By One Vote,* 28–32.

54. R. M. Stimson to Rutherford B. Hayes, June 14, 1875, Hayes Papers.

55. *Appleton's Annual Cyclopaedia,* 1875, 606–7; Rutherford B. Hayes to A. T. Wikoff, Sept. 20, 1875, and to John Sherman, July 5, 1875, Hayes Papers; Hayes, *Diary and Letters,* 3:274 (July 3, 1875); Seip, *The South Returns to Congress,* 215–16; Unger, *The Greenback Era,* 263–64.

56. McAfee, *Religion, Race, and Reconstruction.*

57. Rutherford B. Hayes to W. D. Bickham, July 10, 1875, Hayes Papers; DeCanio, "State Autonomy and American Political Development."

58. Garfield, *Diary,* 3:137–38 (Aug. 30–31, 1875); *Ashtabula Sentinel,* June 24, 1875; Morton, "Ohio's Gallant Fight," 192–208; Holt, *By One Vote,* 54–66.

59. "Speech of Hon. Allen G. Thurman, Delivered at Cleveland Ohio," August 28, 1875, newspaper clipping in Allen G. Thurman Papers, Ohio Historical Society; Benjamin F. Wade to Edward C. Wade, Oct. 18, 1875, broadside, American Antiquarian Society; *Appleton's Annual Cyclopaedia,* 1875, 607; McPherson, *A Hand-Book of Politics,* 1876, 255. On the ethnocultural basis of politics, see Kleppner, *The Cross of Culture.*

60. *Congressional Record,* 44th Cong., 1st sess., 175–81 (Dec. 7, 1875); DeCanio, "State Autonomy and American Political Development."

61. J. E. Cooley to Samuel J. Tilden, Oct. 20, 1875, Tilden Papers, box 8; *Cincinnati Enquirer,* Oct. 13, 1875. The biblical reference is to Luke 16:19–31.

62. Rable, *But There Was No Peace,* 154–62; Simpson, *The Reconstruction Presidents,* 185–89, 189 (quotation); Gillette, *Retreat from Reconstruction,* 155–60, 159 (quotation); *New York Tribune,* Oct. 12, 1865.

63. See, e.g., *Harper's Weekly,* May 27, 1876, 419ff.

64. Garfield, *Diary*, 3:211 (Jan. 5, 1876).

65. James C. Madigan to Charles P. Kimball, Nov. 11, 1875, Tilden Papers, box 8.

66. Summers, *The Press Gang*, 279–97; Summers, *The Era of Good Stealings*, 259–73.

67. William Brodie to John H. Harmon, May 2, 1876, Tilden Papers, box 9; John Bigelow, Diary, April 28, 1876, John Bigelow Papers, series 6, vol. 50, New York Public Library; *Appleton's Annual Cyclopaedia*, 1876, 785–86; Holt, *By One Vote*, 96–118.

68. Summers, *The Era of Good Stealings*, 257–58, 267–69.

69. John Sherman to A. M. Burns, Jan. 21, 1876, Hayes Papers.

70. *Appleton's Annual Cyclopaedia*, 1876, 779–85; Wittke, "Carl Schurz and Rutherford B. Hayes"; Slap, *The Doom of Reconstruction*, 232–37.

71. S. Bassell French to Samuel J. Tilden, Nov. 21, 1875, Tilden Papers, box 8; Holt, *By One Vote*, 107–8.

72. Wittke, "Carl Schurz and Rutherford B. Hayes."

73. *Appleton's Annual Cyclopaedia*, 1876, 781–82; Unger, *The Greenback Era*, 293–308; Ritter, *Goldbugs and Greenbacks*, 123–36; DeCanio and Smidt, "Prelude to Populism"; Buck, *The Granger Movement*.

74. *Congressional Record*, 44th Cong., 1st sess., 444 (Jan. 17, 1876), 1815 (March 20, 1876), 2862 (May 1, 1876), 5230–32 (Aug. 5, 1876); Unger, *The Greenback Era*, 281, 289–91.

75. George L. Miller to Samuel J. Tilden, Feb. 20, 1876, Tilden Papers, box 9.

76. *Appleton's Annual Cyclopaedia*, 1876, 787–90; McPherson, *A Hand-Book of Politics*, 1876, 222–24; Unger, *The Greenback Era*, 308–12; Polakoff, *The Politics of Inertia*, 108–12; Holt, *By One Vote*, 112–18.

77. Abram S. Hewitt to Samuel J. Tilden, July 6, 19, and Aug. 8, 1876, Tilden Papers, box 9.

78. Rutherford B. Hayes to James A. Garfield, June 28, 1875, Garfield Papers, series 4, vol. 40; Hayes to Carl Schurz, June 27, 1876, Hayes, *Diary and Letters*, 3:329–30.

79. *Appleton's Annual Cyclopaedia*, 1876, 392–93, 407–9; Holt, *By One Vote*, 74–75, 86–87; Rutherford B. Hayes to James Blaine, Sept. 14, 1876, Hayes Papers.

80. Act of Feb. 12, 1873, ch. 131, 17 Stat. 424; Ulysses S. Grant to "Mr. Cowdrey," Oct. 3, 1873, in McPherson, *A Hand-Book of Politics*, 1874, 134–35.

81. *Congressional Record*, 44th Cong., 1st sess., 2085, 2088, 2130 (March 30–31, 1876); Weinstein, *Prelude to Populism*, 82–91.

82. This act remonetized the silver dollar and authorized the coining of between 2 to 4 million dollars of silver coins every month. Barreyre, "Les échelles de la monnaie."

83. On this idea that the law was enacted without congressmen being aware of its content, see Nugent, *Money and American Society*, 162–72; Weinstein, *Prelude to Populism*, 8–32; and DeCanio, "Populism, Paranoia, and the Politics of Free Silver."

84. Flandreau, *L'or du monde*, 251–86; Nugent, *Money and American Society*, 181–204; Weinstein, *Prelude to Populism*, 82–123.

85. Garfield, *Diary*, 3:262, 333 (April 31, Aug. 9, 1876); *Congressional Record*, 44th Cong., 1st sess., 4213–15, 4563 (June 28, July 13, 1876); Weinstein, *Prelude to Populism*, 118–19.

86. John Sherman to Rutherford B. Hayes, June 26, 1876, Hayes Papers.

87. Gillette, *Retreat from Reconstruction*, 251–52; Garfield, *Diary*, 3:203–4 (Dec. 20, 1875); Martis et al., *The Historical Atlas of Political Parties*.

88. Garfield, *Diary*, 3:215–17 (Jan. 13–17, 1876); Summers, *The Press Gang*, 279–81; Coulter, "Amnesty for All except Jefferson Davis."

89. Higham, *Strangers in the Land*, 28–34.

90. Rutherford B. Hayes to James A. Garfield, Aug. 5, 1876, Hayes Papers.

91. John Sherman to A. M. Burns, Jan. 21, 1876, Hayes Papers.

92. Foner, "Reconstruction Revisited"; Gillette, *Retreat from Reconstruction*, 308–9; Zuczek, *State of Rebellion*, 163–65.

93. William H. Smith to Rutherford B. Hayes, July 1, 1876, William H. Smith Papers, Hayes Presidential Center; Rutherford B. Hayes to W. K. Rogers, Aug. 13, 1876, Hayes Papers.

94. Hayes, *Diary and Letters*, 3:373 (Nov. 7, 1876).

95. Ibid., 3:375.

96. The electoral crisis has been told many times, often in a very biased way. The best account to date is Holt, *By One Vote*, 175–243.

97. Twelfth Amendment.

98. Garfield, *Diary*, 3:435 (Feb. 7, 1877). Hayes was actually sworn in a first time, in the White House, the previous day, lest the inauguration ceremony be disrupted.

99. Hayes, *Diary and Letters*, 3:390 (Dec. 17, 1876); Polakoff, *The Politics of Inertia*, 106–61.

100. Telegram, Jan. 17, 1877, Tilden, *Letters and Literary Memorials*, 2:534; James A. Garfield to Rutherford B. Hayes, Jan. 19, 1877, Hayes Papers; Calhoun, *Conceiving a New Republic*, 111–12.

101. James Comly to Rutherford B. Hayes, Jan. 8, 1877, Hayes Papers; Garfield, *Diary*, 3:415, 423 (Jan. 14, 24, 1877).

102. James A. Garfield to Rutherford B. Hayes, Dec. 13, 1876, Garfield Papers, series 6A, vol. 18; Hayes to William H. Smith, Dec. 24, 1876, and Jacob D. Cox to Hayes, Jan. 31, 1877, both Hayes Papers; Polakoff, *The Politics of Inertia*, 232–324.

103. Ibid., 315–24; Simpson, *The Reconstruction Presidents*, 203–19.

Epilogue

1. I develop this reflection on space and politics in Barreyre, "Les échelles de la monnaie."

2. Linden, "'Radicals' and Economic Policies."

3. Polakoff, *The Politics of Inertia*. For a discussion of the role of the federal government after Reconstruction, see Bensel, *Yankee Leviathan*, 405–36; Bensel, *The Political Economy of American Industrialization;* and Balogh, *A Government out of Sight*, 277–351.

4. In chronological order: the Dakotas, Montana, Washington, Idaho, and Wyoming.

5. On the persistence of the composition of presidential tickets, see Polakoff, *The Politics of Inertia*, 315–24.

6. Nugent, *Money and American Society,* 243–50; Ritter, *Goldbugs and Greenbacks,* 152–207.

7. Harris, "Right Fork or Left Fork?"

8. Bensel, *The Political Economy of American Industrialization,* 457–500; Reitano, *The Tariff Question in the Gilded Age.*

9. On financing pensions, see Skocpol, *Protecting Soldiers and Mothers.*

10. Of course, the Democratic deal collapsed when in 1895, the Supreme Court declared the income tax unconstitutional. On the tariff in the early twentieth century, see Wolman, *Most Favored Nation.*

11. On the end of federal enforcement of elections, see Calhoun, *Conceiving a New Republic,* 226–88, and Brandwein, *Rethinking the Judicial Settlement of Reconstruction,* 184–205.

BIBLIOGRAPHY

Primary Sources

PERIODICALS

Alton Telegraph (Illinois)
Ashtabula Sentinel (Ohio)
Bankers' Magazine and Statistical Register
Chicago Inter-Ocean
Chicago Republican
Chicago Times
Chicago Tribune
Cincinnati Commercial
Cincinnati Enquirer
Cincinnati Gazette
Cleveland Herald
Cleveland Leader
Free-Trader
Harper's Weekly

Hine's Quarterly
Hunt's Merchants' Magazine and Commercial Review
Joliet Republican (Illinois)
Joliet Signal (Illinois)
Jonesboro Gazette (Illinois)
Marietta Register (Ohio)
Merchants' Magazine and Commercial Review
Nation
New Century
New York Times
North American
Quincy Whig (Illinois)
U.S. Record and Gazette

CAMPAIGN NEWSPAPERS (FROM THE AMERICAN ANTIQUARIAN SOCIETY COLLECTION)

1866: *Campaign Post* (Boston), *Old Flag* (Chambersburg, PA)
1868: *Campaign Gazette* (Little Rock), *Campaign Post* (Boston), *Father Abraham* (Lancaster, PA), *Jacksonian* (Lewiston, ME), *National Democrat* (Philadelphia), *National Radical* (Washington, DC), *Worcester Sentinel* (MA)
1870: *Labor Reform Dispatch* (Concord, NH)
1872: *Plaindealer* (Concord, NH), *Reformer and Campaign Times* (Boston)
1876: *Bremen Gazette* (Indiana), *Campaign Press* (Dover, NH), *Chronicle* (Harrisburg, PA), *Daily Madison Patriot* (Wisconsin), *Herald of Liberty* (Des Moines), *National Illustrated Weekly* (Chicago), *Pueblo Republican* (Colorado), *Republican Leader* (Aurora, IN), *Spirit of the Campaign* (New York), *Uncle Sam* (New York), *Uncle Samuel* (Lancaster, PA)

PAPERS OF INDIVIDUALS

John Bigelow, New York Public Library
John A. Bingham, Ohio Historical Society
George S. Boutwell, American Antiquarian Society
Guy M. Bryan, University of Texas Library
James M. Comly, Ohio Historical Society
Jacob D. Cox, Oberlin College Library
David Davis, Chicago Historical Society and Illinois State Historical Library
James A. Garfield, Library of Congress
Joshua R. Giddings and George W. Julian, Library of Congress
Rutherford B. Hayes, Hayes Presidential Center and Library of Congress
John A. Logan, Library of Congress
Robert C. Schenck, Hayes Presidential Center and Miami University Library
Carl Schurz, Library of Congress
John Sherman, Hayes Presidential Center and Library of Congress
William H. Smith, Hayes Presidential Center and Ohio Historical Society
Charles Sumner, Library of Congress
Allen G. Thurman, Ohio Historical Society
Samuel J. Tilden, New York Public Library
John A. Trimble, Ohio Historical Society
Lyman Trumbull, Illinois State Historical Library and Library of Congress
Benjamin F. Wade, Library of Congress

Garfield, James A. *The Diary of James A. Garfield*. Edited by Harry James Brown and
    Frederick D. Williams. 4 vols. East Lansing: Michigan State University, 1967.
————. *The Works of James Abram Garfield*. Edited by Burke A. Hinsdale. 2 vols.
    Boston: James R. Osgood, 1882.
Garfield, James A., and Burke A. Hinsdale. *Garfield-Hinsdale Letters: Correspondence
    between James Abram Garfield and Burke Aaron Hinsdale*. Edited by Mary L. Hins-
    dale. Ann Arbor: University of Michigan Press, 1949.
Grant, Ulysses S. *The Papers of Ulysses S. Grant*. Edited by John Y. Simon et al. 32
    vols. Carbondale: Southern Illinois University Press, 1967–2012.
Hayes, Rutherford B. *Diary and Letters of Rutherford Birchard Hayes, Nineteenth Pres-
    ident of the United States*. Edited by Charles Richard Williams. 3 vols. Columbus:
    Ohio State Archæological and Historical Society, 1922.
Johnson, Andrew. *The Papers of Andrew Johnson*. Edited by LeRoy P. Graf et al. 16
    vols. Knoxville: University of Tennessee Press, 1967–2000.
Lincoln, Abraham. *Speeches and Letters of Abraham Lincoln, 1832–1865*. Edited by
    Merwin Roe. New York: E. P. Dutton, 1907.
Sherman, John, and William T. Sherman. *The Sherman Letters: Correspondence be-
    tween General and Senator Sherman from 1837 to 1891*. Edited by Rachel Sherman
    Thorndike. New York: Charles Scribner's Sons, 1894.

Strong, George Templeton. *The Diary of George Templeton Strong.* Edited by Allan
Nevins and Milton Halsey Thomas. 4 vols. New York: Macmillan, 1952.

Tilden, Samuel J. *Letters and Literary Memorials of Samuel J. Tilden.* Edited by John
Bigelow. 2 vols. New York: Harper and Brothers, 1908.

Welles, Gideon. *Diary of Gideon Welles, Secretary of the Navy under Lincoln and
Johnson.* Edited by Edgar Thaddeus Welles. Vols. 2–3. Boston: Houghton Mifflin,
1911.

OFFICIAL PUBLICATIONS

Boutwell, George S. *A Manual of the Direct and Excise Tax System of the United States
Including the Forms and Regulations Established by the Commissioner of Internal
Revenue, the Decisions and Ruling of the Commissioner, Together with Extracts from
the Correspondence of the Office.* Boston: Little, Brown, 1864.

———. *The Tax-Payer's Manual; Containing the Entire Internal Revenue Laws, with
the Decisions and Rulings of the Commissioner, Tables of Taxation, Exemption, Stamp-
Duties, &c., and a Complete Alphabetical Index.* Boston: Little, Brown, 1865.

Buell, James. *Statement of James Buell. Committee on Banking and Currency. February
9th, 1874.* Washington, DC: Government Printing Office, 1874.

Schurz, Carl. *Report on the Condition of the South.* Washington, DC: Government
Printing Office, 1865.

*Statistical Abstract of the United States. First Number. 1878. Finance, Coinage, Com-
merce, Immigration, Shipping, the Postal Service, Population, Railroads, Agriculture,
Coal and Iron. Prepared by the Chief of the Bureau of Statistics, Treasury Department.*
Washington, DC: Government Printing Office, 1879.

U.S. Bureau of the Census. *Historical Statistics of the United States from Colonial Times
to 1970.* 2 vols. Washington, DC: Government Printing Office, 1970.

U.S. Commissioner of Internal Revenue. *Annual Report of the Commissioner of Internal
Revenue.* Washington, DC: Government Printing Office, 1865–77.

U.S. Comptroller of the Currency. *Annual Report of the Comptroller of the Currency.*
Washington, DC: Government Printing Office, 1865–77.

U.S. Congress. *Bills and Resolutions of the House and the Senate.* Washington, DC:
Government Printing Office, 1865–77.

———. *Congressional Globe.* Washington, DC: Blair and Rives, 1865–73.

———. *Congressional Record.* Washington, DC: Government Printing Office, 1874–77.

———. *Congressional Serial Set.* Washington, DC: Government Printing Office,
1865–77.

———. *Journal of the Executive Proceedings of the Senate of the United States.* Washington, DC: Government Printing Office, 1865–77.

———. *Journal of the House of Representatives of the United States.* Washington, DC:
Government Printing Office, 1865–77.

———. *Journal of the Senate of the United States.* Washington, DC: Government
Printing Office, 1865–77.

———. *Revised Statutes of the United States.* Vol. 18. Washington, DC: Government Printing Office, 1878.

———. *The Statutes at Large and Proclamations of the United States of America.* Vols. 14–17. Boston, Little, Brown, 1868–73.

———. *The Statutes at Large of the United States of America.* Vol. 19. Washington, DC: Government Printing Office, 1879.

U.S. Monetary Commission. *Report of the United States Monetary Commission.* Washington, DC: Government Printing Office, 1877.

U.S. Secretary of the Treasury. *Annual Report of the Secretary of the Treasury.* Washington, DC: Government Printing Office, 1865–77.

Walker, Francis Amasa, ed. *Statistical Atlas of the United States, Based on the Results of the Ninth Census 1870, with Contributions from Many Eminent Men of Science and Several Departments of the Government.* New York: J. Bien, 1874.

PRINTED PRIMARY SOURCES

Adams, Charles Francis. "The Currency Debate of 1873–1874." *North American Review* 119 (1874): 111–65.

Adams, Henry Brooks. "The Legal Tender Act." *North American Review* 110 (1870): 299–327.

———. "The Session." *North American Review* 111 (1870): 29–62.

Appleton's Annual Cyclopaedia and Register of Important Events. Embracing Political, Military, and Ecclesiastical Affairs; Public Documents; Biography, Statistics, Commerce, Finance, Literature, Science, Agriculture, and Mechanical Industry. New York: D. Appleton, 1865–78.

Atkinson, Edward. *An Argument for the Conditional Repeal of the Legal-Tender Act.* Boston: A. Williams, 1874.

———. *Discussion on Finance. Greenbacks a Legal Tender for All Debts, Public and Private, Excepting Only, Interest on the Public Debt and Duties on Imports. National Bank Notes a Legal Tender in Payments to and from the Government for All Demands, Excepting Only, Interest on the Public Debt and Duties on Imports. Read the Law!* New York, 1869.

———. *The National Debt, a Decrease of 802 Millions in Three Years, Important and Interesting Facts: Speech of Edward Atkinson, of Brookline, Mass. Delivered at Worcester, Mass., Sept. 9, 1868.* Washington, DC: Gibson Brothers, 1868.

———. *On Cotton.* New York: American Geographical and Statistical Society, 1866.

———. *On the Collection of Revenue.* New York: American Free Trade League, 1869.

Barclay, John M. *Constitution of the United States of America, with the Amendments Thereto. To Which Are Added Jefferson's Manual of Parliamentary Practice, the Standing Rules and Order for Conducting Business in the House of Representatives and Senate of the United States, and Barclay's Digest.* 2 vols. Washington, DC: Government Printing Office, 1871.

Bigelow, John. *Mr. Tilden's War Record. An Authoritative Statement. The Ground Taken by Samuel J. Tilden on Public Questions during the War. — His Unswerving Loyalty to the Government*. New York: N.p., 1876.

Blaine, James G. *Twenty Years of Congress from Lincoln to Garfield. With a Review of the Events Which Led to the Political Revolution of 1860*. 2 vols. Norwich, CT: Henry Bill, 1884.

Bloss, G. M. D. *Life and Speeches of George H. Pendleton*. Cincinnati: Miami Printing, 1868.

Boutwell, George S. *Reminiscences of Sixty Years in Public Affairs*. 2 vols. New York: McClure, Phillips, 1902.

Breen, J. W., and Francis Amasa Walker. "Claims of the Anti-Bondholders, and Reply." *Lippincott's Magazine of Literature, Science and Education* 2 (1868): 636–41.

Burchard, Horatio C. *Tariff Reduction — Should Able-Bodied Men Be Pensioned? — Tariff Bounties — Who Receive Them. Speech of Hon. Horatio C. Burchard of Illinois, April 27, 1872*. Washington, DC: Government Printing Office, 1872.

Campbell, Alexander. *The True American System of Finance: The Rights of Labor and Capital, and the Common Sense Way of Doing Justice to the Soldiers and Their Families; No Banks, Greenbacks the Exclusive Currency*. Chicago: Evening Journal Book and Job Print, 1864.

———. *The True Greenback; or, The Way to Pay the National Debt without Taxes, and Emancipate Labor*. Chicago: Republican Book and Job Office, 1868.

Carey, Henry C. *The Finance Minister, the Currency, and the Public Debt*. Philadelphia: Collins, 1868.

———. *The Harmony of Interests, Agricultural, Manufacturing and Commercial*. Philadelphia: H. C. Baird, 1868.

———. *Monetary Independence. Letter of Mr. H. C. Carey to the Hon. Moses W. Field, Chairman of the Committee of Invitations for the Detroit Convention*. Philadelphia: N.p., 1875.

———. *The Public Debt, Local and National: How to Provide for Its Discharge While Lessening the Burthen of Taxation. Letter to David A. Wells, Esq., Chairman of the Board of Revenue Commissioners*. Philadelphia: Henry Carey Baird, 1866.

———. *Reconstruction: Industrial, Financial, and Political. Letters to the Hon. Henry Wilson, Senator from Massachusetts*. Philadelphia: Collins, 1867.

———. *Resumption! How It May Profitably Be Brought About*. Philadelphia: Collins, 1869.

Cole, Cornelius. *Memoirs of Cornelius Cole, Ex-Senator of the United States from California*. New York: McLoughlin Brothers, 1908.

Cook, Theodore P. *The Life and Public Services of Hon. Samuel J. Tilden, Democratic Nominee for President of the United States, to Which Is Added a Sketch of the Life of Hon. Thomas A. Hendricks, Democratic Nominee for Vice-President*. New York: D. Appleton, 1876.

Cooke, Jay. *How Our National Debt Can Be Paid: The Wealth, Resources, and Power of the People of the United States*. Philadelphia: Sherman, 1865.

Cornell, William Mason. *The Life of Hon. Samuel Jones Tilden, Governor of the State of New York; with a Sketch of the Life of Hon. Thomas Andrews Hendricks, Governor of the State of Indiana.* Boston: Lee and Shepard, 1876.

Davenport, John I. *The Elections and Naturalization Frauds in New York City, 1860–1870.* 2nd edition. New York: N.p., 1894.

Deshler, John G. *A Financial System for the "Granger," with the Argument.* Columbus: Ohio State Journal, 1874.

Donnelly, Ignatius. *The American People's Money.* Chicago: Laird and Lee, 1876.

———. *Facts for the Granges. The Necessity for Co-Operation among the Farmers, Patent Laws against Them, Railroad Legislation against Them, the Robberies of the High Tariff against Them, the Evils of a Paper Currency against Them. Their Remedies, Cheap Transportation, Ship Canals, Specie Payments and Low Tariff. Extracts from Speeches before the Granges of Dakota, Rice, Goodhue, Fillmore, Mower, Olmsted, Winona, and Washington Counties during March, April, May, and June 1873.* Saint Paul: N.p., 1873.

Elder, William. *How Our National Debt Can Be Paid: The Wealth, Resources, and Power of the People of the United States, Issued by Jay Cooke.* Philadelphia: Sherman, 1865.

Fessenden, Francis. *Life and Public Service of William Pitt Fessenden.* 2 vols. Boston: Houghton, Mifflin, 1907.

Field, Moses W. *Greenbacks, Money and Labor. Hard Times, Their Cause & Remedy.* N.p.: N.p., 1877.

Flagg, W. C. *Aim and Scope of the Farmers' Movement, Speech at Riggs' Grove, Winchester, Scott County, August 7, 1873.* Chicago: Prairie Farmer, 1873.

Fluctuations in Gold, Stocks, Exchange and Government Securities National Bank Statements from 1863 to 1868 Inclusive, Treasure Movement at New York for Ten Years, an Extract from the Annual Review of Commercial and Financial Chronicle. New York: W. Dana, 1869.

Foster, Lillian. *Andrew Johnson, President of the United States; His Life and Speeches.* New York: Richardson, 1866.

Fuller, Corydon Eustathius. *Reminiscences of James A. Garfield, with Notes Preliminary and Collateral.* Cincinnati: Standard Publishing, 1887.

Garfield, James A. "The Currency Conflict." *The Atlantic Monthly* 37 (1876): 219–36.

———. *Honest Money, Speech Delivered at Faneuil Hall, September 10, 1878.* Boston: N.p., 1878.

Groom, Wallace P. *Currency Needs of Commerce. National Paper Money, Interchangeable with Government Bonds, Advocated.* New York: N.p., 1873.

Hall, James. *Letters from the West: Containing Sketches of Scenery, Manners, and Customs, and Anecdotes Connected with the First Settlements of the Western Sections of the United States.* London: H. Colburn, 1828.

Harris, Edward. *Memorial of Manufacturers of Woolen Goods to the Committee of Ways and Means of the House of Representatives, Showing That the Present High Duties on*

Wool Are Destroying That Branch of Industry Together with a Statement of Facts and Statistics, Sustaining the Allegations of the Memorial, by Edward Harris, of Woonsocket, R.I. Washington, DC: M'Gill and Witherow, 1872.

Heath, B. S. *The Greenback Dollar, Its History and Worth.* Chicago: M. M. Pomeroy, 1877.

Howells, William Dean. *Sketch of the Life and Character of Rutherford B. Hayes; Also a Biographical Sketch of William A. Wheeler, with Portraits of Both Candidates.* New York: Hurd and Houghton, 1876.

Julian, George W. *Political Recollections, 1840 to 1872.* Chicago: Jansen, McClurg, 1884.

Kelley, Oliver H. *Origin and Progress of the Order of the Patrons of Husbandry in the United States: A History from 1866 to 1873.* Philadelphia: J. A. Wagenseller, 1875.

Kelley, William D. *Speeches, Addresses and Letters on Industrial and Financial Questions. To Which Is Added an Introduction, Together with Copious Notes and an Index.* Philadelphia: Henry Carey Baird, 1872.

Kellogg, Edward. *A New Monetary System: The Only Means of Securing the Respective Rights of Labor and Property, and of Protecting the Public from Financial Revulsions.* 6th edition. Philadelphia: Henry Carey Baird, 1878 (1849).

Kendrick, Benjamin B. *The Journal of the Joint Committee of Fifteen on Reconstruction: 39th Congress, 1865–1867.* New York: Columbia University, 1914.

Kerr, Winfield Scott. *John Sherman, His Life and Public Services.* Vol. 1. Boston: Sherman, French, 1908.

Lester, C. Edwards. *Lives and Public Services of Samuel J. Tilden and Thomas A. Hendricks.* New York: Frank Leslie's, 1876.

Lieber, Francis. *Notes on the Fallacies Peculiar to American Protectionists; or, Chiefly Resorted to in America.* New York: American Free Trade League, 1869.

Logan, John A. *Removal of the Capital. Speech of Hon. John A. Logan, of Illinois, Delivered in the House of Representatives, January 22, 1870.* Washington, DC: F. & J. Rives & Geo. A. Bailey, 1870.

McCabe, James D. *The Life and Public Services of Horatio Seymour: Together with a Complete and Authentic Life of Francis P. Blair, Jr.* New York: United States Publishing, 1868.

McCulloch, Hugh. *Men and Measures of Half a Century: Sketches and Comments.* New York: Charles Scribner's Sons, 1888.

McKee, Thomas Hudson. *Manual of Congressional Practice. (The U.S. Red Book.).* Washington, DC: Thos. H. McKee, 1891.

McPherson, Edward. *A Hand-Book of Politics.* Washington, DC: Philp and Solomons, 1868–1872; Solomons and Chapman, 1874–1878 (biennial).

Morgan, John T. "The Political Alliance of the South with the West." *North American Review* 126 (March 1878): 309–22.

The National Banks, the System Unmasked, Greenbacks Forever. Cincinnati: I. A. Hine, 1869.

Newcomb, Simon. *A Critical Examination of Our Financial Policy during the Southern Rebellion*. New York: D. Appleton, 1865.

Nichols, Thomas. *Honest Money: An Argument in Favor of a Redeemable Currency*. Chicago: Honest Money League of the Northwest, 1878.

Nicolay, John G., and John Hay. *Abraham Lincoln: A History*. 10 vols. New York: The Century Company, 1890.

Official Proceedings of the National Democratic Convention, Held at New York, July 4–9, 1868. Boston: Rockwell and Rollins, 1868.

Pendleton, George H. *Payment of the Public Debt in Legal Tender Notes!! Speech of Hon. George H. Pendleton, Milwaukee, November 2, 1867*. Milwaukee: Office of the Milwaukee News, 1867.

———. *Speech of Hon. George H. Pendleton, at Loveland, O., August 22, 1871*. N.p.: N.p., 1871.

Perry, Arthur Latham. *Elements of Political Economy*. New York: Charles Scribner, 1866.

Poore, Benjamin Perley. *The Life and Public Services of John Sherman*. Cincinnati: Sherman Club, 1880.

Proceedings at the Mass Meeting of Citizens in the Cooper Institute, New York, Tuesday Evening, March 24th, 1874, on National Finances. New York: Comes, Lawrence, 1874.

Proceedings of the National Commercial Convention Held in Boston, February, 1868. Boston: J. H. Eastburn's Press, 1868.

Salter, William. *The Life of James W. Grimes, Governor of Iowa, 1854–1858: A Senator of the United States, 1759–1869*. New York: D. Appleton, 1876.

Sharp, Isaac S. "Stay and Exemption Laws." *The American Law Register* 20 (1872): 201–7.

Sherman, John. *National Finances—Specie Payments. Speech of Hon. John Sherman, of Ohio, in the Senate of the United States, March 6, 1876*. Washington, DC: Government Printing Office, 1876.

———. *Recollections of Forty Years in the House, Senate and Cabinet*. 2 vols. Chicago: Werner, 1895.

———. *Sherman on Pendleton. Reply to His Clifton Speech. Delivered at Marietta, September 24th*. Cincinnati: Cincinnati Chronicle, 1867.

Smith, Samuel. *Three Letters on the Silver Question*. Liverpool: Joseph A. D. Watts, 1876.

Smith, Theodore Clarke. *The Life and Letters of James Abram Garfield*. 2 vols. New Haven, CT: Yale University Press, 1925.

Some Facts about the Life and Public Services of Benjamin Helm Bristow, of Kentucky, Designed as a Reply to Inquiries Often Made Respecting the Leading Events of His Life. New York: Evening Post Steam Presses, 1876.

Spaulding, E. G. *A Resource of War—The Credit of the Government Made Immediately Available: History of the Legal Tender Paper Money Issued during the Great Rebellion,*

Being a Loan without Interest and a National Currency. Buffalo: Express Printing, 1869.

Stewart, William M. *Reminiscences of Senator William M. Stewart, of Nevada.* New York: Neale Publishing, 1908.

Sylvis, James C. *The Life, Speeches, Labors and Essays of William H. Sylvis, Late President of the Iron-Moulders' International Union; and Also of the National Labor Union.* Philadelphia: Claxton, Remsen, and Haffelfinger, 1872.

Taylor, James. *American Currency, the Political Issue of the Day.* Chicago: Taylor, 1876.

Thomas, J. H. "Homestead and Exemption Laws of the Southern States." *The American Law Register* 19 (1871): 1–17, 137–50.

Thurman, Alan G. *The Campaign in Ohio. Speech of Hon. Allen G. Thurman, at Sandusky, Ohio, September 7th, 1868.* Columbus: Crisis Printing, 1868.

Tilden, Samuel J. *The New York City "Ring": Its Origin, Maturity and Fall, Discussed in a Reply to the New York Times.* New York: J. Polhemus, 1873.

[Townsend, Samuel P.] A Patriot. *Our National Finances. A Mirror in Which "Trees Can Be Seen as Men Walking."* New York: MacDonald and Swank, 1868.

———. *Our National Finances. No. 10–13.* New York: Baker and Godwin, 1865–67.

Vallandigham, James L. *A Life of Clement L. Vallandigham.* Baltimore: Turnbull Brothers, 1872.

Walker, Francis Amasa. "Claims of the Bondholders." *Lippincott's Magazine of Literature, Science and Education* 2 (1868): 206–12.

———. "An Elastic Currency." *Lippincott's Magazine of Literature, Science and Education* 1 (1868): 316–24.

———. "The National Finances." *Lippincott's Magazine of Literature, Science and Education* 1 (1868): 202–8.

———. "Trade and Currency." *Lippincott's Magazine of Literature, Science and Education* 1 (1868): 86–91.

Walker, George. *La dette américaine et les moyens de l'acquitter.* Paris: E. Dentu, 1865.

Wells, David A. *The Cremation Theory of Specie Resumption.* New York: G. P. Putnam's Sons, 1875.

Willson, Hugh Bowlby. *A Plea for Uncle Sam's Money; or, Greenbacks versus Bank Notes.* New York: John Medole, 1870.

Secondary Sources

Abbot, Richard H. *The Republican Party and the South, 1855–1877: The First Southern Strategy.* Chapel Hill: University of North Carolina Press, 1986.

Alston, Lee J., Jeffery A. Jenkins, and Tomas Nonnenmacher. "Who Should Govern Congress? Access to Power and the Salary Grab of 1873." *Journal of Economic History* 66, no. 3 (2006): 674–706.

Anbinder, Tyler. *Nativism and Slavery: The Northern Know Nothings and the Politics of the 1850's.* Oxford: Oxford University Press, 1992.

Anderson, Benedict. *Imagined Communities: Reflections on the Origin and Spread of Nationalism.* Rev. edition. New York: Verso, 1991.

Anderson, Eric, and Alfred A. Moss, eds. *The Facts of Reconstruction: Essays in Honor of John Hope Franklin.* Baton Rouge: Louisiana State University Press, 1991.

Anderson, George L. "The National Banking System, 1865–1875: A Sectional Institution." Ph.D. dissertation, University of Illinois, 1933.

———. "The South and Problems of Post-Civil War Finance." *Journal of Southern History* 9, no. 2 (1943): 181–95.

———. "Western Attitude toward National Banks, 1873–74." *The Mississippi Valley Historical Review* 23, no. 2 (1936): 205–16.

Anderson, Lee F., Meredith W. Watts, and Allen R. Wilcox. *Legislative Roll-Call Analysis.* Evanston, IL: Northwestern University Press, 1966.

Anderson, Margo J. *The American Census: A Social History.* New Haven, CT: Yale University Press, 1988.

Andreano, Ralph. *The Economic Impact of the Civil War.* 2nd edition. Cambridge, MA: Schenkman, 1967.

Appleby, Joyce O. *Liberalism and Republicanism in the Historical Imagination.* Cambridge, MA: Harvard University Press, 1992.

Atack, Jeremy, and Peter Passell. *A New Economic View of American History: From Colonial Times to 1940.* 2nd rev. edition. New York: Norton, 1994.

Ayers, Edward L., Peter S. Onuf, Patricia N. Limerick, and Stephen Nissenbaum. *All over the Map: Rethinking American Regions.* Baltimore: Johns Hopkins University Press, 1996.

Bacon, Donald C., Roger H. Davidson, and Morton Keller, eds. *Encyclopedia of the United States Congress.* 4 vols. New York: Simon and Schuster, 1995.

Baker, Jean Harvey. *Affairs of Party: The Political Culture of Northern Democrats in the Mid-Nineteenth Century.* Ithaca, NY: Cornell University Press, 1983.

Baker, Paula. *The Moral Frameworks of Public Life: Gender, Politics, and the State in Rural New York, 1870–1930.* Oxford: Oxford University Press, 1991.

Balinski, Michel L., and H. Peyton Young. *Fair Representation: Meeting the Ideal of One Man, One Vote.* 2nd edition. Washington, DC: Brookings Institution Press, 2001.

Balogh, Brian. *A Government out of Sight: The Mystery of National Authority in Nineteenth-Century America.* New York: Cambridge University Press, 2009.

Barreyre, Nicolas. "Les échelles de la monnaie: Souveraineté monétaire et spatialisation de la politique américaine après la guerre de Sécession." *Annales: Histoire, Sciences Sociales* 69, no. 2 (2014): 439–67.

———. "Lire l'opinion publique dans les États-Unis de la Reconstruction (1865–1877)." In *S'exprimer en temps de troubles: Conflits, opinion(s) et politisation de la fin du Moyen Age au début du XXe siècle,* edited by Laurent Bourquin, Philippe Hamon, and Pierre Karila-Cohen, 327–42. Rennes: Presses Universitaires de Rennes, 2011.

———. "The Politics of Economic Crises: The Panic of 1873, the End of

Reconstruction, and the Realignment of American Politics." *Journal of the Gilded Age and Progressive Era* 10, no. 4 (2011): 403–23.

———. "Réunifier l'union: Intégrer l'ouest à la Reconstruction américaine, 1870–1872." *Revue d'Histoire Moderne et Contemporaine* 49, no. 4 (2002): 7–36.

Baum, Dale. *The Civil War Party System: The Case of Massachusetts, 1848–1876.* Chapel Hill: University of North Carolina Press, 1984.

Beale, Howard K. *The Critical Year: A Study of Andrew Johnson and Reconstruction.* New York: Harcourt Brace, 1930.

Beard, Charles A., and Mary R. Beard. *The Rise of American Civilization.* 2 vols. New York: Macmillan, 1927.

Beckert, Sven. *The Monied Metropolis: New York City and the Consolidation of the American Bourgeoisie, 1850–1896.* Cambridge: Cambridge University Press, 2001.

Belz, Herman. *Emancipation and Equal Rights: Politics and Constitutionalism in the Civil War Era.* New York: Norton, 1978.

———. *Reconstructing the Union: Theory and Practice during the Civil War.* Ithaca, NY: Cornell University Press, 1969.

Bender, Norman J. *New Hope for the Indians: The Grant Peace Policy and the Navajos in the 1870s.* Albuquerque: University of New Mexico Press, 1989.

Bender, Thomas. *A Nation among Nations: America's Place in World History.* New York: Hill and Wang, 2006.

———. *Toward an Urban Vision: Ideas and Institutions in Nineteenth Century America.* Baltimore: Johns Hopkins University Press, 1975.

Benedict, Michael Les. *A Compromise of Principle: Congressional Republicans and Reconstruction, 1863–1869.* New York: Norton, 1974.

———. *The Impeachment and Trial of Andrew Johnson.* New York: Norton, 1973.

———. "Preserving the Constitution: The Conservative Basis of Radical Reconstruction." *Journal of American History* 61, no. 1 (1974): 65–90.

———. "The Rout of Radicalism: Republicans and the Elections of 1867." *Civil War History* 18, no. 4 (1972): 334–44.

Benedict, Murray R. *Farm Policies of the United States, 1790–1950: A Study of Their Origins and Development.* New York: Twentieth Century Fund, 1953.

Bensel, Richard Franklin. *The American Ballot Box in the Mid-Nineteenth Century.* Cambridge: Cambridge University Press, 2004.

———. "The American Ballot Box: Law, Identity, and the Polling Place in the Mid-Nineteenth Century." *Studies in American Political Development* 17, no. 1 (2003): 1–27.

———. "Congress, Sectionalism, and Public-Policy Formation since 1870." In *Encyclopedia of the American Legislative System: Studies of the Principal Structures, Processes, and Policies of Congress and the States Legislatures since the Colonial Era,* edited by Joel H. Silbey, 3:1361–77. New York: Charles Scribner's Sons, 1994.

———. *The Political Economy of American Industrialization, 1877–1900.* Cambridge: Cambridge University Press, 2000.

———. *Sectionalism and American Political Development: 1880–1980.* Madison: University of Wisconsin Press, 1984.

———. "Sectionalism and Congressional Development." In *The Oxford Handbook of the American Congress,* edited by Eric Schickler and Frances E. Lee, 761–86. Oxford: Oxford University Press, 2011.

———. *Yankee Leviathan: The Origins of Central State Authority in America, 1859–1877.* Cambridge: Cambridge University Press, 1990.

Berlin, Ira, et al, eds. *Free at Last: A Documentary History of Slavery, Freedom, and the Civil War.* New York: The New Press, 1992.

Bernstein, Iver. *The New York City Draft Riots.* Oxford: Oxford University Press, 1990.

Berwanger, Eugene H. *The West and Reconstruction.* Urbana: University of Illinois Press, 1981.

Billington, Ray Allen, and Martin Ridge. *Westward Expansion: A History of the American Frontier.* 6th edition. Albuquerque: University of New Mexico Press, 2001.

"Biographical Directory of the United States Congress, 1774–Present." bioguide.con gress.gov/biosearch/biosearch.asp.

Blair, William. "The Use of Military Force to Protect the Gains of Reconstruction." *Civil War History* 51, no. 4 (2005): 388–402.

Blank, Charles. "The Waning of Radicalism: Massachusetts Republicans and Reconstruction Issues in the Early 1870's." Ph.D. dissertation, Brandeis University, 1972.

Blight, David W. *Race and Reunion: The Civil War in American Memory.* Cambridge, MA: Belknap Press of Harvard University Press, 2001.

Blondheim, Menahem. *News over the Wires: The Telegraph and the Flow of Public Information in America, 1844–1897.* Cambridge, MA: Harvard University Press, 1994.

Bogue, Allan G. "Bloc and Party in the United States Senate: 1861–1863." *Civil War History* 13, no. 3 (1967): 221–41.

———. *The Congressman's Civil War.* Cambridge: Cambridge University Press, 1989.

———. *The Earnest Men: Republicans of the Civil War Senate.* Ithaca, NY: Cornell University Press, 1981.

———. "Senators, Sectionalism, and the 'Western' Measures of the Republican Party." In *The United States Congress in a Partisan Political Nation, 1841–1896,* edited by Joel H. Silbey, 2:525–51. Brooklyn: Carlson, 1991.

Bonadio, Felice A. *North of Reconstruction: Ohio Politics, 1865–1870.* New York: New York University Press, 1970.

Bordin, Ruth. *Women and Temperance: The Quest for Power and Liberty, 1873–1900.* Philadelphia: Temple University Press, 1981.

Bowers, Claude G. *The Tragic Era: The Revolution after Lincoln.* New York: Blue Ribbon Books, 1929.

Bowersox, Laverne. "The Reconstruction of the Republican Party in the West, 1865–1870." Ph.D. dissertation, Ohio State University, 1931.

Boyer, Robert, and Benjamin Coriat. "Innovations dans les institutions et l'analyse monétaires américaines: Les greenbacks 'revisités.'" *Annales: Économies, Sociétés, Civilisations* 39, no. 6 (1984): 1330–59.

Brandwein, Pamela. *Rethinking the Judicial Settlement of Reconstruction.* Cambridge: Cambridge University Press, 2011.

Bridges, Amy. *A City in the Republic: Antebellum New York and the Origins of Machine Politics.* Cambridge: Cambridge University Press, 1984.

Brock, W. R. *An American Crisis: Congress and Reconstruction, 1865–1867.* New York: St. Martin's Press, 1963.

Brown, A. Theodore, and Charles N. Glaab. *A History of Urban America.* 3rd edition. New York: Macmillan, 1983.

Brown, Thomas J., ed. *Reconstructions: New Perspectives on the Postbellum United States.* New York: Oxford University Press, 2006.

Brownlee, W. Elliot. *Federal Taxation in America: A Short History.* 2nd edition. Cambridge: Cambridge University Press, 2004.

Buck, Solon J. *The Granger Movement: A Study of Agricultural Organization and Its Political, Economical and Social Manifestations 1870–1880.* Cambridge, MA: Harvard University Press, 1913.

Burke, Albie. "Federal Regulation of Congressional Elections in Northern Cities, 1871–94." *American Journal of Legal History* 14, no. 1 (1970): 17–34.

Burnham, W. Dean, Jerome M. Clubb, and William Flanigan. "State-Level Congressional, Gubernatorial and Senatorial Election Data for the United States, 1824–1972." Ann Arbor, MI: Inter-university Consortium for Political and Social Research, 1991. http://dx.doi.org/10.3886/ICPSR00075.v1.

Caldwell, Gary Lee. "The Rise of the Stalwarts and the Transformation of Illinois Republican Politics, 1860–1880." Ph.D. dissertation, University of Virginia, 1976.

Calhoun, Charles W. *Conceiving a New Republic: The Republican Party and the Southern Question, 1869–1900.* Lawrence: University Press of Kansas, 2006.

Callow, Alexander B. *The Tweed Ring.* Oxford: Oxford University Press, 1965.

Campbell, Ballard C. *Representative Democracy: Public Policy and Midwestern Legislatures in the Late Nineteenth Century.* Cambridge, MA: Harvard University Press, 1980.

Carey, John M. "Competing Principals, Political Institutions, and Party Unity in Legislative Voting." *American Journal of Political Science* 51, no. 1 (2007): 92–107.

Carothers, Neil. *Fractional Money: A History of the Small Coins and Fractional Paper Currency of the United States.* New York: John Wiley, 1930.

Carruthers, Bruce G., and Sarah Babb. "The Color of Money and the Nature of Value: Greenbacks and Gold in Postbellum America." *American Journal of Sociology* 101, no. 6 (1996): 1556–91.

Carter, Dan T. *When the War Was Over: The Failure of Self-Reconstruction in the South, 1865–1867.* Baton Rouge: Louisiana State University Press, 1985.

Carwardine, Richard J. *Lincoln.* London: Pearson Longman, 2003.

Cayton, Andrew R. L., and Susan E. Gray, eds. *The Identity of the American Midwest: Essays on Regional History.* Bloomington: Indiana University Press, 2001.

Cayton, Andrew R. L., and Peter S. Onuf. *The Midwest and the Nation: Rethinking the History of an American Region.* Bloomington: Indiana University Press, 1990.

Cayton, Mary K., Elliott J. Gorn, and Peter M. Williams, eds. *Encyclopedia of American Social History.* 3 vols. New York: Macmillan, 1993.

Cimbala, Paul A. *The Freedmen's Bureau: Reconstructing the American South after the Civil War.* Malabar, FL: Krieger, 2005.

———. *Under the Guardianship of the Nation: The Freedmen's Bureau and the Reconstruction of Georgia, 1865–1870.* Athens: University of Georgia Press, 1997.

Cimbala, Paul A., and Randall M. Miller, eds. *The Freedmen's Bureau and Reconstruction: Reconsiderations.* New York: Fordham University Press, 1999.

Clark, Christopher. *The Roots of Rural Capitalism: Western Massachusetts, 1780–1860.* Ithaca, NY: Cornell University Press, 1990.

Clark, John G. *The Frontier Challenge: Response to the Trans-Mississippi West.* Lawrence: University Press of Kansas, 1971.

———. *The Grain Trade in the Old Northwest.* Urbana: University of Illinois Press, 1966.

Clubb, Jerome M., William H. Flanigan, and Nancy H. Zingale. *Partisan Realignment: Voters, Parties, and Government in American History.* London: Sage, 1980.

Coben, Stanley. "Northeastern Business and Radical Reconstruction: A Re-Examination." *Mississippi Valley Historical Review* 46, no. 1 (1959): 67–90.

Cohen, Nancy. *The Reconstruction of American Liberalism, 1865–1914.* Chapel Hill: University of North Carolina Press, 2002.

Cohen, Roger A. "The Lost Jubilee: New York Republicans and the Politics of Reconstruction and Reform, 1867–1878." Ph.D. dissertation, Columbia University, 1975.

Coleman, Charles H. *The Election of 1868: The Democratic Effort to Regain Control.* New York: Columbia University Press, 1933.

Collins, Robert M. "The Originality Trap: Richard Hofstadter on Populism." *Journal of American History* 76, no. 1 (1989): 150–67.

Conzen, Kathleen Neils. *Immigrant Milwaukee, 1836–1860: Accommodation and Community in a Frontier City.* Cambridge, MA: Harvard University Press, 1976.

Cook, Robert J. *Civil War Senator: William Pitt Fessenden and the Fight to Save the American Republic.* Baton Rouge: Louisiana State University Press, 2011.

Cooper, William J., Michael F. Holt, and John McCardell, eds. *A Master's Due: Essays in Honor of David Herbert Donald.* Baton Rouge: Louisiana State University Press, 1985.

Cooper, William J., and James M. McPherson, eds. *Writing the Civil War: The Quest to Understand.* Columbia: University of South Carolina Press, 1998.

Coulter, E. Merton. "Amnesty for All except Jefferson Davis: The Hill-Blaine Debate of 1876." *Georgia Historical Quarterly* 56, no. 4 (1972): 453–94.

Cox, Gary W., and Keith T. Poole. "On Measuring Partisanship in Roll-Call Voting: The U.S. House of Representatives, 1877–1999." *American Journal of Political Science* 46, no. 3 (2002): 477–89.

Cronon, William. *Nature's Metropolis: Chicago and the Great West.* New York: Norton, 1991.

Crouch, Barry A. "A Spirit of Lawlessness: White Violence; Texas Blacks, 1865–1868." *Journal of Social History* 18, no. 2 (1984): 217–32.

Current, Richard Nelson. *Old Thad Stevens: A Story of Ambition.* Westport, CT: Greenwood Press, 1980.

———. *Those Terrible Carpetbaggers: A Reinterpretation.* Oxford: Oxford University Press, 1988.

Curry, Richard O. "The Abolitionists and Reconstruction: A Critical Reappraisal." *Journal of Southern History* 34, no. 4 (1968): 527–45.

———. *Radicalism, Racism, and Party Realignment: The Border States during Reconstruction.* Baltimore: Johns Hopkins University Press, 1969.

Daniel, Pete. "The Metamorphosis of Slavery, 1865–1900." *Journal of American History* 66, no. 1 (1979): 88–99.

Davis, Lance E. "The Investment Market, 1870–1914: The Evolution of a National Market." *Journal of Economic History* 25, no. 3 (1965): 355–99.

Dawson, Joseph G., III. *Army Generals and Reconstruction: Louisiana, 1862–1877.* Baton Rouge: Louisiana State University Press, 1994.

DeCanio, Samuel. "Populism, Paranoia, and the Politics of Free Silver." *Studies in American Political Development* 25, no. 1 (2011): 1–26.

———. "Religion and Nineteenth-Century Voting Behavior: A New Look at Some Old Data." *Journal of Politics* 69, no. 2 (2007): 339–50.

———. "State Autonomy and American Political Development: How Mass Democracy Promoted State Power." *Studies in American Political Development* 19, no. 2 (2005): 117–36.

DeCanio, Samuel, and Corwin D. Smidt. "Prelude to Populism: Mass Electoral Support for the Grange and the Greenback Parties." *Party Politics* 19, no. 5 (2013): 798–820.

Destler, Chester McA. "The Origin and Character of the Pendleton Plan." *Mississippi Valley Historical Review* 24, no. 2 (1937): 171–84.

Dewey, Davis Rich. *Financial History of the United States.* 12th edition. New York: Longmans Green, 1934.

Di Nunzio, Mario R. "Lyman Trumbull, United States Senator." Ph.D. dissertation, Clarke University, 1964.

Dodd, Donald B. *Historical Statistics of the States of the United States: Two Centuries of the Census.* New York: Greenwood Press, 1993.

Donald, David Herbert. *Charles Sumner and the Rights of Man.* New York: Knopf, 1970.

———. *Liberty and Union.* Boston: Little, Brown, 1978.

———. *Lincoln.* New York: Simon and Schuster, 1995.

Donald, David Herbert, Jean Harvey Baker, and Michael F. Holt. *The Civil War and Reconstruction.* New York: Norton, 2001.

Dorfman, Joseph. *The Economic Mind in American Civilization,* volume 3, *1865–1918.*
   New York: Viking Press, 1946.
Downey, Matthew T. "Horace Greeley and the Politicians: The Liberal Republican
   Convention in 1872." *Journal of American History* 53, no. 4 (1967): 727–50.
Downs, Gregory P. *Declarations of Dependence: The Long Reconstruction of Popular
   Politics in the South, 1861–1908.* Chapel Hill: University of North Carolina Press,
   2011.
Doyle, Don Harrison. *The Social Order of a Frontier Community: Jacksonville, Illinois,
   1825–70.* Urbana: University of Illinois Press, 1978.
Dubin, Michael J. *United States Congressional Elections, 1788–1997 : The Official Re-
   sults of the Elections of the 1st through 105th Congresses.* Jefferson, NC: McFarland,
   1998.
DuBois, W. E. B. *Black Reconstruction in America.* New York: S. A. Russell, 1935.
Dunning, William A. *Essays on the Civil War and Reconstruction and Related Topics.*
   New York: Macmillan, 1898.
———. *Reconstruction, Political and Economic, 1865–1877.* New York: Harper and
   Brothers, 1907.
Dykstra, Robert R., and Harlan Hahn. "Northern Voters and Negro Suffrage: The
   Case of Iowa, 1868." *Public Opinion Quarterly* 32, no. 2 (1968): 202–15.
Earle, Carville. "Regional Economic Development West of the Appalachians,
   1815–1860." In *North America: The Historical Geography of a Changing Continent,*
   edited by Robert D. Mitchell and Paul A. Groves, 172–97. Totowa, NJ: Rowman and
   Littlefield, 1987.
Easterlin, Richard A. "Interregional Differences in Per Capita Income, Population,
   and Total Income, 1840–1950." In *Trends in the American Economy in the Nineteenth
   Century,* edited by William N. Parker, 73–140. Princeton, NJ: Princeton University
   Press, 1960.
Edling, Max M. *Hercules in the Cradle: War, Money, and the American State,
   1783–1867.* Chicago: Chicago University Press, 2014.
———. *A Revolution in Favor of Government: Origins of the U.S. Constitution and the
   Making of the American State.* Oxford: Oxford University Press, 2003.
Edwards, Rebecca. *Angels in the Machinery : Gender in American Party Politics from the
   Civil War to the Progressive Era.* Oxford: Oxford University Press, 1997.
Egnal, Marc. "The Beards Were Right: Parties in the North, 1840–1860." *Civil War
   History* 48, no. 1 (2001): 30–56.
Einhorn, Robin L. *American Taxation, American Slavery.* Chicago: University of Chi-
   cago Press, 2006.
———. *Property Rules : Political Economy in Chicago, 1833–1872.* Chicago: University
   of Chicago Press, 1991.
Engelbourg, Saul. "The Impact of the Civil War on Manufacturing Enterprise." *Busi-
   ness History* 21, no. 1 (1979): 148–62.
Engerman, Stanley L., and Robert E. Gallman, eds. *The Cambridge Economic History*

of the United States, volume 2, *The Long Nineteenth Century.* Cambridge: Cambridge University Press, 2000.

Ericson, David F., and Louisa B. Green, eds. *The Liberal Tradition in American Politics: Reassessing the Legacy of American Liberalism.* New York: Routledge, Chapman and Hall, 1999.

Erie, Steven P. *Rainbow's End: Irish-Americans and the Dilemmas of Urban Machine Politics, 1840–1985.* Berkeley: University of California Press, 1988.

Etcheson, Nicole. *The Emerging Midwest: Upland Southerners and the Political Culture of the Old Northwest, 1787–1861.* Bloomington: Indiana University Press, 1996.

Fairman, Charles. *Reconstruction and Reunion, 1864–1888.* 2 vols. New York: Macmillan, 1971.

Faragher, John Mack. *Sugar Creek: Life on the Illinois Prairie.* New Haven, CT: Yale University Press, 1986.

Farmer-Kaiser, Mary. *Freedwomen and the Freedmen's Bureau: Race, Gender, and Public Policy in the Age of Emancipation.* New York: Fordham University Press, 2010.

Fels, Rendigs. "The Long-Wave Depression, 1873–97." *Review of Economics and Statistics* 31, no. 1 (1949): 69–73.

Fenton, John H. *Midwest Politics.* New York: Holt, Rinehart and Winston, 1966.

Field, Phyllis F. *The Politics of Race in New York: The Struggle for Black Suffrage in the Civil War Era.* Ithaca, NY: Cornell University Press, 1982.

Finkelman, Paul. *Slavery and the Law.* Madison, WI: Madison House, 1997.

Finkelman, Paul, and Donald R. Kennon, eds. *Congress and the Emergence of Sectionalism: From the Missouri Compromise to the Age of Jackson.* Athens: Ohio University Press, 2008.

Fischer, Roger A. *Them Damned Pictures: Explorations in American Political Cartoon Art.* North Haven, CT: Archon Books, 1996.

Fitzgerald, Michael W. *Splendid Failure: Postwar Reconstruction in the American South.* Chicago: Ivan R. Dee, 2007.

Flaherty, Jane. "'The Exhausted Condition of the Treasury' on the Eve of the Civil War." *Civil War History* 55, no. 2 (2009): 244–77.

———. *The Revenue Imperative: The Union's Financial Policies during the American Civil War.* London: Pickering and Chatto, 2009.

Flandreau, Marc. "The French Crime of 1873: An Essay on the Emergence of the International Gold Standard, 1870–1880." *Journal of Economic History* 56, no. 4 (1996): 862–97.

———. *L'or du monde: La France et la stabilité du système monétaire international, 1848–1873.* Paris: L'Harmattan, 1995.

Foner, Eric. *Free Soil, Free Labor, Free Men: The Ideology of the Republican Party before the Civil War.* Oxford: Oxford University Press, 1970.

———. *Reconstruction: America's Unfinished Revolution, 1863–1876.* New York: Harper and Row, 1988.

———. "Reconstruction Revisited." *Reviews in American History* 10, no. 4 (1982): 82–100.

Ford, Lacy K., ed. *A Companion to the Civil War and Reconstruction*. Malden, MA: Blackwell, 2005.

Foster, Gaines M. *Moral Reconstruction: Christian Lobbyists and the Federal Legislation of Morality, 1865–1920*. Chapel Hill: University of North Carolina Press, 2002.

Freehling, William W. *Slavery, the Civil War, and the Reintegration of American History*. Oxford: Oxford University Press, 1994.

Friedman, Lawrence J. *Gregarious Saints: Self and Community in American Abolitionism, 1830–1870*. Cambridge: Cambridge University Press, 1982.

Friedman, Milton. "The Crime of 1873." *Journal of Political Economy* 98, no. 6 (1990): 1159–94.

Friedman, Milton, and Anna Jacobson Schwartz. *A Monetary History of the United States, 1867–1960*. Princeton, NJ: Princeton University Press, 1963.

Gallagher, Gary W. *The Union War*. Cambridge, MA: Harvard University Press, 2011.

Gallman, J. Matthew. *The North Fights the Civil War: The Home Front*. New York: Ivan R. Dee, 1994.

Gambill, Edward L. *Conservative Ordeal: Northern Democrats and Reconstruction, 1865–1868*. Ames: Iowa State University Press, 1981.

———. "Who Were the Senate Radicals?" *Civil War History* 11, no. 3 (1965): 237–44.

Geary, James W. *We Need Men: The Union Draft in the Civil War*. Dekalb: Northern Illinois University Press, 1991.

Gerber, Richard Allan. "The Liberal Republicans of 1872 in Historiographical Perspective." *Journal of American History* 62, no. 1 (1975): 40–73.

Gerring, John. *Party Ideologies in America, 1828–1996*. Cambridge: Cambridge University Press, 1998.

Gienapp, William E. *The Origins of the Republican Party, 1852–1856*. Oxford: Oxford University Press, 1986.

Gillette, William. *Retreat from Reconstruction, 1869–1879*. Baton Rouge: Louisiana State University Press, 1979.

———. *The Right to Vote: Politics and the Passage of the Fifteenth Amendment*. Baltimore: Johns Hopkins University Press, 1965.

Gjerde, Jon. *From Peasants to Farmers: The Migration from Balestrand, Norway to the Upper Middle West*. Cambridge: Cambridge University Press, 1985.

———. "Midwest." In *Reader's Guide to American History*, edited by Peter J. Parish, 454–55. London: Fitzroy Dearborn, 1997.

———. *The Minds of the West: Ethnocultural Evolution in Rural Middle West, 1830–1917*. Chapel Hill: University of North Carolina Press, 1997.

Glasner, David, and Thomas F. Cooley, eds. *Business Cycles and Depressions: An Encyclopedia*. New York: Garland, 1997.

Goldberg, Michael L. *An Army of Women : Gender and Politics in Gilded Age Kansas*. Baltimore: Johns Hopkins University Press, 1997.

Goodwyn, Lawrence. *Democratic Promise: The Populist Moment in America*. Oxford: Oxford University Press, 1976.

———. *The Populist Moment: A Short History of the Agrarian Revolt in America.* Oxford: Oxford University Press, 1978.

Grant, Susan-Mary. *North over South : Northern Nationalism and American Identity in the Antebellum Era.* Lawrence: University Press of Kansas, 2000.

Grantham, Dewey W. *The South in Modern America: A Region at Odds.* New York: HarperCollins, 1994.

Green, Fletcher M. "Origins of the Crédit Mobilier of America." *Mississippi Valley Historical Review* 46, no. 2 (1959): 238–51.

Gutman, Herbert G. "The Tompkins Square 'Riot' in New York City on January 13, 1874: A Re-Examination of Its Causes and Its Aftermath." *Labor History* 6, no. 1 (1965): 44–70.

Haeger, John Denis. *The Investment Frontier: New York Businessmen and the Economic Development of the Old Northwest.* Albany: State University of New York Press, 1981.

Hahn, Steven, and Jonathan Prude. *The Countryside in the Age of Capitalist Transformation: Essays in the Social History of Rural America.* Chapel Hill: University of North Carolina Press, 1985.

Halloran, Fiona Deans. *Thomas Nast: The Father of Modern Political Cartoons.* Chapel Hill: University of North Carolina Press, 2012.

Hammarberg, Melvyn. *The Indiana Voter: The Historical Dynamics of Party Allegiance during the 1870s.* Chicago: University of Chicago Press, 1977.

Hammond, Bray. *Sovereignty and an Empty Purse: Banks and Politics in the Civil War.* Princeton, NJ: Princeton University Press, 1970.

Hansen, Stephen L. *The Making of the Third Party System: Voters and Parties in Illinois, 1850–1876.* Ann Arbor: UMI Research Press, 1980.

Hardwick, Kevin R. "'Your Old Father Abe Lincoln Is Dead and Damned': Black Soldiers and the Memphis Race Riot of 1866." *Journal of Social History* 27, no. 1 (1993): 109–28.

Harris, Carl V. "Right Fork or Left Fork? The Section-Party Alignments of Southern Democrats in Congress, 1873–1897." *Journal of Southern History* 42, no. 4 (1976): 471–506.

———. "Spotlight on State Legislatures." *Reviews in American History* 10, no. 1 (1982): 78–83.

Harris, William C. *Lincoln's Rise to the Presidency.* Lawrence: University Press of Kansas, 2007.

———. *With Charity for All: Lincoln and the Restoration of the Union.* Lexington: University Press of Kentucky, 1997.

Havel, James T. *U.S. Presidential Candidates and the Elections: A Biographical and Historical Guide.* New York: Macmillan, 1996.

Haynes, George H. *The Senate of the United States: Its History and Practice.* Boston: Houghton Mifflin, 1938.

Heffer, Jean. "L'âge classique de la dette publique américaine (1789–1916)." In *La dette publique dans l'histoire,* edited by Jean Andreau, Gérard Béaur, and Jean-Yves

Grenier, 365–92. Paris: Comité pour l'Histoire Économique et Financière de la France, 2006.

———. "L'âge d'or du protectionnisme américain." *Histoire, Économie et Société* 22, no. 1 (2003): 7–22.

———. *Le Port de New York et le commerce extérieur américain, 1860–1900.* Paris: Publications de la Sorbonne, 1986.

Higgs, Robert. *The Transformation of the American Economy, 1865–1914: An Essay in Interpretation.* New York: Wiley, 1971.

Higham, John. *Strangers in the Land: Patterns of American Nativism, 1860–1925.* 2nd edition. New Brunswick, NJ: Rutgers University Press, 1988.

Hild, Matthew. *Greenbackers, Knights of Labor, and Populists: Farmer-Labor Insurgency in the Late-Nineteenth-Century South.* Athens: University of Georgia Press, 2007.

Hine, Robert V., and John Mack Faragher. *The American West: A New Interpretive History.* New Haven, CT: Yale University Press, 2000.

"Historical Census Browser." University of Virginia, Geospatial and Statistical Data Center. mapserver.lib.virginia.edu/collections/stats/histcensus/index.html.

Hobsbawm, Eric J. *The Age of Capital, 1848–1875.* New York: Charles Scribner's Sons, 1975.

Hogue, James Keith. *Uncivil War: Five New Orleans Street Battles and the Rise and Fall of Radical Reconstruction.* Baton Rouge: Louisiana State University Press, 2006.

Holmes, William F. "Populism: In Search of Context." *Agricultural History* 64 (1990): 26–58.

Holt, Michael F. *By One Vote: The Disputed Presidential Election of 1876.* Lawrence: University Press of Kansas, 2008.

———. "Change and Continuity in the Party Period: The Substance and Structure of American Politics, 1835–1885." In *Contesting Democracy: Substance and Structure in American Political History, 1775–2000,* edited by Byron E. Shafer and Anthony J. Badger, 93–115. Lawrence: University Press of Kansas, 2001.

———. *The Political Crisis of the 1850s.* New York: Norton, 1978.

———. *Political Parties and American Political Development from the Age of Jackson to the Age of Lincoln.* Baton Rouge: Louisiana State University Press, 1992.

———. "Reconceptualizing Reconstruction," "Reassessing Presidential Reconstruction," and "The Specter of Realignment: Revisiting the Politics of the 1870s." Fleming Lectures, Louisiana State University, Baton Rouge, 1999.

———. *The Rise and Fall of the American Whig Party: Jacksonian Politics and the Onset of the Civil War.* Oxford: Oxford University Press, 1999.

Hoogenboom, Ari Arthur. *Outlawing the Spoils: A History of the Civil Service Reform Movement, 1865–1883.* Urbana: University of Illinois Press, 1961.

———. *Rutherford B. Hayes: Warrior and President.* Lawrence: University Press of Kansas, 1995.

House, Albert V. "The Speakership Contest of 1875: Democratic Response to Power." *Journal of American History* 52, no. 2 (1965): 252–74.

Hubbard, Charles M. *The Burden of Confederate Diplomacy*. Knoxville: University of Tennessee Press, 1998.

Hunt, Gaillard. *Israel, Elihu and Cadwallader Washburn: A Chapter in American Biography*. New York: Macmillan, 1925.

Huntington, Andrew T., and Robert J. Mawhinney. *Laws of the United States Concerning Money, Banking, and Loans, 1778–1909*. Washington, DC: Government Printing Office, 1910.

Huret, Romain D. *American Tax Resisters*. Cambridge, MA: Harvard University Press, 2014.

Huston, James L. *The Panic of 1857 and the Coming of the Civil War*. Baton Rouge: Louisiana State University Press, 1987.

Hütter, Jean-Paul. "La question de la monnaie d'argent aux États-Unis: Des origines à 1900." Ph.D. dissertation, Université de Paris, 1938.

Hyman, Harold M. *A More Perfect Union: The Impact of the Civil War and Reconstruction on the Constitution*. New York: Knopf, 1973.

Hyman, Harold M., and William M. Wiecek. *Equal Justice under Law: Constitutional Development 1835–1875*. New York: Harper Torchbooks, 1982.

Inter-university Consortium for Political and Social Research. "Historical, Demographic, Economic, and Social Data: The United States, 1790–1970." Ann Arbor, MI: Inter-university Consortium for Political and Social Research, 197?. http://dx.doi.org/10.3886/ICPSR00003.v1.

Irwin, Douglas A. "Antebellum Tariff Politics: Regional Coalitions and Shifting Economic Interests." *Journal of Law and Economics* 51, no. 4 (2008): 715–41.

———. "Tariff Incidence in America's Gilded Age." *Journal of Economic History* 67, no. 3 (2007): 582–602.

Jackson, John Brinckerhoff. *American Space: The Centennial Years, 1865–1876*. New York: Norton, 1972.

James, John A. *Money and Capital Markets in Postbellum America*. Princeton, NJ: Princeton University Press, 1978.

James, Joseph B. *The Framing of the Fourteenth Amendment*. Urbana: University of Illinois Press, 1956.

———. *The Ratification of the Fourteenth Amendment*. Macon, GA: Mercer University Press, 1984.

Jarman, Baird. "The Graphic Art of Thomas Nast: Politics and Propriety in Postbellum Publishing." *American Periodicals: A Journal of History, Criticism, and Bibliography* 20, no. 2 (2010): 156–89.

Jaynes, Gerald David. *Branches without Roots: Genesis of the Black Working Class in the American South, 1862–1882*. Oxford: Oxford University Press, 1986.

Jellison, Charles A. *Fessenden of Maine, Civil War Senator*. Syracuse, NY: Syracuse University Press, 1962.

Jenkins, Jeffery A., and Timothy P. Nokken. "Partisanship, the Electoral Connection, and Lame-Duck Sessions of Congress, 1877–2006." *Journal of Politics* 70, no. 2 (2008): 450–65.

Jensen, Richard. "The Religious and Occupational Roots of Party Identification: Illinois and Indiana in the 1870s." *Civil War History* 16, no. 4 (1970): 325–43.

———. *The Winning of the Midwest: Social and Political Conflict 1888–1896.* Chicago: University of Chicago Press, 1971.

John, Richard R. "Affairs of Office: The Executive Departments, the Election of 1828, and the Making of the Democratic Party." In *The Democratic Experiment: New Directions in American Political History,* edited by Meg Jacobs, William J. Novak, and Julian E. Zelizer, 50–84. Princeton, NJ: Princeton University Press, 2003.

———. "Ruling Passions: Political Economy in Nineteenth-Century America." *Journal of Policy History* 18, no. 1 (2006): 1–20.

Johnson, David Alan. *Founding the Far West: California, Oregon and Nevada, 1840–1890.* Berkeley: University of California Press, 1992.

Jones, James Pickett. *John A. Logan, Stalwart Republican from Illinois.* Tallahassee: University Press of Florida, 1982.

Kaczorowski, Robert J. "To Begin the Nation Anew: Congress, Citizenship, and Civil Rights after the Civil War." *American Historical Review* 92, no. 1 (1987): 45–68.

Katz, Irving. *August Belmont: a Political Biography.* New York: Columbia University Press, 1968.

Keith, LeeAnna. *The Colfax Massacre: The Untold Story of Black Power, White Terror, and the Death of Reconstruction.* New York: Oxford University Press, 2008.

Keller, Morton. *Affairs of State: Public Life in Late Nineteenth-Century America.* Cambridge, MA: Belknap Press of Harvard University Press, 1977.

———. *The Art and Politics of Thomas Nast.* Oxford: Oxford University Press, 1968.

Keyssar, Alexander. *The Right to Vote: The Contested History of Democracy in the United States.* New York: Basic Books, 2000.

Killian, Johnny H., George A. Costello, and Kenneth R. Thomas. *The Constitution of the United States of America: Analysis and Interpretation; Analysis of Cases Decided by the Supreme Court of the United States to June 28, 2002.* Washington, DC: Government Printing Office, 2002.

Kindahl, James K. "Economic Factors in Specie Resumption the United States, 1865–79." *Journal of Political Economy* 69, no. 1 (1961): 30–48.

Klein, Maury. *The Life and Legend of Jay Gould.* Baltimore: Johns Hopkins University Press, 1986.

———. *Union Pacific,* volume 1, *1862–1893.* Garden City, NY: Doubleday, 1987.

Kleppner, Paul. *The Cross of Culture: A Social Analysis of Midwestern Politics, 1850–1900.* New York: Free Press, 1970.

———. *The Evolution of American Electoral Systems.* New York: Greenwood Press, 1981.

———. *The Third Electoral System: Parties, Voters and Political Cultures, 1853–1892.* Chapel Hill: University of North Carolina Press, 1979.

————. *Who Voted? The Dynamics of Electoral Turnout, 1870–1980.* New York: Praeger, 1982.

Klingaman, David C., and Richard K. Vedder, eds. *Essays in Nineteenth Century Economic History: The Old Northwest.* Athens: Ohio University Press, 1975.

————. *Essays on the Economy of the Old Northwest.* Athens: Ohio University Press, 1987.

Kousser, J. Morgan, and James M. McPherson, eds. *Region, Race, and Reconstruction: Essays in Honor of C. Vann Woodward.* Oxford: Oxford University Press, 1982.

Krehbiel, Keith. "Paradoxes of Parties in Congress." *Legislative Studies Quarterly* 24, no. 1 (1999): 31–64.

Kromkowski, Charles A. *Recreating the American Republic: Rules of Apportionment, Constitutional Change, and American Political Development, 1700–1870.* Cambridge: Cambridge University Press, 2002.

Krug, Mark M. *Lyman Trumbull, Conservative Radical.* New York: A. S. Barnes, 1965.

Kutler, Stanley I. *Judicial Power and Reconstruction Politics.* Chicago: University of Chicago Press, 1968.

————. *The Supreme Court and the Constitution: Readings in American Constitutional History.* 3rd edition. New York: Norton, 1984.

Labbé, Ronald M., and Jonathan Lurie. *The Slaughterhouse Cases: Regulation, Reconstruction, and the Fourteenth Amendment.* Lawrence: University Press of Kansas, 2003.

Lambert, Jacques. *Histoire constitutionnelle de l'Union américaine,* volume 2, *Les conflits entre sections.* Lyon: A. Rey, 1934.

Lane, Charles. *The Day Freedom Died: The Colfax Massacre, the Supreme Court, and the Betrayal of Reconstruction.* New York: Henry Holt, 2008.

Larson, Henrietta M. *Jay Cooke, Private Banker.* Cambridge, MA: Harvard University Press, 1936.

Larson, John Lauritz. *Internal Improvement: National Public Works and the Promise of Popular Government in the Early United States.* Chapel Hill: University of North Carolina Press, 2001.

Lebergott, Stanley. *The Americans: An Economic Record.* New York: Norton, 1984.

Levinson, Sanford. *Constitutional Faith.* Princeton, NJ: Princeton University Press, 1988.

Levy, Jonathan. *Freaks of Fortune: The Emerging World of Capitalism and Risk in America.* Cambridge, MA: Harvard University Press, 2014.

Linden, Glenn M. "'Radicals' and Economic Policies: The Senate, 1861–1873." *Journal of Southern History* 32, no. 2 (1966): 189–99.

Litwack, Leon F. *Been in the Storm So Long: The Aftermath of Slavery.* New York: Knopf, 1979.

Long, John H. *Historical Atlas and Chronology of County Boundaries, 1788–1980.* Boston: G. K. Hall, 1984.

Lowe, Richard. *Republicans and Reconstruction in Virginia, 1856–1870.* Charlottesville: University Press of Virginia, 1991.

Mach, Thomas S. *"Gentleman George" Hunt Pendleton: Party Politics and Ideological Identity in Nineteenth-Century America.* Kent, OH: Kent State University Press, 2007.

———. "George Hunt Pendleton, The Ohio Idea and Political Continuity in Reconstruction America." *Ohio History* 108 (1999): 125–44.

Maizlish, Stephen E. "The Meaning of Nativism and the Crisis of the Union: The Know-Nothing Movement in the Antebellum North." In *Essays on American Antebellum Politics, 1840–1860,* edited by William E. Gienapp et al., 166–98. College Station: Texas A&M University Press, 1982.

———. *The Triumph of Sectionalism: The Transformation of Ohio Politics, 1844–1856.* Kent, OH: Kent State University Press, 1983.

Maltz, Earl M. *Civil Rights, the Constitution and Congress, 1863–1869.* Lawrence: University Press of Kansas, 1990.

Martis, Kenneth C. *The Historical Atlas of United States Congressional Districts, 1789–1983.* New York: Free Press, 1982.

———. "Sectionalism and the United States Congress." *Political Geography Quarterly* 7, no. 2 (1988): 99–109.

Martis, Kenneth C., Ruth Anderson Rowles, and Gyula Pauer. *The Historical Atlas of Political Parties in the United States Congress, 1789–1989.* New York: Macmillan, 1989.

McAfee, Ward. *Religion, Race, and Reconstruction: The Public School in the Politics of the 1870s.* Albany: State University of New York Press, 1998.

McCaslin, Richard B. *Andrew Johnson: A Bibliography.* Westport, CT: Greenwood Press, 1992.

McCormick, Richard L. *The Party Period and Public Policy: American Politics from the Age of Jackson to the Progressive Era.* Oxford: Oxford University Press, 1986.

McCurdy, Charles W. "Legal Institutions, Constitutional Theory, and the Tragedy of Reconstruction." *Reviews in American History* 4, no. 2 (June 1976): 203–11.

McFeely, William S. *Grant: A Biography.* New York: Norton, 1981.

———. *Yankee Stepfather: General O. O. Howard and the Freedmen.* New Haven, CT: Yale University Press, 1968.

McGerr, Michael E. *The Decline of Popular Politics: The American North 1865–1928.* Oxford: Oxford University Press, 1986.

———. "The Meaning of Liberal Republicanism: The Case of Ohio." *Civil War History* 28 (1982): 307–23.

McGuire, Robert A. "Economic Causes of Late Nineteenth Century Agrarian Unrest: New Evidence." *Journal of Economic History* 41, no. 4 (1981): 835–52.

McKitrick, Eric. *Andrew Johnson and Reconstruction.* Chicago: Chicago University Press, 1960.

McMath, Robert C. *American Populism: A Social History, 1877–1898.* New York: Hill and Wang, 1993.

McPherson, James M. *Abraham Lincoln and the Second American Revolution.* Oxford: Oxford University Press, 1991.

———. *Battle Cry of Freedom: The Civil War Era*. Oxford: Oxford University Press, 1988.

McSeveney, Samuel T., and Joel H. Silbey, eds. *Voters, Parties, and Elections: Quantitative Essays in the History of American Popular Voting Behavior*. Lexington, MA: Xerox College Publishing, 1972.

Meinig, Donald W. *The Shaping of America: A Geographical Perspective on 500 Years of History*. 4 vols. New Haven, CT: Yale University Press, 1986–2004.

Merrill, Horace Samuel. *Bourbon Democracy of the Middle West, 1865–1896*. Baton Rouge: Louisiana State University Press, 1953.

Miller, George H. *Railroads and the Granger Laws*. Madison: University of Wisconsin Press, 1971.

Mitchell, Wesley C. *Gold, Prices & Wages under the Greenback Standard*. Berkeley: University of California Press, 1908.

———. *A History of the Greenbacks, with Special Reference to the Economic Consequences of Their Issue, 1862–1865*. Chicago: University of Chicago Press, 1903.

Mohr, James C. *The Radical Republicans and Reform in New York during Reconstruction*. Ithaca, NY: Cornell University Press, 1973.

———. *Radical Republicans in the North: State Politics during Reconstruction*. Baltimore: Johns Hopkins University Press, 1976.

Montgomery, David. *Beyond Equality: Labor and the Radical Republicans, 1862–1872*. New York: Knopf, 1967.

———. *Citizen Worker: The Experience of Workers in the United States with Democracy and the Free Market during the Nineteenth Century*. Cambridge: Cambridge University Press, 1993.

Moore, Clifford. "Ohio in National Politics, 1865–1986." *Ohio Archaeological and Historical Publications* 37 (1928): 220–427.

Moore, Geoffrey H. "Business Cycles, Panics, and Depressions." In *Encyclopedia of American Economic History: Studies in the Principal Movements and Ideas*, edited by Glenn Porter, 1:151–56. New York: Charles Scribner's Sons, 1980.

Morrison, Michael A. *Slavery and the American West: The Eclipse of Manifest Destiny and the Coming of the Civil War*. Chapel Hill: University of North Carolina Press, 1997.

Morton, Jack Devon. "Ohio's Gallant Fight: Northern State Politics during the Reconstruction Era, 1865–1878." Ph.D. dissertation, University of Virginia, 2005.

Motz, Marilyn Ferris. *True Sisterhood: Michigan Women and Their Kin, 1820–1920*. Albany: State University of New York Press, 1983.

Murdock, Eugene C. *One Million Men: The Civil War Draft in the North*. Madison: State Historical Society of Wisconsin, 1971.

———. *Patriotism Limited, 1862–1865: The Civil War Draft and the Bounty System*. Kent, OH: Kent State University Press, 1967.

Mushkat, Jerome. *The Reconstruction of the New York Democracy, 1861–1874*. Rutherford, NJ: Fairleigh Dickinson University Press, 1980.

Nelson, Scott R. *A Nation of Deadbeats: An Uncommon History of America's Financial Disasters*. New York: Knopf, 2012.

———. "A Storm of Cheap Goods: New American Commodities and the Panic of 1873." *Journal of the Gilded Age and Progressive Era* 10, no. 4 (2011): 447–53.

Nelson, William E. *The Fourteenth Amendment: From Political Principle to Judicial Doctrine*. Cambridge, MA: Harvard University Press, 1988.

Nevins, Allan. *The War for the Union*. 4 vols. New York: Charles Scribner's Sons, 1959.

Noll, Mark A. *Religion and American Politics from Colonial Period to the 1980s*. Oxford: Oxford University Press, 1990.

Nord, David Paul. *Communities of Journalism: A History of American Newspapers and Their Readers*. Urbana: University of Illinois Press, 2001.

Nordin, Dennis S. *Rich Harvest: A History of the Grange, 1867–1900*. Jackson: University Press of Mississippi, 1974.

Nouailhat, Pierre-Yves. *Évolution économique des États-Unis du milieu du XIXe siècle à 1914*. Paris: SEDES, 1982.

Novak, William J. "The Legal Transformation of Citizenship in Nineteenth-Century America." In *The Democratic Experiment: New Directions in American Political History*, edited by Meg Jacobs, William J. Novak, and Julian E. Zelizer, 85–119. Princeton, NJ: Princeton University Press, 2003.

———. *The People's Welfare: Law and Regulation in Nineteenth-Century America*. Chapel Hill: University of North Carolina Press, 1996.

Noyes, Alexander Dana. *Forty Years of American Finance: A Short Financial History of the Government and People of the United States since the Civil War, 1865–1907*. New York: G. P. Putnam's Sons, 1909.

Nugent, Walter T. K. *Money and American Society, 1865–1880*. New York: Free Press, 1968.

———. *The Money Question during Reconstruction*. New York: Norton, 1967.

Oberholtzer, Ellis P. *Jay Cooke, Financier of the Civil War*. 2 vols. Philadelphia: G. W. Jacobs, 1907.

O'Leary, Cecilia Elizabeth. *To Die For: The Paradox of American Patriotism*. Princeton, NJ: Princeton University Press, 1999.

O'Malley, Michael. *Face Value: The Entwined Histories of Money and Race in America*. Chicago: University of Chicago Press, 2012.

———. "Specie and Species: Race and the Money Question in Nineteenth-Century America." *American Historical Review* 99, no. 2 (1994): 369–95.

Onuf, Nicholas G., and Peter S. Onuf. *Nations, Markets, and War: Modern History and the American Civil War*. Charlottesville: University of Virginia Press, 2006.

Onuf, Peter S. *Statehood and Union: A History of the Northwest Ordinance*. Bloomington: Indiana University Press, 1987.

Osterud, Nancy Grey. *Bonds of Community: The Lives of Farm Women in Nineteenth-Century New York*. Ithaca, NY: Cornell University Press, 1991.

Ostler, Jeffrey. *Prairie Populism: The Fate of Agrarian Radicalism in Kansas, Nebraska, and Iowa, 1880–1892*. Lawrence: University Press of Kansas, 1993.

Oubre, Claude F. *Forty Acres and a Mule: The Freedmen's Bureau and Black Land Ownership*. Baton Rouge: Louisiana State University Press, 1978.

Palen, Marc-William. "Foreign Relations in the Gilded Age: A British Free-Trade Conspiracy?" *Diplomatic History* 37, no. 2 (2013): 217–47.

Paludan, Phillip Shaw. *A Covenant with Death: The Constitution, Law, and Equality in the Civil War Era*. Urbana: University of Illinois Press, 1975.

———. *A People's Contest: The Union and Civil War, 1861–1865*. 2nd edition. Lawrence: University Press of Kansas, 1996.

Parish, Peter J. *The North and the Nation in the Era of the Civil War*. Edited by Adam I. P. Smith. New York: Fordham University Press, 2003.

Parsons, Stanley B., William W. Beach, and Michael J. Dubin. *United States Congressional Districts and Data, 1843–1883*. Westport, CT: Greenwood Press, 1986.

Patterson, Robert T. *Federal Debt-Management Policies, 1865–1879*. Durham, NC: Duke University Press, 1954.

Paullin, Charles O. *Atlas of the Historical Geography of the United States*. Washington, DC: Carnegie Institution of Washington, 1932.

Paulson, Ross Evans. *Liberty, Equality, and Justice: Civil Rights, Women's Rights, and the Regulation of Business, 1865–1932*. Durham, NC: Duke University Press, 1997.

Perman, Michael. *The Coming of the American Civil War*. Lexington, MA: D. C. Heath, 1993.

———. "Eric Foner's Reconstruction: A Finished Revolution." *Reviews in American History* 17, no. 1 (1989): 73–78.

———. "Honoring the Fathers." *Reviews in American History* 15 (1987): 533–42.

———. *Major Problems in the Civil War and Reconstruction*. 2nd edition. Boston: Houghton Mifflin, 1998.

———. *Reunion without Compromise: The South and Reconstruction, 1865–1868*. Cambridge: Cambridge University Press, 1973.

———. *The Road to Redemption: Southern Politics, 1869–1879*. Chapel Hill: University of North Carolina Press, 1984.

Peskin, Allan. *Garfield: A Biography*. Kent, OH: Kent State University Press, 1978.

———. "Was There a Compromise of 1877?" *Journal of American History* 60, no. 1 (1973): 63–75.

Piper, Richard J. "Party Realignment and Congressional Change: Issue Dimensions and Priorities in the United States House of Representatives, 1871–1893." In *The United States Congress: The Electoral Connection, 1789–1989*, edited by Joel H. Silbey, 1:165–96. Brooklyn: Carlson, 1991.

Pitkin, Thomas M. "Western Republicans and the Tariff in 1860." *Mississippi Valley Historical Review* 27, no. 3 (1940): 401–20.

Polakoff, Keith Ian. *The Politics of Inertia: The Election of 1876 and the End of Reconstruction*. Baton Rouge: Louisiana State University Press, 1973.

Poole, Keith T., and Howard Rosenthal. *Congress: A Political-Economic History of Roll Call Voting*. Oxford: Oxford University Press, 1997.

Potter, David M. *The Impending Crisis, 1848–1861.* New York: Harper and Row, 1976.

Rable, George C. *But There Was No Peace: The Role of Violence in the Politics of Reconstruction.* Athens: University of Georgia Press, 1984.

Ransom, Roger L. *Conflict and Compromise: The Political Economy of Slavery, Emancipation, and the American Civil War.* Cambridge: Cambridge University Press, 1989.

Redlich, Fritz. *The Molding of American Banking: Men and Ideas.* 2 vols. New York: Johnson Reprint, 1968.

Reitano, Joanne R. *The Tariff Question in the Gilded Age: The Great Debate of 1888.* University Park: Pennsylvania State University Press, 1994.

Renda, Lex. *Running on the Record: Civil War Era Politics in New Hampshire.* Charlottesville: University Press of Virginia, 1997.

Reti, Steven P. *Silver and Gold: The Political Economy of International Monetary Conferences, 1867–1892.* Westport, CT: Greenwood Press, 1998.

Rhodes, James Ford. *History of the United States from the Compromise of 1850.* 7 vols. New York: Macmillan, 1893.

Richardson, Heather Cox. *The Death of Reconstruction : Race, Labor, and Politics in the Post–Civil War North, 1865–1901.* Cambridge, MA: Harvard University Press, 2001.

———. *The Greatest Nation of the Earth: Republican Economic Policies during the Civil War.* Cambridge, MA: Harvard University Press, 1997.

———. *West from Appomattox: The Reconstruction of America after the Civil War.* New Haven, CT: Yale University Press, 2007.

Ritter, Gretchen. *Goldbugs and Greenbacks: The Antimonopoly Tradition and the Politics of Finance in America.* Cambridge: Cambridge University Press, 1997.

Rockoff, Hugh. "The 'Wizard of Oz' as a Monetary Allegory." *Journal of Political Economy* 98, no. 4 (1990): 739–60.

Rohrbough, Malcolm J. *The Land Office Business: The Settlement and Administration of American Public Lands, 1789–1837.* Oxford: Oxford University Press, 1968.

———. *The Trans-Appalachian Frontier: People, Societies, and Institutions, 1775–1850.* Oxford: Oxford University Press, 1978.

Ron, Ariel. "Developing the Country: Agricultural Reform and Tariff Protection." Paper presented at the Policy History Conference, Columbus, June 2010.

Rosenthal, Howard L., and Keith T. Poole. *United States Congressional Roll Call Voting Records, 1789–1990.* Ann Arbor, MI: Inter-university Consortium for Political and Social Research, 2000. dx.doi.org/10.3886/ICPSR09822.v2.

Rosentone, Steven J., Roy L. Behr, and Edward H. Lazarus. *Third Parties in America: Citizen Response to Major Party Failure.* Princeton, NJ: Princeton University Press, 1984.

Roske, Ralph J. *His Own Counsel: The Life and Times of Lyman Trumbull.* Reno: University of Nevada Press, 1979.

———. "The Seven Martyrs?" *American Historical Review* 64, no. 2 (1959): 323–30.

Ross, Dorothy. *The Origins of American Social Science.* Cambridge: Cambridge University Press, 1991.

Ross, Steven Joseph. "Freed Soil, Freed Labor, Freed Men: John Eaton and the Davis Bend Experiment." *Journal of Southern History* 44, no. 2 (1978): 213–32.

Rothman, David J. *Politics and Power: The United States Senate, 1869–1901.* Cambridge, MA: Harvard University Press, 1966.

Rouberol, Jean, and Jean Chardonnet. *Les Sudistes.* Paris: Armand Colin, 1971.

Royster, Charles. *The Destructive War: William Tecumseh Sherman, Stonewall Jackson, and the Americans.* New York: Knopf, 1991.

Ryan, James Gilbert. "The Memphis Riots of 1866: Terror in a Black Community during Reconstruction." *Journal of Negro History* 62, no. 3 (1977): 243–57.

Ryan, Mary P. *Civic Wars: Democracy and Public Life in the American City during the Nineteenth Century.* Berkeley: University of California Press, 1997.

Sandage, Scott A. *Born Losers: A History of Failure in America.* Cambridge, MA: Harvard University Press, 2005.

Sanders, Elizabeth. *Roots of Reform: Farmers, Workers, and the American State, 1877–1917.* Chicago: University of Chicago Press, 1999.

Sawislak, Karen. *Smoldering City: Chicagoans and the Great Fire, 1871–1874.* Chicago: University of Chicago Press, 1995.

Sawrey, Robert D. *Dubious Victory: The Reconstruction Debate in Ohio.* Lexington: University Press of Kentucky, 1992.

Scheiber, Harry N. *Ohio Canal Era: A Case Study of Government and the Economy, 1820–1861.* Athens: Ohio University Press, 1969.

Schell, Herbert S. "Hugh McCulloch and the Treasury Department, 1865–1869." *Mississippi Valley Historical Review* 17, no. 3 (1930): 404–21.

Schlesinger, Arthur M., and Fred L. Israel, eds. *History of American Presidential Elections, 1789–1968.* Vol. 2. New York: Chelsea House, 1971.

Schneirov, Richard. "Thoughts on Periodizing the Gilded Age: Capital Accumulation, Society, and Politics, 1873–1898." *Journal of the Gilded Age and Progressive Era* 5, no. 3 (2006): 189–224.

Schor, Paul. *Compter et classer: Histoire des recensements américains.* Paris: Éditions de l'École des Hautes Études en Sciences Sociales, 2009.

Scott, John Anthony. "Justice Bradley's Evolving Concept of the Fourteenth Amendment from the Slaughterhouse Cases to the Civil Rights Cases." *Rutgers Law Review* 25 (1971): 552–70.

Sefton, James E. *The United States Army and Reconstruction, 1865–1877.* Baton Rouge: Louisiana State University Press, 1967.

Seip, Terry L. *The South Returns to Congress: Men, Economic Measures, and Intersectional Relationships, 1868–1879.* Baton Rouge: Louisiana State University Press, 1983.

Selgin, George A., and Lawrence H. White. "Monetary Reform and the Redemption of National Bank Notes, 1863–1913." *Business History Review* 68, no. 2 (1994): 205–43.

Sexton, Jay. *Debtor Diplomacy: Finance and American Foreign Relations in the Civil War Era, 1837–1873.* Oxford: Oxford University Press, 2005.

Shafer, Byron E. *The End of Realignment? Interpreting American Electoral Eras.* Madison: University of Wisconsin Press, 1991.

Shafer, Byron E., and Anthony J. Badger. *Contesting Democracy: Substance and Structure in American Political History, 1775–2000.* Lawrence: University Press of Kansas, 2001.

Shannon, Fred A. *The Organization and Administration of the Union Army, 1861–1865.* 2 vols. Cleveland: Arthur H. Clark, 1928.

Sharkey, Robert P. *Money, Class, and Party: An Economic Study of Civil War and Reconstruction.* Baltimore: Johns Hopkins University Press, 1959.

Shefter, Martin. "The Emergence of the Political Machine: An Alternate View." In *Theoretical Perspectives on Urban Politics,* edited by Willis D. Hawley et al., 14–44. Englewood Cliffs, NJ: Prentice-Hall, 1976.

Shortridge, James R. *The Middle West: Its Meaning in American Culture.* Lawrence: University Press of Kansas, 1989.

Silber, Nina. *The Romance of Reunion: Northerners and the South, 1865–1900.* Chapel Hill: University of North Carolina Press, 1993.

Silbey, Joel H. *The American Political Nation 1838–93.* Stanford, CA: Stanford University Press, 1991.

———. "Congressional and State Legislative Roll-Call Studies by U.S. Historians." *Legislative Studies Quarterly* 6, no. 4 (1981): 597–607.

———. "'Delegates Fresh from the People': American Congressional and Legislative Behavior." *Journal of Interdisciplinary History* 13, no. 4 (1983): 603–27.

———, ed. *Encyclopedia of the American Legislative System: Studies of the Principal Structures, Processes, and Policies of Congress and the State Legislatures since the Colonial Era.* 3 vols. New York: Charles Scribner's Sons, 1994.

———. *The Partisan Imperative: The Dynamics of American Politics before the Civil War.* Oxford: Oxford University Press, 1985.

———. *A Respectable Minority: The Democratic Party in the Civil War Era.* New York: Norton, 1977.

———, ed. *The United States Congress in a Partisan Political Nation, 1841–1896.* 3 vols. Brooklyn: Carlson, 1991.

Silbey, Joel H., et al., eds. *The History of American Electoral Behavior.* Princeton, NJ: Princeton University Press, 1978.

Simpson, Brooks D. "Grant's Tour of the South Revisited." *Journal of Southern History* 54, no. 3 (1988): 425–48.

———. *Let Us Have Peace: Ulysses S. Grant and the Politics of War and Reconstruction, 1861–1868.* Chapel Hill: University of North Carolina Press, 1991.

———. *The Reconstruction Presidents.* Lawrence: University Press of Kansas, 1998.

Sklansky, Jeffrey. *The Soul's Economy: Market Society and Selfhood in American Thought, 1820–1920.* Chapel Hill: University of North Carolina Press, 2002.

Skocpol, Theda. *Protecting Soldiers and Mothers: The Political Origins of Social Policy in the United States.* Cambridge, MA: Belknap Press of Harvard University Press, 1992.

Slap, Andrew L. *The Doom of Reconstruction: The Liberal Republicans in the Civil War Era.* New York: Fordham University Press, 2006.

———. "'The Strong Arm of the Military Power of the United States': The Chicago Fire, the Constitution, and Reconstruction." *Civil War History* 47, no. 2 (2001): 146–63.

Smith, George Winston. *Henry C. Carey and American Sectional Conflict.* Albuquerque: University of New Mexico Press, 1951.

Smith, Gregor W., and R. Todd Smith. "Greenback-Gold Returns and Expectations of Resumption, 1862–1879." *Journal of Economic History* 57, no. 3 (1997): 697–717.

Smith, Jean Edward. *Grant.* New York: Simon and Schuster, 2001.

Smith, Michael Thomas. "The Most Desperate Scoundrels Unhung: Bounty Jumpers and Recruitment Fraud in the Civil War North." *American Nineteenth Century History* 6, no. 2 (2005): 149–72.

Sproat, John G. *The "Best Men": Liberal Reformers in the Gilded Age.* Oxford: Oxford University Press, 1968.

Stampp, Kenneth M. *The Era of Reconstruction, 1865–1877.* New York: Knopf, 1965.

Stanley, Robert. *Dimensions of Law in the Service of Order: Origins of the Federal Income Tax, 1861–1913.* Oxford: Oxford University Press, 1993.

Stanwood, Edward D. *American Tariff Controversies in the Nineteenth Century.* 2 vols. Boston: Houghton Mifflin, 1903.

Stowe, Lyman Beecher. *Saints, Sinners and Beechers.* Indianapolis: Bobbs-Merrill, 1934.

Studenski, Paul, and Herman E. Krooss. *Financial History of the United States: Fiscal, Monetary, Banking, and Tariff, Including Financial Administration and State and Local Finance.* 2nd edition. New York: McGraw-Hill, 1963.

Summers, Mark W. *A Dangerous Stir: Fear, Paranoia, and the Making of Reconstruction.* Chapel Hill: University of North Carolina Press, 2009.

———. *The Era of Good Stealings.* Oxford: Oxford University Press, 1993.

———. *The Gilded Age; or, The Hazards of New Functions.* Upper Saddle River, NJ: Prentice-Hall, 1997.

———. *Party Games: Getting, Keeping, and Using Power in Gilded Age Politics.* Chapel Hill: University of North Carolina Press, 2004.

———. *The Press Gang: Newspapers and Politics, 1865–1878.* Chapel Hill: University of North Carolina Press, 1994.

———. *Railroads, Reconstruction, and the Gospel of Prosperity: Aid under the Radical Republicans, 1865–1877.* Princeton, NJ: Princeton University Press, 1984.

———. *Rum, Romanism & Rebellion: The Making of a President, 1884.* Chapel Hill: University of North Carolina Press, 2000.

Swenson, Philip David. "The Midwest and the Abandonment of Radical Reconstruction, 1864–1877." Ph.D. dissertation, University of Washington, 1971.

Swierenga, Robert P. *Beyond the Civil War Synthesis: Political Essays of the Civil War Era.* New York: Greenwood Press, 1975.

Swinney, Everette. "Enforcing the Fifteenth Amendment, 1870–1877." *Journal of Southern History* 28 (1962): 202–18.

Taussig, Frank W. *The History of the Present Tariff, 1860–1883.* New York: G. P. Put-
    man's Sons, 1888.
———. *Some Aspects of the Tariff Question: An Examination of the Development of
    American Industries under Protection.* 3rd edition. Clifton, NJ: Augustus M. Kelley,
    1972 (1931).
———. *The Tariff History in the United States: A Series of Essays.* New York: G. P.
    Putman's Sons, 1889.
Thernstrom, Stephan. *Harvard Encyclopedia of American Ethnic Groups.* Cambridge,
    MA: Belknap Press of Harvard University Press, 1980.
Thompson, Elizabeth Lee. *The Reconstruction of Southern Debtors: Bankruptcy after
    the Civil War.* Athens: University of Georgia Press, 2004.
Thompson, Margaret Susan. *The "Spider Web": Congress and Lobbying in the Age of
    Grant.* Ithaca, NY: Cornell University Press, 1985.
Thompson, Richard W. *The History of Protective Tariff Laws.* 3rd edition. Chicago:
    R. S. Peale, 1888.
Thornton, Mark, and Robert B. Ekelund. *Tariffs, Blockades, and Inflation: The Eco-
    nomics of the Civil War.* Wilmington, DE: Scholarly Resources, 2004.
Timberlake, Richard H. "Ideological Factors in Specie Resumption and Treasury Pol-
    icy." *Journal of Economic History* 24, no. 1 (1964): 29–52.
———. *Monetary Policy in the United States: An Intellectual and Institutional History.*
    Chicago: University of Chicago Press, 1993.
Tontz, Robert L. "Memberships of General Farmers' Organizations, United States,
    1874–1960." *Agricultural History* 38, no. 3 (1964): 143–56.
Trefousse, Hans L. *Andrew Johnson: A Biography.* New York: Norton, 1989.
———. *Benjamin Franklin Wade, Radical Republican from Ohio.* New York: Twayne,
    1963.
———. *Carl Schurz: A Biography.* Knoxville: University of Tennessee Press, 1982.
———. *Historical Dictionary of Reconstruction.* Westport, CT: Greenwood Press, 1991.
———. *Reconstruction: America's First Effort at Racial Democracy.* Malabar, FL:
    Krieger, 1999.
Trelease, Allen W. *White Terror: The Ku Klux Klan Conspiracy and Southern Recon-
    struction.* New York: Harper and Row, 1971.
Trentmann, Frank. *Free Trade Nation: Commerce, Consumption, and Civil Society in
    Modern Britain.* Oxford: Oxford University Press, 2008.
Truettner, William H. *The West as America: Reinterpreting Images of the Frontier,
    1820–1920.* Washington, DC: Smithsonian Institution Press, 1991.
Tuchinsky, Adam-Max. *Horace Greeley's New-York Tribune: Civil War–Era Socialism
    and the Crisis of Free Labor.* Ithaca, NY: Cornell University Press, 2009.
Tuffnell, Stephen. "'Uncle Sam Is to Be Sacrificed': Anglophobia in Late Nineteenth-
    Century Politics and Culture." *American Nineteenth Century History* 12, no. 1 (2011):
    77–99.
Turner, Frederick Jackson. *The Significance of Sections in American History.* New York:
    H. Holt, 1932.

———. "The Significance of the Frontier in American History." *Annual Report of the American Historical Association* (1893): 199–227.

Ufland, Peter. "The Politics of Race in the Midwest, 1864–1890." Ph.D. dissertation, University of Illinois at Chicago, 2006.

Unger, Irwin. "Business and Currency in the Ohio Gubernatorial Campaign of 1875." *Mid-America, An Historical Review* 41, no. 1 (1959): 27–39.

———. "The Business Community and the Origins of the 1875 Resumption Act." *Business History Review* 35, no. 2 (1961): 247–62.

———. "Business Men and Specie Resumption." *Political Science Quarterly* 74, no. 1 (1959): 46–70.

———. *The Greenback Era: A Social and Political History of American Finance, 1865–1879.* Princeton, NJ: Princeton University Press, 1964.

Valelly, Richard M. "Deflecting the Ex-Post Veto Player: The Strategy of the 14th Amendment Dred Scott Override." Paper presented at the Wepner Symposium, University of Illinois at Springfield, October 2010.

———. *The Two Reconstructions: The Struggle for Black Enfranchisement.* Chicago: University of Chicago Press, 2004.

Van Atta, John R. *Securing the West: Politics, Public Lands, and the Fate of the Old Republic, 1785–1850.* Baltimore: Johns Hopkins University Press, 2014.

Vilar, Pierre. *Or et monnaie dans l'histoire, 1450–1920.* Paris: Flammarion, 1974.

Vorenberg, Michael. *Final Freedom: The Civil War, the Abolition of Slavery, and the Thirteenth Amendment.* Cambridge: Cambridge University Press, 2001.

Voss, Kim. *The Making of American Exceptionalism: The Knights of Labor and Class Formation in the Nineteenth Century.* Ithaca, NY: Cornell University Press, 1993.

Waller, Altina L. "Community, Class and Race in the Memphis Riot of 1866." *Journal of Social History* 18, no. 2 (1984): 233–46.

Wang, Xi. "The Making of Federal Enforcement Laws, 1870–1872." *Chicago-Kent Law Journal* 70, no. 3 (1995): 1013–59.

———. *The Trial of Democracy: Black Suffrage and Northern Republicans, 1860–1910.* Athens: University of Georgia Press, 1997.

Waugh, Joan. *U.S. Grant: American Hero, American Myth.* Chapel Hill: University of North Carolina Press, 2009.

Weil, François. *A History of New York.* New York: Columbia University Press, 2004.

Weinstein, Allen. *Prelude to Populism: Origins of the Silver Issue, 1867–1878.* New Haven, CT: Yale University Press, 1970.

White, Richard. *Railroaded: The Transcontinentals and the Making of Modern America.* New York: Norton, 2011.

Wicker, Elmus. *Banking Panics of the Gilded Age.* New York: Cambridge University Press, 2000.

Wiecek, William M. "The Great Writ and Reconstruction: The Habeas Corpus Act of 1867." *Journal of Southern History* 36, no. 4 (1970): 530–48.

Williams, Lou Falkner. *The Great South Carolina Ku Klux Klan Trials, 1871–1872.* Athens: University of Georgia Press, 1996.

Wilson, Mark R. *The Business of Civil War: Military Mobilization and the State, 1861–1865*. Baltimore: Johns Hopkins University Press, 2006.

Wittke, Carl. "Carl Schurz and Rutherford B. Hayes." *Ohio Historical Quarterly* 65, no. 4 (1956): 337–55.

Wolman, Paul. *Most Favored Nation: The Republican Revisionists and U.S. Tariff Policy, 1897–1912*. Chapel Hill: University of North Carolina Press, 1992.

Woodman, Harold D. "Sequel to Slavery: The New History Views the Postbellum South." *Journal of Southern History* 43, no. 4 (1977): 523–54.

Woods, Thomas A. *Knights of the Plow: Oliver H. Kelley and the Origins of the Grange in Republican Ideology*. Ames: Iowa State University Press, 1991.

Woodward, C. Vann. *Reunion and Reaction: The Compromise of 1877 and the End of Reconstruction*. Garden City, NY: Doubleday, 1956.

———. "Yes, There Was a Compromise of 1877." *Journal of American History* 60, no. 1 (1973): 215–23.

Woolfolk, George R. *The Cotton Regency: The Northern Merchants and Reconstruction, 1865–1880*. New York: Bookman Associates, 1958.

Wright, Gavin. *Old South, New South: Revolutions in the Southern Economy since the Civil War*. New York: Basic Books, 1986.

Wrobel, David M., and Michael C. Steiner, eds. *Many Wests: Place, Culture, and Regional Identity*. Lawrence: University Press of Kansas, 1997.

Zipf, Karin L. "'The Whites Shall Rule the Land or Die': Gender, Race, and Class in North Carolina Reconstruction Politics." *Journal of Southern History* 65, no. 3 (1999): 499–534.

Zuczek, Richard, *State of Rebellion: Reconstruction in South Carolina*. Columbia: University of South Carolina Press, 1996.

INDEX

Italicized page numbers refer to illustrations.

CPSIA information can be obtained
at www.ICGtesting.com
Printed in the USA
LVHW091154120821
695152LV00001B/62